Belarus

the Bradt Travel Guide

Nigel Roberts

edition
I

www.bradtguides.com

Bradt Travel Guides Ltd, UK
The Globe Pequot Press Inc, USA

LATVIA

Braslav Lakes NP
page 184

National Memorial Complex, Khatyn
page 131

LITHUANIA

Architecture, Grodno
page 165

Minsk
page 95

Fortress, Mir
page 125

Smargon

Moladezhnaya

La

Voranava

Lida

MINSK

Grodno

Novogrudok

Nyoman

Voikavyusk

Baranavichy

Slyutsk

Slonim

POLAND

Njasvizh (UNESCO
World Heritage Site)
page 127

Saligorsk

Dudutki Folk Museum
page 129

Pruzhany

Luninyets

Kobryn

BREST

Pinsk

Byelovezhskaya
Puscha NP
page 154

Pinsk
page 151

Brest Fortress
page 147

Pripyatsky NP
page 211

Belarus
Don't
miss…

Soviet architecture
Brest train station in Stalinist
'wedding-cake' style
(JS) page 141

Forests and lakes
Between Grodno and Brest
(NR) page 157

Minsk
Victory obelisk on
Victory Square
(JS) page 122

**Russian
orthodoxy**
Orthodox Cathedral,
Grodno
(JS) page 167

Memorials
Great Patriotic War
Memorial, Gomel
(NR) page 208

top left   Flowers offered by wedding couples at Afghan War Memorial, Minsk (BY/PCL) page 122

top right   Catholic Church of Sts Simon and Helena, Minsk (JS) page 123

above left   Bread shop sign, Minsk (JS) page 115

above right   Victory Day decorations, Minsk (JS)

top left **Wooden church, Vetka**
(NR) page 209

top right **St Nikolai's Orthodox Church, Brest**
(NR) page 150

left **Orthodox priest**
(NR) page 25

AUTHOR

For the last five years, **Nigel Roberts** has been actively engaged on sustainable development projects with rural communities in Belarus blighted by the Chernobyl catastrophe. By profession a lawyer, he is also a Russian speaker. His interest in the former Soviet Union was kindled as a boy and since then he has researched and travelled widely in the area. This is his first book.

AUTHOR STORY

It was during my second visit to this much misunderstood country that I convinced myself that here was a book just waiting to be written. It made no sense at all that I seemed to be the first to have this thought. And when I decided that I would be the one to write it, there was only one publisher to whom I was prepared to entrust the task of opening the door to the land and people that I had come to love. Bradt's enviable reputation not only for responsible travel writing, but also for being in the vanguard of blazing a trail to new destinations, has ensured that this is the very first book in the West to feature Belarus as a single subject. It's a real delight to be able to share my experiences with you.

I'm writing this story in a flat in the city of Brest, overlooking the main railway line west. It's been a remarkable day. I borrowed a car for a road trip from the brother of a friend of a friend, who drove for two hours at dawn to deliver it to me. He's charging me $25 a day, plus a bottle of vodka. I filled the tank with fuel for $20, then drove all the way across the country on the main highway west from the city of Gomel, mostly on single carriageway, for 7½ hours and with very few cars for company, before arriving in Brest to find not a single hotel room to be had anywhere. Undeterred, my travelling companion Olya bought a newspaper, turned to the classifieds and within five minutes, had found us a flat in a residential block of crumbling Soviet concrete in a suburb five minutes from the centre, fully furnished and with all mod cons, for $30 a night. We drove straight there after one short phone call, handed over the cash and took immediate possession of the keys. We've been out for a sumptuous Indian meal, as good as any that I've tasted anywhere, for $12 each, including drinks, and then finished the evening at a late-night store, where we bought bread, cheese and yoghurt for breakfast, two litres of soft drinks and a litre of beer, all for $6. And as I gaze across the tracks from the balcony, dogs barking in the yard below, I wouldn't want to be anywhere else in the whole world. It feels like I've packed a week's living into one day and it's the best $100 that I've spent in a very long time indeed. There's so much to discover in this country, most of it to do with the people who live here: unconditional hospitality, genuine warmth of spirit and a real desire to engage positively and fraternally with *inostranyets* (foreigners). It's your turn now; don't miss out.

PUBLISHER'S FOREWORD
Adrian Phillips, Editorial Director

The first Bradt travel guide was written in 1974 by George and Hilary Bradt on a river barge floating down a tributary of the Amazon. It was followed by *Backpacker's Africa*, published in 1979. In the 1980s and '90s the focus shifted away from hiking to broader-based guides to new destinations – usually the first to be published on those places. In the 21st century Bradt continues to publish these ground-breaking guides, along with guides to established holiday destinations, incorporating in-depth information on culture and natural history alongside the nuts and bolts of where to stay and what to see.

Bradt authors support responsible travel, with advice not only on minimum impact but also on how to give something back through local charities. Thus a true synergy is achieved between the traveller and local communities.

* * *

When we first announced that we'd commissioned a guide to Belarus, I received a phone call from a journalist with just one question: 'Why would anyone want to go there?' I suspect his was not an unusual reaction. While other former Soviet republics looked westwards, Belarus remained entrenched in the past; for most outsiders, the country represents that bleak, utilitarian 'greyness' so frequently associated with communist states. However, as Nigel Roberts passionately demonstrates, such preconceptions are hugely unfair. He introduces us to lush forests and clear lakes, to quaint churches and intriguing museums, and to warmly welcoming people. It doesn't sound grey to me – in fact, I rather want to go there!

First published May 2008

Bradt Travel Guides Ltd, 23 High Street, Chalfont St Peter, Bucks SL9 9QE, England
www.bradtguides.com
Published in the USA by The Globe Pequot Press Inc, 246 Goose Lane,
PO Box 480, Guilford, Connecticut 06475-0480

Text copyright © 2008 Nigel Roberts   Maps copyright © 2008 Bradt Travel Guides Ltd
Illustrations © 2008 Individual photographers and artists

ISBN-10: 1 84162 207 9   ISBN-13: 978 1 84162 207 1
British Library Cataloguing in Publication Data
A catalogue record for this book is available from the British Library

Photographs Les Bourg (LB), John Devries/TIPS (JD/TIPS), Jean Drake/TIPS (JDr/TIPS), Bruno de Faveri/TIPS (BF/TIPS), Howard Jarvis (HJ), Patti McConville/TIPS (PM/TIPS), Bildagentur RM/TIPS (BR/TIPS), Nigel Roberts (NR), Jonathan Smith (JS), Markus Varesvuo (MV), Bruce Yuan & Yue Bi/PCL (BY/PCL)
Front cover Sculpture of stargazer by Vladimir Zhbanov, Mogilev (A Stepanenko/travel-images.com)
Back cover Archetypal Russian Orthodox dome (NR), Neoclassical KGB building, Minsk (JS)
Title page Soviet propaganda in the metro, Minsk (JS), Roof detail, St Simeon Orthodox Cathedral, Brest (NR), Straw doll GUM store (BY/PCL)
Illustrations Carole Vincer   **Maps** Dave Priestley
Typeset from the author's disc by Wakewing
Printed and bound in India at Nutech Photolithographers

Acknowledgements

The trail leading to this book began a very long time ago. Like many others before me, I grew up in the 1960s with a sense of foreboding, just waiting for the day when the Russians would come. It's difficult now to explain this to those who are too young to know what it was like to live through the Cold War. Bit by bit, a sense of scepticism about Western propaganda began to emerge in my thinking and for this I thank my first Russian teacher at Tudor Grange School, Dave Walton. He opened my mind to the culture, politics and socio-economics of the Soviet Union and encouraged me to look deeper than the answers given in the Western media. Thanks to him, a raw January night found me sitting in a freezing school hall with a handful of other 16 year olds, watching Eisenstein's classic work of revolutionary propaganda *Battleship Potemkin*, wide-eyed and open-mouthed. As Western politics lurched inexorably to the right through the 1970s and 1980s, I sought out alternative views of world politics and spent many a wet London afternoon browsing the shelves of the much-mourned Collett's bookshop.

To my dear old dad and my late ma, grateful thanks for love, unconditional support and for pushing me kicking and screaming all the way to Cambridge, where my mind was truly opened at last. To Tatyana Hopkins, for reigniting the spark of my Russian on Wednesday nights at the Brasshouse Language Centre in Birmingham and for giving me the confidence to speak it again; to Jo Jones, my unofficial editor in this venture, who read every single word for me and pointed me in the right direction when I couldn't see the wood for the trees; and to my very dear friends and colleagues in the West Oxfordshire Vetka Association ('WOVA'), for encouraging and indulging my enthusiasm, for their ideas, for supporting me and keeping me going every step of the way in the writing of this book and perhaps most of all, for truly inspiring me with their idealism. In particular, I dedicate this finished manuscript to the late Brian Hodgson, a dear friend and WOVA comrade who encouraged me all the way with the concept and detail of this book. Brian was eagerly awaiting its publication and I was eagerly awaiting his critique, but he sadly passed on before my work was finished. Brian's idealism, commitment to righting injustice wherever it was to be found at home or elsewhere in the world, his loyalty and good humour are an inspiration to many. Wherever you are, Brian, I hope there's a bookshop. And as I write these words, a candle is burning brightly for you in Saint Nikolai's Church in the heart of the hero-fortress in the city of Brest, scene of astonishing acts of courage and bravery in the resistance against the Nazi hordes.

There are so many people in Belarus that I count as true friends and without whom this book would not have been possible. Viktor Burakov and Yuri Goncharov of Vetka Executive Committee, both true and loyal partners with an unswerving commitment to making life better for families in Belarus; Tatyana Paramonova and Nina Kekukh, my mentors in sustainable development and in navigating a path through Belarusian civic administration and regulation; Doctor

Vladimir Xoxa, chief surgeon at Mozyr General Hospital, performing miracles daily in the most burdensome of circumstances; and finally, all of the families in Vetka who welcome me as a long-lost son every time I visit; to Oleg and Galina, Nikolai and Diana, Yulia, Alicia and Ksusha, but most of all, my adoptive family – Tanya, Valeri, Olya and Anton. I love you as if my own.

The greatest debt of gratitude that I owe is a very large one indeed. First, to my children, Harriet and George, for total inspiration, love and an uncanny knack of keeping my feet firmly on the ground. Kids, nobody has ever believed in me like you do. And finally, to the woman I love with all my heart. She has held my hand through many testing and challenging times and we continue to walk the path together, hand in hand. May it always be so.

FEEDBACK REQUEST

The timing is undoubtedly right for this astonishing country to be 'discovered' some time very soon. Sadly, this will inevitably have consequences that might not necessarily be in the best interests of Belarus and its people. Although still relatively rare, each succeeding visit that I make to Minsk reveals more neon and designer-product advertising. And on my last trip, I noted with resignation and a heavy heart that it now boasts the country's first 'drive-thru' fast-food emporia. The pace of change just might be about to accelerate, a development that will bring new challenges in maintaining up-to-date information.

Please bear this in mind as you embark upon your preparation for your first visit. In short, there is a real paucity of reliable information, particularly with regard to opening hours, telephone numbers and prices for restaurants, bars, clubs and museums. I have personally established and checked the accuracy of the information provided in this guide, or else corroborated data from a number of different sources. Even so, there remains the risk of anomaly; for example, I came across one restaurant in Brest advertising different opening hours on two different windows! The primary difficulty is that there is hardly any concept in this country of consumer-based data for the edification of travellers, tourists and users of leisure facilities. Most trips and visits for non-nationals take place under the aegis of a state agency (there is also a rapidly growing number of independent ones), but very few local people travel around the country for recreation purposes. I very much hope that nothing herein is so utterly 'off the wall' as to be unreliable, but if you have the chance to check for updates or amendments as you go, I advise you to avail yourselves of the opportunity so to do. Don't be spooked, though; it's all part of the great adventure! And if you are participating in an organised trip, then everything will be arranged for you and all facilities included in the specification will be open, whatever the 'official' opening times!

For now, it is rare to meet kindred spirits and road companions in Belarus, but it is my fervent wish that this book will introduce a new breed of traveller to its riches. The tales that I tell in these pages are taken from my own experiences and travels, but one of the chief pleasures that I take from sharing them is the expectation that those who will find new experiences on their own travels may in turn be motivated to share their stories. I very much hope that there will be future editions of this guide, in which case your feedback, comments and criticism will be most gratefully received and acknowledged.

Please write to me c/o Bradt Travel Guides, 23 High Street, Chalfont St Peter, Bucks SL9 9QE, UK; e info@bradtguides.com.

Contents

LIST OF MAPS

Introduction

When my dream to visit the old Soviet Union was first realised in the late 1980s, Belarus existed not as a sovereign state, but as Byelorossia ('White Russia'), one of the constituent republics of the USSR. Other than to those with more than a passing interest in the politics of the area, it was simply a nameless constituent of the vast swathe of red that formed the eastern half of the Cold War map of the world. With the fall of the Berlin Wall and the consequent disintegration of the USSR, a national identity for Belarus began to emerge. But as the other former Soviet republics turned their gaze westwards to embrace political and economic reform through either evolution or revolution, Belarus remained (and remains still) fiercely embedded in the past. Its neighbours to the west and north (Poland, Lithuania and Latvia) are now member states of the European Union, while those to the east and south (the Russian Federation and Ukraine) move ever closer to embracing Western commercialism and the economics of the free market. But Belarus, the most westerly republic of the old USSR, clings steadfastly to the ideals of Soviet communism. It prides itself on being situated in the heart of Europe, at the crossroads of ancient trade routes from west to east and from north to south. The first-time visitor might be forgiven for expecting things to be little different from the rest of eastern Europe, but even before leaving home, there are clues aplenty to suggest that this will not be so. Before this one, no guidebooks devoted to Belarus alone could be found on the shelves of Western bookshops. Maps could only be purchased in specialist travel stores or online. Information anywhere, paper or electronic, is conspicuous by its absence and needs actively to be searched for. In so many respects, it is an unknown land; yet it is much more than this. It is an undiscovered box of gems, with a history rich in heroism, tragedy and despair, natural wonders of great beauty and a people who have endured such privations over the centuries, but whose hospitality is like no other that I have encountered.

I first visited the country in November 2001, arriving at Minsk in the dark of night. First impressions were intimidating, with an edge of danger. Then, the process of entry via customs and immigration was interminable. Stern-faced officials in khaki uniforms were less than welcoming. Emerging into the night, I was led hurriedly to the waiting transport for a six-hour journey down to the southeastern corner of the country, on unlit roads through mile after mile of silver birch forest, stretching away into impenetrable blackness. Stopping briefly to stretch our legs in the middle of nowhere, the raw cold took my breath away as I gazed up into a dazzling panoply of stars, unpolluted by unnatural reflected light from below. As the first snows of winter began to fall, we arrived in Vetka and, over dirt tracks, we came to the old part of town, where wooden houses stood sentinel against the biting cold, windows rattling in ill-fitting frames as flurries of snow danced amongst the eaves. The front door to the house of my hosts opened with a dazzling burst of light and heat as I was ushered into warmth and safety. My life has never been the same since that day and every time I return, it is to the same family, to the same bedroom and it always feels like coming home.

It's a cliché, I know, but a visit to this astonishing country really is one of those life-defining experiences. It is so completely unspoilt by the trappings of modern tourism and Western materialism that it's very easy to feel a sense of having slipped into another time and dimension. In many ways, the country is a living museum of Soviet communism, but to treat it that way would be a gross disservice to the astonishing resilience of its people. Twenty years on from the crippling and catastrophic consequences of the nuclear accident at Chernobyl, Belarusians still feel like the forgotten people of Europe, overlooked and shunned by an international community that links aid and assistance to political reform.

So it is with the greatest of pleasure that I share with you everything that I have come to know and love about Belarus: the natural splendour of primeval green forests, clear rivers and blue lakes; rare flora and fauna; cities that rose from the flames of Nazi barbarism as monuments to post-war Soviet urban planning; stunning museums crammed with rare artefacts unseen elsewhere, empty of visitors but with guides on hand to conduct personal tours; rich culture and tradition; historical sites dating from the Middle Ages to modern times; beautiful churches and the mysteries of Russian Orthodoxy; and most of all, a people whose warmth, honesty and open hospitality must be experienced to be believed. But whisper all this softly, for we must guard but not spoil these riches.

Black stork

Part One

GENERAL INFORMATION

Location Eastern Europe. Borders Russian Federation, Ukraine, Poland, Latvia and Lithuania. The country is completely landlocked.

Size Total state border length 2,969km; area 207,600km²; maximum width west to east 650km; length 560km north to south

Geography Lowland terrain, with a mean elevation above sea level of only 160m, the highest point being 345m. Natural vegetation over nearly 70% of area, of which 38% is forest. Also 20,000 rivers and streams and 11,000 lakes, with significant areas of marsh territory.

Climate Moderately continental, with cold winters and warm summers. Average temperature January –6.7°C, July 17.8°C. Annual rainfall 550–750mm.

Status Republic

Administrative divisions Six regions (*oblasts*), comprising 118 administrative districts

Capital city Minsk

Other major cities Gomel, Brest, Vitebsk, Grodno and Mogilev

Population 9,724,723 (density 49/km²)

People Ethnic Belarussians (81%), Russians (11%), Poles (4%), Ukrainians (2%) and the remaining 2% comprising Jews, Lithuanians, Tatars, Azerbaijanis, Armenians, Latvians, Koreans, Germans, Georgians, Ossets, Moldavians and travelling people

Life expectancy Male 64 years, female 75 years (2006 estimates)

Languages Belarusian and Russian have equal status as state languages

Religion Russian Orthodox, Roman Catholicism and Judaism

Economy Largely unchanged since Soviet times and currently around 80% state controlled

GDP US$79.13 billion in total, US$7,700 per capita (2005 estimates)

National airline/airport Belavia/Minsk International

Currency Belarusian rouble (BYR)

Exchange rate £1 = BYR4,191, US$1 = BYR2,154, €1 = BYR3,169 (February 2008)

International dialling code +375

Time GMT +2

Electrical voltage 200 volts

Flag Two broad horizontal stripes of red and green, red being double the area of green, with traditional patterning of red on a white border down the left-hand side

National anthem Мы, Беларусы ('We Belarusians')

National flower Flax

National bird/animal Black stork/European bison

National sport Ice hockey

Public holidays 1 January (New Year's Day), 7 January (Orthodox Christmas), 8 March (Women's Day), Orthodox Easter, Catholic Easter, 1 May (Labour Day), 9 May (Victory Day, a glorious celebration of the end of the 'Great Patriotic War'), 3 July (Independence Day), 7 November (October Revolution Day), 25 December (Catholic Christmas) and Radaunista (Ancestors' Remembrance Day) on the ninth day after Orthodox Easter

Background Information

GEOGRAPHY AND CLIMATE

Whether you fly over the country or drive across it, the impression you get is always the same; it's very flat and there are lots of trees. The country has no sea borders and it sits in the heart of the mid-European plain between the Baltic Sea to the north and the Black Sea to the south. It borders Poland to the west, Lithuania to the northwest, Latvia to the north, Russia to the northeast and east and finally, Ukraine to the south. The capital of the republic is Minsk and the distances to the capitals of its neighbours are as follows:

Capital city	Warsaw	Vilnius	Riga	Moscow	Kiev
Distance (km)	550	215	470	700	580

The country covers a surface area of 207,600km². The maximum distance from west to east is 650km and from north to south, 560km. The total length of its borders is 2,969km. It ranks 13th of all European countries (excluding Russia) in area size. In all, it is slightly smaller than the United Kingdom, more than twice the size of Portugal and Hungary and no fewer than five times bigger than Holland and Switzerland. But if you look at the map, you will see that it is dwarfed by its gigantic neighbour Russia to the east, a rich metaphor if ever there was one. The plain upon which the country is located extends some way beyond the country's borders and in times of war this has been a distinct disadvantage, rendering it all too easy in geographical terms to invade and subjugate. In times of peace however, this has meant that transport links, whether by road or rail, have been easy to establish and the trade routes that have passed in the direction of the four compass points have at times brought prosperity and multi-culturalism to these lands.

Those hills that exist here are barely hills at all; the mean elevation above sea level is only 160m, with the highest point being Mount Dzherzhinskaya in Minsk *oblast* at just 345m, although it is sufficiently elevated for there to be an emerging winter sports resort. The lowest is the valley of the Nieman River in Grodno *oblast* at just over 80m.

Lakes (11,000 of them) and rivers (totalling 91,000km in length) are the major features, with significant areas of marshland in between. The area of the Polyesye, the largest of the marsh territories, runs along the southern boundary of the country and is one of the biggest in Europe. In the north is the country's lakeland area. Five major rivers run through the territory of Belarus, the Nieman, the Dnieper, the Berezhina, the Sozh and the Pripyat, the last of which flows adjacent to the site of the former nuclear complex at Chernobyl in Ukraine, scene of the world's worst commercial nuclear catastrophe in April 1986. Approximately one-fifth of the territory of Belarus, mostly in the southeast, continues to be affected by radioactive fallout.

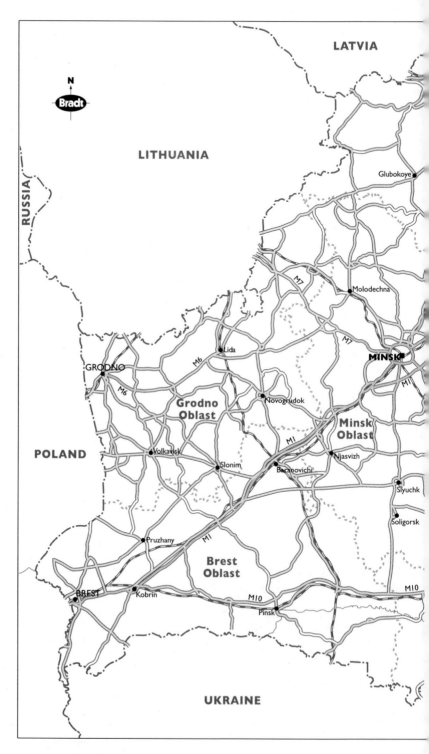

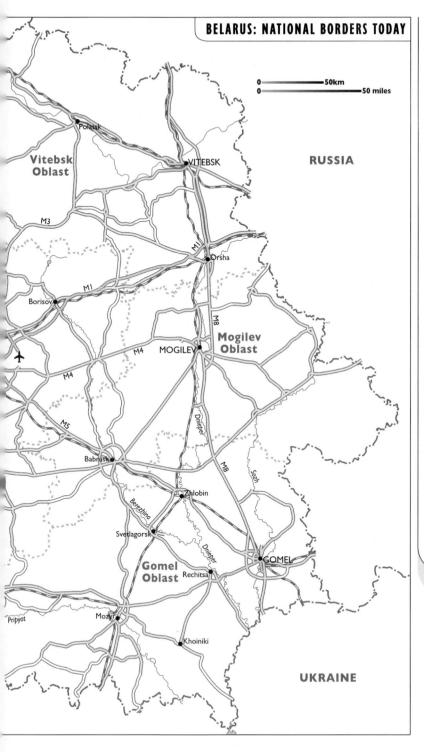

0 — 50km
0 — 50 miles

RUSSIA

Vitebsk
Oblast

Polatsk

VITEBSK

M3

M1

Orsha

M1

Borisov

M8

Mogilev
Oblast

M4

MOGILEV

M4

Dnieper

M5

M8

Sozh

Babruisk

Zhlobin

Berezhina

Svetlagorsk

Gomel
Oblast

Dnieper

Rechitsa

GOMEL

Pripyat

Mozyr

Khoiniki

UKRAINE

Over a third of the total landscape (38%) is covered by forest, much of it forming part of the vast primeval wood that once covered the whole of central Europe. Not only is it a valuable source of timber, it also performs other ecological functions, such as water conservation and soil protection, as well as being home to a rich variety of wildlife and also shelter for much revered supplies of plants used for medicinal and food purposes (particularly mushrooms and berries). Other natural resources include an abundance of peat fields (although these have been significantly depleted by intensive extraction) and small reserves of oil and natural gas, although production is insignificant . There are also 63 separate sources of mineral water supplying a significant number of sanatoria and spas throughout the country. Farmland accounts for around 44% of the republic's area, with 27.3% being arable.

The climate is moderately continental, ranging from unforgiving winters, when the mean January temperature is –6.7°C, to warm summers, when the mean in July is +17.8°C. The annual level of precipitation is 550–650mm in the low country and 650–750mm at higher elevations. The average vegetation period is 184–208 days. Generally, the climate is favourable for growing cereal crops, vegetables, potato and fruit.

HISTORY

No student of modern-day Belarus can hope to gain an insight into the mystery and enigma that characterise the national psyche without first engaging in at least a rudimentary study of all that has gone before. But there is very little to be found specifically about the country in Western books, although there is much to read on the subject of Holy Mother Russia and the former Soviet Union, both of which subsumed it at various times as an integral element of their empires.

There is one theme in particular that spans the centuries: that of suffering and privation. Whether subjugated to the yoke of Lithuanian, Pole, Tsar, Frenchman, Bolshevik, Communist, Nazi, Communist again or latterly oligarch, heroism and tragedy can be found on most of the pages of the country's history, as drama and melodrama unfold in the never-ending struggle to resist pain, anguish, grief and suffering. For generation after generation, there seems to have been no sanctuary from constant oppression, with the identity of the oppressor being largely irrelevant. Further, the media of oppression are many and varied: fear, dogma, hunger, poverty, lack of education, geography, climate and in recent times, Chernobyl. Each succeeding generation has developed defences to resist every challenge that comes along, such that the people of today are characterised by an astonishingly stoical resilience.

ANCIENT TIMES Indications are that early civilisations began to populate the territory that is now Belarus from the middle Palaeolithic period, or 100,000–40,000 years BC, while available evidence suggests that the first significant settlements emerged 24,000–27,000 years ago.

EARLY CIVILISATIONS The area was then settled by the Dryhavichy, Kryvichy and Radzimichy peoples between the 7th and 9th centuries AD, when the first Slavic alliances were formed. This was followed by the first state formations in the principalities of Polotsk, Turov and Smolensk. The town of Polotsk itself, founded by the Kryvichy at the confluence of the Palota and Western Dzhina rivers, is known to have existed since AD862 and it is still regarded as the first capital of the lands now recognised as Belarus. It is also still regarded as the spiritual cradle of the country. Its first chronicled prince, who ruled in the late 10th century, was

Rogvolod. In the following century, the principality reached the zenith of its power and influence under Prince Vseslav Brachyslavavich, who is believed to have ruled for an incredible 72 years from 1029 to 1101. He was known as 'the magician' for his remarkable talents as military leader and statesman. At that time, the extent of Polotskian influence stretched from the Baltic Sea in the west and north to Smolensk in the east. This geographical location held the key to the non-aligned lands between the opulent extravagance of the Byzantine Empire in the east and the warlike Norse tribes of Scandinavia (known to the Slavic peoples as the Varangians) and allowed Polotsk to gain many benefits from trade with Byzantium, the Baltic countries and Scandinavia. At the same time, Byzantine Christianity began to spread across these territories, doubtless as a result of trade links, so stimulating the development of culture through the arts and literature, along with the emergence of stone-based architecture.

A golden age of creativity had begun. The Turovsky Gospels were written in the 11th century and then between 1050 and 1070, the first major architectural structure, the imposing Cathedral of Saint Sophia, was built in Polotsk. It quickly became the very manifestation of the state's might and significance, for at times, foreign ambassadors were officially received here, both war and peace were declared here and it was also treated as the place of safekeeping for the public purse and sacred relics. Sister (later Saint) Ephrosynia, the heavenly 'mediatress' of Belya Rus whose selfless labour has long since passed into legend, was born at the beginning of the 12th century, around the time when master craftsmen were known to be working at the cathedral, such as the architect Johannes and the jeweller Lazar Bogsha. In 1161, Bogsha created the 'Cross for the Enlightener Saint Ephrosynia of Polotsk', a unique masterpiece of eastern Slavonic applied art. And among many contemporary Christian preachers and writers of note, Kirill Turovsky was particularly well known.

THE GRAND DUCHY OF LITHUANIA The 13th century marked a key phase in the history of modern Belarus. In its first half, the foundations of the Belarusian language began to form. This coincided with the establishment of the Grand Duchy of Lithuania, which brought together a number of Belarusian lands and principalities, primarily to meet the threat of invasion from crusading Teutonic knights to the west, Turks from the south and the Golden Horde of Mongol Tartars from the east. Many famous victories were won. The core lands of the duchy at this time were the territories around Kernave, Trakai and Samogitia, together with the city of Vilnius.

The coronation of the ruler Mindaug took place in 1253 and at the same time Novogorodok (now known as Novogrudok) became the capital of the Lithuanian duchy. In 1323, this status was transferred to Vilno (now Vilnius). Under the rule of Vitautis, the duchy reached the peak of its power and influence, expanding its frontiers and gaining international prestige. On 2 February 1386, Grand Duke Jogaila was crowned King of Poland and a personal union under one single monarch was established. Then at the famous battle of Grunwald in 1410, the joint forces of Poland and Lithuania inflicted a crushing defeat on the Teutonic Order, an event of critical importance to the consolidation of the new state, whose power now extended all the way from the Baltic Sea in the north to the Black Sea in the south. The next significant stage of the state's development was the formation (by formal union) in 1569 of the Polish-Lithuanian Commonwealth and consequent creation of a new federative state known as Rzeczpospolita. It was ruled by the grand duke and Rada Polish landowners jointly, with the state being divided into provinces and administrative districts known as povets. The representative body of the feudal lords of the Polish gentry was known as the Sejm, with its deputies being elected at the regional councils of the povet, although simultaneously, the former Lithuanian grand duchy maintained its own government, financial system, army and emblem.

The competing struggle for influence in the eastern Baltic region had instigated the Livonian War in 1558 against the state of Muscovy. This war lasted until 1583. The formal settlement of the 1569 union eventually enabled the new state to win the Livonian War, thereby returning areas of land that had been lost and most importantly, consolidating and securing power and influence in the eastern Baltic.

From early on in the 16th century, massive agrarian reform ('*volochnaya pomera*') had been taking place against a background of almost constant warfare, culminating in the embodiment of the concept of serfdom in a 1588 statute, one of three during the century that codified the fundamental elements of the grand duchy's status, the other two being passed in 1529 and 1566. At the same time, those towns that had assumed self-government under Magdeburg Law since the end of the 14th century were now developing at an intense rate, with the establishment of urban crafts and consequent guild protection. This was an exciting time for those engaged in commercial interests.

THE CHURCH During the 16th century, the lands which now form Belarus saw the establishment of Lutheranism, Calvinism and other Protestant doctrines under the influence of the Reformation. This was a period of considerable religious tolerance and stability, but by the end of the century, the Counter-Reformation had begun. Orthodoxy and Catholicism reached a compromise that resulted in the Brest Church Union of 1596, under which the Orthodox Church of the Grand Duchy of Lithuania recognised the supremacy of Rome, while maintaining its own rites, doctrines and customs. Inevitably, there was reluctance on the part of Orthodox believers to accept religious subjugation under the Union and this, along with inevitable economic pressures on the peasantry and the urban lower classes, resulted in considerable internal strife and opposition to feudalism.

THE RISE AND INFLUENCE OF RUSSIA Neighbouring Russia gleefully seized the opportunity to capitalise on these domestic difficulties within the state of Rzeczpospolita and launched a new war on its territory, which endured from 1654 to 1667. A large portion of modern-day Belarus was occupied and severe economic and demographic crises ensued. The population was reduced by half, whole towns fell into decay and there were many adverse consequences for all levels of society, but most notably the gentry and urban dwellers.

From 1700 to 1721, these lands formed the battleground in the North War waged by the Swedes on Russia and Rzeczpospolita. This war brought about decades of economic ruin which only began to be overcome by the middle of the century, with the revival of commerce and business in the form of a rudimentary market economy. Of more serious consequence even than warfare was the protracted political crisis that was wrought by consequent anarchy in the country and the growing power and influence of neighbouring nation states. The last single King of Poland and Grand Duke of Lithuania, Stanislav August Ponyatovsky (1764–95), tried in vain to consolidate central power, but he was confronted by an active opposition that sought aid and support from abroad. The situation was ripe for exploitation, and the neighbouring states of Russia, Prussia and Austria capitalised on these circumstances by taking advantage of the inequality of Orthodox and Protestant believers in relation to Catholics within Rzeczpospolita. All of this led to the first division of the country in 1772, following which the land that is now eastern Belarus was annexed and incorporated into the Russian Empire. A second division was effected in 1793, as a result of which central Belarus was also

BELARUSIAN TERRITORIES (16TH CENTURY)

KEY
Border of modern Belarus —·—·—
Border of Reczpospolita ········

Baltic Sea

MOSCOW▪

KÖNIGSBERG▪

VILNIUS▪

●Polatsk
●VITEBSK

Pomerania GDANSK▪

GRODNO ●Lida

MINSK▪ MOGILEV●

NOVOGRUDOK

Berezina Dnieper Sozh

Babrusk●

●POZNAN

BERYESTYE● Pripyat
Pinsk Mozyr

RECHITSA● ●GOMEL

RUSSIA

WARSAW▪

N
Bradt

Bohemia ●KRAKOW

▪BRNO

HUNGARY

Ottoman
Empire

annexed. There was a limited degree of patriotic resistance, leading to the uprising led by Kostyushko, but in 1795, the third and final division of the country took place, with Russia subsuming the western lands of Belarus. Rzeczpospolita was never to exist again as a sovereign state and the administrative divisions, taxes and duties of the Russian Empire were finally imposed across all of its lands.

There followed a long period of Russian domination. During the Napoleonic invasion of Russia in 1812, the territory was the major theatre of war, resulting in huge losses and a significant diminution in the population. After the war, in the vacuum created by social and administrative disintegration, democratic ideas began to flourish, leading to the development of the first national liberation movement. As a consequence there was an uprising in 1830–31 to re-establish the state of Rzeczpospolita and restore the national boundaries that existed in 1772, the date of its first division. Inevitably, the uprising was suppressed, but the position of the gentry and of Catholicism had been weakened. Roman Catholic churches and monasteries were closed, while the lands, estates and possessions of the rebels were confiscated by the state. Other contextual events included the closure of the University of Vilno and the annulment of the statute of 1588, which had codified the autonomous Grand Duchy of Lithuania's governance arrangements. For every purpose, the lands of modern Belarus now existed only as the north-western region of the Russian Empire.

In the 19th century, broader issues within the empire began to take effect and as the Tsars sought to cling on to power and perpetuate the subjugation of the people (in the face of increasing challenges through assertion of democracy and enfranchisement), Russian influences from the establishment grew incrementally stronger. By way of example, the compromise reached under the Brest Church Union of 1596 was reversed and the Uniate Church ceased to exist, allowing traditional Russian Orthodoxy to once more reign supreme. And while the peasants tended the fields, the landed gentry, the privileged classes and the re-established Church saw to it that any attempts to assert a specific identity for the Belarusian people were systematically suppressed, oftentimes with brutality. Among the many forms in which this suppression manifested itself was the proscription of the use of the Belarusian language in written form. Despite (and probably because of) this official denial of an independent Belarusian identity, nationalist ideas continued to flourish underground. The promotion of Belarusian literature, art, folklore and language began to take hold in the minds and consciousness of the people, notwithstanding the perpetuation of the prejudice and lack of opportunity suffered by native Belarusians in terms of access to significant administrative and governance positions of influence within the Russian empire; as had earlier been the case for centuries, across ceaseless periods of Lithuanian and Polish dominance.

Hand in hand with cultural development was increasing economic well-being, most notably in respect of the industrialisation of the country's richest natural resource (timber), although progress was only gradual and there remained painfully little change in the high rate of rural deprivation, which for the most part, was worse than anywhere else in the Empire. The majority of the population by far was still to be found on the land, maintained in a position of unrepresented subservience through poverty, ignorance, effective disenfranchisement and the power of privilege. Then in 1861, peasant reform abolished serfdom. The first underground newspaper *Peasant's Truth* was established between 1862 and 1863, then later that year and into 1864, the national liberation movement in the Empire rose up against tsarism in the lands that are now Poland, Lithuania and Belarus, although brutal suppression once more ensued and a codified legal regime was enforced that was to endure into the 20th century.

In the 1880s, however, the revolutionary organisation Gomon was established by Belarusian students who had trained at the higher education establishments of Saint Petersburg. This name became synonymous with the ideals and rights of an emerging Belarusian nation, while a fledgling national identity was again assumed through the media of language, culture and literature. An upsurge in democratic and national liberation ideas and thinking was now creating real conditions for the establishment of Belarusian statehood. Also this century, an important demographic development occurred that was to have very significant and tragic consequences for future generations and society in general. Belarusian lands were included in the Pale of Settlement, the territorial area into which Jews from all over the empire were forced to re-locate their homes and communities, such that by the time of the German invasion in 1941, the population of some of the towns that fell under Nazi oppression and tyranny were up to 70% Jewish.

THE 20TH CENTURY The first national political party (the Belarusian socialist Gromada party) was created in 1903, with the objectives of overthrowing autocracy and bringing about a Russian federation of democratic republics. Each of these republics was to be a separate nation with statehood, cultural and national autonomy and the inalienable right to independent self-determination. After the abolition of serfdom in the wider Russian empire in 1861, there had been slow but effective reform of the means of land allocation, but this did not prevent the mass displacement of the peasant classes from the lands of modern-day Belarus to Siberia. Approximately 335,000 people took this option between 1907 and 1914, while many more from the privileged classes dispersed further afield into Western Europe and beyond to America.

LATVIA

POLAND

Polatsk

●VITEBSK

RUSSIAN SSR

MINSK■

MOGILEV●

BELARUS SSR

Babrusk●

●GOMEL

Mozyr●

POLAND

UKRANIAN SSR

N

As had been the case on countless occasions in the past, Belarusian territory was again a battleground when hostilities broke out in 1914, with bloody and brutal clashes between opposing armies of the German and Russian empires. After Russia's entry into the war, martial law was declared in Belarus. As with other conflicts across the centuries, there was widespread destruction and mass occupation, this time by troops under the German flag. Then in November 1917, the armed uprising in Petrograd (formerly Saint Petersburg) and the homecoming to Russian territories of the Bolshevik leader Vladimir Iliych Ulyanov (the revolutionary Lenin) hastened the end of tsarism in the empire. Political activity in Belarus intensified and the first independent Belarusian democratic republic was established on 25 March 1918, despite the continuing German occupation. The influence of the Bolshevik revolution was acquiring significant momentum and the German occupation came to an end, but the declaration of the new republic's status could not prevent the proclamation of Soviet power in Minsk. As a result, the Belarusian Soviet Socialist Republic (BSSR) came into existence in Smolensk on 1 January 1919.

The Russians subsequently occupied much of Lithuania and as a result, the new state became the Lithuanian-Belarusian Soviet Socialist Republic in February 1919, the capital of which was Vilnius. War between Poland and the emerging Soviet Union ensued, during which the territory of much of the nascent country was under Polish occupation (including Minsk). Then on 31 July 1920, the BSSR was proclaimed for a second time after the expulsion of Polish troops. Unfortunately for the new state, however, the 1921 Treaty of Riga resulted in the annexation by Poland of the western territories and the flickering flame of the emerging Belarusian identity was extinguished. Elsewhere, the rump of the BSSR, under Bolshevik control, continued to exist in the form of six administrative districts of the province of Minsk, with a total population of 1.5 million people. It joined the Union of Soviet Socialist Republics (USSR) on 30 December 1922 and its territories were expanded first in 1924, then again in 1926, when 17 western districts of the Russian SSR were added, the people of which were predominantly Belarusian. These districts remain part of modern-day Belarus.

In the years that followed (leading up to the outbreak of war once more in Europe in 1939), Soviet social policy made a dramatic volte face. In a very short space of time, the USSR emerged as a massive world power, bringing together diverse cultures, races and former nation states across an enormous geographical area (and several time zones!). At first, the concept of ethnicity was encouraged throughout the Union, with active promotion of disparate cultures and traditions, as if to show the world that "the Revolution" truly was an international movement that could transcend barriers of class, language and background. The Party also saw this as the best form of protection against so-called pernicious Western influences. Against that background, traditionalism and the concept of a specific identity were allowed to flourish in the Belarusian SSR. Things proved to be very different in the 1930s. The Georgian Georgi Djugashvili (Stalin) had incrementally (and by design) inherited stewardship of the Revolution from Lenin as the 1920s drew to a close and a dark period in the history of these lands ensued, as the fear of internal opposition and the paranoia of the Soviet leader took hold. Millions were incarcerated, tortured and murdered across the USSR in Stalin's infamous purges. As many times before in history, Belarusian nationalists were cruelly suppressed. The features and horrors of this dark period of world history are widely documented elsewhere, but the terrible contradiction of the huge advances proclaimed by the Soviet Union at the time in terms of astonishing economic growth against a background of mass murder and social re-engineering on a scale previously unimagined in the modern world is a grim one indeed. The new dawn of hope for Belarusian culture that had been so joyously celebrated in the 1920s proved to have been a very false one indeed as the 1930s drew to a close.

Following the notorious and shameful 1939 pact of mutual non-aggression, German and Soviet tanks simultaneously rolled across Poland from the West and the East respectively. The state boundary that had existed immediately prior to the 1921 Treaty of Riga was quickly restored as the western territories and their communities were forcibly snatched back from Polish control and sovereignty. When the Nazis dissolved the pact in spectacular fashion by invading the Soviet Union in 1941 under Operation Barbarossa, which was designed to deliver Hitler's avowed intention to wipe the USSR from the face of the earth, the Soviet Union responded by entering the global fray. The 'Great Patriotic War' had begun. As the most westerly of the SSRs, Belarus was quickly overrun by the Nazis, in just two months. The occupation that followed was cruel and brutal. It was resisted by a mass movement of guerrilla and partisan activity throughout the republic involving many thousands of active volunteers, backed by many thousands more in reserve. The occupying forces were actively and ruthlessly opposed, but in turn, this led to yet more atrocities on the part of the invaders. Almost 25% of the population were brutally murdered in hundreds of punitive operations that brought about the deaths of men, women and children through the systematic burning and destruction of thousands of villages and hamlets under the pretext of fighting guerrillas. Today, this tragic loss of life and brutal destruction of whole communities is commemorated at the memorial complex of Khatyn in Minsk province, the site of one such village burnt with its residents, a haunting and deeply moving memorial that is described elsewhere in this book.

In July 1944, amidst scenes of unparalled patriotic fervour and wild abandon, Marshall Zhukov's Red Army completed the liberation of the country following a major offensive. The cost was enormous, both economically and in terms of loss of life. The capital Minsk had been almost completely destroyed and today, very few pre-war buildings are still standing. And of the 2 million Belarusian people who lost their lives in the war, many died in the concentration camps of the Third Reich across occupied Europe. In addition, almost 380,000 had been removed to Germany for the purpose of enforced labour. Incredibly, it was not until 1971 that the country's population again reached its pre-war level, although the Jewish community had been all but wiped out and never recovered.

In August 1945, under the Soviet-Polish Treaty, 17 districts of Byelostock and three of Brest (but not the city itself) were formally transferred to Poland, although the majority of western Belarus was retained by the Soviet Union. Also in 1945, the Belarusian SSR was one of the 51 signatories to the founding of the United Nations Organisation. It says much about the national psyche that within the republic itself, as with others in the USSR, this act was regarded as an acknowledgement on the part of the international community of the contribution made by the USSR to the crushing defeat of Hitler's Nazi Germany. It is difficult to argue with this standpoint. Between 1939 and 1945, conservative estimates place the war dead of the USSR at an incredible 24 million people. Some place the actual figure at 30 million. This astonishing statistic is topped only by the fact that even the lower of these two figures exceeds the *total* of war dead of every other country in the world, on both sides of the conflict.

The damage and destruction of the war years was reversed in spectacular fashion and at an incredible pace by means of a rigidly enforced series of plans of regeneration through industrialisation and collective farming, all on a massive scale. A new Minsk, rising from the ashes of the old, was at the very heart of this process of re-birth and renewal. The BSSR established itself as a major centre of manufacturing within the USSR and the consequent creation of jobs brought in a huge immigrant population from the Russian Federation SSR, including into positions of influence within the government of the republic. As in earlier times, this process of mass immigration was said to be a form of "protection"; as the most westerly of the Soviet republics, the BSSR was Stalin's first line of defence (both militarily, culturally and ideologically) against the perceived moral bankruptcy of the West. But as had been the case in the 1930s, one consequence of this process of social engineering was that traditional Belarusian culture came under threat once more.

THE CHERNOBYL LEGACY The consequences of the accident which occurred in the early hours of 26 April 1986 at the Chernobyl nuclear power plant, then in the Soviet Union and now within the territory of Ukraine, have proved to be nothing

CHERNOBYL CAESIUM-137 CONTAMINATION (2001)

KEY

Caesium–137 contamination
(curies per km²)

| 1–5 | 5–15 | 15–40 | 40+ |

N

Bradt

VITEBSK

MINSK■   MOGILEV

●GRODNO

Babrusk●

Vetka

●GOMEL

●BREST   Pinsk●

Mozyr●

0 ———50km
0 ———50 miles

Chernobyl

short of a catastrophe for Belarus, and in terms of the economic, ecological and social impacts, it is universally regarded as the worst incident in the history of commercial nuclear power.

During the course of tests to determine the ability of the fourth reactor to power safety systems if the external electricity supply was lost, a steam explosion occurred, triggering a fire, a further series of explosions and then a nuclear meltdown, in which the core of the reactor was destroyed. As the roof of the reactor was blown into the sky, the consequent inrushing of oxygen reacted with the extremely high temperature of the reactor fuel to produce a graphite fire, which then hastened the spread of radioactive material. The fallout exceeded that generated by the explosion over Hiroshima in 1945 and was 16 million times greater than the release in the accident at Three Mile Island in Pennsylvania in 1978. As local people watched from the balconies of their flats in the nearby city of Pripyat, just 2km away, the explosion and the deadly cloud that billowed out in its wake (which is said to have been actively glowing) hurled nuclear fuel, intensely radioactive (but short-lived) isotopes, primarily iodine-131 and other long-lived isotopes such as caesium-137, strontium-90, americium-241 and plutonium-238, 239, 240 and 241 high into the night sky and the atmosphere. It must have been quite a sight. And how chilling it is to reflect now that the onlookers can have had no understanding at all of the mortal danger in which the fates had placed them.

In 1986, Pripyat, Chernobyl and Belarus were all part of the USSR. Pripyat and Chernobyl are now in Ukraine. The city was once home to over 50,000 people, but today it is a ghost town, a snapshot in time, left exactly as it was when residents were evacuated later that day, with the remains of everyday life still to be seen all around.

Emergency measures that were immediately put into place succeeded in extinguishing the fires on the roof of the reactor, but the fire crews who rushed to the scene were not told of the extreme radioactivity of the smoke and debris. All of the fire-fighters received fatal doses, while the fire inside the reactor was not finally extinguished until helicopter crews had dropped large amounts of sand, lead, clay and boron onto it. By the end of the year, a concrete sarcophagus had been erected over the reactor, but it was always intended to be an interim measure only. It stands there still and lately cracks have begun to appear. The international community has come together to design a much more sophisticated tomb to encase the plant more effectively, but the cost will be immense. To date, no works have begun.

The immediate response of the Soviet authorities was to say and do nothing by way of aid for local people. This proved to be a catastrophic abrogation of social responsibility. For example, informed opinion suggests that had the authorities made supplies of non-radioactive iodine quickly available to the population, the absorption of radioactive iodine into the thyroid gland of many, with the long-term deleterious health effects that followed, would have been avoided.

In the days that followed, the evacuation of residents in the locality of the plant was stepped up, but people were not told why they were being moved. The international community began to hear rumours of a nuclear disaster, but every story was categorically denied by the authorities. Meanwhile, soldiers and workers known as 'liquidators' were sent in to mount a huge clean-up campaign. This began with the removal of debris in the vicinity of the plant, then spread to the large-scale sluicing down of buildings in an ever-increasing radius. All that this achieved, of course, was to ensure the spread of radioactive material into the ground.

In the immediate aftermath of the explosion, several hundred people, mostly workers and liquidators, were hospitalised, of whom 31 subsequently died (28 from acute radiation exposure). Around 135,000 people were evacuated from the locality and between 300,000–600,000 liquidators were involved in the decontamination of the 30km evacuation zone around the plant. Subsequently, hundreds of thousands more people were evacuated as the authorities began to comprehend the scale of the disaster and the area of land that had been affected.

The initial risk to health came from the concentration of radioactive iodine, which has a half-life of eight days. Iodine is readily absorbed into the thyroid gland. This happened both directly and also longer term as, for example, children drank supplies of contaminated milk. As a result, the incidence of thyroid cancer (and lesser conditions) has risen sharply over the years. Over 500,000 people in Belarus alone are thought to have thyroid pathology. Of greater impact on the infrastructure of society was the effect of contamination of the soil with caesium-137 (half-life 30 years) and strontium-90 (half-life 28 years). Indeed, 21% of the total area of Belarus is thought to have been contaminated with caesium-137. Where it is present in the soil, it is absorbed by plants, insects, grazing animals and crops, and by these means enters the local food supply.

The long-term effects of the catastrophe have been subject to much speculation and conflicting hypotheses. It is true that relatively few people died directly as a result of the *explosion* itself. It is also true that the number of cancers and birth defects directly attributable to radiation has been very difficult to measure. Indeed, a report of the Chernobyl Forum (comprising a number of UN organisations, the World Health Organization, the International Atomic Energy Agency, the Belarusian government and others) sought to minimise the consequences of the accident. This report met with heavy criticism, particularly from those organisations working directly with communities in the affected areas. A subsequent report (TORCH), commissioned by a German MEP, predicted far greater consequences. Then in 2006, Greenpeace issued its own report to coincide with the 20th anniversary of the disaster, predicting yet more significant effects not simply from increased rates of cancer, but also from intestinal, heart, circulatory and respiratory problems, as well as damage to the immune system.

It is also widely accepted that in addition to specific health problems of this nature, those exposed to the radiation (and indeed, many who were not) continue to exhibit many of the symptoms that commonly manifest themselves in the aftermath of trauma, such as fear, stress, anxiety, depression, physical symptoms that are hard to explain and a feeling of hopelessness.

The state has sought to address all of these issues (at very significant cost to the economy) and is particularly concerned with the health and well-being of children living in contaminated areas. Many sanatoria and rehabilitation centres in so-called 'clean' areas exist to facilitate this. Charities and non-governmental organisations have been established in many of the countries in western and northern Europe to offer recuperation holidays to children. Working in partnership with local administrations in Belarus, these organisations have been able to offer almost 220,000 children the opportunity to leave their irradiated homeland for varying lengths of time. It is widely accepted that these breaks have a very positive effect on health.

Today, however, the reality of life in Belarus is that almost two million people continue to inhabit areas that were (and still are) subject to radioactive contamination to some degree.

THE CULTURAL CHERNOBYL Later in 1986, the policies of sweeping and institutional reform instigated by the Soviet President Mikael Gorbachev (the conventional English spelling has been used throughout this guide, although a more accurate phonetic translation would be Gorbachov) afforded the Belarusian people an opportunity to reassert their national identity and rail back against the so-called Russification policy that had been followed since the early days of the Cold War (see above). Formal representations were made, including by way of petition, to expose and highlight the long-term suppression of Belarusian culture and heritage. In the climate of the times, social commentators dubbed this turn of events the 'cultural Chernobyl'. By now, the seeds of unrest and revolution were beginning to fall from the trees all across the lands of the Warsaw Pact. Then in June 1988, the bodies of as many as 300,000 of Stalin's victims were discovered in mass graves, although claims as to numbers, responsibility and even as to whether or not these murders ever occurred at all, have been the subject of denial and counter-denial ever since the discovery of the site. Whatever the truth of the situation, the proponents of Belarusian nationalism used it as proof that the Soviet state did indeed engage in a deliberate policy of cultural and ethnic suppression. The socio-economic consequences of these events were such that political opposition began to achieve momentum that was ultimately irresistible during the last years and eventual break-up of the USSR, notwithstanding that Belarus was (and still is) considered to be one of the most traditionally communist of the union's republics. As the USSR lurched towards disintegration and nationalist voices began to be heard once more, the BSSR steadily began to assert its sovereignty.

The last throw of the dice for the ailing USSR was the bungled coup to remove Gorbachev (Yeltsin's finest hour!) in 1991. It failed within days and soon after, on 25 August, Belarus declared full independence. Then on 19 September, the BSSR was officially renamed the Republic of Belarus, when the heads of the governments of the Russian, Ukrainian and Belarusian SSRs signed the Act on Denunciation of the Union Treaty of 1922. From that day, the USSR ceased to exist and a newly independent sovereign state of Belarusian peoples was born within the nascent Commonwealth of Independent States, in which it was joined by the Russian Federation and Ukraine.

On 15 March 1994, the Supreme Council of the Republic of Belarus adopted a new constitution, under which the country was proclaimed a unitary democratic legal state. On 10 July that year, Alexander Grigoryevich Lukashenko was elected the first president of the new republic. A firm opponent of the Gorbachev reforms, his background was state farm administration and he was swept to power on a ticket to restore stability. Against a background of mass insecurity and fear for the future, he promised a return to the safety of a regime whose loss was already being mourned. He captured the mood of the times perfectly. He holds the position of president to this day, following sweeping victories with very large majorities in the presidential elections of 2001 and 2006.

GOVERNMENT, POLITICS AND ADMINISTRATION

First, the official facts: the head of state is the president, who is directly elected by the people for a five-year term of office, although this period was effectively extended to seven years as a consequence of a presidential referendum in 1996. The office holder is also the guarantor of certain inalienable rights and institutions, including the constitution and the rights and freedoms of individual citizens. In addition, the position carries with it a wide-ranging portfolio of rights, including to call national referenda, dissolve parliament, determine the structure of government, dismiss the heads of judicial and other bodies, conduct negotiations on and execute international treaties, declare states of emergency, impose martial law and abolish governmental acts. The president can also issue decrees and instructions of lawful and binding force throughout the country. The parliament is the National Assembly, which consists of two chambers: a lower house (the House of Representatives, with 110 members) and an upper house (the Council of Ministers of the Republic of Belarus, with 64 members). The Council is the core function of state administration, exercising executive power on behalf of the people. In so doing, the Council is responsible and accountable to both the President and the Parliament. It consists of the Prime Minister, Deputies of that office, Ministers and Chairs of the various State Committees. All of them are presidential appointees and there is no requirement that they be members of the legislature. The powers of the House of Representatives include to appoint the Prime Minister, propose constitutional amendments, call for a vote of confidence in the Prime Minister and make suggestions on domestic and foreign policy. The Council of the Republic has the power to select various government officials, conduct an impeachment trial of the president and to accept or reject bills passed from the House of Representatives. Each chamber may veto any law passed by local officials if contrary to the country's constitution. The Judiciary consists of the Supreme Court and various other specialised courts, such as the Constitutional Court (comprising 12 judges 'elected' for an 11-year term of office), to deal with specialist issues relating to the constitution. The President himself appoints judges to this Court, with appointments being confirmed by the Council of the Republic.

In the USSR, the political system was a single-party one: the Communist Party of the Soviet Union. When the system began to unravel as an unintended consequence of Mikael Gorbachev's sweeping reform by way of restructuring (*perestroika*), the plurality of the political landscape had already begun to emerge as, one by one, the former constituent republics declared independence. So it was that by the second half of 1993, the Ministry of Justice in Belarus had registered 12 political parties and seven non-governmental and political movements, including (amongst others), the Belarusian People's Front For Revival (1989), the United

Democratic Party of Belarus (1990), the Belarusian Peasants' Party (1991), the Belarusian Social & Democratic Party Gromada (1991), the Party of Communists of Belarus (1991), the Belarusian Christian & Democratic Union (1991), the Slavic Assembly Belaya Rus (1992) and the Green Party of Belarus (1992). Generally, all of them had few members, pursued different political objectives and goals, followed different ways of attaining them and were organised along different lines. Many did not stand the test of time due to lack of popular support, while others joined forces. But the general characteristic of the 'opposition' as being a disparate array of disjointed and poorly organised groups was as true then as it is today.

The office of president was first established in 1994, following the adoption of a new constitution in March of that year. Six contenders for the presidency were presented to the people in June and Alexander Lukashenko secured 45.1% of the popular vote, the highest of the six. In a second ballot run-off in July between Lukashenko and the second-placed candidate, former prime minister Kyebich, a self-styled 'traditionalist', Lukashenko secured more than four times as many votes as his opponent. Less than a year later, the first of a number of referenda was held, in which 83.3% of those who voted (64.8% of the electorate) agreed to the Russian language being granted official status of equality with Belarusian. A similar number agreed with the president's avowed policy of pursuing economic integration with Russia, whilst a lesser number (but still an overwhelming majority) agreed to adopt a new flag and to grant the president power to discontinue the Supreme Council.

The next referendum was held in November 1996, when 70% of those who voted agreed to new constitutional arrangements enabling the incumbent president's term of office to be extended to seven years and permitting the dissolution of parliament through the office of president. Western governments questioned the legitimacy of this referendum, but allegations of electoral impropriety have always been robustly denied by the Belarusian government.

Parliamentary elections were held in 2000 and 2004. The third national referendum was also held in October 2004, continuing the theme of increasing consolidation of presidential power. Almost 80% of voters are said to have agreed with the removal of the constitutional restriction on the number of terms for which an elected president could serve. All of these ballots attracted allegations of unfair practices on the part of international observers, claims that were hotly denied by the Belarusian government.

Further elections took place on 19 March 2006, including for president. The candidates were the incumbent Alexander Lukashenko, who was able to stand again following the constitutional reforms legitimised by the 2004 referendum; Alexander Milinkevich, the head of a loose federation of opposition parties (and still regarded today as the unofficial 'leader of the opposition'; and Alexander Kazulin, a Social Democrat. Several aspects of the administration of the election and of the campaign itself led to concern amongst Western governments and independent election monitoring bodies that there had been systemic failures in the process of democracy. There were allegations of intimidation and police brutality following several clashes between demonstrators and the authorities, including the forcible removal during the hours of darkness of a tented camp in central Minsk. On the other side, observers sent by the Commonwealth of Independent States, declared themselves satisfied that all was in order and that the interests of transparency, lawfulness and democracy had been fully met. Senior Belarusian government sources hotly disputed claims of irregularity, entertainingly rebuffing the allegations in robust fashion by countering with claims of a similar nature in respect of the re-election of George Bush to the White House. Whatever the reality, a landslide victory was declared for the incumbent president, with over 80% of the popular vote. Milinkevich polled just 6%.

The Council of Europe, which monitors democracy and human rights, has barred the country from membership since 1997. And the European Union has imposed travel bans on the president and other senior members of the government, along with punitive economic sanctions. Observers have also criticised the Belarusian government for human rights violations in respect of actions against non-governmental organisations, independent journalists and opposition politicians. And in testimony to the United States Senate Committee on Foreign Relations, Secretary of State Condoleezza Rice famously labelled Belarus as being one of six nations on the United States' list of 'outposts of tyranny'. In response, the Belarusian Foreign Ministry denounced this statement as 'a poor basis' for effective Belarusian–American relations. Indeed, all of the claims of administrative, constitutional and democratic irregularity are vehemently denied by the Belarusian government, which seeks to draw on the apparent hypocrisy of the international community in its response to conflict and its alleged interference in areas such as the Middle East and Afghanistan. Meanwhile, the political rhetoric around the globe continues apace.

As for present opposition to the government within the country, there is very little. A number of disparate groups exist, loosely headed by Alexander Milinkevich, but they cannot agree on a platform and while they periodically hold rallies in Minsk, at which inevitably there are clashes between demonstrators and police, they cannot call on popular support. The reality of life in modern Belarus is that prevailing circumstances do not encourage the development of a properly organised and credible opposition that can offer a real alternative to the present government. Indeed, most of the population regard those opposition groups that exist as little more than agitators and many people are distrustful of their motives. And all the while, the president continues to nurture popular support from the 'old guard' with agricultural subsidies and the prompt payment of pensions and salaries to the militia and the armed forces. To this day, there remains a fond and almost romantic affection for what are seen as the good old days of the Soviet Union. While statues of former Soviet leaders were torn down throughout the former Soviet Union as the Berlin Wall itself was reduced to rubble, Lenin still stands sentinel on a plinth of granite in every Belarusian town and city. And indeed, the policy of the government remains firmly to bring about ever closer relations with the Russian Federation, if not formal union with the state that many regard fondly as Mother Russia, whose President Putin continues to juggle many balls (if not flaming clubs) all at once, in his pursuit of closer relations with Western democracies. For international observers of diplomacy, these are interesting times indeed.

In administrative terms, the country is divided into six provinces, known as *oblasts*, each of which is named after the city serving as its administrative centre, with the *city* of Minsk, which is situated in the *province* of Minsk, having its own unique status. This form of administrative division is a clear inheritance from the days of the Soviet Union. The *oblasts* are further subdivided into *raions*, commonly translated as districts. Local legislative authorities are elected by the residents of each district, while local executive committees are appointed by higher executive authorities. The same applies to each *oblast*, with the leader of the executive authority being appointed by the president himself. The seven administrative provinces are Minsk city, Brest, Gomel, Grodno, Mogilev, Minsk and Vitebsk.

ECONOMY

The Belarusian economy is still believed to be around 80% state-controlled and has progressed little since the days of the Soviet Union. And indeed, considerable reliance is still placed on the supply of raw materials from the country's gigantic neighbour Russia. Every now and again Vladimir Putin flexes Russian muscles and reminds Alexander Lukashenko who is in charge by turning off the tap on the supply of natural gas. Most of the industrial and agricultural enterprises in Belarus remain in state hands, although there have been experiments with more market-based ventures on an ad hoc and ill-conceived basis, largely with spectacularly unsuccessful results. This is not least because the old-style Soviet mentality of the bosses and the workforce is ill-equipped to survive, let alone flourish, in global markets that are becoming ever more competitive and cut-throat. On its own, Belarus simply does not have the clout, the money, the influence or even the nous to muscle into the marketplace. So it does not try to be something it manifestly is not and as a result, it still has one of the last remaining state-controlled and rigidly monopolistic economies, certainly in Europe.

Today, collective farming dominates agriculture, which is based on pig breeding, the cultivation of potato, beet, grain and flax (the country's national flower) and also the processing of wood from the vast areas of forestation in the country. During the 1960s, heavy industry and mechanical engineering, most notably the manufacture of tractors (for which the country was famed) made a significant contribution not only to the country's own economic stability, but also to the economy of the USSR. In those terms, it was punching well above its weight, for notwithstanding its modest size, the Belarusian SSR was one of the most industrially advanced of the Soviet republics. All of that ended with the fall of the USSR and the disappearance overnight of the patronage and protection of its immediate neighbour, the Russian Federated SSR. Rudimentary market structures with non-existent governance arrangements meant that there was a free-for-all in state trading between the component former republics. It was all just a little like the Wild West for a while. Bit by bit, traditional industries rallied in Belarus after independence, even to the point of modest but incremental growth in the 1990s. But there has been little institutional reform since 1995, when the president took the first tentative steps in leading the country down the road of so-called 'market socialism'. This practice has seen the establishment and tightening of administrative, bureaucratic and market controls over both prices and currency exchange. At the same time, law reform has expanded the jurisdiction of the state over the management of business ventures, such that direct intervention is very much a reality. To underpin this monopolistic approach, a towering bureaucratic monolith of decree, regulation and statutory obligation has been created, such that not only businesses of every size and profile, but also charitable non-governmental organisations are subject to a rigorous and oftentimes debilitating regime of increasing interference on the part of the state. This has taken the form of random changes to the law, some of which have retrospectively applied fresh requirements and a burdensome process of complex inspection and monitoring. The state also has extensive power to 'hire and fire' senior company executives. Not surprisingly, this policy of state economic control and the West's perception of a need for political reform have made it difficult for the state to attract foreign investment. Would-be financiers are understandably nervous. It's just as well, then, that even though the tap is periodically turned off, the trade in oil and natural gas with Russia delivers a valuable commodity to Belarus at a knock-down and heavily discounted price, which it then sells on the open market at considerable profit.

Indeed, the advent of the 21st century saw economic policy shift into reverse gear in terms of market initiatives and during 2005, state control was increased when a number of significant private companies were renationalised. Interestingly, official government statistics show that in that year, there was 8% economic growth. And for a number of years now, it has been claimed that inflation has been steadily dropping. The estimated GDP in 2005 of US$79.13 billion (agriculture

9%, industry 32% and services 59%) should have equated to an annual income of around US$7,700 per head, but if you were to ask the average Belarusian for details of his or her income that year, the answer in most cases would be around 10% of that figure. Western observers placed the rate of inflation in 2005 at approximately 8–9%, while the United Nations believes that during the last ten years, average monthly income has grown from US$20 to US$225. Discussion with the man in the street paints a very different picture and in 2003, 27% of the population were assessed as being below the poverty line. As ever, statistics can be used to supposedly prove and disprove any theory or hypothesis.

At the end of 2005, the labour force was estimated to be 4.3 million, of whom 14% were then engaged in agriculture, 35% in industry and 51% in services. Only 1.6% of the population were at that time officially registered as unemployed, although there is a strong perception that a sizeable proportion of the labour force is under-utilised, thin on work and considerably less productive than it might be.

In today's market-driven world, where global corporations exercise greater power and influence than nation states, the health of a country's economy is linked to the response of international governments and financial organisations to its political direction. For Belarus, the most cursory examination of any international funding stream or source of aid, particularly those of the European Union, the World Bank and the International Monetary Fund, shows that compared with other countries in the region, it has been treated extremely partially. In effect, the people of the country find themselves at the sharp end of economic sanctions. And the man at the top is not exempt from this. In May 2006, the European Union passed a resolution freezing the assets of Alexander Lukashenko personally, along with a number of his colleagues in government. Travel and visa bans to the countries of the EU were also imposed at the same time. These sanctions were a direct consequence of the EU's belief that the election in March 2006 and the preceding suppression of opposition groups had been unlawfully conducted, fraudulent and improper.

The effect of all of this is to strengthen the president's belief that the interests of the country and its people lie in ever closer alignment with the systems and structures of the Russian Federation. At the opening ceremony of the first Belarusian–Russian economic forum in Minsk on 6 September 2005, Alexander Lukashenko addressed participants using these words: 'Without losing either country's sovereignty, we aim to develop a unified legal, economic and administrative system to become the foundation for our union state.' Only time and the government of the Russian Federation will determine the accuracy of this prediction.

From the very beginning of his presidency, Alexander Lukashenko made clear his avowed intention to deliver integration with the Russian Federation and he embarked on developing policies to achieve this outcome. One of his proposals was to introduce a single currency for a united Russia and Belarus. The change to a common currency would have meant the creation of a united central bank or agency and not surprisingly, the location and control of this was always contentious. As might be expected, the main debate was whether it should be in Moscow, Minsk or both at the same time.

After the election of Vladimir Putin to the presidency, Russia took a less positive position on the question of integration with Belarus and became decidedly lukewarm. In 2000, the National Bank of Belarus was forced into taking urgent measures to shore up the economy and the Belarusian rouble was significantly devalued. In December 2002, at a meeting of prime ministers of the two countries, it was jointly declared that integration was still a common goal and that at inception, the Russian rouble would be introduced as the common currency. It was intended that it would completely replace the Belarusian rouble on 1 January 2004 and that in 2007 or 2008, a new common currency would be introduced. But although the necessary technical and economical conditions were declared to have been created, Belarus never introduced the Russian rouble, with progressive postponements of steps towards transition. The position remains the same today.

PEOPLE

Official figures released in July 2007 estimate the population of the country at that time as 9,724,723. The earlier census taken in February 1999 showed the figure to be 10,045,237 at that date, with the subsequent count in December 2005 showing 9,750,500. All of this means that the negative growth rate is currently –0.06%. News that the population is continuing to fall will come as no surprise to those who know the country, for the leading ambition of many Belarusians, particularly the young, is to find a 'better life' elsewhere, usually in the West.

Government figures suggest that over 130 nationalities call Belarus their home, with by far the largest demographic group being that comprising native Belarusians, who make up 81% of the total population. Russians come next, with 11%, then Poles and Ukrainians, accounting for 4% and 2% respectively. Roughly 80% of the people are classed as belonging to the Russian Orthodox Church and around 10% are believed to be Roman Catholic, with the remaining 10% being Protestant, Jewish or Muslim.

Estimates also show that 3–3.5 million native Belarusians reside outside the country's borders, most of them in the United States of America, Russia, Ukraine and Poland.

The population density is around 49 per km² and over 70% of people live in urban areas. Not surprisingly, the most densely populated area is Minsk *oblast,* with 81 people per km², while the most sparsely inhabited area is in the north of Vitebsk *oblast,* where the figure is fewer than ten. Approximately 24% of the urban population, 1,758,000 people live in the capital city Minsk. Then come Gomel (506,000), Vitebsk (361,000), Mogilev (360,000), Brest (293,000) and Grodno (277,000).

Some 15.7% of the population is aged 14 years and under, with 69.7% being between 15 and 64. Those aged 65 and over account for the remaining 14.6%. The median age is currently 37.2 years. The birth rate is 11.16 births per 1,000 people and the death rate is 14.02 deaths per 1,000 people. The infant mortality rate is 13 deaths per 1,000 live births (as compared with 18.9 in 1994), with the life expectancy at birth being 69.08 years (64 for males and 75 for females). The size of the average family is 3.2 people. In 2003, there were 88 males for every 100 females living in the country. Interestingly, there has been a significant drop in fertility rates from 1.88 children per female in 1994, to 1.43 in 2007.

But all of these statistics (collectively and individually) are just numbers on a page. However commentators choose to interpret them, they say nothing about the national characteristics of the Belarusian people, and only by getting to know individuals and by earning their trust and respect can this be revealed. There are many features. Resilience, self-respect, pride, self-discipline, stoicism, hospitality, warmth, generosity, humour and the ability to sing and drink the night away are only some of them. A visit to this extraordinary country leaves many indelible imprints on the memory from things that are seen, but the ones that last the longest are memories of ordinary encounters with everyday people.

Belarusians live close to the earth and their relationship with nature and the seasons is intense. Spring, summer and autumn are spent tending the land and in

One day, perhaps soon, I shall sit down to write a travelogue by way of homage to the truly astonishing people that I have met; it may or may not include the aged *babooshka* whom I was foolish enough, in a moment of utter madness and entirely baseless bravado, to challenge to a drinking contest. After an evening of sumptuous but simple provender in a rural homestead close to the Russian border, we sat down to exchange traditional songs, tell stories and debate big issues. Almost everyone you meet has an enviable grasp of significant international affairs. The level of intellectual debate on matters of relevance to the future of the planet and to society puts us to shame in the West. One toast followed another as each topic of conversation came to a head, then we reached the point at which only she and I had yet to refuse the inevitable invitation for our glasses to be filled to the brim. My exhortations for the granny to drain hers met with a nonchalant look of utter indifference. Her timing was perfect; having milked the moment for every last drop of drama, she proceeded to raise the glass to her lips, then slowly but steadily, drank to the bottom before returning it to the table with precision and a further look of indifference, this time, bordering on contempt. I should have seen the signs and backed away in shame. But I persisted. And as my foolish bravado led me on, she maintained her steady hand, inscrutable visage and a clear resolve to see me off. I'm told that it was wonderful spectator sport and that I didn't admit defeat for at least four toasts after the first look of fear came into my eyes. And the *babooshka*? The only indication of any slight effect of the vodka was that she sang louder and louder, but no less melodiously. That apart, not a single word passed between us.

preparation for the long, dark winter. Those who live in the town will spend as much time as they can at a modest wooden cottage (*dacha*) owned by someone in their family, while rural dwellers will have their own extensive plot of land at home. The stockpile of produce from the year's labours will then be shared within the community. Indeed, the concept of the extended family is alive and well in Belarus. Whenever I sit down to eat at the table of my Belarusian family, the man of the house will reach for a slice of bread, close his eyes, bring the bread to his nose, inhale deeply, then look solemnly into my eyes and nod his head with a smile of understanding. The sense of a real fondness for and dependence upon the land is a palpable one.

LANGUAGE

Both Russian and Belarusian have equal status as formally adopted national languages. Belarusian is one of three historic eastern Slavonic languages and not surprisingly, it shares many vocabulary and grammatical similarities with the language of its state neighbours , especially Russian, Ukrainian and Polish. Further, some observers attribute similarities to the Baltic and Slavic languages as evidence that both are descended from a common ancestor, while others believe that this is simply due to geographical proximity and social convergence. Old Belarusian completed its formation between the 13th and 16th centuries with strong Polish influences and towards the end of that period, it became the third Slavic language (after Czech and Polish) in which printing had begun in state administrations. The end of the 18th century is widely regarded as the cross-over point between Old and Modern Belarusian, since when it has been strongly influenced by contrasting political and social changes and considerations. In particular, the promotion of Belarusian culture, language and literature in the 1920s was markedly reversed in the following decade. Under Stalin in 1933, one of the intended outcomes of the Soviet Union's grand 'Reform of Belarusian Grammar' was to cleanse the language of unwelcome historical interference and in particular, to remove the influences of earlier Polonisation, the archaisms and quaint colloquialisms promoted by so-called anti-state 'national democrats' and any artificial barriers between the Russian and Belarusian languages. There was further reform in 1959 and this revision holds good today. During *perestroika* ('restructuring') in the final days of the Soviet Union, Belarusian met with a significant revival. Indeed in 1990, it was envisaged that all administrative and official documentation of the then Belarusian SSR would be switched to Belarusian by the year 2000. Interestingly, this was halted after the election of Alexander Lukashenko as president in 1994, shortly after which the Russian language was afforded equal status. Latterly, there has been talk of further grammatical review and reform of the Belarusian language , but there do not appear to be any firm plans to do this and no further announcements have been made.

The Belarusian alphabet is based on the Cyrillic script, from the alphabet of the Old Church Slavonic language. The current form dates from 1918 and has 32 letters. The rules of modern grammar date from the 1959 reform.

Today, the untutored ear and eye would discern very little difference between Belarusian and Russian. And for observers of eastern European politics, it will be interesting to see how the two languages develop in terms of the current differences between the two. In particular, will linguistic convergence follow any future union between the two nation states?

RELIGION AND EDUCATION

Across history, Belarusian lands have been at the crossroads of culture and ideology, where two worlds collide. Both the West and the East have influenced social, political and ideological development and this applies to religious beliefs as much as to anything else. For most of history, there has been peace between the two major Christian faiths in Belarus (Orthodoxy and Catholicism), with relations between the two being characterised by at best tolerance and peaceful co-existence and at worst a tacit acceptance on the part of both of the presence of the other. This has certainly been so since compromise resulted in the Brest Church Union of 1596, under which the Orthodox Church of the Grand Duchy of Lithuania ceded the spiritual high ground by recognising the supremacy of Rome, the price of this self-imposed subjugation being the right to maintain its own rites, doctrines and customs. Initially (and inevitably), though, there was still reluctance on the part of Orthodox believers to accept a higher authority in this way. Before the Union, the Orthodox population was very much in the majority, in contrast not only to Catholic believers, but also Jews, Muslims and Protestants. But from the 17th to the 19th centuries, most followers of the Orthodox Church were gradually converted to the Uniate, which maintained many Orthodox traditions and rites. By the end of the 18th century, in fact, Uniate believers made up almost 70% of the population, although today only a small community remains. The balance of 30% comprised 15% Roman Catholics, 7% Jews, 6% Orthodox believers and 2% Protestants and others. The union eventually came to an end in 1839 when the Uniate Church merged with the Russian Orthodox Church, after which the Orthodox population again predominated, comprising over 60% of the population by the early 20th century.

As traditional Belarusian culture acquired a new prominence towards the end of the 20th century with the seismic changes in politics and dogma, so the Church came to be regarded both by people and state as a medium for the spiritual foundation of the community. Old eparchies were revived and new ones founded, under the administration of a synod headed by the Minsk and Slutsk Metropolitan Filaret, the patriarchal exarch of all Belarus. And by January 2002, the doors of 983 Orthodox churches were open for worship, with 135 new churches also under construction. In all, there were 1,119 priests, compared with 399 in 1988.

And yet today, a very significant section of the Orthodox community still consists of Старовери ('Old Believers'), who first appeared on Belarusian territory in the late 17th century. They adhere to the Orthodox canons that existed in Russia prior to the major reforms of the time. Under Catherine the Great of Russia, they were widely persecuted for their beliefs. Today most live in the Gomel region, with a particularly large community in the district of Vetka.

The most revered of Orthodox symbols are the saints of the Church, with nearly every place of worship claiming the body or a physical remnant of at least one, as well as prominently displaying significant numbers of icons. Different saints are identified as being associated with different needs or specialisms. At any hour on any day, local people will visit specific icons of particular saints in their local church, praying, incessantly crossing themselves and lighting beeswax candles before them as a sign of faith and by way of an offering. Every church will have at least one corner in which *babooshkas* take charge of stalls selling a huge range of relics, from candles of varying length and girth, to icons of every size and form, for the home, office and even the car.

Indeed, icons are ubiquitous and every home will have a corner of a living room opposite the door as a shrine, in which the most revered and favoured family saint is portrayed in iconic form at the highest point of the room, as close to the ceiling as possible, reverently gazing down from on high to bless the family and its home. At their most ornate, they are painted on wood and covered with gold and silver plate. Not only are they revered, but also feared, with believers vesting them with mysterious and mystical powers. Today, most motorists will proceed about their journeys with a simple icon on the dashboard, or attached to the rear-view mirror.

Orthodox church buildings were traditionally built in the shape of a Greek cross and even newly constructed ones bear the hallmark of the familiar onion dome embossed with gold colouring, topped by the familiar Greek cross. Originally built of wood, no nails were ever used in the construction, the whole being held together by the intricacies of the design. Inside, the iconostasis, a sacred wall covered in icons, holy murals and other pictures of saints, closes off the public area from the section in which only priests are allowed.

On most days of the week, churches are a hive of activity. Participating in an Orthodox service is a stirring and emotionally charged experience. Priests in flowing robes and with the deepest of baritone voices chant prayers and intonations while vigorously swinging incense holders, with an unseen choir making rousing interventions by means of soaring responses. All the time, believers stand in rapt concentration (there are no chairs), constantly crossing themselves and joining in with the responses. This is absolutely not to be missed, but visitors must be sure to treat the occasion with the utmost respect. Without fail, men should remove hats and women cover their heads. Taking photographs is not a good idea, while purchasing and lighting a candle before an icon will always be regarded favourably.

One of the most moving sights is to witness a less formal ritual involving a junior priest and perhaps one or two *babooshkas*. This is a particularly common event. The priest will recite certain prayers and the ladies will respond with light, beautiful and haunting harmonies. Even sceptical hearts will miss a beat.

Given the history of Catholicism in the area and with Polish Catholics on the western border of the country, it is no surprise to find a significant community still in Belarus. Around one in five of the population is Roman Catholic, most of whom are ethnic Poles. Not unexpectedly, the biggest enclave of Catholicism is to be found in Grodno, bordering Poland in western Belarus. In 2002, there were 482 such communities in the country, 170 of which could be found in the Grodno region. In all, there are 285 Roman Catholic priests throughout the country.

Protestantism (in the form of Lutheranism, Calvinism and Evangelical Christianity) is slowly but incrementally expanding from west to east, although it remains a small community consisting mostly of ethnic Germans.

Judaism in Belarus can be traced back as far as the 9th century and its influence was most significant early in the 20th century, when the Jewish population was in the majority (sometimes up to 90%) in many small towns throughout the country. By the end of the Great Patriotic War, however, the community had been all but wiped out as part of the Nazis' 'final solution'. It has never recovered and only a tiny number of synagogues remain.

There was a thriving Islamic population at the time of the Golden Horde in the Middle Ages, but in modern times, only modest numbers of Tatars still live in the country, although small numbers of new mosques have opened in recent times.

The system of education in Belarus is state-administered and funded directly from the budgets of local tiers of government, to which schools report. The structure consists of first kindergarten education, then school education and training, vocational and technical education, secondary special education, higher education, training of scientific and scientific pedagogical personnel and the re-training and self-development of adults. In 2002, almost 71% of pre-school children were in full-time education in nurseries and kindergartens. The two state languages of Belarusian and Russian are used equally for teaching and training. The whole process is overseen by the state Ministry of Education, which has developed a curriculum that consists of compulsory and optional disciplines. The compulsory modules are society and humanitarianism, nature and science, culture and the arts and physical and sports development. Within this overarching structure, there is a surprising degree of autonomy for schools locally to design their own media for teaching, based on capacity, resources and the wishes of parents. Much of the learning is done by rote. The commitment of teaching staff to the education of the state's children is admirable and beyond question, but it is clear that in terms of strategic educational planning, there is much progress to be made.

CULTURE

Across the centuries, the maintenance of 'traditional' Belarusian culture has been problematic. Indeed, the first difficulty is to establish the characteristics of that culture, so diverse were the founding influences and the means of suppression under various regimes.

DRESS The origins of traditional Belarusian dress are as difficult to establish as any area of culture. At different points in history, various sources have been claimed to suit particular political expediency. It is likely, however, that today's antecedents date back as far as the time of the Varangian princes in the 9th century, but not surprisingly, dress also displays the influence of cultures from the neighbouring countries (Poland, Lithuania, Latvia and Russia) to which at various times throughout history, Belarus has been linked in terms of government and society. Primarily made from wool and hand–produced linen, its key features are straight lines and white and red colouring, often with intricate patterns at the edges (as with the national flag), dependent upon the place of origin. There are many subtle variances of design from region to region and even from district to district. Historically, variances from village to village were not uncommon. The rules of society used to dictate which garments were to be worn on which occasions. For example, it was considered indecent for a man to go outdoors without wearing a particular form of jacket over his shirt. It was also prohibited for married women to go out unless wearing a headdress and apron. For both, it was also considered decent for the neck, elbows and knees to be covered. Special attention was paid to female clothing at festival times, reflecting the status of women in Belarusian culture as mothers and home-keepers. Today, national dress is most frequently worn at festivals and special occasions such as weddings. It remains the most prominent embodiment of traditional culture and can most often be seen at public commemorations of special events in history or in state processions.

CRAFTS Traditional crafts include pottery, wood engraving and plait work with straw, willow, root and bark. The most notable and uniquely attributable example of Belarusian folk art is the *rushnik*, or ceremonial towel. Flaxen threads are woven together, usually on looms of historic design, to form delicate silvery white and grey geometric patterns, with ancient symbols featuring in the woven or embroidered decoration of symbolic red colouration at the edges. These sacred items have a very significant place in the hearts and lives of Belarusians. Not only have they long been used for practical and decorative purposes, but they also have an important role in the performance of certain rites, such as those at family meals on national holidays, weddings, christenings, funerals and for welcoming guests to the home with bread and salt. *Rushniki* are commonly to be found draped over icons, both in church and at home.

CUISINE Traditional cuisine displays the same diversity of influence as dress and crafts, although it is widely held to mostly resemble that of Lithuania. Travellers in other parts of eastern Europe will encounter much that they have seen before and little that they will not have seen. Great significance has always been attached to bread, both as a staple foodstuff, but also as an important symbol in many rituals. The potato forms the basis for many meals (historically referred to as 'second bread') and the plentiful supply of mushrooms in the forests that extensively cover the land ensures their prominence in many recipes. The most well-known dish is *draniki* (potato pancakes), usually served with a rich pork stew in pots and liberally lubricated with the ubiquitous elixir of life, vodka. Only moderate seasoning is used in cooking.

LITERATURE Many of the chronicles written in the 12th and 13th centuries endure today as both historical records and also works of great literature in their own right. The only earlier examples of literature that are known to have existed are religious works from the 11th century. The ancient Belarusian language was granted state legitimacy when Belarusian lands were subsumed within the Grand Duchy of Lithuania, a significant event that made a real contribution to the development of literature in the 14th to the 16th centuries. The earliest literary figure of repute was the humanist and scientist Francysk Skaryna, who was a well-known writer and translator in the ancient city of Polotsk. Between 1517 and 1519, he translated much of the Bible into the ancient Belarusian written language for the first time, then published his work in Prague and Vilnius. This was one of the first acts of mass printing in book form in Europe. In 1562, the philosopher Simon Budny, a renowned figure of the European Reformation as a publicist and translator, published the first printed book in ancient Belarusian on the territory of modern Belarus.

In the 1600s, Belarusian–Russian poet, playwright and enlightener Simeon Polotsky was a prolific figure. He introduced the grand Baroque style of writing, which was followed up to the first half of the 19th century, when new trends of romanticism began to reflect the living language and folklore of the population, in a sentimental homage to the perceived idyll of self-styled 'traditional' bucolic life. The most prominent figure of this movement was the great Polish-Belarusian poet Adam Mitskevich. He was born in the district of Novogrudok and he dedicated his great epic poetic work *Pan Tadeush* to his homeland. At the same time, Vincent Dunin-Martinkevich, who is considered by many to be the father of modern Belarusian literature, began to consolidate his reputation with the publication of notable collections of verses. Another prominent figure at the end of the 19th century was Frantishek Bogushevich, a poet who is credited as being the first national writer of folklore. The first nationalist newspapers to be granted lawful status, *Nasha Dolya* ('Our Lot') and *Nasha Niva* ('Our Cornfield'), served as a useful public platform to promote the works of such eminent writers as Yanka Kupala, Yakub Kolas, Eloisa Paskevich, Maxim Bogdanovich, Maxim Goretsky and others, in the form of plays, prose and romantic and dramatic poetry imbued with the romantic and patriotic ideal of independent nation statehood.

After the October Revolution in Russia in 1917, national and revivalist themes dominated Belarusian literature as part of the movement to encourage Belarusians to adopt greater self-awareness and identification of their heritage. This was dealt a severe blow by the ideological repressions of the 1930s, but as is often the case, suppression and persecution wrought a number of magnificent works in the form of poetry and drama created by artists such as Vladislav Golubok, Mikhas Charot, Vladimir Dubovka, Kondrat Krapiva and Pavlyuk Trus. During the Great Patriotic War, art and satire were particularly powerful tools, as well as poetry and heroic novels. The theme of the war, particularly in the context of suffering and misery, dominated the Belarusian and Soviet literary landscape for a long time, notable examples in prose form being *Deep Flow* and *Troubled Happiness* (Ivan Shamyakin), *Unforgettable Days* (Mikhas Lynkov), *Khatyn Story* (Ales Adamovich) and *Neidorf* (Ivan Ptashnikov). Classic epic poems included *Blockade* by Rygor Borodulin and *It Doesn't Pain the Dead* by Vasil Bykov. As the destruction of wartime was replaced by regeneration and rebuilding in the peace that followed, the perceived idyll of rural life began to be promoted again, generally with an abundance of over-sentimentality, this time in the works of Melezh, Adamchik, Streltsov and others, while historical themes and heroic traditions again found a voice as well, the most famous proponent being the brilliant Vladimir Korotkevich. The 1950s through to the 1970s saw the emergence of many notable poets, novelists and dramatists, such as Sergei Zakonnikov, Viktor Kozko and Nikolai Matukovsky. Then after 1986, the Chernobyl catastrophe began to feature as a dark and sombre theme, most notably in the works of Shamyakin, Alexeevich, Karamazov and Buravkin.

MUSIC Musically, Belarus boasts a mixture of artists and styles. Folk music, which derives from the culture of the East Slavic tribes, the Kryvichy, Dryhavichy and Radzimichy, is particularly prominent; consistent themes through the ages have included the adventures of dynastic families and also a celebration of farming through the seasons. As with so much of the tradition and culture of the Belarusian people, the historical realities of suppression and of life inextricably linked to the land have been the inspiration for many an epic song chronicling the lives of farm labourers, peasants, workers and revolutionaries. A new form of musical expression, that of the stirring melody and heroic lyric, was born out of the escapades of the partisans and guerrillas in the Great Patriotic War. Today, a number of higher education establishments in the country are devoted to the promotion and study of the theory, history and practice of musical folklore. *Skomorokhs* (travelling minstrels) were the first to perform secular music in the early Middle

Ages, but they were also prominent in promoting ritualistic songs and chants (such as canticles and psalms) which formed part of religious ceremonies.

The tide of Belarusian musical culture was to ebb and flow over the course of the 20th century according to the prevailing political circumstances of the times. In more recent years, new groups have formed, such as Pesnyary, Syabry, Palats, Krama and Troitsa, all of whom inject a more modern rock feel to traditional songs, but without losing sight of their heritage. The number of festivals devoted to ethnic music has also increased, attracting significant popular support not only through attendance at the events themselves, but also through high profile television networking. A number of the more prominent Belarusian performers are showcased regularly in Poland and Lithuania, where substantial Belarusian communities still exist, as a result of the many changes in national boundaries in this part of Europe over the centuries. Of more dubious worth culturally is that since 2004, Belarus has been an enthusiastic participant in the pan-European 'Eurovision Song Contest'.

THEATRE Traditional theatre was based on folk rituals and games, relying originally upon the work of strolling minstrels to spread its influence. This is not unique to Belarus, of course; far from it. Puppet theatres were particularly popular in the 16th century, a tradition that continues to this day, with most towns boasting their own. Popularity with children here is still very high indeed. Theatre schools gained wide support in the 16th to 18th centuries and in the latter half of the 18th century, performances were regularly given by theatre companies that were established and sponsored by rich magnates and estate owners, under whose patronage many of them flourished. Some of these companies consequently acquired professional status. The National Academic Theatre was established in 1920 under F. Zhdanovich, followed by the second Belarusian State Theatre in 1926, in the town of Vitebsk. The 1930s saw steady progress in the staging of plays devoted to historical events, but during the Great Patriotic War, most troupes suspended their theatre-based activities, preferring instead to take their shows on the road wherever possible to visit active army units at the front and to maintain focus on keeping the morale and spirits of troops and civilians alike as high as possible. Today, festivals promoting the dramatic arts are regularly held all over the country, featuring artists from home and abroad.

The history of professional ballet dates back to the middle of the 18th century and in modern times, the National Academic Bolshoi Theatre of Ballet of the Republic of Belarus has gained an enviable reputation, notwithstanding the higher profile of its equivalent in Moscow. Today, every town of significance size will have its own flourishing opera and ballet theatre. Any opportunity to attend a performance of Belarusian ballet in Minsk should be eagerly taken; the standard is high, the price of admission ridiculously cheap by Western standards and there is a degree of informality about proceedings that lends itself to a most enjoyable experience. The audience is always full of children and families, with the dress code being relaxed in the extreme. No-one stands on ceremony, but unfortunately this has a downside; it is particularly unnerving, for example, to hear mobile phones ringing intermittently throughout a performance and then hugely irritating when they are inevitably answered.

FINE ARTS The history of fine art as a synthesis of cultures from the East and the West can be traced back to the second half of the 14th century. The development of icon painting and the production of book miniatures were greatly influenced by the art and folklore traditions of Byzantium, including a high level of manuscript illumination art. After the October Revolution in 1917, the town of Vitebsk, still renowned for its links with the arts, became the centre of the revolutionary avant-garde movement, enabling brilliant and talented artists to forge their reputations. Perhaps the most famous of them all was Marc Chagall. Born in Vitebsk in 1887, Chagall gained his primary artistic education in the studio of the well-known painter Jeguda Pen, before studying in France. Upon his return to Vitebsk, he founded, lived and worked at an arts school which attracted all of the best talent of the day from around the country. Today, the house where Chagall spent his youth is a popular visitor destination. For more on Chagall and his significant influence on Belarusian culture, see page 179. When the ideological oppression of the Soviet Union was lifted in the early 1990s, artistic life became more dynamic and much more diverse. Design, photography and computer graphics became new media for expression, while the avant-garde movement of the Vitebsk art school also found new life.

NATURAL HISTORY AND CONSERVATION

Natural vegetation covers over 70% of the area of Belarus, 38% of which is forest. Farmland takes up 43.9% of the land mass, which includes arable land extending to 26.8% of the total. The best way to truly understand the extent of the Belarusian **forest** is to fly over the country, when the clear impression gained is that mile after mile of territory is covered by a green blanket that is only occasionally broken by concentrated areas of farmland connected by ribbon-like roads. True there are subtle variances; in the north, the area of lakes, water is a contrasting feature, while in the south, the Pripyat River is cloaked in the Polyesye marshland. But still the overriding feature is the tree. In the north, pines and other conifers predominate, while in the south, forestry is primarily deciduous (most notably oak). Birch knows no geographical boundaries and can be found all over the country. Indeed, in those areas where active forestation has been undertaken, particularly of pine, you will see that every stand of pine trees is surrounded by a protective ring, square or rectangle of silver birch. This is because birch grows faster and as it matures, it shelters the more delicate pine from the excesses of the weather, including the sun. Centuries ago, these areas of forestation together formed part of the great European primeval forest, most of which no longer exists, but here, such that remains is preserved as a natural treasure. Indeed, as well as having significance as a natural timber resource, it also forms an undisturbed habitat for a rich variety of wildlife and increasingly, it is a resource for leisure and ecological tourism.

The Belarusian people are particularly proud of their **national parks**. In 1992, 340km south west of Minsk, the **Belavezhskaya Puscha** National Park was included in the list of World Heritage Sites by UNESCO and one year later, UNESCO granted it the status of a Biosphere Reserve. This means that it is one of the sites monitored by ecologists to assess environmental changes taking place around the globe. Then at the end of 1997, the Council of Europe recognised the park as one of the most conservation-conscious reserves on the continent. The characteristics and profile of the locality were first mentioned in chronicles in 983AD, while the first attempts at establishing a formal reserve on this site were made early in the 15th century. The total area exceeds 90,000ha. The largest population of European bison roam free here; once to be found in abundance throughout the forests of Europe, the species is now extremely rare and the very fact of their existence in Belarus is something of a success story for the country's conservation policies. Also to be found in this reserve are red deer, wild boar, roe deer and elk. Natural predators include wolf, fox, lynx, badger, marten and otter. Birdlife is equally diverse and includes the greater spotted eagle and the aquatic warbler. Experts have estimated that around 1,000 of the oaks in the park are between 300 and 700 years old, with some of the ash being 450 years old, certain of the pines being 220 and a number of junipers as old as 150. There are also white firs, spruce and pine.

In the south of the country is a wide lowland area consisting of hollows, plains, forests and marshes, pierced by many rivers and creeks flowing to the Pripyat River, a tributary of the Dniepr, which itself flows into the Black Sea. In the area lying between the Pripyat, Stviha and Ubort rivers is the significant marsh wetland known as the Polyesye that is home to around 265 species of bird, including heron, the rare black stork (and the more common white), grey crane, eagle owl, serpent eagle and marsh owl. Indeed, both white and black storks can be seen extensively in and around the villages in the south of the country and the first sighting of one of these birds on the wing is a great experience. Within the region of the Polyesye, the total area of the **Pripyat** National Park (established in 1996) exceeds 83,000ha and its territory extends for 64km east to west. Of particular interest are the areas around the banks of the river. The spring melt causes it to rise by 10–15cm each year and the floodplains have their own unique vegetation, with oak and ash further from the river being replaced by black alder and willow adjacent to it. Some 826 species of plant are to be found here, including an astonishing 200 different mosses.

In the northeast of the country, the **Berazhina** Biosphere Reserve was created in 1925 to preserve the natural primeval landscape as well as game and other wild animals, such as the river beaver. Today, many animals and birds that are extremely rare or even extinct elsewhere live here, such as the brown bear. Much of this reserve (extending over 82,000ha) is covered by forest, most of it pine and spruce, with the remainder being largely marshland interspersed with wooded islands. The main river that flows through the reserve (for 110km) is the Berazhina, on much of which navigation and rafting are not permitted.

Narach National Park boasts the largest lake in the country, bearing the same name. The country's renowned Blue Lakes are also situated here. The largest concentration of ecological resorts and recreation complexes in the whole country is situated within the wider Narach area, including a total of 18 sanatoria and recuperation centres. There are also several natural springs and the area is famed for its mineral waters. The park itself was only established in 1999. It covers 94,000ha, 37,900 of which are forest, including the country's largest concentration of pine. Its 42 lakes have a total area of 18,300ha.

Completing the list is **Braslau Lakes** Park, where large numbers of lakes are surrounded by picturesque hilly landscapes. Brooks, rivers and channels, most of them navigable, form a water-bound labyrinth through which the visitor can cast off the trappings of modern life and meander undisturbed. Signs of life from ancient times, such as burial mounds, places of worship and evidence of settlements, complement the natural wonders of the area. Located in the northwest, the park was created in 1995 and its territory covers around 70,000ha. The lakes themselves extend over an area of 183km^2, the deepest of them, South Volos, extending to 40.4m. Lake Struso is particularly beautiful; at the centre is the Isle of Chaichyn, which has its own small inner lake. The water ecosystems here are particularly interesting and 20 of the 800 species of plant are on the endangered list (and consequently subject to special protection measures). Of 30 varieties of fish, eel are the most common and are extensively farmed. Badger, lynx, brown bear, squirrel, elk, wild boar and roe deer all live in the park.

Overall, ecological tourism is a significant growth sector of the economy, although much remains to be done in terms of establishing a viable infrastrucure if it is to be commercially competitive (see *Chapter 2, Living the good life*, page 72). As mentioned several times in a number of contexts throughout this book, the people of the country have an extremely close relationship with (and affinity for) the land and the seasons. This theme dominates life in the rural areas and it only serves to highlight the tragedy and consequences of the Chernobyl catastrophe.

It would be impossible to make even a cursory and passing reference to ecological matters in Belarus without discussing Chernobyl (see *History*, page 13). Prevailing weather conditions immediately after the explosion blew the deadly radioactive cloud over mainland Europe in a predominantly northwesterly direction. The region of Gomel in Belarus was directly in its path. Contamination was spread on an irregular basis as dictated by the weather. For example, there remain particularly radioactive hot spots today where rain fell at the time. It is generally acknowledged that Belarus received about 60% of the fallout sustained by the Soviet Union.

Anyone interested in travelling to Belarus will be concerned to know just how safe it is in terms of radiation exposure. In the past, reliable information has not been easy to find, but it is now widely accepted as scientific fact that the risk of prejudice to heath is minimal. In fact, it is even possible today to join a tour to Pripyat (in Ukraine) that will take participants to within 100m of the nuclear plant. In 2006, an Australian film crew went inside the reactor buildings to film, although for a few minutes only and even then wearing fully protective clothing. You can stand 100m away with a Geiger counter and the reading when it is pointed into the atmosphere is steady, but if you then point it at the reactor, it goes off the scale.

In Belarus, it is not possible to visit any of the hot-spot areas without official permission from the government and even then, only if accompanied by 'officials'. Whole villages stand abandoned to the elements. Most of them have their own cemeteries, but only once a year are the bereaved permitted to return to tend the graves of their loved ones.

The perceived wisdom is that a day in Pripyat will lead to radiation exposure that is actually less than is experienced on an eight-hour flight. It has also been said that a week there is like having one chest X-ray. Given that current levels of radiation diminish incrementally as the distance from the plant increases, the danger for the short-term visitor to Belarus is negligible. Indeed, it is an unavoidable fact of modern life that radiation is all around us, whether from the sun, mobile phones, natural levels of radon gas or many other sources. The internet is now a mine of information on the impact of Chernobyl radiation and authoritative materials that seek to give reassurance to the short-term visitor are easily found. Be cautious and don't be foolhardy by venturing where you are not permitted to go, but look upon the consequences of the accident as a unique educational opportunity concerning some of the biggest issues facing society today and the future of the planet, in an environment that is literally like no other on earth.

2

Practical Information

WHEN TO VISIT

The likely assumption for the uninitiated is that since Belarus used to be part of the Soviet Union, the weather will always be grey, featureless and in winter, bitingly cold. This is only partly correct. Each of the four seasons is distinct and boasts its own features. Winter is indeed bitingly cold for the most part, with the first snows tending to fall in late November. Given the close relationship that most Belarusians have with the land, it is no surprise that this is an event greeted with deep spirituality and romanticism. But the temperature does not plummet until the turn of the year. December is grey, wet and slushy. Come January, the thermometer can freefall to the minus 30s, with long periods of snow accompanied by bitter winds. The scenery can be dramatic; clear blue skies, a watery sun, heavy frosts and thick, immovable, impenetrable ice. But these conditions tend to be the exception rather than the rule and for the most part, the temperature averages around –7°C with consistent and regular snowfall. It is a time when most people remain indoors unless necessity drives them outside to work or study.

Spring is a time of intense activity in the fields, with an abundance of new growth to be found all around. This is also the time to see storks on the wing and nesting atop the high poles that are erected in villages for this very purpose. The temperature is generally warm and welcoming. Summers can be surprisingly hot and in forests and near to water, biting insects are voracious. Be sure to wear long trousers and clothing buttoned to the neck and wrists, accompanied by some form of insect repellent, particularly at dusk. But don't be discouraged; this is a time of long days, balmy evenings, glorious sunrises and sunsets, a verdant landscape and fresh produce in the markets and by the roadside. As if to store up reserves of fresh air and sunshine for those long winter nights, people spend as much time outdoors as they possibly can. In rural areas, this means tending the fields, while in the town, the promenade remains a favoured pastime.

Autumn is a glorious time to be in Belarus. Summers tend to last well into September, but come harvest time in October, the colours of the fields and forests simply take your breath away. There is no real diversity of colour, but almost everywhere as far as the eye can see, a golden scene stretches into the distance. One Sunday pre-dawn morning in October, I left Mozyr in the south by car in pitch darkness to catch a lunchtime flight from Minsk. As the first rays of the sun began to illuminate the landscape with a deep and warm glow, followed by brilliant bursts of gold, the song 'Fields of Gold' was playing on the radio. This may sound a little kitsch, but the experience was intensely moving and one that I am very pleased not to have missed.

The intensity of the Belarusian people's relationship with the land (and by association, with the seasons) means that holidays and festivals are imbued with heavy symbolism and significance. Orthodox Christmas is celebrated on 7 January, when Grandfather Frost brings traditional presents and sweets for children. Anyone who is horrified by the cynical commercialism of Christmas is encouraged to spend this time of year in Belarus, just to restore a little faith. In recent times, fireworks have become a widespread feature on the evening of 6 January, though the safety precautions leave a little to be desired. But the atmosphere is light and jolly, as families promenade in the streets. Then on the night of 13 January, the symbolic passing of the old year is celebrated. Known as 'the Generous Night' (Kolyada), young people parade in fancy dress, often as animals, singing traditional Kolyada songs as they pass from one house to another, with homeowners treating them to edible delicacies as they go.

In late February or early March comes the ritualistic observance of the passing of winter (Maslenitsa). People traditionally bake pancakes, the shape and colour of which symbolise the growing strength of the sun.

Orthodox Easter takes place on the weekend that follows Catholic Easter. It is the biggest festival in the religious calendar. In rural communities especially, the woman of the house will spend all day on Easter Saturday preparing food to be blessed by the priest, before taking it by hand (and generally on foot) to church. At midnight, families congregate at their local church and parade three times around the outside of its perimeter in solemn procession behind the priest, carrying beeswax candles and thinking positive thoughts for good fortune. After returning home in the early hours, everyone except the matriarch (who has much still to prepare and cook) will go to bed, then wake to a sumptuous feast that has by then received the blessing.

The first day of May (Labour Day) and 9 May (Victory Day) are celebrated exuberantly with all the pomp and ceremony that used to be associated with the Soviet Union. Town centres are taken over by parades of young people, war veterans, local dignitaries, the emergency services, the army and every conceivable representative body of civic society. Independence Day on 3 July receives similar treatment. The long days of summer then form the backdrop to many outdoor festivals celebrating the folklore and traditions that are the bedrock of modern

Belarus. Kupalye, celebrated over the night of 6–7 July, is the most pagan and mysterious of them all. Legend has it that at midnight on this date and no other, the flower of a particular variety of fern unfolds and that the one who finds it will be blessed with eternal youth, happiness and foresight. In rural areas, young men set off into the forests hoping that this is the year when a miracle will occur and they will find the mythical flower. Meanwhile, girls pick field flowers, bind them into wreaths and float them down streams, trying to discover their destiny and learn of the one whom they will marry.

HIGHLIGHTS

Belarus offers much more to experience and to see than a single visit will allow, but a week would make for an fascinating, if intense first trip. It is not possible to see all of the key centres of interest in that time, so be selective. The best advice is to visit Minsk and probably at least one other of the big towns, plus as much of the rural hinterland in between as can be accommodated in the time available. Below are some of the top sights, in no particular order.

- **Minsk**, a major capital city and living monument to the grandeur of post-war Soviet urban planning, where expansive boulevards and vast green areas guard the last piece of the old town that the Nazis could not destroy. It's also home to 17 museums, 12 theatres and 38 palaces and centres of culture.
- The national memorial complex at **Khatyn**, just 54km from the capital, which commemorates the hundreds of villages the Nazis razed to the ground in the Great Patriotic War.
- The museums of folk history and life at **Dudutki**, **Strotchitsy** and **Oziartso**, all within a radius of 40km from the capital, where traditional trades and crafts continue to flourish.
- The ancient Russian settlement of **Zaslavl**, only 27km from Minsk, with its historical and cultural museums, 16th-century Transfiguration church and traditional buildings.
- The museum towns of **Mir**, **Nesvizh** (both UNESCO World Heritage Sites), **Novogrudok**, **Polatsk** and **Pinsk**.
- The frontier fortress town of **Brest**, in the southwest of Belarus, where religious history was made in the 16th century (see page 8) and where eastern and western Europe meet, at the symbolic gateway to the old Soviet Union.
- **Grodno**, near the Polish border on the eastern bank of the River Nieman, with its beautiful architecture (including the stunning Polish cathedral) and historic Lithuanian connections.
- The village community and micro-economy of **Komorovo**, close to the Lithuanian border, where the administration is run strictly along sustainable development lines, based on traditional crafts and cottage industries.
- **Vitebsk**, birthplace of the painter Marc Chagall, with its many summer arts festivals and artistic traditions.
- **Mogilev**, with its historical centre and the beautiful Leninskaya Street, a favourite of residents and visitors alike.
- **Gomel**, the country's second-largest city, which is home to the impressive park, palace and cathedral complex founded by Prince Rumyantsev in the 18th century.
- The town and district of **Vetka**, home to 'old believers', with its world-class museum of iconography, the traditional weaving school at Nyeglubka, historic churches and locations of considerable ecological interest.

- The national parks of **Belavezhskaya Puscha** (the third UNESCO World Heritage Site in Belarus), **Berazhina**, **Braslau Lakes**, **Narach** and **Pripyats**, where the wilderness and biological diversity of the country can be enjoyed and where ecological tourism is beginning to take hold.

SUGGESTED ITINERARIES

Although the main tourist sites (identified above) form a good basis for the structure of a visit, the best way to get to the heart of the country and its greatest treasure, its people, is to strike out alone. The task should not be underestimated, for to do so is not in the least easy. One of the hang-ups from the days of the old Soviet Union is a complete lack of understanding of the concept of the independent traveller. It also says much for the hospitality of the Belarusians that they are keen to share their country's riches by offering personal guides to everything that there is to experience. This means that guided tours will certainly show you a great deal, although the level of control over the structure and pace of arranged itineraries will not suit the traveller with an urge for personal discovery. Overall, in the context of discovering and experiencing as much as possible, the arguments in favour of either independent or guided travel are very finely balanced, but perhaps the safest option, certainly if you are on a first visit and don't have contacts in Belarus, is to stick to the main travel agencies. A major advantage of this option is that the process of obtaining an entry visa will be considerably simplified (see *Red Tape* below). Here are some alternatives.

THREE DAYS
- Cities, history, the arts and folklore: Minsk – Khatyn – Dudutki – Vitebsk – Minsk
- Cities and history: Minsk – Grodno – Brest – Minsk
- Cities, ecology and sustainable development: Minsk – Berahzina and Narach national parks – Komorovo – Minsk
- Cities and museum towns: Minsk – Mir – Novogrudok – Pinsk – Minsk

ONE WEEK
- Western Belarus: Minsk – Grodno – Brest – Pinsk – Minsk
- Eastern Belarus: Minsk – Polatsk – Vitebsk – Gomel – Minsk

Both of these week-long trips would include visits between cities to ecological and historical sites of interest.

TWO WEEKS The following will deliver the full experience of city and nature, arts and culture, history and society; you might just need a holiday to get over it!

- Three nights: **Minsk** (with day trips to **Khatyn**, **Dudutki**, **Strotchitsy** and **Oziartso**)
- Two nights: **Grodno** via **Mir** and **Novogrudok**
- Two nights: **Brest** via **Belavezhskaya Pushcha National Park**
- One night: **Mozyr** via **Pinsk** and **Pripyats National Park**
- Two nights: **Gomel** (with day trips to **Vetka** and locations affected by Chernobyl)
- One night: **Mogilev**
- Two nights: **Vitebsk** (with day trip to Polatsk)
- One night: **Minsk** (with a final round-up of activities, including a performance of the State Ballet Company) via **Berazhina National Park**

There are few tour operators in the UK offering programmes for visits to Belarus.

Baltics and Beyond I Amy St, Bingley, W Yorks BD16 4NE; ☏ 0845 094 2125; e info@ balticsandbeyond.com; www.balticsandbeyond.com. This company offers a very comprehensive programme of tours, including 'the Big Belarus Tour', Minsk city breaks, combined city breaks to Minsk & Vilnius, a Minsk & country guesthouse tour & specialist, tailor-made itineraries.

Regent Holidays Mezzanine Suite, Froomsgate Hse, Rupert St, Bristol BS1 2QJ; ☏ 0845 277 3387; e regent@regent-holidays.co.uk; www.regent-holidays.co.uk. Offers 3-night city breaks in Minsk from £395 pp, inc return flights with Czech Airlines from London or Manchester via Prague, with accommodation & b/fast.

The paucity of agency support will present no obstacle to the intrepid traveller, however, as the internet is a mine of information on travel within Belarus. Recommended websites are www.belarusguide.com, www.belarus.net, www.ac.by/country, www.belarustoday.info, www.belarus-online.com, www.minsk.gov.by and www.belarus-misc.org.

Additionally, the Belarusian embassies in the UK and the USA will have information on Belarusian tour operators as well as stocks of brochures, leaflets and business cards (see *Embassies*, page 43).

IN BELARUS In Belarus itself there are many tour operators, all acting under the **National Tourist Agency of the Republic of Belarus**, which exists as a web-based resource (*www.belarustourism.by*). It was established by the state Ministry of Sport and Tourism in December 2001 to co-ordinate overall support for the tourism market. It aims to develop the tourism potential of Belarus, certify hotels and tourist services and train tourism professionals.

The agency's website is an extremely detailed and informative resource. Most important of all, it signposts consumers to many other sites, including the full range of tourist operators.

The marketplace for local tourist agencies is beginning to flourish and there are now hundreds of organisations, with new ones opening all the time. However, do take care to check credentials and bonding arrangements before making any financial or contractual commitments. The following are the largest companies in operation; they are well known and all have good reputations.

AlatanTour 21 Yanki Kupala St, Minsk, 220030; ☏ +375 17 227 7417; f +375 17 226 1304; e incoming@alatantour.com; www.welcomebelarus.com

Association of Agro- and Eco-tourism 6 Dunina-Marshinkyevicha St, Minsk; ☏/f +375 17 251 0076/252 2781; e info@ruralbelarus.by; www.ruralbelarus.by. This is the co-ordinating body for ecological tourism, but in truth, there is no infrastructure to speak of. Three years ago, a directory of properties & facilities at each was produced in Russian & English, although I have it on good authority that only 500 copies were printed & never properly distributed, if at all. The last 2 annual directories were published in Russian only, while the organisation's website is only in Russian also. All of the Belarusian tourist agencies

will have details of available properties, however. The key player in ecological tourism in the country is Eduard Voitekhovich, a forward-thinking visionary who has helped many small enterprises throughout Belarus to develop small, micro-economies in rural tourism. Eduard is the director of the LLC Development Centre of Rural Entrepreneurship at Komorovo in the north of the country, a splendid facility, where traditional crafts & ways of living are encouraged to flourish (14 Zelenaya St, Komorovo, Myadel district, Minsk region; ☏ +375 17 973 7394/7304 or 29 627 2789; e center@komarovo.com; www.komorovo.com). See *Living the good life* (page 72).

Belarus Tour Service 89–20a Rosa Luxemburg St, Minsk, 220036; ☏/f +375 17 200 5675; e service@welcome.by; www.belarustravel.by

Belintourist 19 Masherov Av, Minsk, 220004;
✎ +375 17 226 9840; f +375 17 203 1143;
e marketing@belintourist.by; www.belintourist.by. In
business for over 50 years, Belintourist is the long-
established national tour operator, specialising in visa
support, hotel accommodation, transport & transfers &
booking specialist tours & excursions, inc the
intriguing 'Stalin Line' battlefield & history tour. Other
tours inc 'A Closer Look at Belarusian Folklore', 'The
Beatles Forever' (yes, really!), 'The Ballet/Opera Tour
to Belarus', 'This Fantastic Marc Chagall', 'Waterways
of Belarus', 'Business Tour to Belarus' & 'Recovery of
Body & Soul', each ranging from 4–7 days.

Top-Tour 40 Yakub Kolas St, Minsk; ✎ +375 17 280
1111; f +375 17 280 6237; e toptour@
toptour.by; www.toptour.by
Vneshintourist 8 Melnikaytye St, Minsk, 220004;
✎ +375 17 293 1866; f +375 17 293 1709:
e incoming@mail.bn.by;
www.belarus.vneshintourist.net
Vokrug Sveta 10 Internatsionalnaya St, Minsk, 220035;
✎/f +375 17 226 8392;
e incoming@vokrugsveta.by; www.travel-to-
belarus.com

A brief word now about the availability of tourist information. Don't expect to find anything like as much in the way of leaflets and brochures as you would find elsewhere in the developed world. The embryonic tourism industry still needs to sharpen up its act in terms of marketing and public relations. You will find leaflets relating to accommodation and some eateries, mostly in hotel lobbies, but until recently, there was hardly anything about museums, cultural events and visitor attractions. There is now a free monthly listings magazine called *Where Minsk* that is sporadically available in hotels, containing limited information in English about matters of interest to the visitor, but little else. And there is no concept of the tourist information centre either. The only thing Minsk has that is remotely like one is a counter run by the state tourist agency, Belintourist, attached to the Yubilyenaya Hotel on Prospekt Masherova (*officially* ⊕ *09.00–13.00 & 13.45–18.00 Mon–Thu, 09.00–13.00 & 13.45–16.45 Fri, closed Sat–Sun*). Naturally it's closed at weekends, when tourists might come. In fact, I've never actually seen it open at other times either. But (and I say it cautiously), things are beginning to change for the better. I have met with officials from the State Ministry of Sport & Tourism and they are starting to understand the power of marketing and advertising. The industry now has its own motif that is printed prominently on the front of the growing supply of leaflets and brochures relating to places of interest to the tourist and traveller. Increasingly, they are becoming more and more available in English, although the text is rather quaint. The most frustrating thing of all is that there is a rare and precious commodity to sell in this country in terms of tourism, which is going to be of the greatest interest to a significant constituency of travellers from the West, who will be able to find much that no longer exists in other parts of Europe, all of it less than three hours from London by plane. But the bridge between the two has yet to be built. This means that now really is such a good time to find out for yourself what this astonishing country has to offer (see *Living the good life*, page 72).

RED TAPE

When it comes to bureaucracy, Belarus is a world leader. Inevitably, this is a relic of the old Soviet days. The level of detail, process and checking involved in the most simple of procedures is mind-boggling. Of crucial importance throughout, however, is the ability to smile and to show the utmost patience and civility when coming up against process and procedure. Anger and intolerance are viewed with disdain and will always be greeted with a wry smile, a shrug of the shoulders and a process at least twice as long as the original would have been. Don't be flustered; admire the view and take some time out to relax. And a few words of Belarusian or

Russian never go amiss. An attempt to speak the language, however feeble, will generally melt even the coldest of bureaucratic hearts.

All visitors to Belarus from the UK will require a visa and for UK applicants to obtain a Belarusian visa from the London embassy, the following documents should be submitted to the consular and visa section. These can either be delivered personally by the applicant or on his/her behalf by a visa services company, or sent by Royal Mail or by courier.

- A valid original passport with at least one blank page available for the visa. The passport must be valid not less than 90 days beyond the date of planned departure from Belarus.
- A completed visa application form, which can be downloaded from the embassy website (*www.belembassy.org/uk*).
- A recent passport-sized colour photograph.

A visa application fee must also be paid, full details of which can be found on the embassy's website. Specific additional documentary evidence (for applications for different categories of Belarusian visa) will also be required to be produced as follows:

- **Transit visas** (which are valid for up to one year and which permit a stay in Belarus for not more than 48 hours) require either a valid visa of the country of departure or destination (eg: the Russian Federation), or if such a visa is not required, then a copy of the ticket, itinerary from a travel agency, or any other documents confirming the applicant's trip to the country of destination.
- **Short-term/long-term (business) visas** (which are valid for up to 90 days/one year with a maximum right of stay of 90 days) require a letter of invitation from a company or organisation in Belarus, which is officially registered as a legal entity by the Belarusian authorities, indicating the expected duration of the applicant's stay in Belarus. The company must also provide written guarantees that the applicant will abide by the rules and regulations that apply to foreign citizens.
- **Short-term/long-term (visitor) visas** (valid for up to 90 days/one year with a maximum right of stay of 90 days) require an original letter of invitation that must be presented by friends or relatives of the applicant residing in Belarus at the local passport and visa office of the Ministry of Internal Affairs. Alternatively, an invitation may also be submitted by a Belarusian citizen on a temporary visit to the United Kingdom, who is a husband, wife or a close relative of the applicant.

A DUMMY RUN

Belarusian customs may be tighter than just about anywhere, but one thing that you can bring into the country is a very large lawnmower. I know, because I've done it. My Russian is quite good, but it was tested on that occasion, although not as much as when I took 24 full-size dummy heads through. They were resuscitation aids to help with an injury minimisation programme for schools. The customs official clearly saw a golden opportunity to supplement his income, because he persisted in telling me that there was duty to be paid. One of my Belarusian NGO colleagues came through from the arrivals lounge to assist with the bartering process, but to no avail. That is, until the official got bored and just shrugged his shoulders, before walking away. To look for more sport elsewhere, I guess.

I knew we were in for trouble the moment the two *militia* officers strode out of the airport terminal. They headed for us with far too much purpose and intent for comfort. We had just paid the cab driver and were about to check in for the flight home to London. 'Good day. Passports please.' While one stood sentinel, the other leafed through the pages, one by one. When he came to my immigration document and turned it over to find a blank page, without a stamp, I'm sure that a flicker of a smile played at the edges of his mouth. 'Where is your stamp? This is a very big problem.' All of my visits have been on invitation from one of the regional executive committees and not once in the past had it proved necessary for us to register locally. We were always in the country on official business. But it seemed that the rules had changed and I instantly had a feeling that I knew where this was all leading. We were instructed to pick up our bags and follow the officer into the terminal, where he again looked at my immigration document. Again, 'This is a very big problem.' He took out his mobile, spoke quietly into it and 30 seconds later, another militia officer appeared, this time with a bigger hat. He too looked at the document, shook his head and said to me with grave solemnity that this was 'a very big problem'. What a surprise. The two of them (the third having departed the scene) turned their backs and whispered to each other, before our new-found friend motioned for Richard and I to go with him and to bring our bags with us. It's a very long walk from one end of the departure terminal to the other, particularly when your mind is racing from one scenario to another, as you try to think of a way out of a fast-developing situation. He was actually quite chatty and as we walked past the departure gates, he cheerily pointed out which of them was ours. By now, Richard had turned very pale indeed. As we reached the end of the terminal and passed through a small door, the turn of events that I had started to expect did indeed come to pass. 'Do you have money?' he asked. I replied that I had some roubles, but this clearly wasn't the right answer. 'No. Dollars.' Now that the likely endgame was becoming more apparent, I was able to start thinking a little more clearly about an exit strategy and I could give Richard the reassurance that he clearly needed, even though I wasn't entirely sure myself how this was going to turn out. My big worry had been that we would be detained until our flight had gone, which meant that we would have to stay another night, by which time our visas would have expired. Then we would have been in trouble. Real trouble. We were instructed to follow the officer into a very small and very hot lift, with barely enough room for two nervous travellers, two large bags and a militia man who held every card in the deck. We descended all the way to the bottom and walked out into a vast, gloomy and deserted area. Time for me to make a move. I apologised for our 'error',

- **Short-term/long-term (humanitarian) visas** (valid for up to 90 days/one year with a maximum right of stay of 90 days) require a letter of invitation from the Department of Humanitarian Aid, Ministry of Education, Ministry of Health, Committee on the Consequences of the Chernobyl Catastrophe, or one of the regional executive committees.
- **Short-term (tourist) visas** (valid for up to 30 days) require an original tourist voucher from a registered Belarusian travel agency.
- **Short-term (student) visas** (also valid for up to 30 days) require an original letter of invitation from an educational institution in Belarus.
- **Group visas** (for more than five people who enter and leave Belarus together) also require a list of the people in the group, containing certain information relating to each individual.

Within three working days of arrival in Belarus, visitors should report details of their temporary address and duration of stay to the local police station, so that the stressed that it was entirely unintended and asked what we could do to address the difficulty. 'This is a very big problem for you. The court will impose a very heavy fine. But I can fix it. If you give me a hundred dollars.' The endgame at last. I thought for a few seconds and then nodded. He smiled and indicated that we should join him in the lift again. Just after it began to ascend, he leaned across me, pressed the 'stop' button and with a judder and a bump, we came to a halt. The defining moment had come. Richard had turned grey by this time. It was now very hot indeed and the silence roared in my ears. If I didn't pay up, then it was clear that we weren't getting on our flight. But what if I did offer him money, only for him to announce that now, we were in *real* trouble? 'Breach' of immigration laws was one thing, but attempting to bribe an officer of the state was a different matter entirely. In reality, I'm sure that it took only a few seconds to make the decision, but it felt like hours. I reasoned that US$100 in the officer's back pocket was going to be much more important to him than ensuring observance of the laws of the land. Not entirely with conviction, I reached into my wallet, counted out the last hundred that I had left (a lucky break) and handed over the wad. He smiled, folded it away (it really did go into his back pocket), leaned across me once more and pressed the 'start' button. Richard was still uncomfortable, I could tell. But as we left the lift and walked back into the departure lounge, the mood had palpably changed for the better. Except that we still had two major obstacles to overcome. There were two official procedures to be observed in terms of checking our documents before we could leave and I was starting to envisage two more 'fees' of a hundred dollars each. And I had no more dollars. I mentioned this to my militia friend, but with a smile and a reassuring arm on mine, he told me that everything would be OK. Bless him, he was clearly a man of honour. After a cursory word with a colleague, who went over to have a word with somebody else, we were ushered through at speed. The final check of the papers, before a stern officer in uniform, can often take five minutes and more. He/she will scrutinise every single page of the passport, scan the photograph, occasionally pick up the phone and sometimes summon a colleague to recheck everything, all of the time looking quizzical and glancing up to look into your face. This time? Ten seconds at most. He took my passport, turned straight to the right visa, stamped it triumphantly and handed it back. We were through and out. But Richard didn't relax until our plane had landed at Milan for our connection and he was well inside the terminal on terra firma. The moral of the tale is a statement of the blindingly obvious. Never, *ever* play fast and loose with bureaucracy and red tape in this country. And always have a few dollars spare, just in case you need an upgrade in services.

passport can be registered. If staying in a hotel, this process will be discharged by the hotel's administration services.

IMMIGRATION AND CUSTOMS Procedures can be tortuous in the extreme, although recently rules have relaxed a little and visitors are no longer required to complete a customs declaration form on arrival. However, your first experience of Belarusian officialdom will still be to stand in a long and interminable line, waiting for a uniformed immigration official to scrutinise every last detail of your passport and visa with the deepest suspicion before allowing you entry.

In common with other European countries, there are some things that cannot be brought into or out of Belarus by visitors. The list includes drugs (narcotic and psychotropic), weapons, ammunition, military equipment or clothing, explosives, poisonous or radioactive materials and printed or audio-visual matters that might cause detriment to the interests of the state.

The maximum that a single person can import into Belarus without duty is 50kg of luggage and contents, the value of which does not exceed €1,000 (or 80kg and €1,200 for an indivisible item), although an excess charge for baggage is rarely enforced. Within the limits stated, specific items that can be taken into the country duty free include one litre of spirits for persons aged 18 and over, one litre of beer, 200 cigarettes or 200g of tobacco (also for persons aged 18 and over), five items of jewellery, three items made from natural furs or leather and one watch (!). Again, items in excess of these amounts should attract duty, but the rules rarely seem to be enforced. Other items such as clothes, a laptop, a camera and other portable electronic devices for personal use are permitted without restriction as to cost or weight, but different (more restrictive) rules apply to Belarusian residents. One notable quirk by way of a throwback to the days of the Soviet Union is that when leaving the country with a laptop, compact discs, DVDs or audio-video tapes, travellers are technically required to present these items for inspection up to one week before travelling, in case they contain something threatening to the national security of the state. The official line, however, is that this provision is 'not strictly enforced'.

It is no longer necessary to make declarations as to the amount and origin of currency or to provide details of credit cards in your possession at the beginning and end of visits, but it is not permitted to take Belarusian currency out of the country at the end of a trip.

Medical insurance is required for all foreign citizens travelling to Belarus and to be eligible for emergency medical care, visitors should possess a medical insurance agreement with a Belarusian insurance company, or with an authorised foreign insurance company. The relevant certificate and policy issued by the company must be presented upon entry to the country. The risks covered must meet the requirements of the laws of the state. Should you (unwisely) be travelling without the benefit of insurance, representatives of Belarusian insurance companies will provide the necessary insurance agreements and certificates on any border crossing point, with premiums for foreign citizens ranging from US$1 for a stay of up to two days, to US$85 for a stay of one year. However, medical insurance is not required for tourists with transit visas crossing Belarus, diplomats and official delegations, crew members of air and rail vehicles, citizens of the CIS states or holders of travel documents issued to stateless persons and refugees.

For up-to-the-minute information on the rules relating to immigration, customs, visas, duty and insurance, see the official website of the Belarusian national state tourism agency (*www.belarustourism.by*).

Ⓔ EMBASSIES

BELARUS EMBASSIES ABROAD

Armenia 375009, Erevan, Abovyan St, 23–6; ☏ +374 1 27 56 11; f +374 1 26 03 84; e armenia@belembassy.org

Argentina Gazadores 21 66, CP 1428, Buenos Aires; ☏ +5411 478 893 94; f +5411 478 823 22; e argentina@belembassy.org

Austria 6A–1140 Huttelbergstrasse, Wien; ☏ +431 419 96 30; f +431 419 960 30 30; e austria@belembassy.org

Belgium Av Moliere 192, 1050 Bruxelles; ☏ +322 340 02 70; f +322 340 02 87; e embbel@skynet.be

Brazil Rua Lauro Muller 116, Sala 1606, Botafogo, Rio de Janeiro 22290–160; ☏ +5521 25 41 22 15;

f +5521 22 44 72 08; e consuladodebelarus@terra.com.br

Bulgaria 6 Charlz Darvin St, 1113 Sofia; ☏ +3592 971 34 88; f +3592 973 31 00; e bulgaria@belembassy.org

Canada 600–130 Albert St, Ottawa, Ontario 1P 5G4; ☏ +1613 233 99 94; f +1613 233 85 00; e canada@belembassy.org

China 1 Dong Yi Jie, Ri Tan Lu, Beijing 100600; ☏ +8610 65 32 16 91; f +8610 65 32 64 17; e china@belembassy.org

Cuba Calle 5ta A 3802 e/38 y40, Miramar, Playa la Habana; ☏ +537 204 73 30; f +537 204 73 32; e cuba@belembassy.org

Czech Republic 626 Sadky St, Troja 17100, Praha 7; ✆ +4202 335 40899; f +4202 335 40925; e czech@belembassy.org

Egypt 26 Gaber Ebn Hayan St, Dokki-Giza, Cairo; ✆ +202 338 95 45; f +202 338 95 45; e egypt@belembassy.org

Estonia Magdaleena 3, Sektsion B, 11312 Tallinn; ✆ +372 651 55 00; f +372 655 80 01; estonia@belembassy.org

France 38, Bd Suchet, 75016 Paris; ✆ +331 4414 69 79; f +331 4414 69 70; e france@belembassy.org

Germany Am Treptower Park, 32, 12435 Berlin; ✆ +4930 536 35 90; f +4930 536 359 23; e info@belarus-botschaft.de

Hungary 1126 Agardi ut 3/b, Budapest; ✆ +36 1 214 05 53; f +36 1 214 05 54; e hungary@belembassy.org

India 163 Jor Bagh, New Delhi 110003; ✆ +9111 2469 45 18; f +9111 2469 70 29; e india@belembassy.org

Iran 1 Azar St, Aban St, Shahid Taheri St, Zafaranieyh Ave, Tehran 19887; ✆ +9821 270 88 29; f +9821 271 86 82; e belarus-iri@apadana.com

Israel 3 Reines St, Tel Aviv POB 11129; ✆ +9723 523 12 59; f +9723 523 12 73; e israel@belembassy.org

Italy Via Delle Alpi Apuane, 16, 00141 Roma; ✆ +3906 820 81 41; f +3906 820 02 309; e italy@belembassy.org

Japan 4-14-12 Shirogane, Shirogane K Hse, Minato-ku, Tokyo 108-072; ✆ +813 34 48 16 23; f +813 34 48 16 24; e japan@belembassy.org

Kazakhstan pr-t Respubliki, 17, 473000 Astana; ✆ +3172 32 18 70; f +3172 32 06 65; e astana_belarus@mail.kz

Korea (South) 432–1636 Shindang-dong, Choong-gu, Seoul 100-835; ✆ +822 798 90 0412; f +822 798 93 60; e korea@belembassy.org

Kyrgyzstan 210 Moscovskaya St, Bishkek 720040; ✆ +9963 12 651 365; f +9963 12 651 177; e kyrgyzstan@belembassy.org

Latvia 12 Jezusbaznicas iela 12, Riga LV 1050; ✆ +371 722 25 60; f +371 732 28 91; e latvia@belembassy.org

Libya PO Box 1530 Tripoli; ✆ +21821 361 25 55; f +21821 361 42 98; e libya@belembassy.org

Lithuania Mindaugo 13, 03225 Vilnius-6; ✆ +3705 266 22 00; f +3705 266 22 12; e lithuania@belembassy.org

Moldova MD 2009. str. A. Mateevichi, 35, Kishinev: ✆ +373 22 238 302; f +373 22 238 300

Netherlands Anna Paulownastrat 34, 2518 BE The Hague; +3170 363 15 66; f +3170 364 05 55; e info@witrusland.com

Poland Ul Wierntnicza 58, 02-952 Warszawa; ✆ +4822 742 09 90; f +4822 742 09 80; e poland@belembassy.org

Romania Str Tuberozelor, 6, Sector 1, Bucuresti; ✆ +4021 223 17 76; f +4021 223 17 63; e romania@belembassy.org

Russia 101100 Moscow, Maroseika St 17/6; ✆ +7 095 924 70 31; f +7 095 777 66 33; e russia@belembassy.org

Serbia 11000 Beograd, ul Deligradska, 13; ✆ +38111 36 16 836; f +38111 36 16 938; e sam@belembassy.org

Slovakia 811 06 Bratislava, ul Kuzmanyho, 3/a 3; ✆ +4212 544 16 325; f +4212 544 16 328; e slovakia@belembassy.org

Sweden Herserudsvagen 5, 4th Floor, 181 34 Lidingo Stockholm; ✆ +468 731 57 45; f +468 767 07 46; e sweden@belembassy.org

South Africa 327 Hill St, Arcadia, Pretoria 0083, PO Box 4107, Pretoria 0001; ✆ +2712 430 77 09; f +2712 342 62 80; e sa@belembassy.org

Switzerland Quartierweg 6, 3074 Muri bei Bern; ✆ +4131 952 79 14; f +4131 952 76 16; e swiss@belembassy.org

Syria Mezzah Est Villas 27, Qurtaja St, PO Box 16239, Damascus; ✆ +96311 611 80 97; f +96311 613 28 02; e syria@belembassy.org

Turkey Abidin Daver Sokak 17, 06550 Cankaya, Ankara; ✆ +90312 441 67 69; f +90312 441 66 74; e turkey@belembassy.org

Turkmenistan Ashhabad ul 2011,17; ✆ +993 12 35 07 37; f +993 12 39 64 88; e turkmenistan@belembassy.org

UK 6 Kensington Court, London W8 5DL; ✆ +44 207 937 3288; f +44 207 361 0005; e uk@belembassy.org

Ukraine Vul M Kocubinskogo 3, 01030 Kiev; ✆ +380 44 537 52 00; f +380 44 537 52 13; e ukraine@belembassy.org

United Arab Emirates Villa 434, 26th St, Al Rouada Area, PO Box 30337, Abu Dhabi; ✆ +971 2 4453 399; f +971 2 4451 131; e uae@belembassy.org

USA 1619 New Hampshire Av, NW, Washington, DC 20009; ✆ +1202 986 16 04; f +1202 986 18 05; e usa@belembassy.org; www.belarusembassy.org; 21st Floor, 708, Third Av New York, NY 10017; ✆ +1212 682 53 92; f +1212 682 54 91; e gcny@belembassy.org

Uzbekistan 53 V Vakhidova St, 700031 Taskent;
\ +99871 120 75 11; **f** +99871 120 72 53;
e uzbekistan@belembassy.org

Vietnam 52, Tay Ho Rd, Tay Ho District, Hanoi;
\ +844 829 04 94; **f** +844 719 71 25;
e vietnam@belembassy.org

FOREIGN EMBASSIES IN BELARUS
UK 37 Karl Marx St, Minsk 220030; \ +375 17
210 5920/21/22; **f** +375 17 220 2306 (general),
220 2311 (visa section); **e** britinfo@nsys.by;
www.britishembassy.gov.uk

USA 46 Starovilyenskaya St, Minsk 220002;
\ +375 17 210 1283/217 7347/217 7348
(general), 226 1601 (after hours or in emergency);
f +375 57 234 7853; www.belarus.usembassy.gov

GETTING THERE AND AWAY

✈ **BY AIR** All international flights and most of those from the other CIS countries go to **Minsk International Airport**, otherwise known as 'Minsk-2'. It is situated approximately 40km from the city. Charmless but functional, it was completely remodelled in 2005 and further extensive works are still under way. The terminal building is divided into two wings, with the left-hand side serving flights in and around the CIS countries and the right-hand side for international flights. Arriving passengers are met on the ground floor, with all departure halls located on the first floor. Left-luggage facilities are underground. There are currency-exchange offices on all floors and the larger office on the second floor is the best of them (⊕ *09.00–13.00 & 13.30–20.00*). There are also banking facilities on the ground floor (with ATMs), right by the entrance for passengers of international flights. The bank is open 24 hours a day and as well as converting currencies, it accepts most well-known credit cards. There is also a general inquiry and information desk, together with car-rental facilities. The offices of all airline companies operating in Belarus are on the first floor, along with a restaurant, bars, souvenir stores and a post office. There is also an airport hotel, with single rooms for foreign visitors costing US$22 per night, but considerably less for CIS citizens.

The airport can be reached by taxi, with a single fare to the centre of Minsk costing around US$20, or by bus to the central bus terminal. The bus service is approximately hourly from 06.00 to 23.00, with a one-way ticket costing BYR578 (available for purchase on the ground floor in the left wing of the airport terminal).

For further details of the airport's facilities, go to its rudimentary website (*www.airport.by*).

The other airport, 'Minsk-1', is located well within the city's boundaries (only 3km from the centre) and mostly caters for local and CIS flights, including the daily flight to and from the country's second city, Gomel. It is a functional building of little charm, although it is a prime example of post-war Stalinist design. The only facilities there are a small currency exchange and a café. Access from the airport into the city is straightforward; the easiest option is to take trolleybuses 2 or 18, or bus number 100. Buy a ticket on board for BYR600. Taxis are also available, but they are not cheap and you will need to negotiate a fixed price (which will be tricky if you don't speak the language).

The main cities in Belarus have their own small airports, but services are intermittent.

Only a limited number of carriers fly into the country and as a result tickets are expensive. The national airline is Belavia (*www.belavia.by*), with daily flights around the world, mostly via connections. The Russian airline Aeroflot also has numerous options. From Europe, the main carriers are Austrian Airlines, Alitalia (Italy), Lufthansa (Germany), Lot (Poland), Czech Airlines and Lithuanian Airlines. El Al has flights to and from Israel. The only direct London flight, taking approximately

2¹/₂ hours, is to and from Gatwick on a Sunday via Belavia, increasing to a twice-weekly service over the summer.

Belavia has representative offices as follows:

5 Hobart Pl, London SWI 0HU; ✎ 0207 393 1202;
f 0207 393 1203; e england@belavia.by
Corporation for Professional Conferences in the USA
13 South Carll Av, Babylon, New York, NY 11702;
✎ 631 661 6779/6869; f 631 661 6914;
e cpcus@aol.com or

ECVO Tours in the USA Suite 909, 45 West 34th
St, New York, NY 10001; ✎ 212 563 6394/468
594 91030; f 212 563 6417; e ecvo@
ecvotours.com

An alternative worth considering is to fly to Vilnius. The capital of Lithuania is little over half an hour by road from the Belarusian border, with Minsk around two hours away on the other side. Lithuanian Airlines has excellent rates and flies from many European destinations. You can then take a train or coach direct to the centre of Minsk, or even hire a car. There are said to be no restrictions on taking a hire vehicle across the border into Belarus, although you should check this with the hire firm well before you travel. Another option is to fly to Kiev in Ukraine. Many international airlines fly there, including British Airways. You can then hire a car and enter Belarus from the southeast. The drive to the border from Kiev takes around two hours, with the drive to Gomel on the other side taking no more than 45 minutes. However, whether you enter Belarus from the northwest via Vilnius, or from the southeast via Kiev, in each case there is the unknown factor of waiting times (plus bureaucratic inconvenience) at the land border crossing. Travelling time is not much longer, because you avoid not only the transit time necessary for connecting flights in cities such as Frankfurt, Vienna, Milan and Warsaw (unless flying direct with Belavia), but also the 43km journey from Minsk-2 airport into the city. Also, there are many non-stop flights both to Vilnius and to Kiev, giving you options to integrate the rest of your journey with train and coach timetables. Both train and coach stations are only 20 minutes from the airport by bus. It all depends on how adventurous you are feeling. As you will see from *On the border* (page 48), crossing by land is an experience all of its own. Some will see this as an enhancement to the travelling experience. I certainly do. But you will be wise to allow at least three hours to pass through the interminable checkpoints and when you add this element to the time spent travelling, there is little to choose in terms of expediency. And if there is a problem with your papers, or the guards are in a particularly playful mood (as they can be with nationals of another country), no-man's-land can be a rather lonely place, especially if you don't speak the language. With a degree of hesitancy, therefore, my advice is to save the border crossing adventure until you are comfortable with the language, or have a Belarusian travelling companion with you to assist in times of difficulty.

As for internal flights, it is certainly worth mentioning that there is doubt as to the routine observance of standard maintenance procedures on the part of some local airlines within Belarus. Wherever possible, you should fly directly to your destination on an international flight originating outside the countries of the former Soviet Union and Central Asia.

⚞ BY TRAIN The new railway station is situated in the centre of Minsk and all international trains arrive and depart from this location. Exits from the platforms to cloakrooms, shops and toilet facilities are on the ground floor, while 24-hour booking offices and an information kiosk are on the first floor. On the second floor are shops, a waiting hall, a post office with international telephone services, a drug store and bars.

There is a currency exchange on the first floor in the old station building next door, with further exchange offices across the road. For those in need of a bed on arrival, the Hotel Express is located right next to the station. It is then a relatively straightforward task to reach any part of the city by underground train, bus, trolleybus or taxi from the railway station square.

The website for the state railway system (*www.rw.by*) is very informative but only in Russian text. Some rudimentary information giving an overview of train services within Belarus (including a basic timetable) is available online (*www.allbelarus.com/services/train*).

Minsk itself is situated right at the crossroads of several major European train routes. For example, there are several routes to Berlin and Vienna, via Warsaw and Brest. Other direct routes go to Kaliningrad, Moscow, Odessa, Riga and Vilnius. One day, I'm going to board a train at St Pancras station in London and journey to Minsk via Lille, Brussels, Cologne and Warsaw. Leaving St Pancras at 10.43 and changing only at Brussels, the scheduled arrival time in Minsk is 21.28 on the following day, with a total journey time of just under 35 hours. This includes a four-hour delay at the Belarusian border while rail workers actually elevate the train and change its wheels (with the passengers still onboard!) to accommodate the narrower gauge track that is still used in the countries of the former Soviet Union.

BY COACH There are three bus terminals in Minsk. The central and eastern terminals serve international routes, while the Moscovskaya terminal serves Moscow. The two-floor building of the central terminal is located close to the railway station. Booking offices and an information bureau are located on the ground floor. On the first floor, tickets for international routes and destinations can be booked.

Central terminal 6 Bobruyskaya St; ☎ 227 37 25   **Moscovskaya terminal** 59 Filimonov St; ☎ 219 36
Eastern terminal 34 Vaneyeva St; ☎ 248 08 82/248   22
58 21

The main carrier in Europe is Eurolines and full details of service and cost can be found on the company's website (*www.eurolines.com* or *www.nationalexpress.com*). The very cheapest (if exhausting) route is direct from London Victoria to Minsk, via Warsaw, the journey time being just under two days.

BY CAR The main European route across Belarus for road transport is the E30 motorway from Paris to Moscow, via Berlin, Warsaw, Brest and Minsk.

The main checkpoints for vehicles on Belarusian border crossings are to be found in the following locations:

Belarus–Poland Berestovitsa–Bobrovniky (for vehicles of all types), Peschatka–Polovtsy (for cars driven by Belarusian or Polish citizens), Kozlovichy–Kukuryky (for trucks and heavy goods vehicles), Warsaw Bridge–Terespol (for cars and coaches) and Domachevo–Slovatyche (for cars).

Belarus–Ukraine Tomashevka, Mokrany, Verchny Terebezhov, Novaya Rudnya and Novaya Guta.

Belarus–Latvia Urbany.

Belarus–Lithuania Kamenny Log and Benyakony.

Amsterdam	1,739	Paris	2,129
Berlin	1,120	Prague	1,141
Budapest	1,110	Rome	2,268
Helsinki	1,148	Sofia	1,753
Kiev	580	Warsaw	550
London	2,180	Vienna	1,164
Moscow	700	Vilnius	215

Belarus–Russia Customs checkpoints have been removed and unrestricted access across the border is permitted unhindered, although sporadic checks and controls are occasionally enforced.

As might be expected, stereotypical encounters with border guards are commonplace, particularly as a significant amount of freight carried by road haulage is still being imported as humanitarian aid for those affected by the Chernobyl catastrophe. Long waits are all too common, with officials taking hour after hour (and sometimes days) to authorise official papers. Independent travellers are likely to be detained for longer periods while papers are methodically checked and rechecked, but you should ignore 'private facilitators' who offer to help travellers pass through checkpoints and border crossings. Travellers in groups, particularly on tours where bookings have been made through state tourist agencies such as Belintourist, will find that their party will be waved through much quicker, effectively by jumping the queue.

For drivers of private vehicles, a customs declaration form is required, which must also provide certain information relating to the vehicle itself. British driving- licence holders must possess a valid International Driver's Licence to drive legally in Belarus, available from most (but not all) main post offices, or the major motoring organisations. When travelling by private vehicle, you must be able to produce ownership documents or a letter of 'power of attorney' at customs offices at border crossings. Note that only originals of these documents are accepted. Specific insurance cover will need to be obtained, as the territory of Belarus is not presently included in the validity zone for foreign vehicle insurance policies. Every border crossing checkpoint has its own insurance bureau and in theory, according to official sources, it takes less than ten minutes to obtain the necessary cover. In reality it often takes considerably longer. The cost of the premium depends on the length of stay in Belarus, ranging from €5 for 15 days to €53 for one year. And payment is only accepted in US dollars, euros, or Russian (but not Belarusian!) roubles.

✚ HEALTH *with Dr Felicity Nicholson*

IMMUNISATIONS No specific vaccinations are required for Belarus, although it is recommended that travellers should be up-to-date with the following to remove the risk of contracting contagious diseases. **Hepatitis A, hepatitis B** (if you might be exposed to blood through sexual contact with a member of the local population or medical treatment), **rabies** (if you might be exposed to wild or domestic animals and be more than 24 hours away from medical facilities), **typhoid** and boosters for **tetanus, diphtheria** and **polio**. International Travel Vaccination record cards are readily available from GPs' surgeries in the UK and they are a useful reminder of material medical dates that are all too easy to forget.

It is 19.40 on a dark, wet and windy September night. We have been on the road north from Kiev for the last two hours, with only a vast panoply of stars for illumination. But we are approaching the border area and with a symbolic gesture of descending gloom, it has begun to rain heavily. We are crossing into Belarus from the Ukrainian side by car and a line of long, low buildings has just appeared out of the blackness on the tree line. I guess at their purpose and Tatyana confirms they are the administration and living quarters of the border guards. Beyond them lies deep, impenetrable darkness, with mile upon mile of forest stretching away into the distance. I am quite surprised by how excited I feel. And just a little on edge. I am immediately reminded of a black and white spy drama from the 1960s. A tunnel is opening up before my very eyes, a link in space and time to days long lost and forgotten. The rain beats down on the roof of the car as the gloom intensifies. Tatyana unwittingly heightens the sense of melodrama. 'Sometimes,' she says with a deep sigh, 'people wait here for three days. The queues can be very long.'

Little by little, we inch towards the first obstacle: Ukrainian emigration. Shadowy, non-descript figures drift in and out of the darkness. We reach the head of the queue and an official in uniform, army I think, peers through the car window at our passports. Then we move inexorably but painfully slowly to the next checkpoint, a large, purpose-built, multi-storey monument to officialdom. As we wait, I ask Tatyana about security along the length of the border. 'It's a big stretch to police,' I say. 'How is it patrolled?' She and Yura exchange views in Russian, before agreeing that most of the roads are impassable, save for the official crossing points, other than on foot. And right now, the other official crossings are closed, so that this is the only means of access by road between Ukraine and Belarus.

Plain-clothes officials mingle with uniformed soldiers and militia, all under blazing arc lights. We reach the front of the queue, where two soldiers (one sporting a very large peaked hat indeed) sit impassively at a small table, surrounded by pens, paper, ancient computer hardware and a scanning device. Out jumps Yura to hand over sheaves of passports and stamped paperwork, while uniformed officials patrol up and down, all of them apparently uninterested in us or anyone else at this gloomy and godforsaken place in the middle of nowhere. Another huge hat joins the first at the flimsy table. One of them scrutinises every single page of our passports (my Belarusian visas are well into double figures) and scans in the photographs, before purposefully (but with one finger) pressing keys on his keyboard, occasionally glancing up at his screen as he types. We notice with some amusement that his table, the extent of his domain, is only part protected from the elements by the overhead canopy, so that the many wires coming out of the back of his kit are being liberally rained upon. As we pass by, he stares wistfully at us from under his enormous peaked hat, perhaps longing to be a passenger in a car that takes him away somewhere, anywhere.

And so into no-man's-land. No lights, just darkness stretching into the night. Unexpectedly, ghostly figures emerge from the gloom. All are women, pushing bicycles with one hand, sporting umbrellas in the other and peering through every car window as they pass by, offering coffee and food from their panniers. One by one, engines are switched off and lights extinguished. After 20 minutes, all is dark and all is silent. Tatyana snuggles down for a sleep. The rain stops as suddenly as it began and overhead, the vista is once more a dazzling display of stars. I fall in and out of fitful sleep. Periodically, the headlights of an oncoming car or truck from the Belarus side wake me with a start. 'We should be through ... in the next 24 hours,' offers Tatyana and it is not easy to spot if this is irony or a cheap shot at humour. As I ponder this, the driver of the lorry next to us in the parallel queue fiddles irritably with the aerial of his ten-inch portable television, as the screen changes from images of lurid colour to grainy black and white. Every ten minutes or so, we start to inch forward, just one car's length at a time. Now more shadowy figures criss-cross the lines of traffic, sometimes standing in small groups, their faces eerily lit by a combination of cigarette ends and vehicle tail-lights.

Our progress is mind-numbingly slow. To our right, a bicycle vendor strikes it lucky, as a lorry driver beckons her over and gestures for her to pour coffee into a plastic cup from her flask. Then much to our surprise, our progress quickens and the next booths appear closer and closer, grotesquely backlit by huge overhead arc lights. The guards seem to have decided that the lorries are going nowhere that night, for their queue has ground to a complete halt. But for us, there is a burst of activity. A very large hat indeed appears at the driver's window and Yura offers that he has three 'foreigners' on board, from England. Three immigration forms appear through the open window from an unseen hand. There is much more activity here; more people, more uniforms, more women on bicycles, more noise, more light. There is only one queue now and with painfully slow progress, we reach the front. Our guard is a stunningly beautiful blonde woman, uniformed and fully tooled up for any eventuality. Her relaxed and friendly manner is most unexpected, but deceptive. She peers alternately at our passports and through the open door, softly speaking our names in anticipation of some recognition on our part. 'You have insurance?' she says; 'Yes of course,' we reply.

She motions our vehicle forward and invites us to park up, still on the exit lane, but kind of out of the way, in an 'in the way' sort of way. Yura accompanies her into the office while she scans our passports. Again.

Ten minutes later, Yura returns and opens the door. 'She wants to see your insurance papers.' He scurries off with them, only to emerge moments later to confirm that all is OK, before disappearing inside once more. Then two very big hats indeed walk out with Yura, deep in conversation. Tatyana too is summoned to join the gathering, before she returns to open the car door to enquire sweetly of Richard as to whether or not he has any more photo ID, as the computer is unable to scan his passport photograph. He gazes imploringly into my eyes and I know at once that he has been transported back to our little adventure at Minsk Airport, when it cost me US$100 to get us out of the country (see boxed text *The Platinum emigration service*, page 40). 'Don't worry, this won't be a problem,' I say (he really didn't enjoy the episode at the airport), as I begin to feel the first flutterings of worry myself. Here we go again ...

But it's all a game. Yura returns to move the car forward and perhaps 10cm closer to the kerb, presumably as instructed, before returning back inside. The merry-go-round spins on. Yura keeps pacing to and fro and the hats keep scrutinising our papers. A large hat appears and points the way forward for us, towards the nirvana of customs (and the final control point) 100m in the distance. Our hearts lift, but the dawn is a false one. Yura does indeed drive towards the customs zone, but when we are tantalisingly close, he turns through 180° (as instructed by the hat) and parks up near to the office. He turns off the engine, climbs out and disappears. He is gone maybe 15 minutes and we begin to wonder if we are ever going to escape this scene from the heart of darkness. Then a figure appears from the inky blackness, striding purposefully forward, head down and hand clutching a wad of documents. It is Yura. He flings open the door, climbs in with purpose and we drive around a corner ... and into a queue. Yura is quizzed by a large hat, but this one has the inclination neither for confrontation nor for sport and we are flamboyantly gestured forward into another queue, where another booth and another hat await. But it's only a tease. We are waved perfunctorily on and before we know what is happening, Yura is gunning the car into the black Belarusian night, while an astonishing display of stars stand sentinel and suspended from the firmament overhead, as we leave both the meteorological and the metaphorical gloom behind us in the darkness. The whole experience took two hours 45 from start to finish and I wouldn't have missed it for the world. Long live the revolution, I say.

Hepatitis A vaccine (Havrix Monodose or Avaxim) comprises two injections given about a year apart. The course costs about £100, but may be available on the NHS; it protects for 25 years and can be administered close to the time of departure. **Hepatitis B** vaccination should be considered for longer trips (two months or more) or for those working with children or in situations where contact with blood is likely. Three injections are needed for the best protection and can be given over a three-week period if time is short. Longer schedules give more sustained protection and are therefore preferable if time allows. Hepatitis A vaccine can also be given as a combination with hepatitis B as 'Twinrix', though two doses are needed at least seven days apart to be effective for the hepatitis A component, and three doses are needed for the hepatitis B part.

The newer injectable **typhoid** vaccines (eg: Typhim Vi) last for three years and are about 85% effective. Oral capsules (Vivotif) are currently available in the US (and soon in the UK); if four capsules are taken over seven days it will last for five years. They should be encouraged unless the traveller is leaving within a few days for a trip of a week or less, when the vaccine would not be effective in time.

Like hepatitis B, pre-exposure **rabies** vaccine ideally comprises three doses given over a minimum of 21 days. So ensure that you visit your doctor or travel clinic well in advance of your trip.

Tick-borne encephalitis can be encountered outdoors in Belarus and particularly in heavily forested areas, where the undergrowth is dense. It is caused by a virus and is usually spread by bites from ticks which are infected with the virus.

The incubation time is usually 7–14 days (which means it takes 7–14 days to develop symptoms after being infected). Those affected may initially develop a flu-like illness that lasts about a week. This may progress to a more severe form of the disease and can be fatal in about one in 30 cases. Generally, however, the risk to the average traveller is small and with sensible precautions can be reduced even more.

Anyone liable to go walking in late spring or summer when the ticks are most active should seek protection. Vaccination is one way to proceed and although the vaccine is not licensed in the UK it can be obtained by some GPs or travel clinics on a named-patient basis. It is unavailable in the USA. If you can locate it then a course of three vaccines given over 21 days should suffice. However, taking preventative measures is also very important. When walking in grassy and forested areas, ensure that you wear a hat, tuck your trousers into socks and boots, have long-sleeved tops and use tick repellents containing DEET. It is important to check for ticks each time you have been for a long walk. This is more easily done by someone else. Don't forget to check your head and in particular behind the ears of children. If you find a tick then slowly remove it by using special tweezers, taking care not to squeeze the mouth parts. Go as soon as possible to a doctor as tick immunoglobulin should be available for treatment.

HEALTH INFORMATION AND TRAVEL CLINICS The International Society of Travel Medicine is one of a number of organisations worldwide that has a plentiful supply of excellent information and advice relating to health for travellers (*www.ista.org*). Other informative websites include www.travmed.com, www.cdc.gov, www.aafp.org and www.thetraveldoctor.com. The UK government's Foreign & Commonwealth Office (*www.fco.gov.uk*) and its department of health (*www.dh.gov.uk*) also provide sensible, if generalised advice.

In the **United Kingdom**, www.travelhealth.co.uk is an independent website offering comprehensive advice to travellers, with links to a great many other internet resources. Another good source of practical advice, including details of clinics nationwide in the UK and links to other resources, is the website www.traveldoctor.co.uk.

A full list of current travel clinic websites worldwide is available from the International Society of Travel Medicine on www.istm.org. For other journey preparation information, consult www.tripprep.com. Information about various medications may be found on www.emedicine.com. For information on malaria prevention, see www.preventingmalaria.info.

UK

Berkeley Travel Clinic 32 Berkeley St, London W1J 8EL (near Green Park tube station); ☏ 020 7629 6233

Cambridge Travel Clinic 48a Mill Rd, Cambridge CB1 2AS; ☏ 01223 367362; e enquiries@ travelcliniccambridge.co.uk; www.travelcliniccambridge.co.uk; ⏰ 12.00–19.00 Tue–Fri, 10.00–16.00 Sat

Doctor today walk-in medical centre 182 Finchley Rd, London NW3 6BP; ☏ 020 7433 1444; e enquiries@doctortoday.co.uk; www.doctortoday.co.uk; ⏰ 09.00–20.00 Mon–Fri, 10.00–13.00 Sat

Edinburgh Travel Clinic Regional Infectious Diseases Unit, Ward 41 OPD, Western General Hospital, Crewe Rd South, Edinburgh EH4 2UX; ☏ 0131 537 2822; www.link.med.ed.ac.uk/ridu. Travel helpline (☏ 0906 589 0380) ⏰ 09.00–12.00 weekdays. Provides inoculations & advises on travel-related health risks.

Fleet Street Travel Clinic 29 Fleet St, London EC4Y 1AA; ☏ 020 7353 5678; www.fleetstreetclinic.com. Vaccinations, travel products & latest advice.

Interhealth Worldwide Partnership Hse, 157 Waterloo Rd, London SE1 8US; ☏ 020 7902 9000; www.interhealth.org.uk. Competitively priced, one-stop travel health service. All profits go to their affiliated company, InterHealth, which provides healthcare for overseas workers on Christian projects.

Liverpool School of Medicine Pembroke Pl, Liverpool L3 5QA; ☏ 051 708 9393; f 0151 705 3370; www.liv.ac.uk/lstm

MASTA (Medical Advisory Service for Travellers Abroad) Moorfield Rd, Yeadon LS19 7BN; ☏ 0870 606 2782; www.masta-travel-health.com. Provides travel health advice & vaccinations. There are over 25 MASTA pre-travel clinics in Britain; call or check online for the nearest.

MediClinic 8 Waterden Rd, Guildford GU1 2AP; ☏ 0845 2252 811; 30a Putney Hill, Putney SW15 6AF; ☏ 0845 2252 911; 129 Alexandra Rd, Wimbledon SW19 7JY; ☏ 0845 2252 511; www.mediclinic.co.uk. A private medical practice offering services to deal with all travel vaccination needs from three locations in & around London. Opening hours vary from clinic to clinic.

NHS travel website www.fitfortravel.scot.nhs.uk. Provides country-by-country advice on immunisation & malaria, plus details of recent developments, & a list of relevant health organisations.

Nomad Travel Store/Clinic 3–4 Wellington Terrace, Turnpike Lane, London N8 0PX; ☏ 020 8889 7014; travel-health line (office hours only) ☏ 0906 863 3414; e sales@nomadtravel.co.uk; www.nomadtravel.co.uk. Also at 40 Bernard St, London WC1N 1LJ; ☏ 020 7833 4114; 52 Grosvenor Gdns, London SW1W 0AG; ☏ 020 7823 5823; & 43 Queens Rd, Bristol BS8 1QH; ☏ 0117 922 6567. For health advice, equipment such as mosquito nets & other anti-bug devices, & an excellent range of adventure travel gear.

Samedaydoctor 14 Wimpole St, London W1G 9SX; ☏ 020 7631 0090; e enquiry@ samedaydoctor.co.uk; www.samedaydoctor.co.uk. Walk-In clinic & appointments, ⏰ 08.00–19.00 Mon–Thu, 08.00–18.00 Fri, 11.00–14.00 Sat.

Trailfinders Travel Clinic 194 Kensington High St, London W8 7RG; ☏ 020 7938 3999; www.trailfinders.com/clinic.htm

Travelpharm The Travelpharm website, www.travelpharm.com, offers up-to-date guidance on travel-related health & has a range of medications available through their online mini-pharmacy.

USA

Centers for Disease Control 1600 Clifton Rd, Atlanta, GA 30333; ☏ 800 311 3435; travellers' health hotline 888 232 3299; www.cdc.gov/travel. The central source of travel information in the USA. The invaluable *Health Information for International Travel*, published annually, is available from the Division of Quarantine at this address.

Connaught Laboratories PO Box 187, Swiftwater, PA 18370; ☏ 800 822 2463. They will send a free list of specialist physicians in your state.

IAMAT (International Association for Medical Assistance to Travelers) 1623 Military Rd, 279, Niagara Falls, NY 1 4304-1745; ☏ 716 754 4883; e info@iamat.org; www.iamat.org. A non-profit organisation that provides lists of English-speaking doctors abroad.

International Medicine Center 920 Frostwood Dr, Suite 670, Houston, TX 77024; ☎ 713 550 2000; www.traveldoc.coms available from the Division of Quarantine at this address.

Canada
IAMAT Suite 1, 1287 St Clair Av W, Toronto, Ontario M6E 1B8; ☎ 416 652 0137; www.iamat.org
TMVC Suite 314, 1030 W Georgia St, Vancouver BC

V6E 2Y3; ☎ 1 888 288 8682; www.tmvc.com. Private clinic with several outlets in Canada.

Australia, New Zealand, Singapore
IAMAT PO Box 5049, Christchurch 5, New Zealand; www.iamat.org
TMVC ☎ 1300 65 88 44; www.tmvc.com.au. Clinics in Australia, New Zealand & Singapore, including: *Auckland* Canterbury Arcade, 170 Queen St, Auckland; ☎ 9 373 3531

Brisbane 6th Floor, 247 Adelaide St, Brisbane, QLD 4000; ☎ 7 3221 9066
Melbourne 393 Little Bourke St, 2nd Floor, Melbourne, VIC 3000; ☎ 3 9602 5788
Sydney Dymocks Bldg, 7th Floor, 428 George St, Sydney, NSW 2000; ☎ 2 9221 7133

South Africa and Namibia
SAA-Netcare Travel Clinics P Bag X34, Benmore 2010; www.travelclinic.co.za. Clinics throughout South Africa.
TMVC 113 D F Malan Dr, Roosevelt Park,

Johannesburg; ☎ 011 888 7488; www.tmvc.com.au. Consult website for details of other clinics in South Africa & Namibia.

Switzerland
IAMAT 57 Chemin des Voirets, 1212 Grand Lancy, Geneva; www.iamat.org

IN BELARUS Travellers to new destinations anywhere in the world inevitably encounter scare stories about risks to health. **Radiation** is still present in Belarus following Chernobyl, but with sensible precautions, such as not drinking local water or eating dairy produce, mushrooms and fruits in and around the clearly marked exclusion areas most affected by the fallout, the risk of radiation-related health problems is extremely slight.

HIV/AIDS has seen exponential growth throughout eastern Europe in recent years and Belarus is no exception. HIV is a sexually transmitted virus and AIDS is the life-threatening immune failure that occurs late in the progression of HIV. Very early stages of HIV just after infection resemble flu or other viral infections. There then follows a latent stage, often years long, with various symptoms, many of them non-specific and easy to misdiagnose. AIDS becomes much more characteristic in the latter stages of the disease where immune failure becomes almost total. The profile of the social group that is most at risk tends to include people who actively engage in sexual activity (not only through prostitution) or abuse drugs. The very clear advice for travellers to Belarus is no different from that which applies to travellers the world over. Don't have unprotected sex (and the best advice is to buy condoms or femidoms before you leave home to guarantee quality), avoid multiple sexual partners and don't share needles. If you notice any genital ulcers or discharge, get treatment promptly since these increase the risk of acquiring HIV. If you do have unprotected sex, visit a clinic as soon as possible; this should be within 24 hours, or no later than 72 hours, for post-exposure prophylaxis.

Animals should always be approached with the utmost caution, even in urban areas, where dogs live a very outdoor life and strays often roam the streets in packs, scavenging for food. They are prone to carry disease, rabies being the most obvious risk, and you can never guarantee that they won't attack. The number of cases of rabies has been steadily increasing in Belarus from 27 in 1996 to 1,628 in 2006.

Most cases have been reported in foxes but numbers are also increasing in raccoons. There were two human fatalities from rabies in 2006.

And remember: even if vaccinated, there is still a risk of contracting the disease from bites, scratches or even licks over an open wound. Any affected area should immediately be washed with soap and running water, followed by the application of an antiseptic (or alcohol if none is available, even vodka, which is widely believed by many Belarusians to have effective recuperative and healing powers). You should then seek immediate medical assistance. Having been vaccinated pre-exposure, the number of post-treatment doses will be reduced. The bottom line here is not a pleasant one; if untreated, rabies is not only fatal in every case, but also a terrible way to die.

You can probably expect to contract some form of minor illness or condition at some point in your stay. During visits to rural areas from late spring to late autumn, flying insects of various types can give you a very nasty bite indeed, particularly at dusk. Take the obvious precaution of covering ankles, wrists, legs, arms and your neck, with the added protection of using insect repellent, ideally with DEET (50–55% strength is best).

As for drinks, the best advice is not to drink water unless bottled or boiled. Under no circumstances should you drink village-well water, which is usually heavily contaminated with impurities.

On the law of averages, you are likely to pick up a dose of diarrhoea sometime, but obvious measures like thoroughly washing your hands with soap at every opportunity will help. If you do get it, be sure to take as much clear fluid as possible to facilitate the rehydration process. Rehydration sachets (such as Electrolade) are also a good idea to rebalance any salts lost in the diarrhoea. You can also take one of the usual remedies like Imodium, although there is a body of opinion that says this only makes matters worse by sealing in the infection. Just do as you normally do in circumstances such as these. If you are unlucky enough to develop a fever with the diarrhoea or notice blood or slime in the stool then seek medical help as soon as possible as antibiotics may well be needed.

LOCAL HEALTH CARE The standard of health care available in Belarus is generally below that which might be expected in the UK and the USA. The state endeavours, under significant economic limitations, to provide comprehensive medical support to its citizens. It is usually the case that medical staff, particularly doctors, display very high standards of professionalism and commitment. They are extremely well trained, but there is a chronic shortage of equipment, materials and medicines. I have visited many hospitals boasting gifts of equipment from other nation states in Europe, where instruction manuals, if available, are in a foreign language and where post-delivery support simply does not exist. Thus no training in the use of equipment is available, no spares are supplied and repairs cannot be undertaken. Drugs and medicines supplied by donor countries are often out of date.

Even though most medical treatment is normally free on production of a UK passport the best advice is to ensure that you travel with comprehensive health cover and to take sensible precautions against exposure to risk. If you are normally on any medication, then ensure that you take adequate supplies with you to cover your trip. Be sure also to take a **first-aid and medical kit** with you, which at the very least should include the following:

- first-aid primary care guide
- antiseptic cleansing tissues
- scissors
- basic hypodermic needles and syringes

- wound closure strips (plasters)
- zinc oxide tape
- assorted bandages, dressings, fabric adhesive strips and safety pins of different sizes and dimensions
- disposable latex gloves
- paracetomol/ibuprofen/asprin tablets (both as painkillers and also as anti-inflammatories), insect repellent, antiseptic cream, antihistamine cream and oral rehydration sachets.

A number of ready-made kits are available on the market and one of the best ranges is produced by Lifesystems (*www.lifesystems.co.uk*).

SAFETY

Due perhaps to a strong police (militia) presence on the streets, there is very little crime in Belarus. The country is governed by a strong presidential system, with security forces that are extremely loyal to it. Historically, the authorities have shown little tolerance for their opposition counterparts. Where events organised by opposition groups take place, there is generally heavy-handed use of security forces to disperse and intimidate. As such, you should studiously avoid all demonstrations and rallies. At all other times, visitors are at greater risk of being targeted for crime than locals, so you should be alert to the possibility of mugging, pickpocketing and theft from vehicles and hotel rooms. Extra care is needed when travelling by train, especially alone on sleeper trains, but the risk is still slight. Taxis are also safe, even in the suburbs and rural areas, but you should never pay up front. Common sense should be your byword at all times; for example, don't be ostentatious with your money, or place yourself in a position of vulnerability in higher-risk areas like train or bus stations and marketplaces. It is also a good idea to be on guard when drinking with people you have just met.

To put things in perspective, though, I have never encountered a single crime incident during my time in Belarus. I have been out walking at night on my own and taken solo taxi rides by dark, both in well-known areas and those that are less so. Just be sensible, vigilant and respectful of people that you encounter along the way. There is much apocryphal talk and rumour about Mafia-style organised crime, which probably owes much to tales that originate in neighbouring Russia, but even if true, mobsters will have little or no interest in foreign travellers who stay well away from their 'business'. In the unlikely event that you become a victim of crime, always pause briefly before acting and think things through. If you are travelling with a tourist agency or staying in a hotel, report the crime to the agency and the hotel first. If your passport is stolen, contact the embassy immediately. Only then should you file a police report. Experiences with the local militia can be mixed and it pays to remember that as a foreigner, you will be treated with just as much suspicion as likely miscreants, if not more.

Scams and swindles are on the increase, although again, you are unlikely to encounter any of them. But take great care every time you use a debit or credit card and never let it out of your sight. ATM machines at banks are safe, but increasingly sophisticated means of reading and decoding cards are in operation in Europe and Russia, so Belarus may be next. And you should never, under any circumstances, agree to change money other than through a bank, exchange bureau or reputable hotel. By Western standards, most people in Belarus have pitifully small financial resources at their disposal and travellers from Europe and the USA are seen as fabulously wealthy. In relative terms, they are. Bear this in mind at all times and be studiously discreet with your money, to avoid placing temptation before locals who

Most of your encounters with local people are likely to be positive ones, because of the genuine sense of unconditional hospitality that runs through the whole of Belarusian society. I once attended the consecration of a new church in the small town of Vetka, close to the Russian border. The Metropolitan Filaret of all Belarus was there to perform the ceremony and the church was packed with local people. There was a huge surge as he entered and I was separated from my rucksack, which contained not only all of my personal belongings (passport, wallet, credit cards, cash and the like), but a very substantial sum of US dollars. There is much poverty in and around Vetka, and the contents of my rucksack represented a fortune by local standards. I was separated from my bag for almost an hour and I am ashamed to say that I feared the worst. But I only had to report the loss to my colleagues in the local administration for things to swing into action. The chief executive of the local authority spoke to the chief of police and there was an immediate flurry of activity. Within minutes my bag and I had been reunited. It was instantly apparent that it had not been opened. It was handed to me by a militia man with the broadest grin I have ever seen, who told me with a mischievous wink that the only matter of concern was whether or not I was a terrorist with a bomb, intent on harming the Metropolitan Filaret. It was handed in by one of the locals as soon as he spotted it, and other local people had joined in the search as soon as word got around that my bag was missing.

can only dream of having the amounts routinely found in your wallet. If anything, the greatest risk of all will be encountered before you even arrive, through access to services requiring payment over the internet. Be very cautious of entrusting your personal details, financial or otherwise, to local sites that profess to be secure. Try to make all your arrangements through reputable agencies with appropriate bonding arrangements.

ROAD SAFETY The quality of driving in Belarus is erratic and motorists will find extravagant ways of avoiding obstacles and delays, including mounting the pavement if necessary. Taxi drivers are no exception. You will need to be particularly alert at night in the towns and cities, where many (but not all) junctions with traffic lights have flashing amber for all roads into the junction during the hours of darkness. The mindset of local drivers (without exception) is that come what may, they will keep going. The concept of 'giving way' is not even an afterthought. Local drivers never use seat belts, but you should always use yours, even though you will be encouraged not to and even though some drivers will view it as an adverse comment upon their driving skills and a personal slight. I recall one journey across the country when I was a front-seat passenger, being driven by an eminent physician who began the journey by describing a recent road traffic accident in which a mutual friend had lost his life, in vivid and gory detail. As I reached for my seat belt, he told me, 'That's OK, you don't need to; I'm a good driver.'

But having said all of this, I have criss-crossed the country at the wheel on a number of occasions and always without (significant) incident. If you use your common sense and stay fully alert, I wouldn't expect you to encounter any difficulty. If anything, the experience puts me in mind of motoring 30 years or so ago, when the number of vehicles on British roads was a fraction of the horde that clogs up the highways and byways most days of the week now. The 'motorways' here are in name only when compared with British ones, other than the new

Olya was fed up with her lot. She had finished university early in the summer, had just started her first teaching job at the school where she herself had studied and she was working extremely hard. Life was just a little tough. So when I told her that I wanted to visit the west of the country, along the Polish border, she jumped at the chance to join me. We borrowed a car from the brother of a very good friend of a very good friend of mine (that's how things are done here) and set off on a beautiful autumn morning.

The road from Gomel to Brest is a delight. It runs east to west in a virtually straight line for 538km, through the low-lying marshland of the Poleysye. It carries very little traffic, so the drive is actually very relaxing. The road stretches to the horizon without bend or hump and overtaking is a joy. The only slight inconvenience is that you have to stop periodically to clean the windscreen of ex-mosquitoes, in their hundreds. And even though it is a thriving border town of some 300,000 residents, driving through the city of Brest itself is also a delight. The signs are good (if you can read Cyrillic), the layout of the roads is easy to fathom and your co-motorists are generally courteous. Driving techniques are occasionally quirky, but there is very little aggression or competition and certainly not the vaguest hint of 'road rage'. You just need to be careful to avoid the pot-holes around town, which can be very deep indeed.

The back roads to Grodno are also a delight, with very few cars for company. But however hard I try, I can never find the right road out of Volkavuysk. The signs are less than helpful and I always seem to be going to the opposite point of the compass to the one I expect. It's clearly a Belarusian version of the Bermuda Triangle.

My first night behind the wheel on the streets of Grodno was a bit of a challenge. We had been on the road all day and arrived to find no hotel rooms available. We secured an apartment for the night in one of the suburbs, but try as we might, we couldn't find the right street, let alone the right block. In exasperation, we phoned the landlord and he agreed to come out to meet us. He was a very young man with a very fast car. As dusk approached, he took off into the gloom like a bat out of Hades, leaving me to pursue him

sections of dual carriageway within a radius of 30km or so of the cities, particularly in the west of the country. Yet driving on single carriageways, even on major routes, is a largely relaxed experience, because of the low number of vehicles on the road. There are few bends, other than long ones and for the most part, roads are flat and unendingly straight. This means that you have a good clear view of what lies ahead and can plan overtaking manoeuvres with a good degree of preparation. The busiest roads are those to and from Minsk, especially the M1, M5 and M6 between the capital and Brest, Gomel and Grodno respectively, all of which have a high proportion of long-haul freight passing through the country into and out of Russia and Poland for all points in the European Union.

One other thing: whatever the time of year, even if the sun is beating down from a cloudless blue sky, drivers will have the heater on full, with the blower set to maximum. Be warned.

Belarus 'A-class' highways are in average to good condition. The condition of 'B-class' roads varies considerably and some are impassable for periods in winter. Drivers should note that roadworks and pot-holes are usually poorly marked. Pony and carts are often encountered outside city limits, presenting a specific hazard for drivers in unlit rural areas.

You should observe the speed limit at all times. The standard speed limit is 40 km/h (25mph) through villages and intensely built-up areas, 60km/h (37mph) on the fringes, 90km/h (55mph) outside built-up areas, and 100km/h (62mph) on motorways. Visiting motorists who have held a driving licence for less than two as best I could, all the while watching the road (Grodno drivers are more excitable than their counterparts in Brest), reading the map and checking the signs. In Cyrillic text.

The only dodgy moments of the trip came on the following day. I was clearly tired. Driving around town, I couldn't understand why the car was a little sluggish. And why there was a smell of burning. Then my hand slipped to the handbrake. It was, of course, fully on. Please don't tell my mate's mate's brother. The second episode was more scary. It's interesting the way the thought process works when you're tired and when the evidence of your own eyes doesn't seem to compute. On the road to Minsk, we hit another long, straight stretch and I counted nine huge wagons heading for Poland in the opposite direction, maybe a kilometre ahead. Then all of a sudden, I couldn't see the path of my own road ahead. This confused me, because only a second ago, everything was perfectly clear. I was even more confused when it seemed that one of the wagons was side by side with another. Then it dawned on me. He was overtaking. I felt like an extra in the Circus Maximus, standing before the onrushing chariot race in *Ben Hur*. By this point in the journey we were on single carriageway. With a yank to the right on the steering wheel, we were into the dirt by the side of the road, great clouds of dust billowing behind us as we bounced along. The wagon made it back in, just in time, but it wasn't a risk I was prepared to take. Olya wasn't in the least bit concerned. She slept through it all.

Overtaking can be challenging if the road is busy and there is a long line of cars, wagons, bicycles, tractors and horse-drawn carts on each side of the road, because everyone seems to be pulling out at the same time and trying to overtake the car in front, which has already started its own overtaking manoeuvre. And when I pulled out from behind a truck on the road to Gomel to take a quick look myself to see if it was safe to overtake, I'm not sure who was more surprised, me or the driver of the oncoming militia car.

For the most part, though, it's stress-free motoring. You can relax, enjoy the scenery and wait for the exotic Beamers and Mercs with blacked-out windows to glide effortlessly by and away into the distance. Ah, the joys of the open road.

years must not exceed 70km/h (43mph). These limits are rigidly and ruthlessly enforced by mobile electronic checking, especially in rural areas, where spot fines significantly swell the coffers of the local militia. But this is a country travelled by knights of the road, where the code of chivalry is routinely observed. This means that whenever any driver passes through a militia speed check, he or she will routinely flash every oncoming driver, without exception, for the next 3km or so. Just make sure that you return the compliment! The authorities also operate a zero-tolerance policy when it comes to drink-driving. You should drive with your lights on at all times between November and March.

There are police checkpoints on routes throughout the country. Drivers should stop at these when instructed and have vehicle documentation ready to hand, as otherwise there is a substantial risk of a fine and consequent delay.

Finally, motorists entering Belarus should ensure that they do not overstay the temporary import terms for their vehicles. Violation of the exit deadline may result in confiscation of your vehicle at the Belarusian border or an in-country police checkpoint.

WOMEN TRAVELLERS Any foreign traveller is viewed with considerable curiosity in Belarus, not least because of their rarity. This is even more true of women travellers, who are a very rare sight indeed. But women travelling together should not expect to encounter harassment, as two or more in a group without male company is a not uncommon sight in bars and restaurants in the big cities.

Single women should exercise caution, however. On your own you might find that you are approached for 'business'. Hotel lobbies are notorious for this, where members of staff and prostitutes who are their associates work closely together to ensure that all available 'business' comes their way. Any woman who is not known in these establishments is viewed with the greatest suspicion and even hostility.

As with everything else in a new destination, female travellers should exercise obvious caution and take the same precautions they would in their own country. Avoid being on the street alone late at night, particularly in badly lit or secluded areas. Try not to take cab rides alone in the dark with small taxi firms, but instead always look for signs and phone numbers on taxis, together with formal identification papers for the driver before you step inside. Be alert in subways. Don't go out at night without being sure of where you are going to sleep and how you are going to get there. It's always best to ensure that someone knows where you are and when you expect to be back. In any situation, try to act with confidence but not aggression. A show of helplessness might be viewed as vulnerability. Be careful about accepting drinks from strangers that you have only just met. And it is never a good idea to accept the invitation of a lift or a coffee.

Be wary of travelling alone on overnight trains, as you will have no choice as to your companions in your allotted sleeping compartment (even in first class, you will not have the luxury of sleeping alone). But again, Belarusian hospitality is likely to come to the fore. You will most likely encounter interesting and sociable companions (male and female), without there being any question of an uncomfortable, claustrophobic or threatening atmosphere. And there are clear rules of etiquette that are universally followed. For example, women can expect absolute privacy to change clothing and prepare for bed. In addition, you will always be offered the lower berth for sleeping.

Young Belarusians are extremely fashion conscious. Both sexes have a stereotypical role in society and are keen to emphasise their sexuality. For men, this translates into the promotion of a very 'macho' image, while women tend to accentuate their physical attributes with a dress code that would be viewed as shamefully overt in Western Europe. Very short skirts and low-cut tops are de rigueur. Since this is accepted behaviour in Belarus, women are not harassed because of their dress, but Western visitors might initially be unnerved by what they see.

FOCUS FOR SPECIFIC GROUPS

DISABLED VISITORS Wheelchair users will find that Minsk is not the most accessible of cities, and other cities and towns are less so. Staff in the tourism trade are generally not used to taking care of visitors with specific needs. You may find that some hotels, restaurants and museums have disabled access and facilities, but you should not assume that this will be so. Always check ahead. Sadly, disability awareness still has some way to go and staff are likely to be caught unawares without prior knowledge. But if you are travelling with one of the major tourist agencies and they are advised of your requirements in advance, you can expect to have your needs accommodated.

For further excellent generic advice of a highly practical nature, visit the splendid website www.able-travel.com. The following companies specialise in offering insurance for disabled and older travellers or cover pre-existing medical conditions.

UK

Age Concern Insurance Services Fortis Hse, Tollgate, Eastleigh, Hants SO53 3YA; ✆ 08001692700; www.ageconcern.org.uk. No upper age limit.

All Clear Travel Insurance Services 6th Floor, Regent Hse, Hubert Rd, Brentwood, Essex CM14 4JE; ✆ 08712 088 579;

e info@allcleartravel.co.uk; www.allcleartravel.co.uk. No upper age limit.

Atlas Direct 37 King's Exchange, Tileyard Rd, London N7 9AH; ℡ 0870 811 1700; f 0870 811 1800; e callme@atlasdirect.net; www.atlasdirect.net. Upper age limit for annual policies is 73 & for single trip is 83.

Chartwell Insurance 292–294 Hale Lane, Edgware, Middx HA8 8NP; ℡ 020 8958 0900; f 020 8958 3220; e info@chartwellinsurance.co.uk; www.chartwellinsurance.co.uk;

Direct Travel Insurance Shoreham Airport, Shoreham by Sea, West Sussex BN43 5FF; ℡ 0845 605 2700; e info@direct-travel.co.uk; www.direct-travel.co.uk. Upper age limit is 75

Enroute Insurance Grove Mills, Cranbrook Rd, Hawkhurst, Kent TN18 4AS; ℡ 0800 783 7245; e info@enrouteinsurance.co.uk; www.enrouteinsurance.co.uk. Upper age limit for annual policies is 79 & for single trip is 85.

Free Spirit Travel Insurance (P J Hayman & Company Ltd) Stansted Hse, Rowlands Castle, Hants PO9 6DX; ℡ 0845 230 5000; f 023 9241 9049; e freespirit@pjhayman.comwww.free-spirit.com.

Safaris must be organised in the UK prior to departure & upper age limit is 85.

Freedom Insurance Services Ltd Richmond Hse, 16–20 Regent St, Cambridge CB2 1DB; ℡ 0870 774 3760; e vicky.moses@freedominsure.co.uk; www.freedominsure.co.uk. Upper age limit for single trip is 85.

J & M Insurance Services 14–16 Guilford St, London WC1N 1DW; ℡ 020 7446 7600; e jmi@jmi.c.u; www.jmi.co.uk. Upper age limit is 79 & medical screening is done in house.

Orbis Travel Insurance Charter Hse, 43 St Leonards Road, Bexhill on Sea, East Sussex TN40 1JA; ℡ 01424 220110; f 01424 217107; e cover@orbis-insure.co.uk; www.orbis-insure.co.uk. Upper age limit is 99.

Towergate Risk Solutions 88 Chase Rd, Southgate, London N14 6HF; ℡ 0870 920 2222; f 0870 920 2211; e marrs@marrs.co.ukwww.marrs.co.uk. Upper age limit is 79.

Travelbility Peregrine Hse, Falconry Court, Bakers Lane, Epping, Essex CM16 5BQ; ℡ 01992 566919; f 01922 566901; e servicecentre@jmi.co.uk; www.jmi.co.uk

USA

Travelex Insurance Services PO Box 641070, Omaha, NE 68164-7070; ℡ 1 800 228 9792;

e customerservice@travelex-insurance.com; www.travelex-insurance.com

Australia

In Australia, if pre-existing medical conditions are covered then the usual procedure is for the client to complete a medical assessment with their doctor, which is then reviewed by the insurer's medical assessor to determine the potential risk and premium applicable.

Aon Personal Insurance GPO Box 390D, Melbourne, VIC 3001; ℡ 1300 134 256; ℡ (international direct dial number): +61 3 9918 5609; f 03 9916 3776; e cgu_aonpi@iag.com.au; www.personalinsurance.aon.com.au/travel.htm

CGU Travel Insurance www.cgu.com.au. Medical assessment forms & contact details (depending on in which state you live) can be found on the website.

Travel Insurance Direct ℡ 1300 843 843; www.travelinsurancedirect.com.au; e infoAUS@

travelinsurancedirect.com.au. Upper age limit for single trip is 85.

Travellers Assistance Insurance Jetset Travelworld Insurance Pty Ltd, Level 5, 24 York St, Sydney, NSW 2000; ℡ 1300 787 311; www.travellersassistance.com.au. Cover is available for pre-existing conditions by completing the 'Under 81 Medical form' or 'Over 81 Medical form' that can be downloaded from the website home page (under Documents).

New Zealand

Mike Henry Travel Insurance Ltd Shortland St, Auckland 1010; ℡ 09 377 5958, 0800 657 744;

f 09 309 5473; e info@mikehenry.co.nz; www.mikehenry.co.nz. No upper age limit.

ETHNIC MINORITY TRAVELLERS Belarusian society likes to think that it is tolerant and embracing of multi-culturalism, but the reality is somewhat different. Sadly, incidences of racism are not uncommon. Given that poverty and deprivation are widespread, this may be linked to inequalities of wealth rather than prejudice based purely on skin colour and appearance. Minority ethnic travellers are likely to be stared at and viewed with great curiosity, but this should not be seen as overt racism. Rather, it reflects inquisitiveness on the part of local people towards anyone who is viewed as a foreigner.

GAY TRAVELLERS Notwithstanding its own view of itself as a tolerant culture, intolerance and homophobia remain present in Belarusian society and in a survey undertaken as recently as April 2002, 47% of people questioned thought that gays should be imprisoned. Since March 1994, the law has acknowledged same-sex relationships between consenting partners, but there is no support for gay initiatives or organisations, so gay life is still largely underground. But youth culture, which is trying to break free from the shackles of state oppression, is increasingly tolerant of homosexuality. It remains to be seen whether this becomes a truly broad and unconditional acceptance of diversity, or just a passing fashion. Meanwhile the powerful Russian Orthodox Church, which claims that 80% of the population are active followers, considers homosexual relationships as among the 'gravest of sins'.

The Belarusian League for the Freedom of Sexual Minorities (LAMBDA) actively campaigns for gay rights. Part of the International Lesbian and Gay Association, it chronicles specific instances of discrimination on the part of state authorities and organisations and publishes its own magazine. A successful gay pride festival took place in 1999, but subsequent events have been cancelled.

FAMILIES As there is universal acceptance in Belarusian culture of heterosexuality and the distinct sexual identities of men and women, it is no surprise to find that a husband, wife and children travelling together will be broadly welcome wherever they go. There are no specific obstacles for families and no inconveniences that cannot be encountered elsewhere in the world.

WHAT TO TAKE

In the big cities, it is increasingly common to find consumer goods that will be familiar to those brought up on Western culture. This means that it is no longer necessary to pack as if a trip to Belarus is like entering another dimension. When travelling in the old Soviet Union, it was always the case that you would need your own bath plug in every hotel, no matter how swish. This is not necessary today. The issue of availability of goods seems to relate more to quality. This means that you can buy cosmetics, sanitary products, clothes, gadgets (such as torches, radios and corkscrews) and all the trappings of modern living, but don't expect them to be of anything other than average quality or to last very long. Before you go, make a list of all essentials as well as items which need to be of high quality. One thing that's very useful is a large packet of antiseptic wipes, which are very versatile and serve a number of purposes. Given that photography is an important medium for capturing your experiences, be sure to take more batteries, film and memory cards than you think you will need. You will encounter more things that you will want to record than you expect.

There are also two luxury items that you may consider packing. First, take a supply of powdered milk for tea and coffee, as these drinks are mostly taken black. Don't let this stop you from trying tea without milk Russian-style, preferably with lemon and a spoonful of sugar. It's delicious. Second, find room for two rolls of toilet paper. Hotel rooms will have adequate supplies, but elsewhere you will be lucky to find anything at all, including in restaurants, bars and other public places. Be warned that toilets in Belarus are often smelly, require you to squat instead of sit and have a wastepaper basket for used paper, which is deposited rather than flushed. Here already is one use for those antiseptic wipes. You should also take a first-aid kit (see page 53 for details of what should be within it), plus a sewing kit for emergency repairs.

CLOTHES Belarusians are very conscious of status. They take great pride in their appearance and will take every opportunity to wear their most fashionable items of clothing whenever they can. The best advice is to take things in which you will feel comfortable, but have with you at least one smart outfit. For men, this need be no more than pressed trousers, smart shoes, a laundered shirt and a tie. Don't worry about a jacket unless you feel underdressed without one. It's all a case of personal preference. For women, a dress or skirt and formal blouse are a good idea. Attendance at a formal event is always on the cards and first impressions go a long way towards establishing cordial relationships with your hosts. But ostentatious gear with exclusive designer labels and accompanying 'bling' will have the opposite effect. For outdoor wear, bring practical clothing with several pockets and a pair of sturdy shoes.

Summers can be very hot. Shirts, trousers and long flowing skirts made of baggy cotton will help you to be more comfortable. Button-down sleeves and button-up collars minimise the risk of over-exposure to the sun. But do remember that Belarusians dress to emphasise their sexuality, so you can expect to see both sexes scantily clad when the temperature rises. In rural areas men will often appear topless, but as a foreigner, you will still be expected to display appropriate decorum and restraint.

By contrast, winters can be freezing. Anyone visiting Belarus from November through to March will need lots of warm clothing. Being outdoors in winter is a wonderful experience if you're prepared for it, but it can be extremely uncomfortable if you're not. It's better to wear a large number of thin layers which allow you to adjust your body temperature more easily. In all probability, you will be going in and out of transport and buildings on a regular basis. It is here that the importance of being able to shed layers comes to the fore, because cars, buses, trains and buildings are like furnaces in winter time.

Winter means snow, so strong, waterproof footwear is a must. Take the thickest overcoat that you possess for extra warmth, but also a waterproof jacket for when it rains. An insulated hat, scarf and gloves can also be considered essential.

BOOKS AND MAPS Authoritative and up-to-date guides and maps for Belarus are few and far between. Those that exist are stocked in specialist travel bookshops, such as Stanfords (*www.stanfords.co.uk*), Daunt Books (*www.dauntbooks.co.uk*) and the Map Shop (*www.themapshop.co.uk*). Books play a huge role in Belarusian culture and when you get there you will find that even in small stores, there are lots of glossy paperbacks on the history, culture and ecology of the country. English-language books are increasingly available.

The publisher Roger Lascelles produces an excellent 1:750,000 map covering the whole of Belarus that is available in the UK, while in Belarus itself, the government produces its own 1:800,000 map via its agency Belkarta. It is easy to read, has English translations of place names and sites, contains key pieces of information and best of all, it incorporates plans of the six major cities on the reverse side. The largest scale map in Europe appears to be the 1:600,000 version sold by the Canadian company International Travel Maps and Books (*www.itmb.com*). Inevitably, the most detailed maps are only available for purchase in Cyrillic script in Belarus itself. The tourist industry there still has far to go, but it has begun to sharpen up its public relations of late, so that decent quality hand maps and pocket guides are now starting to be distributed free in some hotels and transport hubs. Just don't count on it, because you might very well find the dispenser empty when you need it most. The very best advice is be prepared for any eventuality by taking your own with you.

Speaking the language You will be surprised at how many metaphorical doors are opened for you if you try a few words of Russian, especially with children and young people, so as a basic 'must do', take a pocket phrasebook with you. It's worth trying to learn the Cyrillic alphabet, because it makes no end of difference if you can at least read place names. For those without even a rudimentary knowledge of the alphabet or how to pronounce the letters, it can be a very intimidating language indeed. But trust me on this; when you can sound out letters, then you can sound out words as well and you will be surprised, first at how easy it can then be to sound out quite long words and secondly, by how many of them you can actually take a good guess at translating.

There are many **phrasebooks** on the market; my two favourites are those published by Rough Guides and Lonely Planet. Both have basic but useful dictionaries within the text, along with practical sections designed to help you get by in the most common everyday situations. There is nothing to choose between them in terms of quality and it's all a matter of personal preference. Either will enable you to deal with most situations you encounter.

When it comes to **basic language courses for self-study**, the market is saturated and you will be spoilt for choice. I find the *Teach Yourself* books (Hodder Headline Limited, *www.teachyourself.co.uk*) particularly useful, because they publish an extensive range of materials to enable the student to prepare through different learning disciplines. There are 'one day courses' where you can learn 50 words with the help of a CD or DVD, 'starter kits', 'instant courses', 'beginner's courses' and then for those with a yearning to go further, books on grammar. Passing no comment on the choice of descriptive term in the title, *Russian for Dummies* (Wiley Publishing; *www.dummies.com*), in audio and book form, is an excellent way to prepare for practical experiences. The layout is imaginative and the style of teaching effective. I also like the *New Penguin Russian Course* (Penguin Books, *www.penguin.co.uk*), which packs a lot of learning into one portable volume. Nowadays, there are a number of books and CDs on the market that profess to be more effective because they use so-called 'new ways of learning'. My own view is that there is no substitute for learning the basics of the alphabet, pronunciation and grammar in the traditional way, if you want things to stick in your mind. This isn't everyone's view and it may very well be that new and different ways of learning suit you best, in which case, just go with whatever suits your preferred style of learning.

A word about **online language courses**. One of the best I have seen is *Master Russian* (*www.masterrussian.com*). The resources available on this site are very comprehensive, including a number of online multiple-choice tests for you to take and submit, with instant feedback on your results. This isn't the only site of course and time spent web-browsing to find one that suits your own tastes best will never be wasted.

When you are ready to take your study to the next stage, you will need to acquire a more technically based **grammar book**. My personal preference is the series produced by Barron's Educational Series in the United States (*www.barronseduc.com/foreign-languages-russian*). The company's books on verbs, grammar, idiom, vocabulary and pronunciation are especially good. And for a single volume to slip into your pocket that is compact but full of essential learning, take *Oxford Russian Grammar and Verbs* (Oxford University Press; *www.oup.co.uk*).

Finally on books, my view is that you cannot do without a **dictionary** once you have moved beyond the elementary stage of study. If you're serious about your learning, then a weighty tome to keep at home or in the office (or wherever you study) is indispensable, in which case the *Oxford Russian Dictionary* (Oxford University Press; *www.oup.co.uk*) is difficult to beat. I also recommend that you acquire a smaller, pocket dictionary to take with you on your travels. My own preferred choice to slip into a pocket is the *Langenscheidt Pocket Russian Dictionary* (Langenscheidt, *www.langenscheidt.com*), although equally good are the *Oxford Colour Russian Dictionary* and the *Berlitz Russian Phrase Book and Dictionary*.

If you are only able to acquire one learning tool both for home study and to take with you, then buy the *Oxford Beginner's Russian Dictionary*. The dictionary section itself is more than comprehensive, but in the same tome you also have a 'learning and lifestyle kit', which includes a great deal of useful tips, as well as some essential background information on lifestyle, etiquette and culture.

My own view is that the very best way to learn any language is to attend a **language school**. If you ensure that your teacher is a native speaker (usually the case, but not always), you will have the opportunity not only to hear the language as it is truly spoken, but also (and just as important) to learn with others in an interactive manner. Many of the course providers will give you the opportunity to enjoy at least a week's learning at a school in Russia, but naturally this comes at a cost. Language Courses and Language Services UK (*www.listenandlearn.org*) offer individual and group courses at many locations throughout the United Kingdom. And if you make enquiries of your local school or college, you will probably be surprised at how easy it is to find a course close to where you live. In my experience, the best course provider is the Brasshouse Language Centre (*50 Sheepcote St, Birmingham B16 8AJ;* ☏ *0121 303 0114; www.birmingham.gov.uk*). Part of Birmingham City Council, it is the largest adult education centre specialising in languages in the country. Twenty-nine languages are on offer here and course fees are extremely competitive. It is possible to start your studies at beginner's level and go all the way to post-graduate standard. I know this place is good, because I studied here for two years in evening classes and I highly commend it to you.

If you have a burning desire to maintain your interest in this country and its people after you return home from your first visit, then I seriously recommend that you embark upon some study of the language. It will call for some commitment, certainly in terms of your time, but the task is one that will give you great satisfaction as your learning develops. And you can do it in the comfort of your own home if you wish!. Just don't set your sights too high to begin with.

ELECTRICITY

As in Russia, electricity in Belarus is 200v, 50Hz (alternating current). All plugs are symmetrical two-pin, typical of those used in Western Europe. It's a good idea to take at least two international adaptor sets with you. For safety, always unplug appliances that are not in use, as power surges causing explosions are not uncommon.

$ MONEY AND BUDGETING

The national currency is the Belarusian rouble (BYR), which is divided into kopeks, with 100 kopeks to the rouble. For practical purposes, however, this is a worthless denomination, because there is no coinage in circulation and the smallest note is worth BYR10. The other denominations are 20, 50, 100, 500, 1,000, 5,000, 10,000, 20,000, 50,000 and 100,000. As at February 2008, US$1 was worth BYR2,154, while £1 equated to BYR4,191 and €1 would buy BYR3,169.

Foreign currency should only be exchanged at banks, kiosks or official bureaux de change and it is wise to retain all receipts. It is best to change money from US dollars, euros, UK pounds sterling or Russian roubles, as travellers may encounter difficulties with other currencies. If you have booked on a tour through Belintourist or another recognised tour operator, then accommodation, transport and meals will already have been paid for, so large amounts of spending money are not necessary. The US dollar is still the most desired currency, with euros and UK pounds sterling next. You may have difficulty exchanging your money if your notes are not new and crisp. Unfortunately, the same cannot be said for the Belarusian currency that you will receive in return. Major credit cards are accepted in most hotels, foreign currency shops and restaurants. Plastic fraud has not yet taken a hold, but doubtless will one day soon, so try not to let your card out of your sight when you pay. Always check your receipt and keep it until you have been able to compare it with your next statement when you return home.

ATMs can now be found all over Minsk and in increasing numbers in other major cities and towns. Most of them will dispense US dollars as well as Belarusian roubles. Travellers' cheques may be accepted at larger banks, but they are treated with suspicion and cash is much easier to exchange. If you must use travellers' cheques, take them only in US dollars or euros, to avoid exchange-rate charges. Sterling travellers' cheques are not widely recognised and may be met with a blanket refusal.

Exercise common sense with your money and you won't go far wrong. It's best to take a supply of crisp US dollar bills or euros, a debit card to access the local currency from an ATM and a credit card to use in hotels, shops and restaurants. Keeping each of them in a separate pocket decreases the risk of total wipe-out by theft. Flourishing a large wad of cash is never a good idea, even in roubles. The pocket money that you have with you is likely to be more than the average Belarusian earns in a month. And to avoid accumulating scores of rouble notes, take a little time to count out the smallest that you have when making a purchase, otherwise you will very quickly build up a large stash of extremely grimy and smelly notes.

The question of how much currency to take with you depends on your tastes and how much you plan to spend. If you are travelling with a party booked through an agency such as Belintourist, most of your payments will be made up front before you travel. If you are going solo, it will still be easy to spend only a little if you are so minded. You can eat and drink very cheaply by avoiding the flashy joints as you would in any capital city, and getting around by car, bus or train is astonishingly inexpensive by European standards. Entrance fees to museums and theatres are also amazingly good value, particularly given the wealth of treasures to be experienced.

If you are travelling independently, it will be possible to stay in a comfortable (but not luxury) hotel, eat well (but not lavishly), take in a museum or two and cover your transport costs, all for US$100–120 per day. This may not be so for much longer, however. As soon as the local economy begins to realise that the number of foreign visitors is on the increase (as will inevitably be so), prices will start to rise. Already, there is one price in Minsk for locals and a higher one for tourists. The gap will continue to grow. The largest item of additional expense is likely to be the purchase of transport and accompanying guides on specific excursions. If you don't understand the language, then self-guided tours will be of little use, as facilities for English-speaking visitors are few and far between at museums and historical sites.

The import and export of local currency is prohibited and all remaining banknotes must be reconverted at the point of departure. The import of foreign currency is unlimited, subject to declaration, while the export of foreign currency is limited to the amount declared on arrival. Foreign banknotes and coins must be exported within two months of import.

As for tipping, most restaurants will include an element for the service charge in the bill (generally 10–15%), although it always goes down well if you leave something extra, but always in roubles. To leave US dollars on the table after your meal would be viewed as the height of arrogance.

Here are three tentative **budgets** for a week (seven days and seven nights) at the luxury end of the scale, living comfortably (but not extravagantly!) and as economically as possible. There is one huge caveat to all of this: prices are changing virtually by the day and although this information is current at the time of writing, things may well be different when you come to travel. Just do your research before you go! You will see that these tables *exclude* air fares, as well as internal travel from city to city. And if your trip is arranged with a tour operator, then much of the expenditure will be included in the basic tour price. So for the purposes of this exercise, my assumptions have been that you are travelling independently and staying in one city, probably Minsk. Prices are given in US$ per person:

Expenditure (type)	Luxury	Comfortable	Economical
Hotel (inc b/fast)	1,750	700	400
Lunch & dinner	280	150	80
Urban travel	105	45	15
Museums, sights & excursions out of town	285	135	20
Theatre & culture	60	20	10
Souvenirs & gifts	200	75	10
Total	**2,680**	**1,125**	**535**

GETTING AROUND

Travellers planning a first trip to Belarus must ask themselves: do I go it alone, or should I book through an agency as part of a group? Each experience will be different and each has its pros and cons. As a former Soviet republic, the country simply does not cater for independent travellers, because in the old days, the state would need to know exactly what locals and tourist groups were doing at any given time. As was the case then, heavy state control remains an aspect of everyday life. If you are part of a group hosted by one of the country's travel operators, the clear instruction given to your guide will be to chaperone you every moment of your stay. Virtually the only time you will be alone is in your hotel room.

If you're part of a tour group, the time you spend waiting around at immigration, customs, restaurants, hotel check-ins, theatres and museums will be considerably less. You will also have the services of an English-speaking guide. But essentially, you will only see what the authorities want you to see. Nowadays this probably has as much to do with Belarusian hospitality as it does state control: people want to show tourists everything of which they are proud. They want you to have a good time and they want you to be impressed.

Independent travel has the advantage of allowing you to do what you want, when you want. And you have greater control over your budget. But if you can't speak the language, you will be at quite a disadvantage. The Cyrillic alphabet bears very little resemblance to that of Western languages and without a rudimentary understanding, communication, especially written, will be impossible. Very few people that you are likely to encounter as you travel around (and with whom you will need to communicate) are going to speak English. Young people generally have enviable language skills, but staff in train and bus stations, hotels, restaurants and shops do not. Very few museums have information available in English. The same applies to menus in restaurants.

✈ **BY AIR** In theory there are domestic flights between Minsk, Brest, Gomel, Grodno, Mogilev, Mozyr and Vitebsk, but the truth is that few of these flights actually get off the ground, owing to fuel restrictions.

Furthermore, although internal flights are cheap, they are not recommended, as there is reason to believe that some local airlines do not observe proper maintenance procedures. For your safety, therefore, you should fly directly to your destination on an international flight originating outside the former Soviet Union and Central Asia.

Information about internal flights is very hard to come by. The best yardstick is that my Belarusian colleagues only ever fly from city to city within the country if time pressures make it absolutely necessary (and then only with the greatest reluctance); they all travel either by car or by train. This means that the following information is supplied untested and you are strongly advised to verify it if possible. The state enterprise **Gomelavia** (☏ *+375 232 531415;* ℻ *+375 232 536414;* ℮ *gomelavia@ivcavia.com; www.gomelavia.com*) is an airline based in Gomel in the southeast of the country. It was established in 1996 and operates domestic scheduled services and regional charters. Its main base is Gomel Airport, situated 8km from the city, which is the second largest in the country. Gomelavia operates domestic flights to Minsk, Grodno and Mogilev and international flights to Moscow and Kaliningrad in Russia. Its operating partners are Aeroflot and Transaero Airlines. From 25 March 2007, airBaltic (*www.airbaltic.com*) began operating three flights per week from Riga to Gomel.

🚃 **BY RAIL** It was always a cliché that under Soviet dictators the one thing upon which absolute reliance could be placed was that the trains always ran on time. In its day, the Soviet rail system was the largest in the world, crossing 12 time zones. In common with its neighbour Ukraine, Belarus inherited its share of the network when the Soviet Union collapsed. Nowadays, as then, trains between major cities are frequent and relatively cheap, but slow. If you have the time to spare, this is no problem at all; gazing out of a train as it lazily meanders across the country is an excellent way to get a feel for the terrain and the environment. And taking the overnight sleeper from Minsk to Gomel, especially in the dead of winter, is an experience not to be missed. This said, booking train tickets can sometimes be problematic, as it is not uncommon to find that timetable information doesn't match what you are told at the booking office.

Although some parts of the rail network have been modernised, many of the trains are fairly old, particularly those running on local services. These older trains have a distinct charm, with wooden frames and white curtains around the windows. The trains are heated in the winter, though they can be draughty. Overnight trains usually have traditionally designed compartments with closing doors, with a bench seat on each side and fold-down shelves above. If you get to choose, always go for the lower-level berth, as the top berths slope inwards (away from the wall) and there's a good chance you'll fall out in the middle of the night. Bed linen is generally included in the price, but you may occasionally be charged a few US dollars on the train. A restaurant car will be available. Each carriage will have its own uniformed conductor, normally a young woman who will be working a punishing schedule. You will not be allowed to board without first showing her your ticket and as she will be providing your bedding, drinks and meals, it's best to greet her with a smile and a few words of basic but welcoming Russian. If you strike up an early rapport, the journey will be much more pleasant.

There is a certain code of etiquette relating to travel by overnight sleeper. Unless you are travelling in a group of four, you will be sharing your compartment with strangers. When you enter your allotted compartment, be sure to introduce yourself. If you have your own food and drink with you, share it around. And if you have beer or better still, vodka, you'll find your new companions won't be strangers for much longer. Just don't expect to get much sleep. If you are male, remember to offer the lower bunks to female companions and don't forget to excuse yourself from the compartment to permit them the privacy of changing their clothes for bed.

Carriages on day trains consist of either compartments without doors or the usual open-plan arrangement with rows of seats. It is normally possible to order tea, coffee and snacks. Local vendors with fresh produce will also be waiting as each train pulls into the platform for scheduled stops. Toilets are available, but they may be closed while the train passes through urban areas or as it crosses a national border.

To access more rural areas, shorter local lines run through small stations that are little more than a platform, seemingly in the middle of nowhere. These trains are almost always packed (mostly with country dwellers travelling to sell their own produce in local markets) and extremely uncomfortable, with people crammed onto hard upright wooden benches. They are so slow, and the carriages so hot in summer and cold in winter, that it's recommended to take buses to these areas.

Buying train tickets is normally a tortuous process. You will first need to locate the information desk or kiosk, most of which are denoted by the symbol 'i' these days. If you can make yourself understood so that you are given the necessary information for your journey, you will then need to join the queue at the relevant ticket counter to buy your ticket. And don't expect to be greeted with an over-abundance of patience on the part of either ticketing staff or those in the queue.

Left-luggage facilities are available at the stations serving the six major cities and some of the others. They will ether be automatic, in which case you will need to buy a token from the nearby booth, or a room with shelves attended by a member of staff, most likely a *babooshka*. These are quite secure, but don't lose the scrappy piece of paper that the attendant gives you, because 'jobsworths' are everywhere to be found in officialdom in this country. No ticket, no luggage!

Unfortunately, internet information in English about the Belarusian rail system is difficult to find. The state railway site (*www.rw.by*) is useful and practical, but only in Russian. Timetables for the whole of the country can be found at www.aditec.ru, but again only in Russian. However, with a dictionary by your side, it is possible to translate enough timetable information to give you a good idea of services and frequency. Then for some useful photographs of the station at Gomel, should you find yourself in need of some orientation there, go to the official website (*www.vokzal.gomel.by*).

BY BUS Generally travel by bus is cheaper and quicker than by train, although you will be compromising on comfort. For longer journeys, your coach might be relatively plush, but it is more likely to be old and rather rickety. For local travel, especially in rural areas, you will be crammed into a claustrophobic minibus. The timetable is always fairly flexible – again, more so in rural areas. Try not to rely on too much forward planning and if you can, just turn up at the bus station and see what time the next one leaves. When on board, don't be surprised if your bus stops wherever it is flagged down. This makes it a true community facility, but it also makes overcrowding much worse. According to official statistics, 4.3 million passengers travel by bus each day along 4,290 routes – so you'll be pretty unlucky not to find a bus to take you where you want to go. Just don't be surprised if it feels like all 4.3 million are travelling on the same bus as you.

BY CAR The supposed difficulties and risks associated with driving in Belarus are frequently exaggerated. Various travel websites will tell you that you'll have to contend with bad roads, on-the-spot fines from traffic police and speeding maniacs in blacked-out BMWs, not to mention that all signs are in Russian or Belarusian. You will read that every other road user drives excessively fast and recklessly, that they ignore pedestrians and traffic lights, that the roads, even the main arterial ones, are full of cavernous holes and that snow, ice and fog in the winter are a major hazard. The last two points have far more truth to them than the first two, but you're unlikely to have any trouble if you keep your wits about you, exercise common sense, observe the rules of the road and act with courtesy at all times. True, I've witnessed some extravagant (and dangerous) overtaking manoeuvres on most of the motorways, which are generally single carriageway except for the sections extending 50 miles out of Minsk and less for the other cities, but you are unlikely to run any risks if you stay alert, although you might want to bear in mind the experiences recited in *On the Road*, see page 56!

The good news is that because of the low population density, traffic queues in Belarus are few and far between, even in the big cities (although you might want to avoid being downtown in any of the six big cities, especially Minsk in the traditional rush hours), and out of town there is a real feeling of liberation and a sense of being back on the open road. In the country, you can drive for miles without passing another vehicle. And the only time you will encounter a toll road will be on the M1 motorway between Brest and Minsk, where the toll is US$3. The arterial road system is undergoing a process of major modernisation. On most of the major routes, particularly around Minsk, large-scale projects are under way.

If you break down, rescue services are available by ringing ⟍ 001 or ⟍ 007, but dust off your insurance policy first and check what you are letting yourself in for as soon as help arrives but before anything is done. The national car rescue service (call ⟍ 002) offers roadside assistance and towing 24 hours a day.

Car hire Until relatively recently, the concept of commercial car hire was totally unknown. It's now more common, predominantly at Minsk-2 International Airport and at the major city hotels. Rates vary considerably and different conditions apply. Big international companies ply their trade side by side with the Belarusian outfits. You can afford to be choosy, so do your research before you arrive, but do book ahead. Once you get there, you are a captive market and the price is adjusted upwards, sometimes outrageously. But if you do the deal before you leave home, pay up front and are content with a modest vehicle, such as a Skoda Fabia, a Volkswagen Jetta or a Peugeot 206, you can pay as little as £130 for a week, with unlimited mileage. Always check the insurance arrangements in advance and don't forget to bring your international driving licence.

One word of caution: although car crime is not endemic, the company details on the vehicle will mark you out as a wealthy foreigner. Park in public places and not in secluded locations.

Auto Arsenal Hotel Orbita, 39 Pushkina, Minsk; ⟍ +375 17 257 63 84; ⏱ 09.00–17.30 Mon–Fri, closed w/ends.

Avis Minsk-2 International Airport, Smolyevichy District, Minsk 222210; ⟍ +375 17 234 79 90; or Hotel Belarus, 15 Storazhevskaya St, Minsk 220029; ⟍ +375 17 234 79 90; www.avis.com. Both ⏱ 08.00–20.00 all week.

Avtocentre RM Market Promyshlyeny 11; ⟍ +375 17 244 66 42; ⏱ 09.00–18.00 all week

BelRentAvto Office 1, 40 Kyubysheva, Sovyetsky District, Minsk; ⟍ +375 17 202 12 70; f +375 202 12 50; www.prazdnik.by (Russian only); ⏱ 24hrs all week

Europcar Gate 5–6, Minsk-2 International Airport, Minsk 220054; ⟍ +375 17 279 22 41; f +375

On the main highways between towns, roadside checks by the local militia are commonplace. In areas of radiation contamination, where it is forbidden to leave the road and venture into long abandoned villages, or walk in the forest to pick mushrooms and berries, a checkpoint will be manned 24 hours a day, seven days a week, just to keep an eye on who is driving through. Elsewhere, checkpoints are more ad hoc. As already mentioned, there is a code of honour among all drivers, so if an oncoming vehicle flashes you like crazy, the chances are that a roadblock awaits just around the bend in the road. You will be waved down by a uniformed officer brandishing a black and white stick. Smile politely, but don't expect a smile in return. Have all of your papers to hand. And this is probably one occasion when it might not be a good idea to try out your Russian. If the officer thinks you speak the language, he will probably ask you a great many more questions and detain you longer. Speak only in English and shrug your shoulders; the chances are it won't be worth his trouble to keep you at the roadside. Whatever you do, though, just don't slip a few banknotes in your passport with a wink and a grin. That will really make him mad. He might very well be supplementing his miserable income with a spot fine or two from local drivers, but he will view the offer of a bribe from a Westerner as a gesture of supreme arrogance. Just don't do it.

17 279 15 66; or Bldg 2, Office 319, 11, Nezhavistimosty Av, Minsk 220050; ☎ +375 17 209 90 09; f +375 17 209 95 98; www.europcar.com
Hertz Hotel Planeta, 31 Masherova, Minsk; ☎ +375 17 226 67 85; f +375 17 226 73 83; or Hotel Minsk, 11–13 Independence Av, Minsk; ☎ +375 17 209 90 91; f +375 17 209 90 91; e rent-car@mail.ru; www.hertz.com; ⊕ 09.00–18.00 Mon–Fri, closed w/ends
Lada Autoprokat Syeryova 1; ☎ +375 17 275 18 05

Hitchhiking Although hitchhiking, the culture of 'on the road' adventures where the traveller sets out to discover as much about him/herself as the land through which the journey takes place is not common, because there is no concept of a free ride from strangers just for the sake of travelling around, you might still find that as a driver, you are flagged down in urban streets and on main highways by people looking for a lift as an entirely practical and expedient means of getting from point A to point B. Your would-be travelling companion will expect to pay, but the best advice is not to take any risks at all by picking up strangers. Interestingly, you will rarely see a car that is not full to bursting with passengers. This is not just because the strong sense of community means that friends and relatives will be offered lifts by a car owner, the driver timing his own arrangements to fit in with those of his passengers, but also because motorists will look to supplement their income by giving lifts to those in need, particularly around transport hubs such as coach and rail stations (and even bus stops). For the reasons above, I cannot recommend Belarus as a destination for hitchhikers, but if you need to get from A to B and know where you're going, if you're feeling adventurous and you want a real alternative to bus or train travel, this is a great way to interact with local people. They will be fascinated to learn that you are a foreigner and will treat you with enormous respect and affection if you try out a few words of Russian on them. The driver will probably take whatever you offer by way of payment, so be generous, but not flash. He might even refuse to accept anything when he knows you are a visitor from abroad, but persist inventively without being overbearing. Suggest that he uses the money to buy something for his wife, children or mother. Just be fully aware of the potential danger of climbing into a car without knowing anything about your travelling companion. Or companions.

Practical Information GETTING AROUND

2

By taxi Taxis are a fairly cheap and reliable way to get around the big cities and towns, but like everywhere else in the world, there are some unscrupulous operators, especially those that lurk outside hotels and train stations. To avoid hassle, look for either the yellow state-run taxis, or those run by one of the new and reliable private competitors, identified by the numbers 007, 052, 057 or 084. These numbers not only show the company affiliation, they are also the short telephone numbers for each company. The going rate per kilometre is around BYR800. Make sure that the meter is switched on before the cab moves off or negotiate a fee before you get in. Even around Minsk, a ride should never cost more than US$8. Services operate 24 hours a day.

Be aware that Belarusian law permits no more than four passengers in a taxi. Drivers might be persuaded to take more if you offer a little extra, but don't do it; the militia are vigilant and you will inevitably be pulled over. It is the driver who will get into trouble rather than you, but you will be made to feel uncomfortable and as if you are about to be arrested, even though you won't be. You will also be significantly delayed on your journey. I know all this, because it has happened to me. Just don't take any risks.

Away from the towns and cities, most cabs are driven by single operators. They look shady and drive beaten old wrecks, but they lack the vulture-like avarice of their big-city counterparts and they can be trusted, though always go with your instincts if you have any doubts about safety.

ACCOMMODATION

Your accommodation costs will easily be the biggest expense on your visit and at the higher end they can be frightening. A star system ranging from one to five is in operation in the country, but it bears little resemblance to anything that you will have seen before. Each hotel has rooms of different class and status, with prices to match. You can expect to be offered, for example, a room that is either economy, standard, business, semi-suite or deluxe, with daily rates starting at US$57 and going all the way up to US$478 and beyond. You will be encouraged to indulge yourself at the top end of the range, but if all you want is somewhere to rest your head, then rooms at the bottom end will be more than adequate. Prices are different for locals and foreign visitors, with tourists having to pay vastly inflated and wholly discriminatory rates. And against that background of partiality, you can even end up paying entirely different rates for the same class of room, dependent on how you booked it and on which day. There appears to be no logic of any sort to the pricing policy. All in all, it's something of a lottery. Part of the problem is the state's near monopoly on the industry, plus the perception in Belarus that if you come from Europe, then you will be fabulously wealthy with money to burn. Things are beginning to change, though, and if you have the time and confidence to shop around a little, you can usually find a reasonable deal on a decent room, sometimes even one with modern furnishings. The cheaper places tend to be some way out of the centre of the cities, but all will have restaurants and bars. Prices are generally quoted in US dollars, but in almost all cases, hotels only accept payment in Belarusian roubles (or credit cards).

Tourist accommodation is no exception to the general rule that everywhere you look, you will still see relics and reminders of the days of the Soviet Union. In the 1960s and 1970s, when the first intrepid European tourists pioneered holidays there through the only medium that was available, the state tourist agency Intourist, they all returned home with tales of having stayed in soulless, monolithic concrete buildings, where the awfulness of the food was matched only by the surliness of the staff, there was no hot water, every fitting was hanging off, there was never a plug for the bath, the windows didn't fit their frames and they were kept awake all night by the cockroaches. Today, things are very different: the food is pretty good, the staff try to smile (some of them, sometimes), you don't need to bring your own bath plug and perhaps most important of all, the cockroaches seem to have gone. But the soulless monolithic buildings are still there, as is the concrete, both more crumbly and neglected than they were back then.

Wherever you stay, you are going to have a fairly comfortable bed, unlimited hot water, clean sanitation, central heating, a television and a lockable door for your room. You'll also have the services of a concierge on your floor (although these services are usually limited to the shrugging of shoulders when you complain that something in your room is either missing or not working), at least one bar and one restaurant, a newspaper stand, currency-exchange facilities and staff with a smattering of basic English. And free entertainment in the hotel lobby during the hours of darkness (see box, *Hotel ladies of the night*, below).

When you check in, you will be asked to present your passport and it will be kept for the duration of your stay. Don't be alarmed. State regulations require that every visitor is formally registered. Someone somewhere in some organ of the state will then cross-check your visa details, the passport itself, the duration of your stay and your itinerary against information supplied or held elsewhere. But your passport will be perfectly safe and will be returned to you when you leave. Behind the desk will be secure safety-deposit facilities, although each room in the more upmarket hotels will have its own safe. Don't be too paranoid. Things left in your room will almost always be safe. Just be sensible and don't put temptation in anyone's way.

HOTEL LADIES OF THE NIGHT

Each hotel will have its own regular group of working girls (I wonder what the most appropriate collective noun would be?!). They meander around the lobby in heels and short skirts, gently smouldering and oozing availability. Every man who passes, whether or not accompanied by colleagues, family, spouse or partner, receives the sultry look and 'come hither' stare. Sometimes the bait is taken, the line is reeled in and the parties repair to the bar to close the deal. Occasionally the deal is struck much more quickly, in hushed and whispered tones. Then with a nod to the lobby staff, the players stroll arm in arm to the lifts. And so it goes on. The security guards also receive their cut of the takings. It is their job to ensure that no interlopers are allowed to muscle in. And so it is that every female who enters the lobby, no matter how respectable and whatever the company she keeps, is given the once over. My visits to Minsk are usually on business and I generally travel with local colleagues of both sexes. On each and every occasion, my female colleagues are challenged. Without proof of identity and their room key, they would not be allowed beyond the lobby. Some nights, business is slow and the girls are under-employed. So when you take your key from reception staff and it is obvious that you are going to bed, your room number is passed to one of the girls, who will then give you a respectable time to get into bed before she comes to call on you. The knock is generally a soft one and she will not persist, although your phone will always ring ten minutes later if you don't answer the knock. If you then answer the phone, you will be offered 'company', but a polite refusal on your part will be an end to the matter. You won't be harassed. But to avoid any embarrassment, just don't answer the phone. Then the following night and every night after that, the merry-go-round in the lobby will spin all night long.

I was keen to try out agro-tourism for myself and with the help of Tatyana, Saturday afternoon saw our arrival at the home of Sergei Staska (↘ 8 02342 61 601 or 8 029 252 8329) in the picturesque village of Parichi, north of the town of Svetlagorsk on the banks of the delightful Berezhina River. His home is large, with quaint outbuildings in the extensive garden, in one of which is to be found the bathhouse. In fairness, there is much to be done at the property in terms of preparedness for visitors and travellers, but if there is any justice in this world, then Sergei will get the help he so richly deserves. He is one of the kindest, most gentle men I have ever met. Nothing was too much trouble for him during our stay. In a country where hospitality is to be found wherever one travels, Sergei still manages to stand out from the rest. A father of three children, life hasn't always been easy. Years of devoted service in the naval forces must surely have contributed to the break-up of three marriages and now he and his aged mother strive to make a life that will be better than hitherto. We were encouraged to treat his home as our own in every way. Food and drink were in plentiful supply at every meal, where the two of them were in constant attendance, alternately serving and clearing away.

One of the purposes of my visit here was to meet with Eduard Voitekhovich, one of the country's leading lights in ecotourism. He was attending meetings in the area and I was anxious to hear from him about tourism generally. Other colleagues from Belarusian NGOs with an interest in community development joined us for the discussion, together with another mother and son from a nearby homestead who offer visitor facilities. And Sergei was to receive some advice, particularly with regard to funding. Things can be really infuriating in this country. I have been trying for some little while to convince the authorities that the time is right for the tourism industry to take greater steps towards meeting the market that already exists. I have been encouraging the production of leaflets and brochures in English. But if you search for information in the major cities, it can be impossible to find. Absolutely the key issue is that the tourism 'product' massively exists already in Belarus, the market is ready and waiting elsewhere, but there is no bridge between the two! I made this point to Eduard, as we all sat around Sergei's table in deep discussion, a large pile of roasted pumpkin seeds before us for general consumption. I didn't even notice that Sergei had gone, until I saw him return bearing a huge pile of leaflets and brochures, which he presented to me with a broad grin and a flourish. I leafed through the pile open-mouthed. Here, in a rural idyll far from the city, in the home of a splendid Belarusian host who didn't speak a word of English, was the bridge for which we

If your hotel booking has been made through one of the country's tourist agencies, they will usually act as the middle man and take payment from you in advance, so you won't need to pay the hotel other than for items purchased during your stay and charged to your room account. Just be sure to check in advance what is included in the stated price (eg: breakfast). If you have to settle an account when you leave, check it scrupulously. Hotels from mid-range upwards now have facilities to take payment by credit or debit card. There will usually be an ATM in the lobby if you prefer to pay by cash, but you will only be able to do so in Belarusian roubles.

Of course, not everyone wants to stay in a hotel. Private apartments are available for rent in all of the big cities and many of the towns, with the advantage that you can self-cater. Rates are usually very competitive. In recent times, I have arrived in both Brest and Grodno in the early evening without booking accommodation in advance, to find that there was not a single hotel room to be had in either town. It's a good job I was travelling with Olya. For the cost of a local newspaper and a few local calls, we rented an excellent apartment in Brest (five minutes from the city had been searching. Information, photographs, descriptions and key facts for visitors. In English. Yes, really. I read page after page of brochures that are nowhere to be found in Minsk or elsewhere. The most infuriating thing of all was the directory of agro-tourism, detailing names and addresses (with photographs) of participants in the scheme, with information as to the facilities on offer. I was given a copy for each of the last three years. The earliest was in English, but when I asked how many copies had been printed and where they had been distributed, Eduard could only shrug his shoulders. At best, there had been 500 copies. I had never seen one before. And the latest two are only in Russian. Poor Sergei. What chance does he have? We later learned that the government has turned down his application for funding under the rural tourism scheme, because Parichi is deemed to be a town and not a village. It looks like a village to me. But Sergei won't give up. And in the light of all the difficulties that face him, the nightly rate of US$15 for dinner, bed and breakfast is but a drop in the ocean. I really, really hope he gets there.

The second day of our visit took us to another eco-project. In a clearing in the forest, half a mile along a bumpy track, stands the country's only original, working windmill. At least it will function, when the works of reconstruction are finished. It was originally built in 1924 and soon after, the Soviet state required the owner to give it to the government. Three times he refused and three times he was imprisoned. He was eventually shot in 1938 in one of Stalin's notorious gulags. His daughter eventually gifted it to our host Volodya in 2004 and it is clear that he will honour the memory and the courage of the original owner. Just before the gift, the government again asked the daughter to donate the windmill to the state. But having seen her father spend 14 years of his life in jail before being murdered by the state, she wasn't about to defile his memory in this way.

Sergei and Vladimir are working on this project also. When complete, there will be a complex of ten self-catering wooden chalets. The first is well on the way to being finished. Even though some structural work has still to be done, such as adding staircases (!), the bedrooms already contain beds that have been laid with fresh linen. We sat outdoors to discuss the future, with cheese, peppers, oranges, peaches, vodka and the refreshing juice of the birch tree. Volodya has invested much of his own money in the project. After initial opposition from the local state authorities, the national decree in 2004 that first encouraged ecotourism came at just the right time. As a result, the bank has been much more benevolent than before the decree and the local authority no longer places obstacles in Volodya's path. He is someone else who deserves to succeed.

centre) for US$30 a night and another in Grodno, equally well located but to a higher specification, for US$70 a night. Bed linen, towels, cutlery and crockery are always provided. And you have the advantage of feeling right at home when you return after a day or evening out. In some parts of the country, health sanatoria have opened their doors to tourists, offering bespoke programmes lasting from one to ten days (see page 185). Since 2004, following a presidential decree, there has been a real move to promote ecological and agro-tourism in rural areas, where visitors have the opportunity to stay 'down on the farm' or in private homesteads, where they can live the good life and engage in various ecological activities. Resourceful homeowners out of the towns are beginning to see that here is an opportunity to supplement their meagre income, particularly as the decree from the president conferred certain tax advantages. The co-ordinating body in Belarus is the Association of Agro- and Eco-tourism (see page 37 for more details). Accommodation is also available in lodges and tents for those interested in activity holidays in the national parks. And down in the southeast of the country, NGOs from the UK and Belarus are working in partnership with local executive authorities in developing a homestay programme, where excursions and visits are designed locally and travellers stay in the homes of local people. This initiative is very much in its early stages, but already it affords the opportunity for visitors to get right to the heart of local communities.

✕ EATING AND DRINKING

DRINK It makes most sense to begin this section with **vodka.** First, the bare facts: vodka is typically a colourless liquid consisting largely of water, but also containing ethanol produced by distilling a fermented substance, typically potatoes or more usually, grain. It can be distilled from any plant matter rich in starch and sugar, although most commercial vodka is produced from grains such as barley, corn, rye and wheat. Historically, the best of these has always been thought to be rye. The word, ьодка (vodka) – meaning 'little water' – shares a root derivative with the Slav word for 'water' (вода in Russian) and this partly explains why the drink has a mythical, if not spiritual place in the hearts and minds of Belarusians.

There is a flourishing moonshine market in home-distilled vodka made from organic material such as potatoes, grapes and sugar beet. It can even be produced relatively quickly by simply fermenting a solution of crystal sugar, with some salts

A BRIEF HISTORY OF VODKA

Russians (and, by implication, Belarusians) passionately maintain that they 'invented' vodka, although a number of other Northern and Eastern European countries make the same claim with equal vigour: most notably, Poland, where the chemical process of producing alcohol seems to have been discovered (by accident, it must be said!) as early as the 8th century. It is understood that people were experimenting with distillation techniques in Russia as long ago as the 12th century. However, commercial production was not established until the 14th century, although Tsar Ivan the Third then imposed significant restrictions on production at the end of the 15th century. Then in the 16th century, Ivan the Terrible found new sport; bored with generally being very unpleasant to people, he established the first state-authorised and controlled monopoly. Only the nobility were authorised to have stills and they produced vodka to a high standard and in vast quantities, often flavoured with all manner of natural substances (even acorns!). And naturally, they maintained rigid control of the market, a direct consequence of which was the establishment of a flourishing underground home-distilling industry that continues to this day.

The practice of flavouring is still widespread, but if you ask a Belarusian about 'real' vodka, he will sniff disdainfully at the concept of additives. And indeed, there is a very practical reason for this. Distilled properly, vodka is largely free of impurities. Adding ingredients for the purpose of flavouring increases the likelihood of introducing such impurities, thereby making the hangover much worse after a session. It's true (and I speak from experience)! Outside Eastern Europe, particularly in the West, the popularity of vodka as a fashionable drink has soared in the last ten years and by far the most popular brands are flavoured with substances such as cinnamon, pepper, honey, grasses and fruits (especially cranberry and lemon).

Succeeding tsars continued to encourage experimentation on their estates and at the end of the 18th century, one enterprising and imaginative soul happened upon the process of filtration by charcoal as a means to further refine the product. Naturally, only birch wood was used for this purpose. By now, the production of vodka in the Russian Empire was at the cutting edge in terms of technique and sophistication. And significantly for the government coffers, income was at an all-time high. Control from the centre became ever more encompassing as the industry's value increased, with refinements in process and equipment being eagerly sought from the West.

substituting for yeast. This is then distilled after just a few weeks. Much of it is surprisingly smooth, but potentially extremely damaging to health.

Every holiday, birthday, wedding, christening and funeral is celebrated with traditional toasts of vodka. Business deals are formally sealed with a vodka flourish. Family events and social gatherings, particularly to welcome new friends and visitors, would be unthinkable without the presence of a half-litre bottle on the table, with plenty more in reserve should (when!) the need arises. To give an indication of the ubiquity of the vodka toast in Belarusian culture, I have drunk it with the Metroplitan Filaret of All Belarus, with a state lawyer at 09.30 (in his office) to celebrate his birthday, with a headmaster in his office during the school day, at breakfast with the father of my host family, and by night on a farm next to a roaring fire with rural elders gathered around, singing songs and exchanging stories. Toast after toast after toast. But I have never drunk home-distilled vodka without knowing its source or being able to trust the founder of the feast. Open-air markets are a source of non-commercially produced alcohol that can literally be a hazard to life, with lethal ingredients like anti-freeze added to increase the potency. Don't ever be tempted.

As a staple alcoholic drink for recreational consumption, **beer** (пиво) is universally available throughout the country. Much of it is bottled or cask-

When the empire fell and the USSR came into existence, state control was rigidly maintained, with the government owning every distillery in production. In time, the availability and consumption of vodka came to be a metaphor of life under the Communists, for party officials and those within the 'inner circle' found that they had access to the highest quality product (usually distilled from rye), while the market for the masses was flooded with a pale imitation of doubtful quality and dubious origin.

Today, vodka production in Belarus is a very big industry indeed, with an equally big range in quality. But out in the country, the culture of home distillation continues unabated. Go into any home, peek into the storeroom and there you will find row upon row of demijohns, their contents at varying stages of readiness for consumption. Every family will have its own ideas on the best means of production. Fathers will whisper their secrets to you in hushed and reverential tones, eager to explain why their vodka is better for you than anyone else's.

Across the centuries, vodka has been entirely inseparable from the fate and privations of the common man and public/social policy in general. True, it has been an obvious source of revenue for succeeding governments, whatever their ideological background; but it has also destroyed many lives and to this day, its effect on family and community life is as pernicious as it has always been. In the rural communities that I know so well, I have seen a number of individuals who pass each day in a state of abject intoxication. For them, it is the perfect antidote to 'life'. I know families deprived of a father through alcoholism; and I have visited many state institutions for children abused by parents of either sex because of drink. But perhaps no other drink could have so reflected the fire and passion of the Russian soul and the heart of 'Holy Mother Russia'. Here, there are no sun-baked vineyards, no terraces for sophisticates to elegantly imbibe fine wines under a cloudless sky. This idyll just does not fit the reality of Russia's interminably long, dark and freezing winters. Vodka, on the other hand, is seen as the ideal conduit to complement the most sullen and morose of moods in the depths of impenetrable winter. Beer is widely consumed and imported wine has a significant place in the market, but there is nothing like a hearty toast, a passionate debate and a sing-song to warm the blood; and it just wouldn't be the same without opening the throat and liberally pouring vodka down it. Ah, the wonders and mysteries of the soul…

Across the ages, vodka has been regarded as something of a contradiction. Certainly, its restorative powers and general worth as a universal panacea is beyond question in the minds of Belarusians (and in wider terms, amongst the peoples of all Slavic nations), but it has also been regarded as the cause of many problems in society and as the harbinger of moral turpitude in general. When the Bolsheviks came to power in 1917, it was banned from sale in markets and until 1936, only vodka containing less than 20% alcohol was lawfully available for purchase. It is a characteristic of Slavs that they tend to be stoical in the extreme and not always capable of seeing things in the most positive of lights. So to assist with diverting the masses from focusing on the privations of life, Stalin subsequently decreed that restrictions and bans should be removed. It was for just this reason that he also permitted many churches to reopen their doors after the Nazi invasion in 1941. In both cases, 'food for the soul' was needed. Vodka was even given to Red Army soldiers as a staple element of their rations to help drive away the Nazi barbarians from the gate.

By the mid-1980s, national production had increased by 100% over the level in 1940, bringing considerable revenue to the state but visiting incalculable cost on society. During that same period, consumption of alcohol generally increased four-fold in the Soviet Union. In the post-war period, many studies were undertaken to prove or disprove any number of theories, both positive and negative, about the drinks industry in the country.

But whatever the vagaries of statistics, some key themes are beyond contradiction and the injurious impact of alcohol consumption on the rise of addiction, prejudice to family life, the physical and mental abuse of spouses and children, divorce statistics, life expectancy, violent crime and plummeting economic and industrial production has long been officially acknowledged and accepted. In the early years of his presidency, Mikael Gorbachev strived to grapple with these issues by cutting production and increasing taxes and prices, but this had exactly the same effect as the early attempts to control the market in the 16th century. The culture of production and consumption was simply driven further underground. And guess what happened next? By the time it was too late for the USSR, restrictions had been lifted and production was in full swing again.

Of course, vodka was not the only reason for the social, moral and economic disintegration that gradually brought the Soviet Union to its knees. The privations of the Great Patriotic War were seamlessly followed by the pointless and abject absurdities of Cold War politics, when slavish adherence to political dogma laid social and economic waste to the entire nation. Ultimately, the utopian dreams of Marx, Engels and Lenin turned into the nightmares visited on the people by Stalin, Krushchev and Brezhnev. Heroic promises of a bright new day turned to dust.

Add to this the catastrophe wrought by the Chernobyl disaster and it is not too difficult to see why many have sought solace at the bottom of a bottle (and continue so to do). And it was not only totalitarian communism that caused vodka to have a dark influence on Russian culture. The state's dependence on revenues from alcohol sales had encouraged alcoholism and abuse for hundreds of years. It was a very effective way for the wealthy to maintain control over the peasantry.

And as two anonymous Russian proverbs would have it (to reflect the totality of the contradiction), 'Vodka spoils everything but the glasses' and 'There cannot be too much vodka, there can only be not enough vodka.'

conditioned with chemicals, but there is a growing trend for local micro-breweries to produce their own diverse beers of high quality. In bars and restaurants, beer from the Baltika brewery is most in evidence. Established in 1990 in St Petersburg, it is acknowledged to be the market leader. It brews nine varieties (unimaginatively numbered from one to nine, each being known by its number rather than by an individual name), ranging from a light ale with an alcohol content of 4.7%, up to a strong lager of 8%, with pale, classic, original, gold, porter, export and wheat beers in between.

No **wine** is produced in Belarus, but women in particular will display their sophisticated tastes by drinking red wine from Georgia and Moldova. Also available cheaply is 'Soviet champagne', a sickly, gaseous and hideous drink that bears no resemblance to the French original.

As an alternative to vodka (not that one is needed), **cognac** from Armenia is very popular. It is also very competitively priced and of a high standard.

Although there's no doubting the Belarusian preference for alcohol, there are non-alcoholic alternatives, of which the most popular and refreshing is *kvas*. Made by fermenting bread baked with wheat, rye or barley, it is sometimes flavoured with herbs (such as mint) or with fruit (particularly strawberries), raisins or birch sap. It is usually served chilled and unfiltered with the yeast still in it, which adds to its unique malted flavour, as well as giving it a high vitamin B content. Commercial *kvas* is now made like any other soft drink, using sugar, carbonated water, malt extract and the full range of sinister but omnipresent flavourings.

Belarusians also bottle *kompote*, a rich essence of home-grown fruit (usually red berries) and boiled water. It's absolutely delicious. A full range of fruit juices is available in restaurants and bars, but most are made from concentrate. The usual international varieties of bottled mineral water are common place. Also served is a Belarusian variety that is highly carbonated and tastes salty and mineral-rich. Definitely an acquired taste..

Coffee (кофе) and **tea** (чай) are drunk throughout the country. Tea is normally taken with lemon and sugar (or even jam or honey), so you can expect a quizzical look if you ask for milk.

FOOD The cuisine of Belarus is an articulation of the people's relationship to the land. For generations, local people have grown their own produce, mainly starchy root vegetables. This is no surprise, for to do so reflects some of the key features of life here: long and unrelenting winters, painfully short growing seasons, political and social tyranny, the intensely physical and demanding workload of the peasantry and cyclical famine. Resilience needs to be fuelled by hot, nourishing and restorative food. It's a simple question of survival.

Although Belarusian cuisine derives from the same cultural sources as those of its neighbours, it is sometimes considered to be more dull and bland. It was not always so, however; for example, in the early 15th century, whole fried aurochs (a very large but now extinct type of cattle, widely regarded as some form of primeval ox) from the Byelavezhskaya forest were sent across Europe as a gift for the German royal family. And as long ago as the 16th century, the candied root of the sweet myrtle plant (grown in abundance in marshland) is known to have been exported further into western Europe. And baked goose with green peppers was still a popular dish for November feasts (All Saints' and St Martin's) by the middle of the 19th century, when it was served by a Belarusian nobleman at one of his social gatherings in Paris. An 18th century cookbook sums up the extravagance of the era thus – 'take fresh aurochs, but if you don't have any, use elk instead'!

The seismic political shift in the Russian Empire during the first part of the 20th century effectively wiped out the former privileged classes whose lifestyle and wealth had enabled them to maintain these exotic self-indulgences. Further, the very idea of a separate Belarusian cuisine was treated with great suspicion during Stalin's purges in the 1930s. Only after the Great Patriotic War ended did the state begin to realise that the artificially proclaimed 'flourishing of national culture' should also extend to the country's cuisine. Not surprisingly, the excesses and extravagance of the former ruling classes were ignored, if not denied and the only 'traditions' that were permitted to be revived had their roots in peasant heritage. It was almost as if the societal move away from the rural lifestyle that had so dominated Russian society in the 1920s and 1930s as a result of the massive industrialisation of the nation had never existed, at least in the context of the culinary history of the country. Then after independence in 1991, this moved up a gear or two as more lost traditions were 'rediscovered'. Yet modern Belarusian cuisine still displays the characteristics more of its recent Soviet past than its own heritage, whatever that might be. This means that restaurants here are more likely to showcase traditional 'Russian' dishes rather than those with more parochial antecedents.

In fact, ask a sample of the people themselves where their preference lies or if they are bothered about their culinary heritage or not and all will probably say that they are more interested in sampling and getting to know international cuisine. On my last road trip with Olya around the country (it was only a flying visit of three days' duration) our evening meals were curry, pizza and pizza, in that order! In fact, the closest reference that I have been able to find on my travels in Belarus to anything approaching adoption of an ethnic Belarusian foodstuff is that, quaintly, when people refer to the potato, they tend not to use the Russian word (картофелъ), but instead, a term that is unique to Belarus: 'bulba' (булъба). Whenever I use the word at table, I am always slapped roundly on the back and treated to broad grins, accompanied by enthusiastic nodding of the head on the part of my fellow diners. It's clearly more a term of fond affection than a simple noun!

The first Belarusian 'state', Polatsk, subsumed its neighbour Lithuania in the 11th century and remained at its centre for the next 200 years. Over time, Lithuania grew in power and roles were reversed when the Grand Duchy came into being. Then after union with the Polish Kingdom created a new 'super-state', influences from wider Europe began to appear in the territory's cuisine, most notably France, Germany and Italy. For example, *lazanki*, a mixture of flour dumplings and stewed meat (still popular today) is related to Italian lasagne.

But the staple diet of those living in rural communities was always related to the potato and other root vegetables, because for those living close to the land, this type of dish made good use of produce that was grown locally. Historically, the timing of meals for peasants always depended upon the beginning and end of their working day in the fields. For breakfast, around dawn, they would boil potatoes, bake pancakes or make an omelette. Dinner was the second meal of the day, usually around noon. A special kind of pot with two compartments, the *sparysh*, was used by children to bring dinner to their fathers working the land. The first course would consist of borsch (beetroot soup) with meat, fat, vegetables, potatoes and mushrooms. In fact, to call this dish 'soup' does it something of an injustice, for the acid test of quality is whether or not a spoon laid flat on its surface will stay on the surface, not because it floats, but because of the sheer volume of solid ingredients in each bowlful. Like Ukrainians, Russians and Poles, Belarusians are still fond of borsch with a very large dollop of sour cream (*smyetana*) and it is particularly warming and nourishing in the depths of winter. Borsch is still omnipresent today on every menu, whether in a restaurant or at home. For the second course at dinner, workers would eat cereal and potato dishes and would finish with *kvas*, *kompote* or sour milk. Supper at home after dusk would inevitably be more potatoes, this time with some form of stock. There was always a plentiful supply of bread, cereals and meat in the autumn and winter. Spring was the hungriest season of all, simply because last year's store of produce would have been consumed during the harsh winter.

It is no surprise, therefore, that modern Belarusian cookery is still based on traditions which have steadfastly survived turbulent political times. Whoever is in power, the land must be worked and mouths must be fed, whatever the privations of the people. For this reason, many dishes still are based on the potato. They are often grated and made into dumplings, which are stuffed with mushrooms or vegetables and baked in the oven; or used in salads. One particular and popular favourite dish is *draniki*, thick pancakes prepared from shredded potatoes, fried with mushrooms and served with sour cream. It's absolutely delicious.

Historically, meat was always in rather short supply and so it is today. In the past, it was only really eaten on the occasion of significant Christian festivals. These days, you will find few beef dishes on the menu (it has never been highly regarded here), but pork has always been a favourite, along with salted pork fat, which is regarded still as a great delicacy. One of the most popular pork dishes is *machanka*, a personal favourite of mine. It is thought to date from the 18th century and consists of chunks of meat in a rich and thick gravy, served in a stoneware pot with pancakes. You can expect to find it on every restaurant menu.

As for fish, modern Belarus has no sea borders and even historically, there is no tradition of seafaring and farming of the oceans from the days when the country was included with other lands bordering the Baltic and Black Seas. Much more common are lake and river fish, notably perch and carp. They are particularly tasty stuffed with vegetables and mushrooms. At home, river fish (locally caught, naturally) are often baked or boiled without seasoning and occasionally fried. Fish is also served in thick chunks in a consommé. Eels, smoked or stuffed, are the speciality of the northern lakeland territories. I have eaten eel with Eduard Voitekhovitch at Komorovo, close to the border with Lithuania, freshly caught, heavily salted and barbecued at dusk. And absolutely delicious.

The intense relationship that the people here still have with the land is reflected in an almost spiritual fondness for mushrooms and berries. Harvesting them is one of the great activities of late summer and autumn. Many dishes include fresh, salted and pickled mushrooms, together with berries such as bilberry, wild strawberry, red whortleberry and cranberry. Mushrooms are also often used in stuffings, sauces or fillings. Most households preserve and pickle fruits and vegetables for the winter months when there is a shortage of fresh produce.

Most people still try to eat a light breakfast and two fairly substantial meals for lunch and supper. Breakfast might just be bread and tea. Lunch will normally be soup, salad and a main course. Supper is usually more of the same, but in larger quantities. As an accompaniment and to fill out a meal, there is always bread on the table. Most people eat rye bread, because rye is more plentiful in Belarus than wheat. There are many traditional holidays in Belarus and there are special dishes for each one. This is particularly so on the occasion of Orthodox Christmas. If the family is honouring the most sacred of traditions, then hay will first be placed on the table, then the tablecloth, then the meal itself, consisting of no fewer than 12 dishes, representing the number of apostles at the Last Supper.

Eating out It is a rarity for many Belarusians to have the privilege of dining out in a restaurant, other than on very special occasions such as weddings. If you eat in a restaurant at lunchtime you may well be the only customer, and even in the evenings, your fellow diners will most likely to be the local nouveau riche, foreign diplomatic staff and businessmen.

Restaurants are increasingly offering international cuisine and traditional dishes (the latter mainly for tourists on group tours). There are also some fast food restaurants in Minsk. The norm, though, is the Soviet-style eatery with synthetic disco music and décor to match, with dubious cabaret entertainment. Apart from a few upmarket restaurants that attempt English translations (often with hilarious results) menus will be in Belarusian. They are frequently the same thickness as a magazine – not because of the range of dishes on offer, but because each part of a meal is priced separately by weight. If you are dining with Belarusians who order for you, expect the process to take an excruciating amount of time. With a disdainful flick of the fingers and a shout of 'девочка!' ('girl!'), a waitress will be summoned to your table and interrogated on the quality of particular dishes and their ingredients, together with the manner of cooking and presentation. At best, answers are greeted with a look of blank uninterest but more usually with a scowl. It's a touch unnerving.

Café culture is considerably more egalitarian in its patronage than are restaurants. Coffee bars are plentiful in the larger towns and cities, where students and young people meet to hang out and look disdainfully superior.

A cheaper but less pleasant alternative to the cafés are the shacks with outdoor seating where loud disco music is played, young waitresses wearing far too much make-up and little else lean on the counter looking very bored and the fare on offer is gassy tasteless beer and tired open sandwiches.

Note: The chapters of this book on the six major cities all include a *Where to eat* section. The price given at the end of each individual restaurant listing is indicative of the starting price for a standard three-course meal (main, starter or sweet, and coffee) without drinks, unless otherwise specified.

🧺 SHOPPING

In the 1970s, there was a rumour that in the Soviet Union shop windows were full of tempting things to buy, but that when you went inside, there was nothing on the shelves. For the most part, this was true. No self-respecting Russian would be seen out on the street without an old and tatty plastic bag, whatever the hour of day or night, just in case they came across something to buy somewhere, whether or not they actually needed or wanted it. But now, especially on the streets of Minsk, there are new designer stores selling exclusive Western labels and pharmacies selling top-range cosmetics, all with flashy billboards to match. By night, the glare of neon is beginning to light up the sky on street corners and at major road intersections. Shopping malls with piped mindless *muzak* and supermarkets are even beginning to appear. And of course, there are high prices in US dollars to match the image.

For a more intriguing shopping experience, try the GUM department store in Minsk. It's a fascinating slice of modern Soviet social history. Typical goods include lacquered inlay caskets and trinket boxes, laminated wooden spoons, framed straw animals, ceramic plates, decorative amber incorporated into pictures of rural scenes, wooden carvings, religious icons, decorated wooden eggs, cheap metal badges with grand Soviet slogans under a portrait of Lenin, embroidered blouses, linen tableware, original samovars and the ubiquitous wooden *matryoshka* doll (many of which have the face of Gorbachev or Reagan instead of the traditional peasant woman).

Elsewhere on the streets, particularly in suburban neighbourhoods, you will find small metal kiosks selling newspapers, magazines, sweets, chewing gum and beer. The vendor will hardly be visible through a tiny hatch opening; the walls and glass frontage are literally plastered with the goods that are available for purchase.

In the big cities, shops are open six days a week but closed on Sundays. Opening hours for food shops are generally from 09.00 (some from 08.00) until 20.00 and sometimes later. Other stores will open from 11.00 (some from 10.00) until 19.00 or 20.00. Occasionally, outlets aimed at the foreign tourist market, particularly in Minsk, will also open on Sundays. Also note that antiquities (such as genuine icons), valuables, works of art and manuscripts other than those offered for sale in souvenir shops require an export licence.

Indoor markets are huge, inexpensive and offer more choice than the shops. The best-known ones in Minsk are called Parking, Impulse, Starazhovsky, Zhdanovichy, Mir Mody ('World of Fashion'), Komorovko and Europa. One of the best is to found at Stadion Dynamo, the home of the much-loved football team Dynamo Minsk. For some of them, you will need to pay a paltry amount to enter.

If you can, it's worth visiting an open-air market, particularly in the smaller towns and villages. Locals will often ride to market in a horse and cart, with the man of the house (usually elderly) up front with a large stick and a *babooshka* at the back, precariously perched amongst piles of turnips, potatoes and beetroots. Dress down as much as possible, and be prepared for some lively bartering.

In both types of market, be aware that 'designer' items and CDs/DVDs sold at very cheap prices will be fakes, and that pickpockets may be about, so keep one eye on your wallet at all times.

ARTS AND ENTERTAINMENT

In all the countries of the ex-Soviet Union, the fine arts (whether classical or more avant-garde) play an important role in everyday life. On Saturday nights, concert halls and theatres across Belarus are filled with the elderly, families and young people, there to celebrate the best of Russian and Belarusian culture. Even the smallest community will have its own theatrical troupe and modest concert hall.

The price that local people pay for tickets is very low (even for best seats at a performance given by one of the state companies in Minsk), though as a tourist you will have to pay considerably more. Don't be put off, as the price is still far less than you would pay at home. Audience knowledge at each performance is very humbling, and more often than not, the quality of the performance will be very high. It's a special moment to be sitting in a theatre in Minsk as the orchestra strikes up the overture to a Tchaikovsky ballet, then to witness the colour and splendour of the set and the athleticism of the dancers. At the end, members of the audience will vie to be the loudest to shout bravo as awe-struck little girls in their finest dress clothes nervously hand bouquets to the principal dancers.

Among the best performances are those by the National Academic Bolshoi Ballet Theatre Company, the National Academic Great Opera Theatre and the Belarusian State Philharmonic. Do try to take in a performance given by one of these companies. If you are travelling with one of the main tourist agencies, this will probably be included as a matter of course, but even if not and you have to book yourself, ticket availability should not be a problem (see *Chapter 3*, page 124 for details).

Puppet theatres and circuses are the children's favourites. The state circus regularly draws large crowds, but although the tumblers, jugglers and clowns are highly polished entertainers, the whole experience is marred by degrading animal acts such as 'flying bears' (yes, really) which may make you feel pretty uncomfortable.

In the larger towns, live music can be enjoyed most nights of the week, ranging from ethnic folk groups playing in intimate, smoke-filled venues to the latest Belarusian group hammering out stadium rock. Many restaurants have live acts, especially at weekends, the style of music reflecting the restaurant's image. Trendy places will put on a cabaret show, 1970s style, while the 'traditional' venues aiming at the tourist market will showcase folk acts, usually solo performers or duets, strumming guitars and singing of unrequited love, historical melodrama, the glory of the peasant lifestyle or the celebration of the potato harvest (often all at once).

Every town will have at least one cinema and in Minsk this includes an open-air drive-in, together with several cinemas with surround sound, state-of-the-art digital projection and air conditioning. The latest releases are regularly shown, although they will be dubbed (badly).

Even in the smallest towns, museums display impressive collections of historical artefacts that tell the story of the locality through the ages. There will be exhibits focusing on the earliest settlements, the evolution of agricultural and industrial practices, folk art and ecology. These can be fairly dry, especially for children. Museum staff will be readily available to chaperone visitor groups and to offer detailed commentaries on the displays. *Babooshkas* are on hand to collect your admission fee and to jealously guard endless rooms of exhibits.

The post-Soviet era has also led to the growth of some less family-oriented distractions. The more shady *'biznizmyeni'* in cities such as Minsk and Gomel have bankrolled numerous casinos, nightclubs, strip joints and lap-dancing clubs, usually adjacent to or incorporated within the larger hotels. The prostitution industry, always lucrative in the past, is now booming.

PHOTOGRAPHY

Always take more film or digital memory cards than you think you are going to need. The larger towns will have these available, but at high cost, and they won't supply much specialist equipment. It's also worth bringing a spare camera battery. For technical tips, see pages 84–5.

People you meet will usually allow you to take photographs, though you should always ask permission first. Even if they readily accept, people will often pose in very stiff and formal ways. Elderly people in particular will stare fiercely into the lens. If you can, make arrangements to send on a printed copy and be true to your word. The photo will take pride of place in a modest home and will be a conversation piece for guests. It's also a good idea to take photos with you of your family and children, as people will take great interest.

Don't be tempted to take pictures of military facilities, soldiers, offices of the KGB (still omnipresent) or government buildings. The first sight of a camera will be greeted by a shrill blast from a member of the militia whom you did not even know was there, and your film or camera may be confiscated.

C MEDIA AND COMMUNICATIONS

MEDIA Ever since the date in 1991 when Belarus came into existence as an independent nation state on the disintegration of the Soviet Union, there have been claims that state control of all forms of media communication (newspapers, journals, periodicals, internet websites, radio and television) has been all-encompassing, just as it was in the days of the USSR. Ironically, this followed a period of relative freedom in the final years of the Soviet Union, when President Gorbachev essayed in vain to bring about real reform of the system through *glasnost* ('openness') and *perestroika* ('restructuring'). But since that time, there has been sustained criticism on the part of human rights and 'media watch' organisations that freedom of speech has been universally suppressed in Belarus and that the state-controlled media outlets have enjoyed privileges that have been denied to independent ones. As an example, it is understood that early in 2007, the Belarusian

Association of Journalists reported that Byelpashta, the state postal service with a monopoly over the distribution of subscription periodicals, had been denying distribution to the major nationwide independent newspapers and to many local independent journals. When editors of the newspapers and journals in question asked for this apparent partiality to cease, the blanket response of Byelpashta's management was reportedly that 'since the law does not oblige the organisation to include a periodical in its catalogue, it is the right of Byelpashta to choose publications for its catalogue'. Against all the odds, some independent publications appear to have survived, but life is not easy for them. Increasing regulation of their activities makes it all too easy for them to run the risk of non-compliance, with closure being an ever-present threat. Meantime, everywhere you look, on television or in newspapers, the state's view of things is omnipresent. Suppression of freedom of speech is firmly denied by the government. The universal mandate given to the president in successive elections is cited as authority for the claim that the people are happy with things as they are. Doubtless, the small and poorly organised opposition see things differently. The context to all of this is that the United States of America and the European Union continue to cry 'foul' and to impose economic sanctions on Belarus both directly and indirectly. By way of example, the European Parliament passed a resolution under reference C157 /465 in July 2005 in which it 'strongly condemns the Belarus regime's indiscriminate attacks on the media, journalists, members of the opposition, human rights activists and any person who attempts freely to voice criticism of the President and the regime'. This and all other criticism has met with robust and withering rebuttals on the part of the Belarusian government, along with suggestions that Western democracies might care to reflect on their own policies and human rights records, domestic and foreign. All the while, the Russian Federation sits impassively in the ambivalence of its own relationship with both ideologies. It's as though the Cold War had never ended. Inevitably, the truth lies somewhere along the great divide. Certainly, there are many pertinent questions to be asked and answered, but the same can be said for many political regimes around the world, including some very close to home. Perhaps the best indicator is the view of the human rights and 'media watch' charities who have critically reviewed the substantial body of evidence of suppression of freedom of speech that they claim exists in abundance.

Press The English-language paper *Belarus Today* (*www.belarustoday.info*) is published weekly. The principal dailies are *Narodnaya Gazeta* and *Respublika*, all printed in Belarusian and Russian. *Sovetskaya Belorossiya* is printed in Russian only and *Zvyazhda* in Belarusian only. *Belaruskaya Delovaya Gazeta*, which temporarily closed in 2003, has since resumed publication and is the main private daily paper. *Belaruskaya Gazeta* is a weekly private publication.

Television The Belarusian National State Teleradio Company operates three channels, including the satellite station Belarus-TV, but it's easy to pick up stations broadcasting from Russia.

Radio Radio Belarus, which is also state-run by the same company, operates three national networks and an external service, broadcasting in Belarusian, Russian, German, Polish and English. Daily transmissions are on air from 17.00– midnight on the frequencies of 7360 and 7390, from 18.20–midnight on 7420 kHz and from 20.00–midnight on 1170 kHz. Online broadcasts began in January 2005, then in September of that year, air time was increased from five to ten hours daily in two separate five-hour slots. To listen and for further information on state television and radio facilities, go to the company's website (*www.tvr.by/eng*).

Ariadne Van Zandbergen

EQUIPMENT Although with some thought and an eye for composition you can take reasonable photos with a 'point-and-shoot' camera, you need an SLR camera if you are at all serious about photography. Modern SLRs tend to be very clever, with automatic programmes for almost every possible situation, but remember that these programmes are limited in the sense that the camera cannot think, but only make calculations. Every starting amateur photographer should read a photographic manual for beginners and get to grips with such basics as the relationship between aperture and shutter speed.

Always buy the best lens you can afford. The lens determines the quality of your photo more than the camera body. Fixed fast lenses are ideal, but very costly. A zoom lens makes it easier to change composition without changing lenses the whole time. If you carry only one lens, a 28–70mm (digital 17–55mm) or similar zoom should be ideal. For a second lens, a lightweight 80–200mm or 70–300mm (digital 55–200mm) or similar will be excellent for candid shots and varying your composition. Wildlife photography will be very frustrating if you don't have at least a 300mm lens. For a small loss of quality, tele-converters are a cheap and compact way to increase magnification: a 300 lens with a 1.4x converter becomes 420mm, and with a 2x it becomes 600mm. Note, however, that 1.4x and 2x tele-converters reduce the speed of your lens by 1.4 and 2 stops respectively.

For photography from a vehicle, a solid beanbag, which you can make yourself very cheaply, will be necessary to avoid blurred images, and is more useful than a tripod. A clamp with a tripod head screwed onto it can be attached to the vehicle as well. Modern dedicated flash units are easy to use; aside from the obvious need to flash when you photograph at night, you can improve a lot of photos in difficult 'high contrast' or very dull light with some fill-in flash. It pays to have a proper flash unit as opposed to a built-in camera flash.

DIGITAL/FILM Digital photography is now the preference of most amateur and professional photographers, with the resolution of digital cameras improving all the time. For ordinary prints a six-megapixel camera is fine. For better results and the possibility to enlarge images and for professional reproduction, higher resolution is available up to 16 megapixels.

Memory space is important. The number of pictures you can fit on a memory card depends on the quality you choose. Calculate in advance how many pictures you can fit on a card and either take enough cards to last for your trip, or take a storage drive onto which you can download the content. A laptop gives the advantage that you can see and edit your pictures properly at the end of each day, and delete rejects, but a storage device is lighter and less bulky. These drives come in different capacities up to 80GB.

Some radio stations target Belarusian listeners from outside the country. For example, Radio Baltic Waves broadcasts from Lithuania, while Radio Ratsyya is based in Poland.

✉ **POST** The state post offers the usual full range of postal services. Just bear in mind that mail that's not in Cyrillic script may very well not reach its destination. If you are sending mail home to the UK or US, then at the very least, write ВЕЛИКОБРИТАНИЯ (Great Britain) or Соединённые Штаты Америки (USA) at the end of each address; that should at least guarantee that your correspondence gets to the UK at some point in time, though not necessarily until after you return home.

Bear in mind that digital camera batteries, computers and other storage devices need charging, so make sure you have all the chargers, cables and converters with you. Most hotels have charging points, but do enquire about this in advance. When camping you might have to rely on charging from the car battery; a spare battery is invaluable.

If you are shooting film, 100 to 200 ISO print film and 50 to 100 ISO slide film are ideal. Low ISO film is slow but fine grained and gives the best colour saturation, but will need more light, so support in the form of a tripod or monopod is important. You can also bring a few 'fast' 400 ISO films for low-light situations where a tripod or flash is no option.

DUST AND HEAT Dust and heat are often a problem. Keep your equipment in a sealed bag, stow films in an airtight container (eg: a small cooler bag) and avoid exposing equipment and film to the sun. Digital cameras are prone to collecting dust particles on the sensor which results in spots on the image. The dirt mostly enters the camera when changing lenses, so be careful when doing this. To some extent photos can be 'cleaned' up afterwards in Photoshop, but this is time-consuming. You can have your camera sensor professionally cleaned, or you can do this yourself with special brushes and swabs made for the purpose, but note that touching the sensor might cause damage and should only be done with the greatest care.

LIGHT The most striking outdoor photographs are often taken during the hour or two of 'golden light' after dawn and before sunset. Shooting in low light may enforce the use of very low shutter speeds, in which case a tripod will be required to avoid camera shake.

With careful handling, side lighting and back lighting can produce stunning effects, especially in soft light and at sunrise or sunset. Generally, however, it is best to shoot with the sun behind you. When photographing animals or people in the harsh midday sun, images taken in light but even shade are likely to be more effective than those taken in direct sunlight or patchy shade, since the latter conditions create too much contrast.

PROTOCOL In some countries, it is unacceptable to photograph local people without permission, and many people will refuse to pose or will ask for a donation. In such circumstances, don't try to sneak photographs as you might get yourself into trouble. Even the most willing subject will often pose stiffly when a camera is pointed at them; relax them by making a joke, and take a few shots in quick succession to improve the odds of capturing a natural pose.

Ariadne Van Zandbergen is a professional travel and wildlife photographer specialising in Africa. She runs the Africa Image Library. For photo requests, visit www.africaimagelibrary.co.za or contact her on ariadne@hixnet.co.za.

✆ TELEPHONE SERVICES The country code is 375 and each number after that should have nine digits. The suffixes for the six regions of the country are as follows:

| Grodno | +375 15 | Minsk | +375 17 | Mogilev | +375 22 |
| Brest | +375 16 | Vitebsk | +375 21 | Gomel | +375 23 |

If you find yourself dialling landlines within Belarus, then don't expect to pay very much. But if you are ringing mobile numbers, then do watch the credit/allowance balance on your own mobile. All hotels now have international dialling facilities direct from your room, but make sure that you carefully scrutinise the final account when you check out. If you are taking your own mobile to Belarus, then buy a local SIM card to put in it. It shouldn't cost more than US$10. But carry your own SIM card with you as a back-up, just in case. Check out the state service website for further details (*www.eng.beltelecon.by/info*).

ꂬ INTERNET According to statistics compiled by international monitors, there are now around 1.4 million internet users in Belarus, around 14% of the total population. And a recent survey indicates that people aged between 20 and 24 are the most active internet users, with 40% of all users being government officials. A majority of all users (45.6%) live in the six regional centres, with 22.9% of these being inhabitants of Minsk, while only 9.8% live in villages. This means that the profile of the average internet user in Belarus is of a young governmental employee in his or her early twenties living in a major city.

BUSINESS

Business hours for offices are 09.00–18.00 Mon–Fri; for banks 09.00–17.00 Mon–Fri; for general stores 09.00–21.00 Mon–Sat, 09.00–18.00 Sun; and for food shops 09.00–20.00 Mon–Sun (with some open 24 hours in the big cities).

These hours will be more variable outside the big cities, and closure for lunch between 13.00 and 14.00 is fairly common.

If you are in Belarus on business, remember that bureaucracy is a major obstacle to fast transactions, so plan ahead as much as you can. If you need to make appointments, do so in plenty of time and always confirm verbal arrangements by email or fax. If you are dealing with an organisation for the first time, try to forge a relationship with an intermediary in advance, preferably someone who you can trust, who speaks English and Belarusian to a high standard and whose credentials have been verified by an independent source.

Belarusians are fairly restrained and will reserve judgement until they are sure of themselves in any situation. So, when doing business, you can probably expect a brief handshake and a curt nod of the head by way of introduction. Meetings are quite formal but with relatively little fanfare. If you are unsure about anything, just watch carefully and follow what others do. Meetings and negotiation sessions can be a little trying. First and foremost, you should observe the usual common courtesies: listen intently, never interrupt or patronise anyone, always acknowledge another person's point of view, then put your own arguments quietly, respectfully and without histrionics. Don't try to suggest that your position is in any way stronger or more imposing. If you do, the shutters will come up and there will be no progress. If you stay calm throughout and with a smile on your face, then you can guarantee that you will be listened to respectfully and if your arguments are persuasive, then they will be accepted. But you must also be prepared to make concessions in an effort to move things along. It helps to show that you regard your counterparts as being of equal status in every way.

Don't show frustration at legal regulations or bureaucracy in general. If you do, then things will always be slowed down and another obstacle placed in your way. It's preferable not to try to steer your own course through this maze; instead hire the services of a local lawyer who can act as an independent consultant and give you the best advice on legal issues.

If and when a decision is made that is acceptable to all sides, the matter does not end there. Decisions are made on levels, so if you manage to gain agreement with one level of an organisation, it does not automatically follow that the rest will agree. Generally speaking, the higher up you go, the easier it is to get a 'yes', but it is not uncommon for matters to proceed a very long way (and right to the point of conclusion), only for everything to be called off without explanation. So always have an alternative plan ready.

Overall, there are early signs that in economic terms, the country is beginning to open up internally and to look outside its borders in terms of trade, business and commerce. Although the economy continues to be run on a planned basis, a growing number of entrepreneurs with professional back-up and guidance are looking to transact business across national borders. And the government is ever keen to encourage foreign investment into the country, although usually on the basis that strategic and practical decisions on the way all monies are spent remain fully in Belarusian hands. Foreign investors should not expect to retain a stakeholder role for themselves in this. Several business centres have been established in Minsk as an initial point of contact for all trade enquiries, each of them offering access to business directory information for would-be trading partners, including names and addresses of individual firms and the nature of their business or trade, contact details, basic economic information and statistics, market research, marketing and merchandise, company formation, sales information, translation services and even arrangements for sightseeing visits. In other words a brokerage and facilitating service to put potential trade partners from outside the country in touch with those within. Critically, they also offer to guide foreign companies through the maze of government regulations that exist here. But standards of the services on offer certainly differ, however. At the bottom end of the scale, there is a facility at the Hotel Planeta that is little more than a desk in a cupboard, seemingly offering no more than basic administrative support. At the other end of the scale, a comprehensive range of services can be found at the Business Communication Centre (*12 Komsomolskaya St, Minsk 220050;* ℓ *+375 17 227 21 27;* f *+375 17 226 58 85;* ◷ *09.00–18.00 Mon–Fri*), which was set up in 1994 and now has nine employees. Its primary area of business appears to be the wood trade, both in terms of supply and also the construction of prefabricated buildings.

That same year, an unexpectedly free-market initiative opened the door for European business interests in the form of a hotel and conference venture that was jointly established with Germany – the Internationale Bildungs-und-Begegnungsstatte (IBB), or International Education and Meeting Centre (*11 Prospyekt Gazyety Pravda, Minsk 220116;* ℓ *+375 17 270 39 94;* f *+375 17 270 39 95;* e *ibb@ibb.by; www.ibb.by/en*). Situated in a southwestern suburb of Minsk, it is no more than 5km from the city centre, with easy access by car to the centre and Minsk-2 Airport.

The IBB has made a name for itself as an open door through which to explore Minsk's (and therefore Belarus's) business opportunities. The informative website (above) has much more detail on this. Among the IBB's permanent business residents with offices at the centre are respected institutions such as the Organisation for Security and Co-operation in Europe and two European banks.

The IBB's state-of-the-art conference facilities certainly establish it as a market leader; there are three well-equipped seminar rooms, a large function room seating 350 and simultaneous translation facilities. And a very good indicator of the outward and forward thinking of its proprietors is that throughout the centre, access is wheelchair-friendly, something of a rarity in Minsk. Training facilities are also on offer in subjects such as economics, politics, culture, the environment, journalism, languages and information technology.

It remains to be seen how much further the country will extend its hand towards the economic markets of Europe and beyond. Neither the European Union nor the United States render conditions favourable for businesses in their countries to trade here, while President Lukashenko shows no sign of abandoning his commitment to a planned and controlled economy in favour of more free- market principles. Most

2

companies remain in state ownership and for those which are not, laws and regulations are complex and all-embracing in the extreme. But the language of every public statement is about opening up trade with the rest of Europe. There are many agendas at work here. Belarus continues to push for greater co-operation and ultimately formal union with the Russian Federation. But President Putin has a fine line to walk. He wants to see Russia playing a full part on the world economic and political stage, but he knows full well that those with the biggest clout, most notably the USA, view Belarus as a market and administration in need of major governmental reform. It is very difficult to forecast how things will go from here.

BUYING PROPERTY

Type 'buying property in Belarus' into a search engine and you will immediately gain access to several websites telling you how easy it is to buy property in Belarus. Don't be fooled. Although the voracious market in land and property deals is focusing increasingly on the former Eastern bloc as the latest source of cheap investment, Belarus is firmly closed for business. There is no real concept of proprietorial land ownership as there is in the West. Many people rent their homes from the state; in the country, there is a distinctly laissez-faire attitude to the delineation of boundaries.

SOCIETY AND CUSTOMS

The characteristics of the Belarusian people are difficult to generalise, but historically there has been a long tradition of calmness and tolerance. This said, people can get very passionate when debating the big issues of the day. You will be expected to play your part in the debate and will be asked a great many questions about life where you come from. Be honest, but be very careful about how you comment on Belarusian society. Derogatory statements will not go down well. Never be critical of the government or of the president, as you never know who might be listening. It's a cliché, but Soviet trains really did run with absolute punctuality, so don't be late to events or meetings.

Despite the legacy of the Soviet era, the outward face of Belarus is youthful, energetic and optimistic. Young people are encouraged to pursue every sport going, from ski-jumping and ice-skating to wrestling and horseriding. In Max Myrni, the country has one of the top men's doubles tennis players in the world and Belarus performs consistently well in Davis Cup tennis. President Lukashenko, a major ice-hockey fan, has decreed that every town is to have its own sports palace, offering a full range of sporting opportunities to the country's youth.

The *banya*, or Belarusian sauna, can be a great way to make friends (see box *The bathhouse culture*). There are communal *banya* in many towns with nominal entrance fees. The format is largely the same as the private *banya*, but the anteroom will be much larger and will contain communal shower facilities, while cold water will be available in a plunging pool outside the steam room. You will inevitably be in the company of strangers here, so the bonding experience of the more intimate private *banya* shared with friends will probably be supplemented with (but not replaced by) macho posturing.

GIVING SOMETHING BACK

When I talk to people about how unspoilt and uncommercialised Belarus is and about how that makes it a destination of rare interest for the visitor, the response is always the same: that nobody will go until budget flights are available.

top **Stone carving, Brest**
(JS) page 147

above **Soviet propaganda in the metro, Minsk**
(JS) page 104

right **Statue of Lenin, Polotsk**
(JS) page 181

top **Typical rural cottage, Parichi village, Gomel *oblast***
(NR) page 73

above **Painted gate, Vetka folk arts museum**
(NR) page 209

left **Victory Day celebrations along Sovyetskaya Street, Gomel**
(NR) page 204

top **China factory, Dobrush**
(NR)

above left **Girls with goat, Polotsk**
(JS) page 181

above right **Babooshka, Vetka**
(NR) page 209

right **Windmill, Dudutki**
Folk Museum
(NR) page 129

top   **Wild boar** *Sus scrofa* (BR/TIPS) page 31

above left   **Wolf** *Canis lupus* (BR/TIPS) page 30

above right   **Beaver** *Castor fiber* (PM/TIPS) page 30

below   **Brown bear** *Ursus arctos* (JD/TIPS) page 31

above left **White stork**
Ciconia ciconia
(MV) page 31

above right **Lynx**
Lynx lynx
(JDr/TIPS) page 30

right **Roe deer**
Capreolus capreolus
(BF/TIPS) page 30

below **European bison**
Bison bonasus
(LB) page 30

top	**Entrance to Brest Hero Fortress** (NR) page 147
above left	**Chernobyl Memorial, Vetka** (NR) page 209
above right	**'The Unconquered Man', Khatyn** (NR) page 132
below	**'Thirst', Brest Hero Fortress** (NR) page 147

THE BATHHOUSE CULTURE

The *banya* (bathhouse) is a distinct feature of rural Belarusian life. Traditionally made of wood, it stands in the open. In a village, it will be in the garden of a dwelling house, but in the depths of the rural hinterland, it will most likely be situated near a lake or river. Inside is a wood-heated stove containing stones. The stove is fuelled up ready for use over the course of the day and when the operating temperature is reached the door to the stove is opened and water is thrown onto the stones to create intense amounts of steam. Participants throw water and sometimes beer onto the hot stove to create a fragrant, steam-filled atmosphere. To enhance the whole experience, they slap each other with a sheaf of oak or birch twigs and leaves tied together in a bundle. This is done firmly and with gusto to exfoliate the skin. Usually, the sheaf has been soaked for a few days previously in natural oils. This intense aroma, when added to the steam, makes for a very heady atmosphere.

Three separate activities make up a complete cycle. First, participants sit in the bathhouse, on wooden slatted benches, to begin the process of perspiration. This initial phase normally lasts for ten to fifteen minutes before everyone takes a breather by sitting in the small anteroom (which is not much bigger than a large cupboard, but considerably cooler than the steam room) and having a beer. To maintain hydration, naturally. In the second phase, guests are invited to lie across a bench, first on their front and then on their back, while the host whacks them with the sheaf. Guests then return the compliment. At this point everyone repairs to the anteroom for another gulp or two of beer. Then it's back in for the final time, to thoroughly wash and rinse your tingling body with soap and water heated by the stove and decanted into a large metal bowl. Cold water will also be at hand and you can expect your hosts to be playful with it. Afterwards, everyone relaxes together in the anteroom with more beer and occasionally vodka, in which case the sensation of intoxication, after all that perspiring, is almost instantaneous. At this point, if you are deep in the country, expect to be invited to jump in the river or lake. If you are really lucky, it will be winter and you will be encouraged to roll in the snow.

That is a very depressing supposition. Put bluntly, there is now a very persuasive argument that the footprint we leave as we depart is equally as important as our hopes and aspirations for ourselves when we arrive.

Since the Chernobyl catastrophe, much of the aid that has been targeted at Belarus and its people has been humanitarian assistance, but sustainable development programmes are on the increase. The idea is to transfer skills and experience that help to build an infrastructure for local people to develop local solutions for their problems.

Your presence in Belarus and the interest you show in the people you meet and all that you see will be a very good start. To give you a few ideas about continued involvement on your return home, you might want to have a look at the following websites. They will give you a broad feel for the types of project that are being supported by the international community. I shall be very surprised if you do not return from your first visit with a burning resolve to put something back into this wonderful country and its people. Plenty of options exist, certainly in the UK and Ireland. The best thing of all is that you can get involved quickly in your own locality and pretty soon you will have the chance to take a direct and active part. My own view is that while humanitarian assistance can certainly help to alleviate some of the hardship that exists in this country, it does little to stimulate growth and development within the regions in sustainable terms. And it is only by this means that communities and individuals will be able to build confidence and self-respect in the search for ownership and control over their destiny. The development work that I have been able to undertake with Belarusian communities over the last six years is *absolutely* the most rewarding and fulfilling thing that I have ever done. At the outset, I had no specialist skills in the field, but by learning with people in the communities themselves (as they progressed their own learning and experience), I have been fortunate indeed to feel that it really is possible to make a difference to (and have a positive impact on) the lives of real people. The work isn't easy and is sometimes very frustrating, but in terms not only of the outcomes delivered in Belarus, but also my own personal development, I wouldn't change a single moment of it. And to feel that I have been taken into the hearts of people in a very different community from my own is truly humbling. Every time my plane touches down at Minsk or I cross the border, it feels like coming home. Over to you now to play your part.

www.un.by/en/undp/ The website dedicated to the United Nations Development Programme in Belarus. The entirety of the programme has global application in the field of sustainable development. There are many initiatives presently underway in Belarus.

www.chernobyl.info The site of an umbrella operation that draws together the work of many charitable organisations & NGOs combating the consequences of the Chernobyl disaster throughout the whole region affected by the fallout.

www.chernobyl-international.com Based in Ireland, the Chernobyl Children's Project International ('CCPI') has undertaken an astonishing amount of work over the last 16 years, raising around €70 million of direct aid to regions affected by the catastrophe & arranging recuperation breaks in Ireland for 15,000 children.

www.chernobyl-children.org.uk/ An umbrella charity established 12 years ago with 30 member organisations in England, Scotland & Wales. Its aims & activities are similar to CCPI & each year, around 400 children are brought to the UK for recuperation.

www.wova.org.uk I make no apology for including this small charity in the directory, even though I am one of the trustees & I do hope that readers will forgive this rather shameful piece of opportunistic advertising. The aim of the organisation is to promote & deliver sustainable development projects jointly with local representative bodies & NGOs in communities affected by Chernobyl in the Vetka region of Gomel oblast.

www.remember chernobyl.org A very useful site providing links to sites of other charities operating in the same field.

A brief word now about local charities and NGOs operating in Belarus that are not related to the alleviation of Chernobyl consequences. They certainly do exist,

STUFF YOUR RUCKSACK – AND MAKE A DIFFERENCE

www.stuffyourrucksack.com is a website set up by TV's Kate Humble which enables travellers to give direct help to small charities, schools or other organisations in the country they are visiting. Maybe a local school needs books, a map or pencils, or an orphanage needs children's clothes or toys – all things that can easily be 'stuffed in a rucksack' before departure. The charities get exactly what they need and travellers have the chance to meet local people and see how and where their gifts will be used.

The website describes organisations that need your help and lists the items they most need. Check what's needed in Belarus, contact the organisation to say you're coming and bring not only the much-needed goods but an extra dimension to your travels and the knowledge that in a small way you have made a difference.

www.stuffyourrucksack.com
Responsible tourism in action

One of the early projects that WOVA chose to support in its infancy was the establishment of a goose-farming co-operative in the village of Svetilovichy, right in the heart of the contaminated zone in southeastern Belarus. A beautiful (but very hot) summer's day saw me standing by a dusty roadside on the edge of the village, waiting to chaperone a flock of goslings to their new homes. After an hour or so, a battered and beaten saloon pulled up. Out clambered the driver, extremely hot and bothered. When he opened up the back I could scarcely believe my eyes, for crammed in from floor to ceiling was tray after tray of two-day old goslings, 750 of them. They had travelled all the way from Minsk, a seven-hour journey, without water or fresh air. Miraculously, all survived, without exception. After a cursory examination, we led the saloon through the village to a small farmstead, where local villagers had been waiting patiently for over two hours in the heat of the midday sun. They formed an orderly queue to the rear of the saloon and each family or individual took charge of 20 inquisitive and noisy birds, some of the villagers stuffing them into wicker baskets for transportation home. Many of the aged babooshkas had tears of gratitude in their eyes and flowing down their cheeks as they headed slowly home with their new charges. Witnessing this scene of real community engagement, it was impossible not to be moved and deeply humbled. The local co-coordinator Anna wept uncontrollably as we stood side-by-side and hand-in-hand to watch the distribution process. I drive through this village regularly on my travels. On one such occasion, our car pulled to the side of the road and there stood Anna, overjoyed to see me again and tearful as ever, to administer hugs and kisses and to press a plastic carrier of gifts for my wife and children into my hand, before pushing me gently (but with purpose) back into the car. The whole encounter took no more than 30 seconds, but she had heard that I was in the locality and had waited by the roadside for my car to pass through, to give me presents for my family. Never have I been so humbled. As for the geese? Ah, that's another story for another book …

undertaking splendid work in the field of community development and the promotion of family health and well-being, but if you type 'charities in Belarus' into your internet search engine, page after page will appear with a Chernobyl theme. I know of many small individual NGOs operating in the regions and indeed, I have worked closely with a number of them on locally focused projects designed to benefit particular communities, or parts of them. The local regulations relating to NGOs are extremely comprehensive and life can be difficult for them. The best way to gain access to their areas of activity is via the United Nations and its constituent bodies, such as UNDP or UNICEF. An hour or two spent on the relevant websites will enable you to locate projects of specific application, including details of local partner NGOs and charities in Belarus itself.

Alternatively, all of the charities whose objects are related to the alleviation of problems and consequences for Chernobyl children and their families have locally based activities and functions throughout the UK, Ireland and many other countries in Western Europe. Offers of help and assistance, particularly with regard to hosting Belarusian children on recuperative holidays, are always gratefully received. Wherever you live, a local branch is unlikely to be far away. I have met many families who have offered their homes to children in this way and entirely without exception, the experience has always been described to me as a life-affirming one. Irrespective of this being a wonderful opportunity for you to 'give something back', it will also greatly enhance your own personal development and that of your family members, particularly children. Kids are rarely burdened with

2

the baggage that only comes with adulthood and to see deep friendships flourish between youngsters, notwithstanding language barriers, is an experience not to be missed. And this can be the door that leads you to other community-based activities for the benefit of families and individuals in Belarus. There are opportunities to support any number of projects that are designed to build capacity and well-being, from investment, funding and monetary donations on the one hand, all the way to more direction contributions on the other, including for example, offering skills and expertise for building projects, driving vehicles bearing humanitarian aid or collecting plant and equipment in your own country for transportation to Belarus. Amongst other things, I have taken through customs a computer modem, medical equipment, toys, books, writing equipment, resuscitation dummies, clothes and a coffee jug. Oh and the lawnmower, of course. Opportunities to make a contribution really are boundless and you won't regret a single moment or a single penny.

European bison

Part Two

THE GUIDE

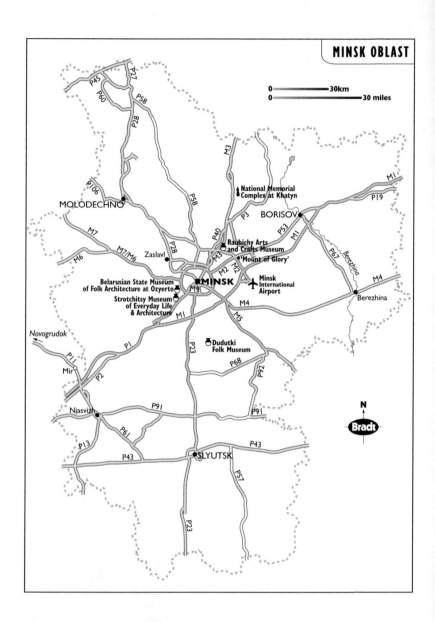

0 ▰▰▰ 30km
0 ▰▰▰ 30 miles

P27
P45
P60
P58
P28

M3

P106

MOLODECHNO

National Memorial
Complex at Khatyn

P58

P3

BORISOV

M1

P19

P40

M7

M7/M6

Zaslavl

Raubichy Arts
and Crafts Museum

P28

M3

M53

M1

P67

Berezhina

M6

M2

'Mount of Glory'

MINSK

Belarusian State Museum
of Folk Architecture at Ozyerto

M9

M2

Minsk
International
Airport

M4

Berezhina

Strotchitsy Museum
of Everyday Life
& Architecture

M1

M4

M5

Novogrudok

P1

Dudutki
Folk Museum

P11

P23

Mir

P2

P68

P92

Njasvizh

P91

P91

P61

P13

P43

SLYUTSK

P43

P57

P23

N

Bradt

3

Minsk City and Oblast
Минск

Minsk (Belarusian **Мінск** and Russian **Минск**) is the capital and largest city in Belarus. As the national capital, it has special administrative status in the country and it is also the administrative centre of Minsk *oblast*. Perhaps surprisingly, given the geographical size and metaphorical significance of its giant neighbour the Russian Federation, Minsk is also the headquarters of the Commonwealth of Independent States (CIS), which was formed on the break-up of the Soviet Union.

First mentioned in the Primary Medieval Chronicles of 1067 and situated on one of the most significant trade routes connecting the Baltic and Black seas, this reconstructed city of expansive boulevards, wide streets, modern and classical architecture, huge shaded parks, fountains and monuments to heroism on the banks of the Svislach River has an appeal all of its own that it will take you some while to articulate, even though you feel it as soon as you set foot there. It has long been regarded as one of the most impressive cities in all of the republics of the former Soviet Union. Almost completely destroyed by the Nazis in World War II (still referred to in the former Soviet republics as 'the Great Patriotic War'), Stalin ordered it to be rebuilt after the conflict ended in a manner that would stand as a testament to the rest of the world of the might, resilience and ingenuity of Soviet communism. As such, it remains the best example of post-war Soviet urban planning on a grand scale (and the only one of the western Soviet republics' capital cities largely untainted, for now, by Western commercialism). Herein lies its appeal and idiosyncrasy, for after a short while there you begin to realise that it is unlike any other capital city that you have visited before.

Minsk is the sort of place where you can feel relaxed and at ease without even knowing it. Most capitals of the world are characterised by a high level of ambient noise and a jumble of activity wherever you look. Not so Minsk. For a city of 1.7 million people, the atmosphere is universally calm. By way of example, ten-lane boulevards are often devoid of traffic. In many cities of the world, there is a feeling of claustrophobia as buildings close in on top of each other. But in Minsk, the skies are huge and there is a real sense of open space. Everywhere you go, there are vast and sweeping panoramas to take in, all with a host of different sights. At times, you can walk for hours in areas of parkland and not see another soul, but without feeling nervous in the process. The streets are spotlessly clean and free from crime. Access to all areas of interest to the visitor by public transport is simple and uncomplicated, not to say impressively efficient. Many of the sights can be reached on foot and in so doing, you will rediscover an activity that is largely lost in the West: that of promenading. This is because walking is seen as so much more than simply a mechanical act of propulsion from A to B. Rather, it is an art form to be savoured, with every footstep to be relished. Everywhere you look, even in the depths of winter and no matter what the time of day or night, you will see people strolling, apparently aimlessly, but locked in conversation and arm in arm. Here in Minsk (and indeed, everywhere in Belarus), teenagers mingle with families, young children, older people and young women on their own or in twos, just taking the air, enjoying the sights, chatting and relishing the fact that they have, for a short while, stepped off the merry-go-round of life.

My favourite day to be in Minsk is on a Sunday, before breakfast. I always set the alarm early and get out on the street as soon as I can lever myself out of bed, just to walk and walk. The grandiose buildings and particularly the monuments to the heroism of the city and its people during the privations of war are all the more impressive if you can enjoy them in solitude and in silence. Inner peace, serenity, a feeling of security and a rare connection with the soul on the streets of a major capital city? Count on it!

GEOGRAPHY AND CLIMATE

As your plane gradually descends on its approach into Minsk, you may be surprised to find relatively dense forest not that far from the airport. It's true that Minsk-2 International is a little way out of town, but a drive through the suburbs of the city also reveals pockets of dense woodland either side of the main routes. They have been ingeniously incorporated into areas of parkland, but the whole effect is to give a very clear impression of the great swathe of primeval forest that once covered the entirety of the central European plain.

The hills across which the city has spread over the centuries and through which the Svislach River gently meanders can hardly be called hills at all, for the mean altitude above sea level struggles to reach 200m. And whether you approach Minsk by land or by air, from any direction, the impression gained is always the same; it's pretty flat.

A cursory glance at the map of Europe shows that Belarus is situated right in the middle of the continental land mass, with the capital city itself right in the middle of the country.

All of these factors combine to produce a moderate continental temperate climate. Prevailing winds are westerly, northwesterly and southwesterly, a consequence of which is the relatively frequent incidence of moist air masses from the Atlantic. So it is that average temperatures for each season and the annual level of precipitation, as both rain and snow, sit in the middle of the average for the whole country.

HIGHLIGHTS

There is a strong commitment throughout Belarusian society to promoting culture and the arts, not only in terms of government public and social policy, but also for ordinary people in terms of their leisure time. Allied to this is a national enthusiasm (if not passion) for sport and outdoor pursuits. It's no surprise then, to find that history, fine art and sport are well represented in terms of public facilities, with something to please every taste. In fact, the unadorned statistics reveal that there are 16 museums, 11 theatres, 20 cinemas, 139 libraries and over 3,000 different sporting facilities in this town! The best of them for the first-time visitor include the following:

MUSEUMS Great Patriotic War Museum, Belarusian State Museum of Folk Architecture, Museum of Ancient Belarusian Culture, National Museum of History and Culture of Belarus, Belarusian National Fine Arts Museum, Maxim Bogdanovich Literary Museum and Yanka Kupala State Literary Museum.

PARKS, OPEN SPACES AND RECREATIONAL AREAS Gorky Park, Central Park, Yanka Kupala Park, Central Botanical Gardens, Victory Park and Chelyuskintsev Culture and Leisure Park.

SQUARES, MONUMENTS AND SIGNIFICANT ARCHITECTURAL FEATURES Victory Square, Pryvaksalnaya Square, Independence Square, Oktyabrskaya Square, Island of Tears, Zaslavskaya Jewish Memorial, Rakauskoye suburb and Traiyetskoye suburb. For something quirky and off-the-wall, see also the newly constructed National Library!

CATHEDRALS AND CHURCHES Cathedral of the Holy Spirit, Church of Saint Simon and Helena, Cathedral of Saints Peter and Paul, Maryinsky Cathedral and Saint Alyeksandr Nyevsky's Church.

THEATRES National Academic Bolshoi Ballet and Great Opera Theatre of the Republic of Belarus and Yanka Kupala National Academic Theatre.

Further information on all of these attractions can be found later in this chapter.

HISTORY

It does not overstate the issue to say that the entire history of Minsk (and indeed, of greater Belarus) is characterised by conflict, invasion and subjugation. It is a quirk of fate or the whim of the gods that it just happens to have been in absolutely the wrong place on so many occasions, caught between the envious gaze of warring and expansionist neighbours on all sides. This is reflected in the history of the city. First mentioned in chronicles as Menesk in 1067, it was founded on the banks of the Svislach and Nyamia rivers, when the population of an older settlement 16km away on the Menka River (from which Minsk derives its name) moved to a more favourable location, the site of the present city. Today, the village of Gorodische is located on that original site. The first settlement was no more than a fortified wooden fortress incorporating the homes of the townspeople, the whole being surrounded by earthen ramparts. It came under the protection of the state of Polatsk, widely regarded as the first ever independent Belarusian state. The first structures of stone had appeared by the middle of the 12th century, by which time the significance of the town was incrementally rising as a consequence of the separation of Polatsk into a smaller number of independent jurisdictions, each under the control of its own prince. Before the split, the territory of the town and the entirety of the area had been scarred by the violence of warfare as opposing princes sought supremacy. Its geographical location at the heart of the European continent, situated on important trade routes by road and by river, ensured its significance as a conquest to be prized.

When it was acquired by the Grand Duchy of Lithuania in 1242, key members of the local elite quickly began to enjoy privileged rank and status in the state's hierarchy and in society. As a consequence, the town soon became one of the largest and most significant in the whole of the duchy. Prince Vasily is mentioned as being ruler in 1325 and then in 1387 Prince Yagyela gifted the town and its surrounding settlements to his brother Skyrgal, who passed them to Prince Vitovt only five years later. Around this time, Minsk was added to the Wilno (now Vilnius) province of the grand duchy, before gaining greater significance as the centre of its own administrative area later that century. The emerging status of the city was recognised further in 1499, when the great Lithuanian Prince Alexander bestowed Magdeburg rights of self-determination upon it. By this time, the population was around 4,000. Warfare and conflict returned again in 1505 when the town was burned and looted by the Mongol Golden Horde, although the fortified castle held out. Two years later, it came under siege again, this time by troops under the command of the Moscow Prince Mikhail Glinsky. But in 1566, it became the capital of its own province upon the formation of the mighty Reszpospolita state (when the Treaty of Lublin united the Grand Duchy with the Kingdom of Poland). It quickly became the largest city at that time on the territory of modern Belarus, incorporating 60 other towns and villages. The Union brought about the first significant societal development of the city for some while, as a significant Polish community settled there and quickly began to influence its culture and administration.

Conflict continued to rage as the struggle for supremacy over this important settlement proceeded unabated. Surrounded by the three mighty states of Poland, Lithuania (which by then had joined into one) and Russia, this is hardly surprising. The Livonian War with Russia under Ivan the Terrible (which had begun in 1558) did not end until 1583, although the city's position as a powerful seat of government was further recognised in 1580 when the Grand Duchy's Supreme Court of Appeal was relocated there, alternating every two years with Wilno and Novogrudok. All the while, the cultural, commercial and spiritual development of the city was proceeding at pace, notwithstanding the constant threat of warfare. As significant architectural features began to spring up all over town, its civic status was recognised when it was granted its own coat of arms (in 1591). Again, armed conflict extracted its price and significant structural damage was suffered in the war between Russia and Reszpospolita that began in 1654. Russian forces occupied the city in 1655, but very few houses survived and the population had been halved (to around 2,000) by the time they were expelled. In fact, the city was under Russian administration until 1667. More was to follow. The extensive works of restoration and rebuilding that were put in train thereafter were then wiped out during the Northern War between Russia and Sweden, first under the occupation of Swedish forces in 1707, then again when the city was retaken by Russian troops under Peter the Great.

A period of relative stability followed throughout the remainder of the 18th century, but the long period of destruction had left its mark and Minsk was by now little more than an insignificant provincial settlement of some 7,000 people. But the days of the once-mighty state of Reszpospolita were numbered and upon the occasion of its second partition in 1793, Minsk became part of another mighty state, this time the Russian Empire. It quickly acquired the status of capital of a Russian province (in 1796) and under the patronage of its powerful new rulers, it began to grow and develop exponentially. The original blueprint for the modern city is recognisable from this time; for example, the main Zakharyevskaya thoroughfare was laid out, which subsequently became Francyska Skoriny Avenue and is today known as Nyezhavizhimosty. At this time, the city's buildings were still predominantly of wooden structure, but three major fires in the period up to 1835 had enabled the pace of redevelopment to quicken. By this time (and inevitably) civic and architectural progress had again been interrupted by warfare, when the 1812 invasion by French troops under Emperor Napoleon decimated the city's population (from 11,200 to just under 3,500). During this time, Minsk was used by the French army as a major base for munitions and weapons, as the frontline moved eastwards towards Moscow.

It is simply astonishing to muse on the contradiction that is inherent in a city trying to grow and develop across the centuries against a backdrop of almost ceaseless destruction and bloodshed. As discussed elsewhere in this book, this contradiction and its consequential privations have gone a long way towards shaping the national psyche of the country and its people.

But as the decades of the 18th century passed, so the march of progress proved irresistible. Minsk was again rebuilt as a network of streets and boulevards was established. The first library was opened in the 1830s, at the same time as the city's first fire brigade was commissioned. This was followed by the establishment of the first theatre company. Broadsheet newspapers began to appear. The population grew to around 30,000 by the middle of the century, as trade, commerce and civic administration helped to bind and strengthen the community in ways never before seen. Not even armed insurrection on the part of nationalists in 1830 and then again in 1863 was able to halt this progress. The significance of the ancient trade routes through the city was emphasised with the construction of major road and rail links, from east to west linking Warsaw and western Europe beyond to Moscow and from north to south linking the Baltic and Black seas. Developments to the commercial infrastructure quickly followed, as supplies of water, telephone, electricity and urban transport were established, along with new factories. In turn, this led to greater community and societal development, as churches, schools and places of entertainment sprang up all over town. As the 20th century approached, the population of the city climbed steadily towards the 100,000 mark.

Then just as the people were getting used to stability and relative affluence, the odour of revolution grew stronger and stronger throughout the Russian Empire, as social and political emancipation gathered pace. In Minsk, major industrial development saw the rise of worker militancy, while the nationalism evidenced by the armed risings of 1830 and 1863 continued to smoulder. Then the flames of destruction burned again as the continent was ravaged by battle and bloodshed during World War I. During 1915, Minsk once again found itself a battle-scarred city right on the front line (Germany's Eastern Front) in a major theatre of warfare, as it had so many times in its history. Minsk was chosen as the location for the headquarters of the Imperial Russian Army, with large infrastructure facilities (such as munitions bases and military hospitals) close by. As before, the city suffered structural damage and a significant diminution in the population as citizens became refugees on the long road east in search of safety in the arms of the Motherland. The revolutionary movement sought to exploit these difficulties and a massive campaign to undermine the morale of the troops proved to be successful. As the Bolsheviks promised bread and peace to soldiers, workers and families alike in the internationalist fight against the global oppression of the ruling classes, matters came to a head when Lenin swept into government following the November Revolution of 1917. A Soviet of Workers was immediately established in the city as the army simply imploded, with disillusioned soldiers deserting in their tens of thousands and trudging home eastwards. At the end of December, the National Belarusian Congress made a formal declaration of the birth of the Belarusian People's Republic, an independent nation state. As a result of the negotiated Treaty of Brest-Litovsk (a staggering piece of exploitative and politically expedient diplomacy on the part of Lenin), which delivered Russia's withdrawal from the war, Minsk fell under the occupation of German troops in February 1918. Then on 25 March, the declaration of independence made in December was formally adopted and the city was pronounced capital of the nascent state. Independence lasted less than 12 months and in December 1918, the Red Army marched into town. Its status as a capital city was reaffirmed in January 1919, but this time of the brand-new Belarusian Soviet Socialist Republic (BSSR). A new order had begun, although further destruction and loss of life followed in the war between the emerging USSR and Poland, as Lenin sought to unite many territories under the red flag. The war was not formally ended until the Treaty of Riga, when (once and for all) Minsk became capital of the BSSR (one of the founding republics of the newly proclaimed USSR), a position that the city held until the break-up of the Soviet Union in 1991, when it became the capital of the newly independent Republic of Belarus.

Throughout the remainder of the 1920s and the 1930s, Minsk (in keeping with the rest of the Soviet Union) benefited from exponential development on a startling scale. An ambitious programme of industrialisation and reconstruction began as soon as hostilities ended and within a short space of time, it had gained pace and momentum never before seen in the Western world. In a few short years, huge new industrial complexes were in full production to deliver the state- controlled objectives of succeeding Five Year Plans, while the workers and citizens themselves began to benefit from ambitiously established social welfare and community facilities in the form of new schools, hospitals and places of entertainment. But nothing was as it seemed, of course. It was only decades later that details of the backdrop of ideological, social and artistic persecution perpetrated by Stalin's brutality in the name of protecting 'the Revolution' began to emerge.

The cyclical view of history is often found to be correct and it was again to be the city's destiny that one yolk of oppression was to be replaced by another. The rise of Nazi barbarism in Germany throughout this time was a cause of great anxiety, both East and West. Prior to the outbreak of hostilities in September 1939, the population of the city was around 300,000, but after Germany unexpectedly tore up the infamous Molotov-Ribbentrop Pact of Non-Aggression by invading the Soviet Union on 22 June 1941 under Operation Barbarossa, Minsk again found itself right on the front line of battle as it had so many times before in its history. The city suffered the horror of aerial bombardment by blitzkrieg on the very first day of the invasion as Hitler sought to subjugate the population through terror and it was no surprise when it fell to the invading German army just six days later. The occupation was to endure for 1,100 days. Stalin's policy had been to buy some time by falling back immediately in the defence of Moscow and as a result, a great deal of plant and machinery from the majority of the factories in the city, along with tens of thousands of people from the civilian population (with the most precious of museum and gallery artefacts), had already been shipped eastwards deeper into the Motherland, for protection, security and to be preserved for future use.

The Nazis immediately declared Minsk the centre of a new Eastern Reichskomissariat and local people were treated with merciless and abject brutality. The context for this was Hitler's absolute belief that the Slavs were a 'sub-human' race that was to be eradicated from the face of the earth. So it was that communists, so-called 'sympathisers', partisans and ordinary men, women and children were imprisoned, tortured and murdered. Public parks became the site of mass hangings. Many more from the local population were pressed into slave labour, both within Belarus and also following transportation to all corners of the Reich. Food became scarce in the extreme as supplies were requisitioned to feed the occupying forces and thousands of civilians starved to death. It is not widely known that the city also became one of the largest of the Nazi ghettos in the war, with up to 100,000 Jews imprisoned there. But by early 1942, the city and its people had begun to fight back, as Minsk became the focal point and pivotal administrative centre of the entire Soviet partisan resistance movement throughout the struggle against oppression in Stalin's Great Patriotic War.

Minsk was eventually liberated by Soviet troops amidst scenes of unbounded joy on 3 July 1944 (now celebrated as the Republic of Belarus National Independence Day national holiday), but the German army had clung on tenaciously throughout the first six months of the year and the destruction was almost total. Most of the houses, factories and administrative buildings had been flattened, while much of the road, rail and bridge infrastructure had been bombed out of use. When the Red Army re-entered the city, it was to find that its population had been decimated from 300,000 at the start of the war in 1939 to little over 50,000 at the cessation of hostilities. Over 70,000 of Minsk's residents had been murdered. When those who lost their lives in the surrounding districts is taken into consideration, the total rises to over 400,000 people.

At first, serious consideration was given to leaving the ruins of the city untouched, abandoning it and moving the national capital to Mogilev, but with the final defeat of the Nazis in 1945, the process of rebuilding began. As far as was possible, this did not mean reconstruction, and every effort was made to restore as much of the city as could be saved. Sadly, precious little was left and today only a small part of the classical architecture remains, concentrated mostly in Old Town (Старий Город), close to the city centre. Even there, much could not be saved. Throughout the late 1940s and 1950s, a new city centre rose from the rubble and ashes of the old one, as imposing new buildings in the grand design that became synonymous with Stalin appeared alongside expansive boulevards and within huge squares. Once more, the city grew and began to flourish, as a result of a process of massive and unprecedented industrialisation, which exceeded even that seen in the 1920s and 1930s. Hand in hand with the re-establishment of the social and administrative infrastructure was exponential population growth, as young people moved to the 'big city' from the rural hinterland. There was also a rigidly planned and controlled state policy to migrate skilled workers into the region from other parts of the Soviet Union to finally deliver regeneration. To meet the consequent housing need, Minsk spread outwards beyond its former city boundaries and upwards in the form of archetypical, high-density and high-rise concrete apartment housing.

But in spite of this fundamental transformation, a grateful nation never forgot the sacrifices made by the people of the city, and with others elsewhere in the USSR, Minsk was bestowed the honour of being officially recognised as 'Hero City (Город Герой) of the Soviet Union' in 1974.

After the fall of the Soviet Union in the early 1990s, the city's evolution continued, but in a different direction. As the new state sought to establish its credentials on the European and global stage, Minsk began to assume the status and the adornments of an international capital city. Embassies and consulates were opened in abundance as governments worldwide sought to present their credentials and establish their interests, while the administrative buildings that formerly supported the Soviet machine now became centres of national republican government. But as the new republic struggled to find its feet in the wake of the consequences of the Chernobyl catastrophe and the large-scale collapse of the institutions of the former USSR, economic instability was everywhere to be seen. Yet since the turn of the century, things have begun to change for the better. The drive into the city from out of town used to be categorised by the sight of half-built and long-abandoned building projects, but today, there is a marked change. On the outskirts of Minsk, new mini-suburbs of residential development (some of them extremely affluent) have sprung up and metro lines have been extended. Further expansion of the system is planned. The road system (including the Minsk orbital motorway and inner ring road) has also been improved dramatically. Much of the city is under government-financed development, a sure sign of growing economic confidence.

GETTING THERE AND AWAY

As you might expect, Minsk is the geographical focal point for all means of transportation into and out of the country. It is the main (and for the most part only) entry and exit point for air travel to Belarus. Major European road and rail links converge on the city from all points of the compass. Details of air routes, carriers and airport facilities can be found in *Chapter 2*, pages 44–7, together with

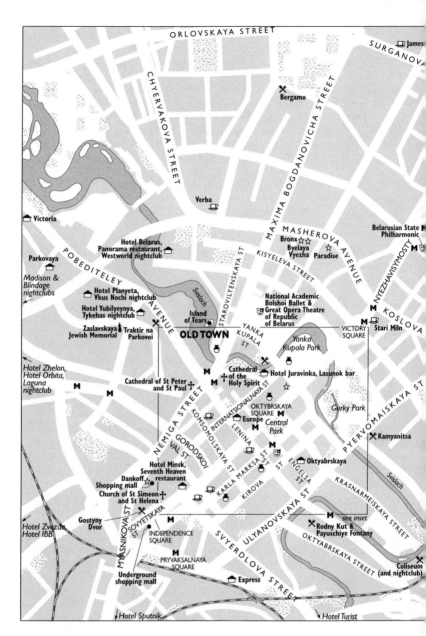

key information on rail travel, access by coach, roads, border crossing points and a few tips on independent travel by car. This should be enough to get you into (and out of) the country.

AIRLINE OFFICES IN MINSK CITY

✈ **Air Baltic** 11 Bogdanovicho; ✆ 234 34 76; www.airbaltic.lv; ⊕ 09.00–18.00 Mon–Fri

✈ **Austrian Airlines/Swissair** 19 Prospyekt Pobyedityelye; ✆ 276 89 70; e auasalesminsk@ aua.com; www.aua.com; ⊕ 09.00–17.00 Mon–Fri

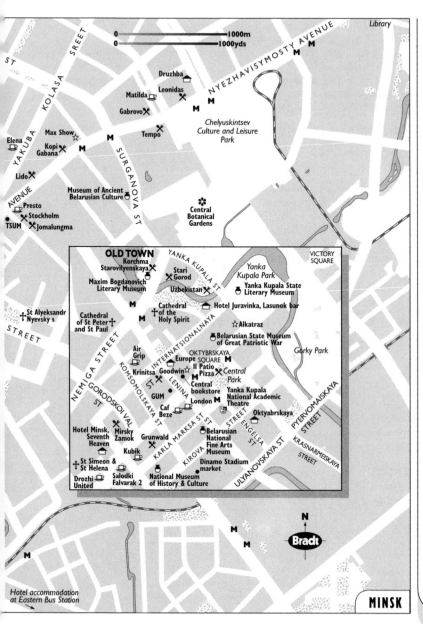

Map labels (Minsk city map):

Library

1000m
1000yds

Druzhba
Leonidas
Matilda
Gabrovo
Max Show
Elena
Kopi Gabana
Lido
Presto
Stockholm
TSUM Jomalungma
Tempo

NYEZHAVISYMOSTY AVENUE

KOLASA STREET
YAKUBA AVENUE
SURGANOVA ST

Chelyuskintsev Culture and Leisure Park

Museum of Ancient Belarusian Culture

Central Botanical Gardens

OLD TOWN
Korchma Starovilyenskaya
Stari Gorod
Maxim Bogdanovich Literary Museum
Uzbekistan
Yanka Kupala Park
Yanka Kupala State Literary Museum
Hotel Juravinka, Lasunok bar

St Alyeksandr Nyevsky s
Cathedral of St Peter and St Paul
Cathedral of the Holy Spirit
Alkatraz
Belarusian State Museum of Great Patriotic War

VICTORY SQUARE

NEMIGA STREET
GORODSKOI VAL ST
KOMSOMOLSKAYA ST
INTERNATSIONALNAYA

Air Grip
Krinitsa
Goodwin
Europe SQUARE
Il Patio Pizza
Central Park
Central bookstore
London
Yanka Kupala National Academic Theatre
GUM
LENINA ST
Caf Beze
Oktyabrskaya

OKTYABRSKAYA

Gorky Park

PYERVOMAISKAYA STREET
KRASNARMEISKAYA STREET
ENGELSA STREET
KIROVA STREET
KARLA MARKSA ST
ULYANOVSKAYA ST

Hotel Minsk, Seventh Heaven
Mirsky Zamok
Grunwald
Belarusian National Fine Arts Museum
Kubik
St Simeon & St Helena
Drozhi United
Salodki Falvarak 2
National Museum of History & Culture
Dinamo Stadium market

N
Bradt

Hotel accommodation at Eastern Bus Station

MINSK

Minsk City and Oblast   GETTING THERE AND AWAY

3

✈ **Aviakassa** 29 Karl Marksa; ☎ 227 62 54;
🕐 08.00–20.00 Mon–Fri, 08.00–18.00 Sat–Sun
(this agency sells all airline tickets)
✈ **Belavia** 14 Nemiga; ☎ 210 41 00;
e info@belavia.by; www.belavia.by; 🕐 09.00–19.00
Mon–Fri, 09.00–17.00 Sat–Sun (also sells tickets for
its partner companies Aeroflot, Austrian Airlines, LOT
Polish Airlines, CSA Czech Airlines & Air Baltic).

✈ **El Al Israeli Airlines** 3 Pyervomayskaya; ☎ 236 35
42; also at 8/18, Komsomolskaya; ☎ 211 26 06; &
at Office 54, 6a, Partisansky; ☎ 229 81 58;
www.elal.co.il; 🕐 09.00–18.00 Mon–Fri
✈ **Estonian Air** 11 Bogdanovicho; ☎ 269 05 54;
www.estonian-air.ee; 🕐 09.00–18.00 Mon–Fri
✈ **flyLAL (Lithuanian Airlines)** 3 Bersona; ☎ 220 74
14; e info-belarus@lal.lt; www.lal.lt;

⊕ 09.00–17.00 Mon–Fri (also represented in Belarus by the travel agency Uzheni, 8/18 Komsomolskaya; ✆ 206 38 60; ⊕ 09.00–18.00 Mon–Fri)
✈ **LOT Polish Airlines** 7 Masherova; ✆ 226 68 28; www.lot.pl; ⊕ 10.00–17.00 Mon–Fri
✈ **Lufthansa** 56 Nyezhavhizhimosty; ✆ 284 71 30; also at Orbita Hotel, 39 Pushkina; ✆ 257 06 39;

www.lufthansa.by; ⊕ 09.00–17.30 Mon–Fri, 09.00–13.00 Sat
✈ **Transaero** 23 Internatsionalnaya; ✆ 289 14 53; ⊕ 09.00–18.00 Mon–Fri (this company manages airline bookings & sales to any destination worldwide)

AIRLINE OFFICES AT MINSK-I AIRPORT
✈ 38/2 Chkalova; ✆ 225 08 77/222 52 31; www.avia.by

✈ **Air Baltic** ✆ 222 51 61; www.airbaltic.lv; ⊕ 09.00–18.00 Mon–Fri

AIRLINE OFFICES AT MINSK-2 INTERNATIONAL AIRPORT
✆ 225 02 31/279 13 00; www.airport.by
✈ **Austrian Airlines/Swissair** ✆ 279 15 39; www.aua.com; ⊕ 09.00–17.00 Mon–Fri
✈ **Belavia** ✆ 279 10 32; e info@belavia.by; www.belavia.by; ⊕ 09.00–19.00 Mon–Fri, 09.00–17.00 Sat–Sun

✈ **Estonian Air** ✆ 234 23 76; www.estonian-air.ee; ⊕ 09.00–18.00 Mon–Fri
✈ **LOT Polish Airlines** ⊕ during take-offs & landings only
✈ **Lufthansa** ✆ 279 17 45; www.lufthansa.by; ⊕ 09.00–17.30 Mon–Fri, 09.00–13.00 Sat

GETTING AROUND

BY METRO, BUS, TRAM AND TROLLEYBUS Public transport in Minsk is extremely cheap and unfailingly reliable, but somewhat overcrowded. If you want to feel like a local, however, then you must give it a try. Other than walking (and most of what you will want to see is accessible on foot), you have considerable freedom of choice, given that any of the options (metro, bus, tram and trolleybus) are all user-friendly. The metro system is very easy to work out and at peak times, trains run every three minutes. During the day, the service is every five minutes, then every ten after 23.00 hours until the system closes for the night at 01.00, before opening for business once more at 05.30, Monday to Sunday. See map on inside back cover and *Chapter 2, Getting around*, page 66 for further details.

BY TAXI Taxis in Minsk are fairly cheap and reasonably reliable, but as in any city in the world, you are at risk of being ripped off by unscrupulous operators, and perhaps more so in Minsk on account of the language difficulty.

TOURIST INFORMATION

This is the right point in the narrative to remind readers of the caveat in the *Feedback request* at the beginning of this guide relating to the shortage of information on opening hours, telephone numbers and prices for restaurants, bars, clubs, museums and the like. In some cases, it has proved almost impossible to ascertain some of the data, but every effort has been made to personally establish and corroborate every last detail. The fact that things are developing so rapidly in this country is another challenge for the visitor. I'm convinced that all of this *will* change for the better, but for now, the key difficulty remains that there is hardly any concept in Belarus of consumer-based data for the edification of travellers, tourists and users of leisure facilities. There should be real comfort, however, in the knowledge that if you are on an organised visit, then you are bound to find that places on the tour *will* be open! And for my part, I always find that a modest degree of ambiguity adds to the value of the adventure and of the experience.

But for now, the tourism industry has yet to sharpen up its public relations act. The only facility that vaguely resembles the sort of tourist information centre that we are used to seeing in the West is run by the state tourism agency Belintourist (*19 Prospyekt Masherova*; ↘ *226 99 00; officially* ⊕ *09.00–13.00* & *13.45–18.00 Mon–Thu, 09.00–13.00* & *13.45–16.45 Fri*). The exterior of the building (which is attached to the Hotel Yubileynya) looks quite promising, with lots of inviting posters covering the windows (which, incidentally, haven't been changed for the last four years). Sadly though, all that they conceal inside is a desk and very little information is available. Astonishingly, it closes for lunch and it's even closed at weekends when tourist business is likely to be at its most brisk. At other times, exercise caution and come expecting to be disappointed, because I've never actually seen it open. I know someone who has, but service was less than helpful. In other words, come to this town prepared and bring your own information with you.

WHERE TO STAY

The biggest percentage of your budget is going to be blown on accommodation costs, so it pays to be choosy. Most hotels are very much of a muchness, the industry standard featuring a monolithic tower block that incorporates varying amounts of crumbling concrete, 1970s décor, a smart (if soulless) lobby and functional facilities. As a visitor from the West, your perceived wealth will be very much in demand, so expect to pay at a much higher rate than is on offer to locals and people of other CIS countries. That said, you will still be paying very much less than in other major European cities. Only recently have a handful of private enterprises emerged to threaten the state's monopoly and with so little competition, there seems to be no impetus to modernise facilities. The safest option for your first visit, but not the cheapest or the most imaginative, is to book through one of the major tour operators. This will give you a feel for the general standard on offer, then you can plan a little more adventurously when you return for subsequent visits. For ease of comparison with other hotels in the rest of Europe and beyond, prices are quoted for the room rate per night in US dollars, including buffet breakfast. Please note, however, that in many of these hotels, an additional registration fee of around US$5–10 per person will be payable for foreign visitors. All luxury and mid-range hotels will now accept payment by credit or debit card, but payment by cash will need to be in Belarusian roubles only, *not* US dollars, the euro or any other currency. And do remember: these are not the only hotels in the city, just a selection. They are, however, ones that have been personally tested, or where there is a wealth of descriptive information available on the growing number of tourism websites to help you make your choice. Like everything else in this country, your hotel will be something of a first-time adventure, so if you adopt that mindset, you won't go far wrong!

LUXURY In this category, you can expect to find something a little out of the ordinary and unusually for this country, each hotel is independently appointed and wholly unlike any of the others. Not surprisingly, though, there are prices to match.

⌂ **Europe** (67 rooms) 28 Internatsionalnaya St; ↘ 229 83 33; f 229 83 34; e reservation@ hoteleurope.by; www.hoteleurope.by. Right in the heart of the city, on the corner of Lenina St & close to a number of key sights, this imposing 7-storey hotel opened in Sep 2007. The country's first genuine 5-star establishment, it is considered to have overtaken the Minsk as the swankiest hotel in town. The best rooms enjoy impressive panoramic views over Old Town. All are extremely well appointed & those at the top of the range are the very latest in luxury. Some of the rooms are non-smoking &, unusually for Belarus, there are also facilities for the less able. In addition to an exclusive restaurant, 5 opulent bars & a nightclub, there is a business centre, secure parking, a laundry service, beauty parlour, gift shop, currency exchange, gym & pool. *Sgl from US$450, dbl from US$597.*

⌂ **Minsk** (258 rooms, 38 of which are classed 'luxury') 11 Independence (Nezhavizhimosty) Av; ☎ 209 90 75/76/00; f 209 90 80/92 32; e hotelminsk@pmrb.gov.by; www.hotelminsk.by. Until the arrival of the Europe, this was the only truly 4-star hotel in the whole country & it's a fairly opulent base for your stay in town. Located downtown, within easy walking distance of many of the sights, this former Soviet hotel was given a major facelift in 2002 with a marble lobby, state-of-the-art conference facilities for 50 people, fitness centre, casino & shops. All rooms are elegantly furnished & all with the usual mod cons, together with 3 restaurants (including one on the 6th floor with fine views of the city), 3 bars & a banqueting hall. There are also 5 suites, some non-smoking rooms & limited facilities for the less able. *Sgl from US$140, dbl from US$180, suite from US$340–880.*

⌂ **Victoria** (169 rooms, 115 sgls, 4 of which are adapted for wheelchair users, 45 dbls, 8 luxury & 1 'Presidential suite') 59 Pobediteley Av; ☎/f 204 88 44 (24hr information line 204 88 55); e office@hotel-victoria.by, or info@hotel-victoria.by; www.hotel-victoria.by. This top-of-the-range 4-star hotel, aimed clearly at the business market, welcomed its first guests on 1 July 2007. Shortly thereafter, the president himself paid a visit, an event that signifies the importance that the state places on the success of the venture. The English-language website is extremely slick & sharp in PR terms. Situated not far from the city centre (but not as close as the blurb would have you believe!) & on the banks of the Svislach River, this hotel seeks to combine state-of-the-art business facilities with luxury accommodation. It's all brand new, shiny & very 'new money'. The business centre itself boasts multi-media projection equipment, high speed Wi-Fi internet access, simultaneous translation facilities, seminar rooms & an 80-seat conference hall, all supported by secretarial & administrative services. All bedrooms are fully AC, with LCD interactive satellite TV, internet access & mini-bar. Facilities also include 24hr on-site underground car parking, beauty centre (with spa),

solarium, massage facility, sauna, hairdresser, laundry, currency exchange, ATM, souvenir/newspaper stand, lobby bar (24hr), vitamin bar & swish restaurant (⏱ 07.00–05.00). If the PR hype is to be believed, then this place is something special, but for the traveller without business interests, its appeal is likely to be limited. *Sgl US$115–175, dbl US$130–185, suite from US$585.*

⌂ **Internationale Bildungs-und-Begegnungsstatte** (33 rooms) 11 Gazety Pravda Av; ☎ 270 39 94; f 270 39 95; e ibb@ibb.by; www.ibb.by. This modern business facility, incorporating state-of-the-art conference facilities in 3 seminar rooms & a function hall seating 350, was constructed in 1994 in partnership with a German venture. It feels classy & has a relaxed & calm ambiance, but this is because it is around 10km from the general brouhaha of the city centre, in a suburb to the southwest. Facilities inc sauna, bar & the excellent Westphalia restaurant. All rooms are well appointed; 3 have been adapted for wheelchair use. *Sgl from US$85, dbl from US$117.*

⌂ **Juravinka** (18 rooms) 25 Yanka Kupala Av; ☎ 206 69 00/13; f 206 69 89/227 55 42; e contacts@juravinka.by; www.juravinka.by. Modern in design (it was built in 2001), luxuriously comfortable, compact & centrally located on the banks of the Svislach River near to Old Town, this is a quirky but stylish venue. There is no lobby; just a desk in front of a lift. The PR blurb describes an entertainment complex (including 10-pin bowling), a casino & 2 restaurants, but they are in a separate building, around the back & across the car park. Within the hotel itself, facilities include a massage room, solarium, fitness centre & 4 bars. All of the bedrooms are on 1 floor, where the carpet is plush & where you will rub shoulders with the city's elite. There are 13 sgls, 4 dbls & an amazing Presidential Suite, boasting 2 jacuzzis, 2 enormous beds, a TV the size of a cinema screen & its own swimming pool. *Sgl from US$152, dbl from US$200, suite US$900.*

⌂ **Parkovaya** (11 rooms) 10 Gvardeyskaya St; ☎ 206 39 89; f 206 39 92; e mail@hotelparkovaya.com; www.hotelparkovaya.com (Russian only). Built in 2001, this small but discreet hotel has only 6 dbl rooms & 5 2-room suites, all of them well furnished. There is also a good restaurant, jacuzzi & a sauna. *Dbl from US$160, suite from US$225.*

MID-RANGE Here, all of the hotels are very much alike: 1970s-style Soviet design with only limited aesthetic appeal. But all are well appointed and comfortable, if wholly interchangeable. Prices are very competitive by Western standards, although each hotel has its own complex pricing structure with countless numbers of categories at differing rates.

🛏 **Belarus** (520 rooms) 15 Storazhevskaya St; 209 75 37/76 93; f 239 12 33; e info@hotel-belarus.com; www.hotel-belarus.com. An imposing 22-floor concrete high-rise, this hotel dominates the skyline, towers over the Minsk Hero City monument & has spectacular views across parkland & the Svislach River towards Old Town & the Island of Tears, particularly by night. The panoramic view from the high-quality top-floor restaurant is stunning. Many of the rooms have their own balcony, but the concrete has passed its sell-by date & alarming cracks are not uncommon. All rooms are well appointed, although the quality of the furniture & décor is not great. There are several bars, plus a noisy disco/club/casino in an adjoining section on the ground floor, a conference hall, business centre, sauna & shops. Most of the rooms have been renovated in recent times & there is a choice of sgls, dbls & suites of various sizes. *Sgl from US$50, dbl from US$65, suite from US$100.*

🛏 **Orbita** (208 rooms) 39 Pushkin Av; 206 77 81; f 257 14 20; e reservation@orbita-hotel.com; www.orbita-hotel.com. Opened in 1991, this is a 14-storey high-rise of 180 sgl & dbl rooms, plus 28 suites. There is a restaurant & a banquet hall, together with several bars, conference facilities, sauna, casino & nightclub. *Sgl from US$52, dbl from US$60, suite from US$110, rising to US$1,410 for the President's Suite.*

🛏 **Planyeta** (310 rooms) 31 Masherova Av; 203 85 87/226 78 55; f 226 77 80; e booking@hotelplaneta.by; www.hotelplaneta.by. Extensive renovation has placed this hotel on a slightly higher quality threshold than the others in this category, although the wall-to-wall pseudo-marble in reception is a little gaudy. Located within a few mins' walk of the Belarus & Yubilyeynya hotels, rooms range from sgls to VIP apts, all of them clean & comfortable. Facilities include a business centre, Hertz car-hire office, shops, meeting/conference rooms, restaurants, bars, sauna & a casino. *Sgl from US$73, dbl from US$115, suite from US$180, rising to US$600 for the VIP apts.*

🛏 **Yubilyeynya** (230 rooms) 19 Masherova Av; 226 90 24; f 226 91 71; e info@hotelyubileiny.by; www.hotelyubileiny.by. Also overlooking the Svislach River, this is a very busy hotel, full of hustle & bustle. Of all the hotels in this category, here is the most bewildering range of differently appointed rooms, from sgls to dbls to suites, each of them either economy, junior or business class. Those at the lower end are a little shabby, whilst the higher-grade ones have recently been decorated. But for sheer value for money, this hotel takes some beating. Facilities include a business centre, 250-seat conference hall, restaurants, bars, sauna, shops, ATM & casino. *Sgl from US$44, dbl from US$62, suite from US$140, rising to US$231 for the best of them.*

🛏 **Oktyabrskaya** (103 rooms) 13 Engels St; 222 32 89; f 227 33 14; e oktyabr@tut.by; www.hotel-oktyabr.by (Russian only). This medium-sized hotel on 8 floors is unexciting but functional, with a host of amenities. The décor is drab, but the rooms are adequate. The excitement value, however, comes from its location next to the office of the President of the Republic, so security is high & the atmosphere a little tense. Whatever you do, don't be tempted to take the opportunity to photograph the office building. Instead, watch out for the president's heavily guarded motorcade leaving at high speed. *Sgl from US$59, dbl from US$74 & the 2 suites US$138 each.*

LOW BUDGET

🛏 **Turist** (173 rooms) 81 Partisansky Av; 295 40 31/05; f 295 41 45; e office@hotel-tourist.com; www.hotel-tourist.com. Located close to large-scale shopping facilities, this is a functional but comfortable 15 storey high-rise. Amenities in-house are limited, but include a conference hall, currency exchange & a hairdresser. Yet the staff are friendly & a stay here represents good value for money. If you want basic facilities & rudimentary comfort without the frills, this is the place for you, although the location is not that convenient for visitor attractions or restaurants. Just make sure that the prices quoted on the website are the ones you will actually pay. There is also a restaurant, banqueting hall, bar & summer pavement café. Rooms comprise sgls, dbls, trpls & even quadruples (!), all in either economy or business class. *Sgl from US$32, dbl from US$43, trpl from US$51 & quadruples from US$55.*

🛏 **Sputnik** (162 rooms) 2 Brilyevskaya St; 229 36 19. Information is scarce & difficult to find, but this hotel is always busy & seems popular with CIS tourists on a budgetary shoestring. *Sgl from US$31, dbl from US$44 & luxury rooms from US$78.*

🛏 **Druzhba** (50 rooms) 3 Tolbukhina St; \/f 280 16 71. A functional but rather tired & very, very Soviet-style hotel in need of a pick-me-up, even though it was supposed to have been renovated in 2005. Some of the rooms at the bottom end of the scale do not have en-suite facilities. There is a restaurant here, but don't expect a gourmet experience. There is also a conference centre & a sauna. *Sgl from US$40, dbl from US$50, trpl from US$33.*

🏠 **Beltransgaz** (30 rooms) 4 Staroborisovsky Trakt; ℣/f 237 01 16; e hotel.max@beltg.gazprom.com. Built in 2003, there are 11 sgls, 16 dbls & 3 trpls. There is also a banquet hall, café, bar & shop. Established primarily for travelling executives of the state gas company, a stay here will get you out of the clichéd Soviet-hotel experience, but the location is some way off the main drag. Yet the rooms are big & well appointed. There is a general air of freshness about the place. Pay extra for b/fast in the café. *Sgl from US$42, dbl from US$59, trpl from US$75.*

🏠 **Aquabel** (116 rooms) 50 Lagoysky Trakt; ℆ 237 91 19/92 22; f 237 91 22; e hotel@aquabel.by; www.aquabel.by. An out-of-town hotel, this little gem is located close to the winter sports centre at Raubichy. Built on 4 floors in 2003, rooms range from sgls to 3-room suites. All are comfortable, bright & well appointed, with modern fittings. Interestingly, there is a touch of Scandinavia about the ambiance of the place. There is also limited wheelchair access. Facilities include a hairdresser, business services (including internet access), restaurant & a bar. A fitness centre & swimming pool are shortly to be added. The real disadvantage here, though, is the location. The only real option for a ride to town is by taxi, which will cost around US$10. *Sgl from US$41, dbl from US$49, suite from US$101.*

VERY CHEAP

🏠 **Zvezda** (88 rooms) 47 Gazyety Izvestia Av; ℆ 270 74 85; f 272 85 42; e hotelzvezda@tut.by; www.hotelzvezda.com. Built in 1982, this establishment (a joint Belarussian–American venture) is a good bet if you are travelling independently & with your own transport. Located in a southwestern suburb of the city, it is 15 mins' drive from the cultural & business centres. There is a café boasting a wide variety of European cuisine, sauna, hairdresser & small meeting room. The website is slick & very Western, but this hotel does not appear to be widely used by visitors from abroad. A cute PR selling point is that rates appear to be the same for Belarusian & foreign visitors alike. Another good selling point that will be familiar to Westerners is the availability of guest packs, including toothbrush, tooothpaste, soap & shampoo, with complementary bottled mineral water on a daily basis. Unusually for a budget facility, you can also pay your bill with most major credit or debit cards, but do bear in mind the relative remoteness of the location. The number 81 bus will take you to the central railway station in 25 mins, a taxi significantly quicker. Whatever the issues, this must be either the best deal in town, or a triumph of marketing. Be the first to find out & tell us! *Sgl from less than US$20, with only modest increases for a dbl at US$30, a trpl at US$35 & 3-room suites at US$40.*

🏠 **Zhelon** (100 rooms) 52 Odoyevskovo St; ℆ 252 94 27; f 252 04 59. Facilities include a 'restaurant', bar & hairdresser. The rooms here are all tired & shabby, but most of them have shared washing facilities. Frankly, it's little more than a dormitory in a remote location. *Sgl & dbl from US$20, trpl US$30. There also appear to be some suites at US$50.*

🏠 **Express** (50 rooms) 4 Pryvakzalnaya; ℆ 225 64 63. Adjacent to the main railway station, this is the place for the budget traveller with no other options for accommodation. Just keep your expectations low & don't expect to be able to book in advance. This is a place to go only as a last resort when you've just arrived in town, tired & with nowhere booked. There is very little information available about this hotel, but all washing & toilet facilities are likely to be shared & of dubious quality. There are sgl, dbl & trpl rooms, but you will almost certainly be sharing with a stranger. There are no English speakers amongst the staff, the whole place is dingy & there is an edge of insecurity here. Frankly, the only reason for listing this establishment is by way of contingency in case you find yourself in an emergency. *Prices start at US$15.*

🏠 **Eastern Bus Station** 34 Vanyeyeva; ℆ 247 63 74. There is rumoured to be a hostel on the top floor of this bus station, which is meant to be for bus drivers in need of somewhere to lay their head between one job & the next, but authentic travellers have also been known to be allowed to stay here. No information is available, so realistically, this is even less of an option than the Express (above).

RENTING APARTMENTS This is becoming an increasingly viable and attractive option, particularly if you are looking to stay for a week or more, although rental by the night is also possible if you need it. In those circumstances, there is simply no comparison on cost and this is much the best way to do it if cost is your only driver. You also have the opportunity to very much please yourself as to your comings and goings. As a resident of the city, albeit a temporary one, you're going to feel much more part of the scenery than as a hotel tourist. But you will need to be on the ball; this market is very much in its infancy and there does not appear to be much of a safety net (if any at all) to regulate the activities of agents who may charge a significant fee, just to put you in direct contact with unknown property owners. It is to the owners that the actual rental will then be payable. So be careful out there; constantly check costs and look diligently for hidden charges. Make sure you know what you are getting for your investment, and do please satisfy yourself as to the arrangements for registering your passport, as required by national laws.

Additionally, a number of American and European companies operate international rental agencies; many of them claim to have access to apartments in Minsk, but a lot of these companies seem to be little more than clearing houses to facilitate contact with the real owners. With that in mind, point your internet search engine at 'apartment rental in Minsk' and browse away to your heart's content!

Belarus Rent Service e info@belarusrent.com; www.belarusrent.com. There is also a London telephone number for enquiries (+44 208 133 0701). This is the most professional & best known of the agencies in this field. As well as offering centrally located apts consisting of 1–4 rooms at very competitive prices (on a daily rate or for longer periods, at the behest of clients), a bespoke service is also on offer to deal with peripheral needs, such as obtaining visas, meeting guests at the airport & arranging transport to their apt, offering guided tours & providing interpreters. 1-room apts for up to 2 people from US$40 per night, rising to around US$80 for a luxury 3-room VIP facility with jacuzzi for up to 5 persons. For the larger apts, there is a reduction on the daily rate for rentals of a week or more.

If you can speak the language with confidence and don't mind being in town without having anywhere booked, the best way to avoid the attentions of agents is to buy a local newspaper when you get there and browse the listings. Dozens and dozens of apartments will be listed and the phone number provided will almost always be the landlord in person. I have done this before, having arrived without a hotel booked and unable to find a room anywhere. I've never had any difficulty in finding an apartment, even for one night. Just don't forget to register your passport as the law requires.

✕ WHERE TO EAT

The restaurant trade is another of the rapidly expanding markets in this fast-developing country, with new eateries opening up all the time. Many of the places listed here are some kind of throwback to the 1970s, particularly in terms of gaudy Soviet-style décor, but the range of cuisine available is diverse and quality is often very high indeed. Overall, prices are lower than in other European cities, but Minsk is catching up fast. With so much choice available, you can afford to experiment and be adventurous. Most of them will have menus in English, but not very informative ones. All of these restaurants should take major credit cards, but do check first. The figure given at the end of each listing is indicative of the starting price for a standard three-course meal (main, starter or sweet and coffee) without drinks, but do remember that things are changing very rapidly. Do your research in advance if you can.

TRADITIONAL BELARUSIAN
✕ **Byelaruskaya Kukhnya** 15 Storozhevskaya St; ☎ 209 75 95; ⏰ 11.00–midnight. A worthy attempt at creating the authentic Belarussian experience in décor, ambiance & food. US$15–20.

✘ **Gostyny Dvor** 17 Sovyetskaya St; ☎ 206 64 17; ⏰ 12.00–midnight. Centrally located near the Red Church, 'Old Russian' cuisine is served here. There is an open fire & live music to complete the experience, along with suits of armour & medieval drapes on the walls. Think Middle Ages & castles, but it's all done with style & the food is very good indeed. US$15–20.

✘ **Grunwald** 19 Karl Marksa St; ☎ 210 42 55; ⏰ 10.00–23.00. Belarusian, Polish & Lithuanian cuisine in a relaxed & friendly atmosphere. It's intimate, classy & reminiscent of Old Europe, but don't expect speedy service. Come prepared to stay for the whole evening & just people-watch while you eat. One of my favourite places to spend a few hours enjoying good food. US$15–20.

✘ **Gubernia** 28 Odoyevskovo St; ☎ 252 79 43; ⏰ 10.00–midnight. Belarusian & Lithuanian cuisine. Located quite some way to the east of the city centre, it's OK if you happen to be in the vicinity, but lacks charm & the food is no better than can be found elsewhere. US$10–15.

✘ **Kamyanitsa** 18 Pyervamaiskaya St; ☎ 294 51 24; ⏰ 12.00–23.00. The proprietor is keen to stress that the food here is prepared to recipes from the days of the Grand Duchy of Lithuania & of the mighty Reszpospolita state. It might be hype, but the setting is authentic, well presented & the food is good, complemented by live roots music in the evening. Worth a visit. US$15–20.

✘ **Korchma Starovilyenskaya** 2 Starovilyenskaya St; ☎ 289 37 54; ⏰ 09.00–23.00. Located in a prime position on the banks of the Svislach in Old Town, the décor represents a worthy attempt at recreating a historical setting, but it's all a little hackneyed. The view over the river is quite splendid though. Belarusian & Italian cuisine. The food is good & in the summer, the atmosphere is relaxed. US$15–20.

✘ **Krinitsa** 2 Lenin St; ☎ 227 08 04; ⏰ 12.00–midnight. One of the most highly regarded & renowned restaurants in the whole of Minsk, the food is outstanding, the décor opulent & the atmosphere intimate. The resident pianist is one of the city's finest. & if all of this were not enough, it's located in the heart of town. US$20–30.

✘ **Mirsky Zamok** 9 Gorodskoi Val St; ☎ 206 53 47; ⏰ 11.00–23.00. This is a really good try at establishing an authentic taste of Old Belarus (whatever that might be). The décor is heavily medieval & reminiscent of the citadel at Mir from which it takes its name. The food is excellent & the service very efficient. It's easy to stay here all day long. US$15–20.

✘ **Rakovsky Brovar** 10 Vityebskaya St; ☎ 206 64 04; f 206 65 25; ⏰ 12.00–midnight. This is a classy restaurant with its own micro-brewery. It's located in the historical part of the city & the décor is a cross between a Belarusian hunting lodge & 19th-century Scandinavia. Think wood panelling, plus drapes & tapestries in abundance. On entry, you will be greeted by a huge sturgeon in a tank, but don't be put off. Behind is a sports bar with big screens backing onto the brewery itself. Al fresco dining is well served by a cosy patio downstairs & a terrace on the top floor. The beer is excellent & the food superb, with service to match. 3 other venues bear the same name (& are in the same ownership), but they are bars & not restaurants. Do give this one a try (it's one of my favourites in the city), but try to book or at least get there early, as its high reputation means that it's popular with locals & tourists alike. US$15–20.

✘ **Rodny Kut** 5 Oktyabrskaya St; ☎ 227 85 61; ⏰ 12.00–23.00. If you have the money to 'push the boat out', this is the place. Located in the city's concert hall, it is spread over 3 main banqueting rooms, all with sumptuous décor. Food & service are simply outstanding, but you will pay for the privilege. US$30–40.

✘ **'Seventh Heaven' (Hotel Minsk)** 11 Nyezhavisymosty Av; ☎ 209 90 66; ⏰ 11.00–02.00. Located on the top floor of the classy Minsk Hotel, the views over the city are splendid, while the cuisine is only a short way behind. There is live music nightly. US$20–30.

✘ **Stari Gorod** 19 Bogdanavicho St; ☎ 286 05 08; ⏰ 11.00–23.00. Located in the reconstructed Old Town, this place might be aimed at the tourist market, but it doesn't cut corners on quality. The cellar is cosy in the winter & the terrace inviting in the summer, while the food is always good & well presented. Give this one a try. US$10–15.

✘ **Traktir Na Parkovoi** 11 Pobyedityelyei St; ☎ 203 82 51; ⏰ 12.00–midnight. Belarusian & Slavonic cuisine is served here in a setting that is modelled on a traditional Belarusian farmstead. There is also a courtyard with a huge open fire for cooking. Shashlik is a particular speciality. Romany music is played by a fiddler or accordionist wandering from table to table & it's impossible not to be seduced by the romance of it all, even though you know it's tacky & clichéd. The only downside is that tourists love it & they all seem to know about it. Just give in to it & indulge yourself. I have! To keep that warm glow going, each diner receives a complimentary liqueur upon leaving. US$15–20.

EASTERN EUROPEAN AND EX-SOVIET

✗ **Chumatsky Shlyakh** 34 Myasnikova St; ☎ 200 90 91; ⏰ 10.00–23.00. Traditional Ukrainian recipes served in a rustic interior by staff in national dress. Live music is played at the weekends & a delivery service is available. There is also a menu for children. Sample Belarusian cooking elsewhere first, then come here to compare notes. US$15–20.

✗ **Gabrovo** 81 Nyezhavisymosty Av; ☎ 287 30 53; ⏰ 10.00–midnight Mon–Fri, 11.00–midnight Sat–Sun. Authentic Bulgarian cuisine in a traditional setting, with seating available outside all year round, serviced by large burners for heating. US$10–15.

✗ **Natvris Jhe** 4 Svyazistov St; ☎ 238 02 55; ⏰ 12.00–midnight Tue–Sun. A truly authentic Georgian experience can be had here, all to the accompaniment of live roots folk music. US$10–15.

✗ **Sofia** 49 Anayeva St; ☎ 297 50 00; ⏰ 11.00–23.00. Bulgarian cooking in a Bulgarian setting. Unremarkable. US$10–15.

✗ **Sovyetsky** 50A Parnikovaya St; ☎ 267 06 76; ⏰ 16.00–midnight Mon–Fri, 14.00–midnight Sat–Sun. The complete Soviet experience to live music, with red caviar in abundance. Outside seating in the summer months. US$20–40.

EUROPEAN

✗ **Admiral** 39 Pushkina; ☎ 257 22 04; ⏰ 11.00–midnight. All is very French here, from the Breton costumes of the waitresses to the impressive selection of seafood, with an excellent wine list to go with it. The décor is intended to recreate either a courtyard or a cobblestone pavement & it works pretty well. All in all, not a bad try. US$15–20.

✗ **Bavaria** 50 Odoyevsky St; ☎ 251 21 00; ⏰ 12.00–23.00. Traditional German fare, German beer & authentically dressed serving staff, so it's all very German indeed. US$10–15.

✗ **Kabachok I2** 38 Kolasa St; ☎ 281 72 16; ⏰ 12.00–02.00. Trendy & hip (so popular), the food is varied & quite good, but the décor is not easy on the eye. Don't come here for a quiet night. US$10–15.

✗ **Lido** 49 Nyezhavisymosty Av; ☎ 288 27 67; ⏰ 11.00–23.00. Tasty Latvian food, but rather too many lightbulbs on the exterior are suggestive of something garish. By contrast, all is relaxed & homely inside. US$10–15.

✗ **Panorama (Hotel Belarus)** 15 Starozhevskaya; ☎ 209 76 99; e panorama_rest@mail.ru; ⏰ 07.00–04.00. Located on the 22nd floor of this unspectacular hotel, the panoramic views of the city are unsurpassed (look out especially for the new library, lit up like a Christmas tree!), whilst the food, from an international menu, is of a consistently high standard. Service is helpful & professional. US$15–20.

✗ **Pechki Lavochki** 22 Skoryny; ☎ 227 78 79; ⏰ 11.00–midnight. The set lunches here are extremely good value & filling. In the evening, the menu is broader & the food of a consistently high quality, with an impressive wine list. Just watch out for the serenading musicians. The vegetarian menu is especially good & probably the best in town. US$10–20.

✗ **Stockholm** 3 Gikalo St; ☎ 284 52 42; ⏰ 12.00–23.00. As might be expected from the name, only Scandinavian dishes are served here. The décor is authentic & the low lighting creates a cosy, intimate atmosphere. The food & service are both excellent, but it's not cheap. US$20–25.

✗ **Westphalia** 11 Gazety Pravda Av; ☎ 270 57 27; www.westfalia.by; ⏰ 07.00–02.00. Some way out of town in the joint Belarusian–German venture IBB hotel & conference complex, this restaurant is well worth a visit nevertheless. The food is exquisite & the wine list (including cocktails) comprehensive. There is live music from Thu–Sun. Excellent value for money. US$10–15.

✗ **Zolotoi Vyek** 8/3 Kirova St; ☎ 227 03 33; ⏰ 12.00–midnight. It's a good attempt at offering a lavish setting, but it just strays into the tacky. Yet the food is varied, specialist & of a very high quality. US$15–20.

ITALIAN

✗ **Bergamo** 37 Kulman; ☎ 234 45 56; ⏰ 10.00–midnight Mon–Sat. Quality Italian food & frequented by staff from the Italian embassy. Enough said? US$10–15.

✗ **Coliseum** 15 Smolyenskaya St; ☎ 285 30 95; ⏰ 12.00–02.00. Almost a nightclub, expect to step right back into the 1970s as you cross the threshold. There is live jazz nightly, along with tacky floor shows. US$15–20.

✗ **Kopi Gabana** 71 Nyezhavisymosty Av; ☎ 292 02 08; ⏰ 10.00–23.00. Ostensibly an Italian venue, it's another place with an identity crisis, because you can also expect to find European (including English!) & Indian menus, plus sushi & 9 varieties of shashlik!

The cocktails are good & the staff extremely friendly & accommodating. US$15–20.

✗ **Patio Pizza** 22 Nyezhavisymosty Av; ☎ 227 17 91; ◷ 11.00–midnight. This is the most popular pizza place in town. Much used by the locals as a place to meet, the high-quality food is complemented by the simple brick décor. In other words, you will only be concentrating on what you eat. The waiters are slick & the cocktail menu comprehensive. There's also a help-yourself all-you-can-eat salad bar, unheard of elsewhere in the city (or the country, for that matter). US$5–10.

✗ **Payuschiye Fontany** 5 Oktyabrskaya St; ☎ 206 64 16; ◷ 08.00–midnight Mon–Fri, 12.00–midnight Sat–Sun. There's a lot going on here. The award-winning Italian chef oversees b/fasts first thing, then business lunches, before serving high-quality evening meals to the accompaniment of live jazz music. This is a classy place, so you might want to dress up. You won't be disappointed. US$15–20.

✗ **Parmigiano** 17/1 Masherova Av; ☎ 288 10 61; ◷ 12.00–02.00. Not just fine Italian dining, but also wine tasting to the sound of live piano. US$20–40.

✗ **Pizza Kiprianna** 14 Bersona St; ☎ 222 42 38; ◷ 11.00–23.00. This Cypriot restaurant offers over 40 different pizzas as well as exotic dishes from the eastern Mediterranean. US$10–15.

✗ **Teatro** 6 Bogdanovicho; ☎ 234 13 52; ◷ 10.00–23.00. Classy & slick, there are 43 different pizzas available here. Just wear black to match the décor. There is also a delivery service. US$10–15.

✗ **Tempo** 78 Nyezhavisymosty Av; ☎ 284 04 92; ◷ 12.00–23.00. Give this one a try. It's always packed with students, so there's a lively buzz about the place & the food is good. A delivery service is available. US$10–15.

MEDITERRANEAN

✗ **Kasbar** 23 Vakzalnaya; ☎ 200 81 55; f 200 25 91; ◷ 12.00–02.00. Billed as a Syrian restaurant, the décor is certainly Arabesque. Shashlik is a speciality, as are the belly dancers. US$15–20.

✗ **Leonidas** 87-A Nyezhavisymosty Av; ☎ 287 38 49; ◷ 11.00–23.00. Acceptable Mediterranean dining in an OK setting. US$15–20.

ORIENTAL

✗ **Brigantina** 42 Nyezhavisymosty Av; ☎ 284 53 04; ◷ 10.00–02.00. Lavishly decorated to look like some kind of fisherman's wharf; the food is uninspiring. US$15–20.

✗ **Jomalungma** 7 Gikalo St; ☎ 280 53 88; www.jomalungma.by; ◷ 12.00–23.00. This is one of my favourites. Indian, Tibetan, Nepalese & Thai cuisine are all on offer here, including a delivery service. So ordering from your hotel room ought to be possible. The food is of a high standard & service is good, with the proprietor in constant attendance. He drives the staff very hard indeed & isn't fussy about closing the kitchen door before tearing them off a strip. Décor & presentation is similar to that on offer in the West & the quality of the food is high, but the 1970s cabaret floor shows are more than a little incongruous! US$10–15.

✗ **Mon Café** 2/4 Myelnykaitye St; ☎ 203 99 57; ◷ 12.00–23.00 Mon–Thu, 12.00–02.00 Fri–Sat. The sushi is good here (& at affordable prices), but there's something of an identity crisis about the place. It seems to be covering too many bases (restaurant, bar, club with resident DJ), so relaxing it isn't. US$10–15.

✗ **Planyeta Sushi** 18 Nyezhavisymosty Av; ☎ 210 56 45; ◷ 12.00–23.00. It's a sushi bar, period (& part of a chain). There are plenty of these at home. US$10–15.

✗ **Uzbekistan** 17 Yanki Kupaly St; ☎ 227 73 14; ◷ 12.00–midnight. Uzbek cuisine is not easy to find, but if you were to guess what it might be like, this would be it. There's a lot going here, with the belly dancing something of a speciality. Renowned also for the quality of the service, the menu is enticing & the whole effect is worth a look. US$15–20.

SOUTH AND CENTRAL AMERICAN

✗ **Novaya Galereya** 3 Kozlova St (Palace of Art); ☎ 288 11 53; ◷ 12.00–02.00. Average Latin-American cuisine against a backdrop of themed evenings, such as 'Beer Mondays' & 'Viva Cuba Thursdays'. US$15–20.

✗ **Varadero** 5 Myelezha St; ☎ 262 14 16; ◷ 11.00–23.00. The interior is in the style of Old Havana, while the food is served under the direction of an internationally renowned chef trained in the best restaurants there. Live music, Cuban rum & very large cigars complete the experience. US$15–20.

ENTERTAINMENT AND NIGHTLIFE

CAFÉS AND COFFEE BARS

Air Grip 19 Komsomolskaya; ☎ 201 37 93; e air_grip@anitex.by; ⏱ 09.00–23.00. Italian ices served al fresco in the garden. Relaxed & pleasing, it's a good place to recharge your batteries.

Bastion 35 Volgogradskaya St; ☎ 280 17 67; ⏱ 12.00–23.00. Cheap & cheerful ethnic Slav dishes in a traditionally styled environment. Pleasant but uninspiring.

Beatles Café 65 Tomiryaskova; ☎ 209 01 48; ⏱ 11.00–23.00. This small & unassuming venue, liberally decorated with 'authentic' memorabilia, pays affectionate & respectful homage to the Fab Four. If you've been to the surreal Depeche Mode theme bar in Tallinn, Estonia, then this is the place for you.

Café Beze 18 Nyezhavisymosty Av; ☎ 206 64 09; ⏱ 10.00–01.00. Quaint & charmingly retro, the richest of desserts are served here, so only come if you have a (very) sweet tooth.

Dalat 40 Zhudra St; ☎ 253 36 48; ⏱ 10.00–23.00. A Vietnamese café specialising in national dishes & snacks. It's a long way out of the city centre, which is a pity, because it has a simple charm all of its own.

Elena 19 Yakuba Kolasa; ☎ 232 01 73; ⏱ 11.00–23.00. A sweet little cellar café that is cheap & cheerful. Always popular, this is just the place to hang out for an intermission during your sightseeing.

James 58 Surganova; ☎ 290 28 88; e restaurant@james.by; www.james.by; ⏱ 12.00–02.00. Yep, this really does have a James Bond 007 theme. Cool, chic & classy, this is a favourite haunt of the Minsk in-crowd. It's also clichéd, crowded & kitsch, but worth it just to be able to sip trademark vodka martinis, as the man himself gazes down upon the wannabes from portraits on every wall. It's just one of those things that simply has to be done, especially if you're on a romantic liaison.

Kalyesa 2 Brestskaya St; ☎ 278 87 56; ⏱ 11.00–23.00. Shashlik & a good selection of other dishes are barbecued to order. Best eaten outdoors.

Kubik 13 Volodarskovo; ☎ 227 79 08; ⏱ 10.00–midnight. This is a great place for a pit-stop, with good coffee & lots of snacks on offer. Trendy, popular & relaxed, all at the same time. Do bear this place in mind if you're dashing around & need a quick break.

London 18 Nyezhavisymosty Av; ☎ 289 15 29; ⏱ 10.00–23.00. A cosy venue offering a huge selection of teas & coffees, with cakes & sweets to match. Just avert your gaze from the tacky souvenirs.

Matilda 7 Kalinina; ☎ 281 76 21; ⏱ 12.00–23.00. Don't miss out on this little gem. The prices are dirt cheap, the ambiance is soothing & the décor is classy.

Presto 56 Nyezhavisymosty Av; ☎ 232 15 79; email; presto@iptel.by; ⏱ 12.00–02.00 Sun–Thu, 12.00–03.00 Fri–Sat. Just a great place to sample a host of different coffees, but only if you like your caffeine served with very loud music. Come here for cocktails in the evening.

Salodki Falvarak 2 Tanka St; ☎ 206 34 11; ⏱ 10.00–23.00. Modelled on a Parisian café, there's a good range of coffee & tea, but the pastries are strictly Belarusian. Only sample if you're in need of an intense sugar rush or extremely hung over.

Salodki Falvarak 2 2 Nyezhavisymosty Av; ☎ 284 30 79; ⏱ 10.00–23.00. More of the same, but in a larger venue with interesting Cubist décor.

Stari Miln 40 Nyezhavisymosty Av; ☎ 284 44 40; ⏱ 11.00–midnight. Very snug & cosy indeed, this favourite of the locals enjoys a well-deserved reputation.

Verba 51 Kropotnika; ☎ 234 69 95; ⏱ 11.00–23.00. Another cosy venue, this time specialising in shashlik. I like this one. It's unpretentious & knows that it's a hip venue, so it doesn't have to try. Another one for your 'must-do' list.

BARS Although only a small number of venues are listed here, many of the places described earlier as restaurants and cafés also double as bars, with most of them readily serving drinking clientele as well as diners. And there are many others out there that haven't even made it into the book at all. So, embark on a voyage of discovery and perhaps you can find somewhere new.

Dhrozhi United 2 Svyerdlova; ☎ 200 54 56; ⏱ 09.00–02.00. Ahem. Even Minsk has its own Irish bar. It's more than a little clichéd, but proper Guinness is served nonetheless & it's worth a visit

3

for the craic. Czech & German beers are also available.

♀ **Galeryea Vin** 23 Masherova Av; ☎ 226 63 90; ⏰ 11.00–23.00 (19.00 Mon). This is a discreet bar at the back of a wine retailer. In a country not known for the quality of its (imported) wine cellars, decent vintage is available in this unexpected oasis of quality.

♀ **Lasunok** 25 Yanki Kupala; ☎ 206 69 13; www.juravinka.by; ⏰ 13.00–03.00 Mon–Thu, 13.00–05.00 Fri, 11.00–05.00 Sat, 11.00–03.00 Sun. Above the restaurant & part of the hotel bearing the same name (the Juravinka), this is a chic place to meet, where you can sit under the glass dome & people-watch. There is an attractive riverside outdoor seating area for the summer.

CASINOS AND CLUBS If you read the publicity blurb that is aimed at enticing would-be punters in search of hedonistic pleasure into these establishments, you would be led to believe that they are the only places in town for aspiring socialites, sophisticates and the well-to-do to be seen. True it is that the country's nouveau riche *biznismyeni* and their glamorous escorts are to be found at leisure here, often until dawn (it's the same world over, after all); but some of these places are also the haunt of the seedy underside of society. In particular, prostitution is rife and ladies of the night can be seen plying their trade amongst the tables. But if you exercise some common sense, then the art of people-watching can richly be served here. Stay sober, keep a tight hold on your wallet, keep your wits about you and you won't go far wrong. You will need to pay an entrance fee just to cross the threshold of these emporia, ranging from US$2–5 for standard club venues, all the way to US$20+ for a more sophisticated and chic experience in the classier locations.

☆ **Alkatraz** 25 Nyezhavisymosty Av; ☎ 227 59 82; ⏰ 12.00–06.00. The usual fare is on offer here: booze, loud music & scantily clad young women cavorting on stage, all within the expected prison theme.

☆ **Blindage** 9 Timiryazheva; ☎ 219 00 10; ⏰ 22.00–06.00. Offering very loud music within a themed militaristic setting, teenagers abound here.

☆ **Byelaya Vyezha** 17 Masherova Av; ☎ 284 69 22; www.belaveja.by; ⏰ 24hrs. This venue likes to think that it is the foremost gaming & entertainment centre in the entire city. It's a boast that is not entirely without foundation. A state-of-the-art dance area equipped with 9m-high video plasma screens stands next to the hip & sassy cocktail bar (with the 'cigar bar' close by!). Go-go dancers & strip shows are a regular feature, while the gaming facilities attract a large crowd of serious punters.

☆ **Bronx Club** 17/1 Masherova Av; ☎ 288 10 61; ⏰ 12.00–02.00 Sun–Wed, 12.00–05.00 Thu–Sat. This is one of the classiest nightspots in town & for once the reality matches the hype. Cheap it most certainly isn't, so be prepared to spend some serious money here. There is a good-quality restaurant & some very trendy bars, together with live music from time to time. Both chic & relaxed at the same time, this is a stylish venue. Expect to find the glitterati here.

☆ **Coliseum** 15 Smolyenskaya St; ☎ 285 30 95; ⏰ 12.00–06.00. Archetypical club, casino & restaurant facilities are on offer here.

☆ **Dankoff Club** 25 Myasnikova St; ☎ 220 24 09; ⏰ 24hrs. A real curiosity. Sophisticated dining, gaming, slot machines, billiards, dancing, striptease & erotic shows are all on offer here, alongside family entertainment & 'fun for kids'! You might want to leave them at home.

☆ **Goodwin** 19 Nyezhavisymosty Av; ☎ 226 13 06; restaurant ⏰ 12.00–22.00, club 22.00–05.00. I've been taken here several times; my Belarusian friends think it's the height of chic. It isn't, I'm afraid. But the food is good & the staff are very friendly. There is loud music on large video screens & 1970s-style disco dancing after 22.00. For the sports-minded, there are also multi-screen presentations of major sporting events.

☆ **Laguna Club** (attached to Hotel Orbita) 39 Pushkina Av; ☎ 252 69 46; ⏰ 21.30–05.30. Restaurant, bar & erotic shows, including 'customised performances' & 'non-stop solo erotic dances all night long'.

☆ **Madison Club** 9 Timiryazheva St; ☎ 219 00 10; www.madisonclub.by; ⏰ 13.00–06.00 Mon–Fri, 09.00–06.00 Sat–Sun. There are 2 cocktail bars here boasting comfortable leather sofas, along with a dance floor & a restaurant, but this club isn't actually as hip & trendy as it thinks it is, although locally, its reputation is high. The admission fee is also on the steep side.

☆ **Max Show** 73 Nyezhavisymosty Av; ☎ 232 00 38; ⏰ 22.00–06.00. More non-stop erotica, but with a twist, for there is also a male show for the delectation of the female audience.

☆ **Paradise** 13 Masherova Av; ☎ 223 55 33; ⏱ 23.00–04.00 (06.00 Sat). For aficionados of the fondly remembered school or youth-club disco, this is the place to go. But it's not cheap, it's gloomy, a tad grimy & full of teenagers.

☆ **Reaktor** 29 Very Khoruzhey; ☎ 288 61 60; ⏱ 22.00–06.00. Pulsating music aimed at the teenage market. Themed on the nuclear age, it also reckons to have its own reactor. Hmmmm.

☆ **Tyekhas** (attached to Hotel Yubilyeynya) 19 Masherova Av; ☎ 226 63 90; ⏱ 22.00–04.00. A small & uninspiring venue offering adult entertainment.

☆ **Vkus Nochi** (attached to Hotel Planyeta) 31 Masherova Av; m 330 53 30; www.tasteofnight.com; ⏱ from 22.00. Accessed through the night bar in Hotel Planyeta, this is strictly a venue for adult entertainment only.

☆ **Westworld Club** (attached to Hotel Belarus) 15a Storazhevskaya; ☎ 293 17 98; ⏱ 20.00–06.00 (closed Mon). Belarusian & other European cuisine is available in the restaurant, but the major draw here is the nightly programme of erotica. It's the most popular venue in town. So it claims. Ghastly & more than a little seedy.

SHOPPING

Western designer goods are becoming increasingly available from new boutiques that are springing up all over the city, but why shop for things that you can get back home? The 'main drag' for shopaholics is **Nyezhavizhimosty Avenue** and in particular, the section northeast of the Hotel Minsk. The two large **state department stores** can be found here: **GUM** (*21 Nyezhavizhimosty Av;* ☎ *227 88 76;* ⏱ *09.00–21.00 Mon–Sat, 10.00–19.00 Sun; nearest metro: Oktyabrskaya/ Kupalovskaya*) and **TSUM** (*54 Nyezhavizhimosty Av;* ☎ *284 21 64;* ⏱ *09.00–21.00 Mon–Sat, 11.00–18.00 Sun; nearest metro: Yakuba Kolasa*). Shop here for all things Belarusian, including ethnic souvenirs and books. Just browsing is an experience in itself. GUM in particular is a must for those on the trail of Soviet-style memorabilia, especially cheap lapel badges which all seem to show Lenin's profile against a variety of backdrops. Part of the massively expansionist building programme at the end of the Great Patriotic War, the architecture and décor are classically Stalinist, even down to the trademark red stars in the glass of the windows and the grand statuettes in heroic poses on the staircases inside. With hammer and sickle motifs all around you, it's like a 1950s time warp. Many other specialist stores can be found on this avenue. Window-shopping is also a fine complement to the art of promenading, particularly when accompanied by an occasional diversion to a pavement café.

For **markets**, visit the **Dinamo Stadium** (*8 Kirova;* ☎ *227 26 11;* ⏱ *08.00–17.00*), where the stalls selling cheap (and often imitation) goods of every variety are permanently located all around the outside of this imposing, grandiose and impressive venue (which is well worth a peek through the gates); and also the **Komarovsky rinok** (*6 Very Koruzhey;* ☎ *232 66 08;* ⏱ *08.00–19.00; nearest metro: Yakuba Kolasa*), where all manner of goods are available for purchase, including an astonishing array of fresh produce. This is a fantastic place to meander and people-watch, but when in either of these markets, keep your wits about you and be on the lookout for pickpockets. Don't allow your carelessness to spoil a truly authentic slice of archetypical Belarusian life.

There is a large **shopping mall** at the junction of Lenin and Nyemiga streets, close to the Nyemiga/Frunzhyenskaya metro entrance (*Na Nyemiga; 8 Nyemiga;* ☎ *220 97 47;* ⏱ *09.00–21.00 Mon–Sat, 10.00–20.00 Sun*), but it's all rather tired and drab. New malls are under construction in many other locations. Recently opened is the major underground shopping centre beneath Independence (formerly Lenin) Square. After stumbling around the hazards of the largest building site I have ever seen for the last few years, I was astonished when last in Minsk to find the work complete. As you enter the complex, it looks just like any other in the

West, with piped *muzak* and shiny fittings. But it hasn't managed to attract the designer-label outlets and the goods on offer are pretty second rate, with a depressingly high number of vacant and un-let units. It's not very promising and scarcely worth a look, notwithstanding all the hype and publicity that has trailed its arrival on the scene.

Probably the best bargains of all by way of souvenirs are books. Glossy pictorial guides are available very cheaply and although many of the tomes are in Russian, there are a significant (and growing) number of English works. But to my mind, Cyrillic printing is a work of art in itself. In any event, you can always look at the pictures and maps to remember your stay. There are many **bookstores** all over town and every one is well stocked, but my personal favourite is the **Central Bookstore** (*19 Nyezhavizhimosty Av;* ☎ *227 49 18/226 10 52;* ☉ *10.00–15.00 & 16.00–19.00 Mon–Fri, 10.00–15.00 & 16.00–18.00 Sat; nearest metro: Oktyabrskaya/Kupalovskaya*) This shop has the largest selection of books in the city, as well as a fine range of Soviet-style posters and calendars.

Otherwise, there is a whole world of discovery by way of retail therapy just waiting for you. Should anything catch your eye in a shop window as you promenade along the boulevards, just step off the pavement and take a look. Shop browsing is a real art in this city and the best thing of all is that you won't be hassled by manic assistants eager to secure their commission on a sale. It's a stress-free experience and a great way to observe an interesting slice of Belarusian life.

OTHER PRACTICALITIES

BANKS Here are the main addresses for a selection of major banks. Most of them also have a considerable number of branches scattered throughout the city (for example, Belagroprombank has 117 and Belvnesheconombank has 62), offering the usual banking, currency and exchange services. Standard opening hours are 09.00–17.00, Monday to Friday, but closing times may vary an hour or so either way, with early closing on Friday. Nearly all will have at least one ATM. Machines are also to be found in other locations, such as the lobbies of the larger hotels, or in major shopping centres.

$ **Belagroprombank** 3 Zhukov Av; ☎ 218 57 77
$ **Belarus National Bank** 20 Nyezhavizhimosty Av; ☎ 219 23 03
$ **Belarusky Narodny Bank** 87a Nyezhavizhimosty Av; ☎ 280 16 63

$ **Belpromstroibank** 6 Mulyavin Bd; 289 46 06
$ **Belarusbank** 32 Myasnikov St; ☎ 218 84 31
$ **Belvnesheconombank** 32 Myasnikov St; ☎ 209 29 44

COMMUNICATIONS

Telephone To make an **international call to Belarus**, dial 375, followed by the city code (minus the first zero), followed by the subscriber's number.

To make an **international call from Belarus**, dial 8, wait for the continuous dialing tone, dial 10, the country code, the city code (minus the first zero), followed by the subscriber's number.

To make a **call within Belarus**, dial 8, wait for the continuous dialing tone, dial the city code (the first digit of which must be 0), followed by the subscriber's number.

To make a **call within the same town in Belarus**, dial 2, then the subscriber's number only.

Cellular (mobile phone) services are supplied by Velcom GSM, Belcel and MTS, all of which provide international roaming services. If you are going to make significant numbers of calls to local mobile numbers on these Belarusian networks from your own mobile, you will save pots of money by purchasing a local SIM card from one of the providers when you arrive.

For **international calls to subscribers of Belarusian mobile networks**, dial +375 29 and the subscriber's number.

Internet facilities can be found in hotels and post offices in any district of the city. There are also a very large number of busy internet cafés.

Fax services are available in all larger hotels.

Emergency telephone numbers

Police ☎ 02	Traffic police in Minsk ☎ 259 14 44
Fire brigade ☎ 01	24hr emergency vehicle breakdown ☎ 268 80 55
Ambulance ☎ 03	

Other useful telephone numbers

Bus services ☎ 004	Pharmacy information ☎ 069 (🕐 weekdays only)
Train services ☎ 005	Minsk information line ☎ 085
Airport and flight services ☎ 006	Speaking clock (in Russian) ☎ 088
Taxi services ☎ 007, 057, 061 or 081	Enquiry services (in English) ☎ 221 84 48
Minsk directory ☎ 009	(🕐 09.00–17.00 only)

Post and courier The main **post office** is situated at 10 Nyezhavizhimosty Avenue (☎ *226 06 82; www.belpost.by;* 🕐 *08.00–20.00 Mon–Fri, 10.00–17.00 Sat–Sun*). Telephone, telegraph, fax, photocopying and internet services are available here.

Telegrams can be sent from hotels or any post office, and regular mail deliveries are also available from hotels or any post office.

Express delivery services are available from:

DHL 18 Brestskaya; ☎ 278 11 08; www.dhl.by. The company also has a number of express centres throughout the city.
EMS 10 Nyezhavizhimosty Av; ☎ 222 65 11; www.belpost.by. This is the state service located at the main post office.

FedEx 15b Zhukovskova; ☎ 226 99 09; e callcenter@mum.by; www.mum.by
TNT 10 Platanova; ☎ 236 80 00; e info@tnt.by; www.tnt.by. Also at Minsk-2 airport; ☎ 279 11 86.
UPS 3 Muzikhalny; ☎ 206 55 80; e minsk@tut.by; www.ups.by

HOSPITALS

✚ **Minsk Clinic Number 10** 73 Uborevich St; ☎ 241 98 11

✚ **Accident & Emergency Hospital** 58 Kizhevatova; ☎ 227 76 21

PHARMACIES

✚ **Belfarmatseya Pharmacy Number 13** 16 Nyezhavizhimosty Av; ☎ 227 48 44; 🕐 24hr Mon–Sat

✚ **Belfarmatseya Pharmacy Number 36** 11 Shevchenko Bd; ☎ 288 97 43; 🕐 24hr Mon–Sat
✚ Medicine Kiosk at **Preston Market Store** 153a Bogdanovich St; ☎ 288 47 34; 🕐 24hr

WHAT TO SEE AND DO

MUSEUMS

The Belarusian State Museum of the Great Patriotic War (*25a Nyezhavizhimosty Av;* ☎ *227 56 11 or 227 76 35 for an English-speaking tour guide;* f *227 56 65;* e *mail@warmuseum.by; www.warmuseum.by;* 🕐 *10.00–17.00 Tue–Sun; nearest metro: Oktyabrskaya/Kupalovskaya; admission BYR5,000, but free on the second Tue of every month!*) This is a truly sombre museum (and for many years, the only one of its kind in the whole of the Soviet Union) chronicling the terrible events of World War II (which continue to dominate the national psyche to this very day) from the perspective of the USSR. Three floors of exhibits contain displays of great detail, but sadly only with Russian captions. Guided tours are also available and if you book in advance, you will be able to secure the services of an English speaker (details as above). Documentary films are constantly showing (but in Russian only). Periodically, war veterans are present to recount their experiences. There is a harrowing scale model of a Nazi concentration camp, plus photo after photo of public executions by hanging in the city's parks. There is also an excellent and extensive featured exhibition devoted to the famous and heroic Belarusian partisan movement, which made such a significant contribution to halting the Nazi invasion and undermining the occupation. Outside is a fine collection of militaria and an imposing statue of Lenin. The website is hugely informative, both on the museum and the on broader context of the conflict, but like the museum itself, the text is sadly only in Russian.

Museum of Ancient Belarusian Culture (*1–2 Surganov St;* ❧ *284 18 82/24 97;* ☉ *10.00–17.00 Mon–Thu; nearest metro: Akademya Nauk; admission free*) As might be expected from the title, the exhibits here are primarily archaeological, including the remains of a Palaeolithic boat excavated from the mud of the Sozh River in the southeast of the country (there is a very similar exhibit in the museum in Vetka, see *Chapter 8, Gomel City and Oblast,* page 209). There are also exhibits of traditional folk art, including clothes, along with a number of icons. Everything is presented in a very traditional, not to say old-fashioned manner, so this is probably one for the specialist.

National Museum of History and Culture of Belarus (*12 Karl Marx St;* ❧ *227 43 22;* ☉ *11.00–19.00, closed Wed; nearest metro: Oktybrskaya/Kupalovskaya; admission BYR7,000*) Some regard this as the foremost historical museum in the whole country, but as with the Museum of Ancient Belarusian Culture (above), everything is displayed in a rather dreary and unimaginative way. Still, if you're a traditionalist when it comes to museums, you won't be disappointed. The bare facts show that there are an incredible 338,000 exhibits grouped into 45 collections that include archaeology, religious relics, weapons, fine arts, icons, photographs, manuscripts, historic printing and much, much more. Don't miss the quaint display of potatoes in the basement. Yes, really.

Belarusian National Fine Arts Museum (*20 Lenin St;* ❧ *227 71 63/45 62;* ☉ *11.00–19.00, closed Tue; admission BYR4,500*) Plundered by the Nazis during the Great Patriotic War, this is the country's largest museum of art. The fate of the vast majority of its original contents remains a mystery to this day, but little by little, its collections were painstakingly reassembled during the post-war years and now include modern Belarusian art, manuscripts and books dating from the 16th century, national Belarusian art dating from the 17th century, west European art and ancient artefacts.

Maxim Bogdanovich Literary Museum (*7a Maxim Bogdanovich St;* ❧ *234 42 69/07 61;* ☉ *10.00–17.00, closed Mon; also closed Sun in summer; admission BYR5,000*) Housed in a beautiful 19th-century building in Old Town, this collection is dedicated to the famous Belarusian poet and includes original manuscripts, books of collected verses printed during the poet's lifetime, photographs and personal belongings. Romance, drama and tragedy abound here. Both general and themed tours are available with the services of a guide, but not yet in English. Literary recitals and musical evenings are also held here.

Yanka Kupala State Literary Museum (*4a Yanka Kupala St;* ⟍ *227 78 66/79 43;* ⏰ *10.00–17.00 Mon–Sat; admission BYR4,500*) Situated in one of the city's most beautiful suburbs, it tells the story of the life and work of the famous Belarusian poet, playwright, translator and author.

PARKS, OPEN SPACES AND RECREATIONAL AREAS
Gorky Park (*22 Nyezhavizhimosty Av;* ⟍ *227 78 42*) The city's oldest park (founded in 1800) and situated on the banks of the Svislach River, the main entrance is off Victory Square. There are many attractions for children, together with an observatory and planetarium, a covered skating rink and a stage for summer concerts. Horseriding and boating are available here and the big wheel has fine panoramic views of Minsk from its 56m high-point. Installed in 2003, it has enclosed cabins, unlike its rather ramshackle predecessor. But although this park boasts an abundance of manmade entertainment features, its generally attractive and relaxed ambiance has more to do with its natural environment. There are groves of lime and maple trees that have stood for 100 years or more, along with rare cedars and pines. It's the ideal location for promenading and people-watching, whatever the season.

Central Park (*Nyezhavizhimosty Av*) Originally laid out in 1872, it contains the city's oldest public fountain, 'A Boy and a Swan', together with a number of significant sculptures, both classical and modern. Immediately following its opening, it became a favourite place of rest and relaxation for intellectuals, which is why a theatre was built in its southwestern corner in 1890. It was never popular with local people, not least because plays in Belarusian, Polish and Hebrew were banned there until 1905. Today, it is the National Theatre and bears the name of the famous poet Yanka Kupala.

Yanka Kupala Park (*Nyezhavizhimosty Av*) Designed in 1962, it is home to the Yanka Kupala monument and museum, along with many other sculptures. Its broad central walkway slopes gently down to the River Svislach, which is 120m wide at this point. Over 4,000 trees and many more shrubs were planted when this park was laid out, making it an oasis of green in the heart of the city and a splendid place for an afternoon's stroll.

Central Botanical Gardens (*2 Surganova;* ⟍ *289 44 84;* ⏰ *10 May–31 Oct 10.00–18.00; admission BYR700*) Founded in 1932 and now under the stewardship of the National Academy of Sciences, there are many varieties of plantlife here, all in a setting that is most pleasing on the eye. The rose garden, alpine garden and landscape park are particularly attractive. It is a very popular place of relaxation for the city's residents. Opening times are rather ad hoc, so do ring in advance to avoid the risk of a wasted journey.

Victory Park Founded in 1945, it contains the huge Komsomolskoe Lake and is a very popular location for promenaders.

Chelyuskintsev Culture and Leisure Park Opened in May 1932 and adjacent to the Central Botanical Gardens, attractions include a children's amusement park and a miniature narrow-gauge railway. There is also a large area of urban forest which gives a clue to the former ecology of the land on which the city now stands.

SQUARES, MONUMENTS AND SIGNIFICANT ARCHITECTURAL FEATURES – A CITY WALKING TOUR The following entries from Pryvaksalnaya Square to Victory Square follow a more or less straight line bisecting the city in a northeasterly

direction along Nyezhavizhimosty (formerly Francyska Skoriny) Avenue. Here lies the heart of the city and a day's amble to take in the sights as listed comes highly recommended. *En route*, you will pass a host of bars and eateries to keep you fortified, as well as any number of diverse shops for a little retail therapy and souvenir hunting along the way.

Pryvaksalnaya Square Originally home to the city's first railway station, constructed of intricate red brick in the 1870s, the impressive new station was built here in the 1990s. The sense of space, air and grandeur is truly astonishing. Archetypical Stalinist granite buildings on a grandiose scale can also be found here, including the two lofty towers known colloquially as the 'City Gates'. Consisting of 11 storeys on three tiers in the style of a wedding cake and positioned at the corners of two five-storey blocks of flats, they form an impressive entrance to this open and sweeping public space, which itself forms an integral part of the post-war spatial planning of the city. Begun in 1948, the final brick was laid in 1956 under the watchful gaze of chief architect Rubyanenko from Leningrad (now St Petersburg). These two dwelling units were something of an exception in social planning terms, for they were entirely self-contained, incorporating their own shops, restaurants, pharmacies and school and medical facilities. When originally built, the two towers were topped with spires, while sculptures stood on the corners of the first tier. Façades were decorated with ornate stucco. Sadly, all of the apocrypha concerning Soviet concrete are true and these adornments are long gone, their crumbling demise a portent of the collapse of the system that created them. All that remains is the country's biggest clock, along with the country's former coat of arms. The new railway station faces you on the other side as you enter the square through the City Gates. The concept of imaginary twin gates replicates in fond homage the design of the original station, which itself featured double-tier pavilions either side of its entrance. But the new structure extends horizontally rather than vertically, with the onlooker's gaze drawn between the imaginary gates to the soft and rounded lines of the central access, which is topped by a simple but impressive pyramidal roof skylight. The whole effect is set off beautifully by the reflection of the entire square in the mirror-like walls of the spacious foyer, giving the visitor the perception of a grand city entrance through triumphal portals.

Independence (formerly Lenin) Square A great many pre-war Stalinist buildings survive here. There is also an imposing statue of Lenin. The best panoramic view of the square can be seen through the arch in Leningradskaya Street, when the buildings on the north side, dominated by the House of Government (with Lenin in the foreground) and the Red Catholic Church of Saint Simon and Saint Helena (of which more below), stand open to the eye in all their glory. Government House is a monument to simplistic symmetry, with several buildings of different height overlooking the central ten-storey structure, the whole being recessed from the square at a distance of 50m, just to add to its imposing and monumental appearance. Built between 1930 and 1934 as a manifestation of civic power and influence, the architectural design of this building was originally intended to be the blueprint for the whole of the city. The eastern side of the square, where Nyezhavizhimosty (formerly Fransyska Skoriny) Avenue begins is flanked by the neo-Classical lines of the magnificent Hotel Minsk, built in 1957 and the Central Post Office, built in 1953. The southern side consists of the Belarusian State University (1962), the Minsk City Executive Council buildings (1964) and the Metro Administration building (1984). In many ways, this magnificent square contains the beating heart of the country. It has survived military occupation by a cruel oppressor, has been the sight of countless processions to celebrate revolution and freedom, hosted demonstrations in the era of *perestroika* as the Soviet Union breathed its last and then, finally, was the location from which the birth of the newly independent republic was proclaimed on 19 September 1991. For many years, the whole experience of standing in this symbolic and visually arresting place was ruined by the presence of a huge and cavernous building site right in the very middle of the square, as an underground shopping complex slowly took shape. Happily, most of the remedial work in the square has at last been completed. Do try to spend a little while in this impressive location and focus your attentions on the splendour of all that can be seen around you.

Nyezhavizhimosty (formerly Francyska Skoriny) Avenue It is the city's main thoroughfare which runs away from Independence Square down to Victory Square and is the axis around which the great works of reconstruction were designed after the war. In 1944, a documentary film was shot to give a bird's-eye panorama of the centre of Minsk. To view it now, especially with the benefit of a visit to the city as it currently stands, is a sobering and sombre experience. Of the 825 major buildings that stood at the outbreak of hostilities, only 60 of stone and 20 of wood survived. One cannot but marvel at the resilience, commitment and civic pride of a country and people who set about the task of regeneration with such gusto. This imposing avenue, which was built anew with geometric precision on the site of the former Sovietskaya Street, is said by many to resemble the famous Nevsky Prospyekt in St Petersburg, not only for its architectural prominence, but also for its human side, represented by a café-style culture. Promenaders stroll hand in hand in an ambiance of relaxed sophistication. Ominously though, on the left-hand (northwestern) side of the street, an entire block is taken up by a yellow building of neo-Classical design, with a grandiose entrance flanked by enormous pillars. This is the home of the KGB. Directly opposite is a long, thin park containing a bust of the much-feared Felix Dzherzhinsky. A native Belarusian and one of Lenin's closest acolytes, he was the founder of the hated Cheka, the forerunner organisation to the KGB. Moving down towards first Oktybrskaya and then Victory Square, you will pass the National Bank building on the right of the street, which is directly opposite the GUM state department store. Built in 1951, 'this shoppers' paradise' (as the official description has it) boasts exquisite décor which is best appreciated from the opposite side of the street. Stop the world at this point and take in the sumptuous view.

Oktyabrskaya (formerly Central) Square This square probably suffered more architectural damage during the war than any other part of the city. There is yet more Stalinist architecture here, including the imposing Trade Unions Palace of Culture (built in 1954) and the more simply designed museum dedicated to the Great Patriotic War. The square was made complete by the construction in 2001 of the dominating Palace of the Republic, which put the finishing touches to the original post-war plan of connecting the historical heart of the city with its new administrative centre, high on a plateau above the River Svislach. It also incorporates Central Park (described earlier) on its southern side. Behind the park is the imposing edifice of the pre-war Communist Party of Belarus Central Committee building, which today is the location of the office of the president. Be very careful when taking photographs here. If spotted by the militia, you will have some explaining to do. Continuing along **Nyezhavizhimosty Avenue**, you pass **Yanka Kupala Park** to the left and **Gorky Park** to the right, both split by the Svislach River (see above for further details). Just after the river on the left is one of the most picturesque thoroughfares in the entire city, Kamunicheskaya Street, with grandly opulent buildings on one side and the landscaped riverbank on the other. For Cold War students, building number 4 is home to the former apartment of one Lee Harvey Oswald, who lived here for a number of years before his return to the United States and notoriety as JFK's assassin (or so it is alleged).

Victory Square Situated further downtown on Nyezhavizhimosty, where this main route out of town in the direction of Minsk-2 International Airport meets Zakharava Street, Victory Square (which used to be round and is now elliptical, such that it alarmingly resembles the chariot scene from the movie Ben Hur in rush-hour traffic – not for the faint-hearted driver) is dominated by the imposing monument to commemorate the nation's losses in the Great Patriotic War. Many Minsk residents still refer to the square as the 'Circus', as it was formerly called before the great obelisk was erected in 1954. At 40m tall, it is topped with the 'Order of Victory', the trademark Soviet red star. On 3 July 1961, an eternal flame was lit at its base. Wedding bouquets are commonly to be seen here, for it is an accepted feature of wedding ritual in this country that the bride and groom (with their full entourage) will pay homage to those who have fallen in war at memorials such as this. It's a necessary and essential photo opportunity for them as part of the day's proceedings. In fact, expect to see a wedding party at any number of locations in the city, arriving at speed in a motorcade, windows down and horns blaring! At the design stage for the monument, many of the best-known Belarusian sculptors of the time were commissioned to contribute to the scenes shown in bas-relief on the four facets at the foot of the column. They are named '9 May 1945 Victory Day', 'Soviet Army during the Years of the Great Patriotic War', 'Belarusian Partisans' and 'Glory to the Fallen Heroes'. If you look carefully here, you will find the site of a neat microcosm of Soviet revisionism. Stalin was already dead by the time these reliefs were sculpted and his profile, not surprisingly was added to the fresco, originally appearing on the flag next to Lenin's portrait. But as the years passed and Stalin's legacy hastened his fall from grace, his profile was quietly and without ceremony transformed into Lenin's ear. The dominance of the column has its best perspective from a distance, but a closer view lends greater appreciation to the scenes depicted at the base. At the same time, take a look around you. The classically constructed houses on the south side, each with beautiful entrances and neat towers, are connected by handsome rows of columns. There is also an underground hall containing commemorative material, which is well worth a visit.

OTHER NOTABLE MONUMENTS AND ARCHITECTURAL FEATURES
Island of Tears Situated on the River Svislach directly opposite Old Town and inaugurated on 3 August 1996, this is a commemorative memorial to the fallen in the USSR's ill-fated and disastrous Afghanistan campaign (1979–88). The central feature is a chapel, upon the walls of which bleak and harrowing images of grieving mothers, widows and sisters are sculpted, all waiting in vain for their loved ones to return. Inside are four altars bearing topical icons, together with small shrines dedicated to the fallen from each of the country's administrative *oblasts*, their names listed on the walls. In the centre, memory bells have been lowered into a sunken recess containing soil from a number of graves, along with a sealed capsule containing soil from the field of battle in Afghanistan where some of the nation's sons fell. This is a highly symbolic and ritualistic gesture, often to be found at memorial locations. Nearby is the statue of a doleful angel in mourning, weeping because he could not save the boys' lives. The Afghanistan fiasco matches the American misadventure in Vietnam for mind-numbing folly. For years after the war ended, veterans received no recognition either from an ungrateful state or from the Party machine. The authorities simply wanted to turn their collective

back and pretend that the madness had never even happened. Access to the chapel is via a short footbridge from Old Town (see below), but beware the street vendor waiting to accost you with tacky souvenirs, including out-of-date calendars. He has an interesting collection of badges from the old Soviet Union though, most of them featuring Lenin's gaunt face atop a Party slogan exhorting the workers to ever greater achievements. The short written guide to the Island of Tears memorial is also worth buying for the photographs alone, as a reminder of your visit.

Zaslavskaya Jewish Memorial This moving and harrowing sculpture of a group of people seen descending a slope marks the very spot where 5,000 Jews from the Minsk ghetto were herded to their death on a single day in March 1942.

Rakauskoye suburb Situated on the western approaches to the city, the earliest settlements were founded here and during the Nazi occupation it became one of Europe's biggest Jewish ghettos. Only 13 individuals out of a population of 100,000 survived to the Soviet liberation.

Traiyetskoye suburb Famous for its bars and taverns since the 13th century, this attractive historic area located close to the hotel district is known as 'Old Town'. Sadly, it's only a reconstruction though. Even so, the rebuilding during the 1980s of the brightly coloured two- and three-storey houses was sympathetically accomplished, enabling the visitor to experience the city as it existed a century or so ago. Then, the dwellings were of stone and the streets were cobbled. It was a non-aristocratic part of the city, housing factory workers, peasants, craftsmen, traders, civil servants of low rank, military personnel and the petty bourgeoisie. Today, their successors are the owners of the offices, shops, cafés, bars and restaurants that occupy the buildings there. Just across the river from here, at the junction of Lenin and Nyemiga streets, stands the Nyemiga metro station. In May 1999, on the day of a local festival, its entrance was the scene of a terrible tragedy, when hordes of excitable youngsters ran into the adjoining pedestrian underpass to shelter from torrential rain: 53 of them were trampled to death. An official plaque commemorates this awful event. More poignant are the personal mementos and reminders left there by friends and loved ones. All who pass by are given to pausing for quiet reflection.

The National Library With the finishing touches to this amazing building having only recently been added, here is an eye-catching sight indeed. Located on Nyezhavizhimosty (formerly Francyska Skoriny) Avenue, a little out of town on the main thoroughfare into the city from Minsk-2 International Airport, it dominates the skyline for miles around, particularly at night, when it is illuminated in a dazzling display of colour. The architects based the whole concept on the shape of a diamond; the problem is, it appears to be perched precariously at ground level on nothing more than one of its points and there is apocryphal rumour amongst local people that it is dangerously unstable in its design. Some 15 million books are eventually to be moved here. The English website www.nlb.by/en is extremely informative, so do pay some attention to this quirky feature before you go, then stop off on your travels for some great photo opportunities (while it's still standing).

CATHEDRALS AND CHURCHES
Church of Saint Simon and Saint Helena (*15 Sovyetskaya*) Known locally to residents simply as the 'Red Church' for its distinctive red-brick construction and 50m-high bell tower, this imposing structure, one of the city's iconic landmarks, is situated on the north side of the recently redeveloped

Independence Square, one of the grandest in the whole city. Erected between 1908 and 1910, it is the best-known place of Roman Catholic worship in Minsk. Just as well, then, that the city's strategic planners did not have their way in the 1960s, when they wanted it to be pulled down and replaced by a wide-screen cinema! Daily services at 09.00 and 19.00, plus 10.00 and 12.00 on Saturdays and 11.00 and 13.00 on Sundays.

Cathedral of the Holy Spirit (*3 Kirilya i Mefodya*) This splendid Eastern Orthodox cathedral was constructed in 1642 and has benefited from many phases of renovation following damage and periods of closure. It is one of the last surviving monuments of Old Minsk. It houses a number of impressive icons, including that of Our Lady, which is said to have miraculously appeared on the bank of the River Svislach in 1500. An essential 'must-see', with a good souvenir shop. Evening services are held at 18.00 every day except Monday.

Maryinsky Cathedral (*9 Svobody*) A survivor of two world wars, but not of Stalin's rebuilding programme, the copper domes of this restored Roman Catholic cathedral are another iconic sight. Evening services are held at 19.00.

Saint Alyeksandr Nyevsky's Church (*11 Kozlova*) This small but imposing red-brick construction with the archetypical domes of gold has been opened and closed time and again with the prevailing political circumstances during its 100-year existence. During the Great Patriotic War, it survived (perhaps with divine intervention?) when a Nazi bomb crashed in front of the altar from on high, but failed to explode. Today, evening services are held at 18.00 and 20.00.

Cathedral of Saints Peter and Paul (*4 Rakovskaya*) Built in 1613 with donations from 52 nobles and inhabitants of the area, the 'yellow church' is the oldest-surviving of the city's places of worship. Evening services are held at 18.00.

THEATRES
National Academic Bolshoi Ballet and Great Opera Theatre of the Republic of Belarus (*1 Paris Commune Sq;* ⟍ *234 06 66/80 74 (ballet), 227 54 03 (opera); www.balet.by (Russian & English); nearest metro: Oktyabrskaya/Kupalovskaya*) Built in 1938, the theatre building itself is presently undergoing works of significant reconstruction. Pending completion, performances of ballet are generally held in the Great Hall of the Palace of the Republic, 1 Oktyabrskaya Square. All start at 19.00 and generally feature popular classics such as *Swan Lake*, *Sleeping Beauty* and *Don Quixote*. Tickets can be purchased from the office at 1 Paris Commune Square (⊕ *09.00–13.00 & 14.00–18.00 Mon–Fri*). Tickets can also be purchased from the following locations: booking office of the Palace of the Republic, on the left-hand side of the central entrance (⟍ *216 22 44*); one of three theatrical booking offices at 13, 19 and 44 Nyezhavizhimosty Square; Central Department Store 54, Nyezhavizhimosty Square (on the second floor); and at one of three metro stations, Yakuba Kolasa Square, 'Institute of Culture' or Oktyabrskaya.

Belarussian State Philharmonic (*50 Nyezhavizhimosty Sq; www.belarusopera.com (Russian & English); nearest metro: Ploschad Yakuba Kolasa*) Opera performances (a mixture of classical and modern) are held at the halls of the State Philharmonic. Tickets can be purchased from the office at 1 Paris Commune Square (⟍ *234 10 41;* f *234 07 72;* e *belarus_opera@tut.by;* ⊕ *15.00–19.30 Mon, 11.30–14.00 & 15.00–19.30 Tue–Sat*); also from the offices of the Philharmonic Society (*50 Independence Av (cash only);* ⟍ *231 16 17;* ⊕ *09.00–20.00*).

Yanka Kupala National Academic Theatre (*12 Engels St;* ℡ *227 60 81/42 02;* *www.kupala-theatre.by; nearest metro: Oktyabrskaya/Kupalovskaya*). Performances are held daily (except Tue) at 11.30 and 19.00.

OUTSIDE MINSK

The best way to visit any of the following places is likely to be by booking a local tour through one of Minsk's agencies (see *Chapter 2, Tour operators*, page 37 for further details). Some of the sites will benefit from a whole day each, while others can be combined. Do shop around, because prices vary significantly. Some companies will offer a cheap flat rate that excludes everything when you get there (admission, meals, separate features, etc), but others will quote an 'all-in' price. For example, a flat-rate half day in Dudutki will cost around US$40 (plus everything else, ie: admission, meals, separate features etc to be paid when you get there) and an all-in excursion around US$100.

MIR Around 90km southwest of Minsk and just 15 minutes off the main M1 motorway to Brest lies the small museum town of Mir and its beautiful 16th-century **fortress** (⊕ *10.00–17.00 Wed–Sun; admission BYR2,660, US$3 for foreign visitors*). Upon leaving Minsk, the terrain very quickly becomes much more reminiscent of western Europe, with rolling wooded hillsides of oak and beech replacing the silver birch that is omnipresent elsewhere in Belarus. Shortly after turning off the motorway, the fairy-tale castle comes into view. Situated on the edge of the town in a delightful setting overlooking a serene lake and built largely of stone and red brick, it is not only a powerful monument to the influence of the princes who commissioned its construction, but also very pleasing on the eye. Since 2000, it has been designated a UNESCO World Heritage Site, one of three in the country.

The settlement of Mir was looted and burned by invading crusaders in 1395. By 1434, it had fallen into the ownership of the 'big baron' Radzivili family, whose patronage ensured a steady increase in the significance of the settlement, as it grew first into a township and then into the administrative centre of Mir County. In the late 16th and early 17th centuries, earthen walls were built around the township and it became a fortress. Four corner gates, the foundations of which have now been excavated, gave access from the four main roads that originally met here. In 1579, the township was granted rights of limited municipal self-determination and government, so that it very quickly attracted craftsmen and tradesmen of various nationalities, including Belarusians, Tartars, Jews and ethnic travelling people. Indeed, the extravagant Duke Carol Stanislav Radzivili bestowed upon a certain Jan Martsynkyevich the grand title of 'King of the Gypsies' of the great principality of Lithuania in 1778, also declaring Mir to be their capital.

Naturally, the mixture of cultures and ethnicities had a defining influence on the community that was established here. It is for this reason that a Roman Catholic church, an Eastern Orthodox church, a synagogue and a mosque were built in close proximity. Very quickly, the township began to attract merchants and their goods from all corners of Belarus, Poland, the Baltic States and Russia.

The walls and towers of the castle (still known today as the 'medieval flower') first appeared in the 1520s, followed by the construction of the Renaissance palace itself between the late 16th and early 17th centuries. After a battering during the war with Russia in 1655 and the later Northern War, it gradually fell further into disrepair, before a revival in the 1730s, when a portrait gallery and ornate banqueting hall were added, together with a beautiful Italianate garden containing citrus, fig, myrtle, cypress, box, mahogany and laurel trees. The scent on the breeze

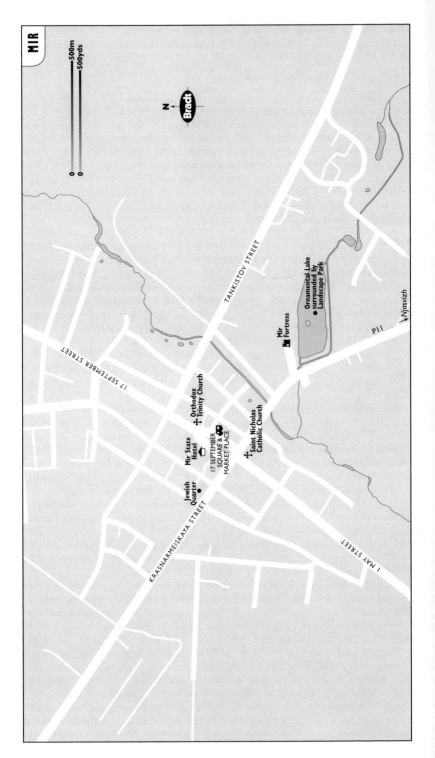

MIR

500m
500yds

N Bradt

TANKISTOV STREET

17 SEPTEMBER STREET

KRASNARMEISKAYA STREET

1 MAY STREET

P11

Njasvizh

Jewish
Quarter

Mir State
Hotel

17 SEPTEMBER
SQUARE &
MARKET PLACE

† Orthodox
Trinity Church

† Saint Nicholas
Catholic Church

Mir
Fortress

Ornamental Lake
surrounded by
Landscape Park

of summer evenings must have been heady indeed. Latterly, the complex suffered extensive damage in the Great Patriotic War. A Cossack regiment was stationed here and a number of engagements took place in the vicinity. A very significant programme of restoration is at last well under way, and when completed, the walled structure of five towers (a fifth was added after the first four for security purposes in the centre of the west wall facing the road to Vilnius, as the only means of access by drawbridge and portcullis) and a courtyard will accommodate a small hotel, conference hall and traditional restaurant in addition to the museum of exhibits currently housed in various rooms throughout the building. Caution is needed when negotiating the steep, narrow and winding staircases which permit access to those parts of the castle that are presently open to the public, with some of the steps being quite large. It is possible to climb to the very top of the southwestern tower, the best preserved of the five, from which there are extensive panoramic views over the town and surrounding countryside. The five floors currently house works of fine art. Around the castle wall at lakeside is a host of souvenir stalls, some tacky, but some with attractive artefacts and books at reasonable prices. In the castle grounds stands a pretty chapel of Modernist style (built in 1904) that serves as a burial vault. Across the lake are remains of the former estate buildings. The landscaped 16ha park around the lake was established at the same time as the chapel. There are many varieties of trees and a wooden bridge that accesses a small islet in the lake. This is an excellent spot to take photographs of the castle and is frequented by newlyweds as part of their 'grand tour' (see page 122).

Other sites in Mir Located behind the trees to the north of the castle is a **monument and burial site** for Jewish victims of the war. A total of 1,600 Mir Jews were executed here on 9 November 1941. A further 850 were imprisoned in the ghetto that was later established in the castle, all of whom were murdered on 13 August 1942.

A few hundred metres to the west, the town's lively **square and marketplace** are well worth a visit. In the middle is a neat garden and some permanent fixtures for the local market, while around the outside are houses, shops, a restaurant and a small state-run hotel. Like the castle, much of the town was destroyed in the war, so these buildings are reconstructions rather than the originals, albeit painstakingly and lovingly restored. However, the original architecture of the **Jewish quarter** dating from the early 19th century, including the *kahal* (the self-government building), two synagogues and the *yeshivah* (a rabbinic academy for the study of Holy Scriptures) is still standing, just off the square. Also there are the original Renaissance **Roman Catholic Church of Saint Nicholas** from the 16th and 17th centuries and the 16th-century **Orthodox Trinity Church**, both of which are worth a look, although their opening hours are somewhat unpredictable.

Getting there By car, take the main M1 motorway (a toll road in part) from Minsk to Brest and take the turn north onto the road signposted Mir for 8km. The town is situated on the bus route from Minsk (departing from the central bus station) to Novogrudok, the ride taking around two hours. However you get here from Minsk, make sure you have a full day available.

NJASVIZH Situated 120km southwest of Minsk and only half an hour from Mir by road is the historic settlement of Njasvizh, one of the oldest in the country. Thought to have first been established as a settlement in the 13th century, historians believe that the town itself was founded around 1446. It retains many of its oldest buildings today. Indeed, the former home of the Radzivili family is widely regarded as the most attractive palace that the country has to offer. It is surrounded by a large park boasting a number of ornamental lakes and sumptuous gardens. The family's ownership of the town began in the middle of the 16th century and was to last for more than 400 years, during which time it gained great fame for its prosperity. In 1586, the town was granted the Magdeburg Right for self-government and determination, which was a catalyst for rapid economic development. Many trade guilds were established and it was no surprise that at the end of the 16th century, it was almost completely rebuilt, the chaotic and haphazard layout of its medieval streets being replaced by the geometric design that remains to this day. The main street crosses the town from east to west. It was originally surrounded by earthen walls that were constructed to make the town a fortress. Some of them, most notably in the southeast, can still be seen. Over the centuries, many severe trials (such as plunder, fire and war) took their toll on the town, but through it all, the mighty Radzivili dynasty survived. The line finally ended in 1939, but not until it had first seen off not only the Great Lithuanian Principality, but also the might of the Russian Empire. In addition to the palace and only a short walk away from it are the stunning **Farny Polish Roman Catholic Church** (designed in early Baroque style by the 16th-century Italian architect Bernardoni, who also designed the palace), the **tower of the castle gates**, **the remains of the town gate** (this is the only one of the original four still to be standing) and the **Benedictine monastery**. A further short distance away is the **town square**, where the **trades hall** and **market houses** are situated. All of these buildings date from the 16th century. Representations of and artefacts from the life of this historic town are collected in the small but engaging **museum** on Leninskaya Street. The outstanding Belarusian Renaissance thinker and humanist Symon Budny is known to have worked in the former **printing house** here. In 1562, he published a number of significant works at this site. His nearby statue marks this key point in the history of Belarusian literature.

The first stone in the construction of the **palace** was laid in 1584. It was rebuilt many times and to this day displays features of the Renaissance, early and late Baroque, Rococo, Classicism, neo-Gothic and Modernism. The complex once numbered around 170 rooms, with a series of underground passages connecting it to the town's monasteries. It was originally encircled by ramparts, ditches, four towers and a series of ponds. It also boasted valuable collections of fine art, weaponry, books and family archives. Today, the only resident is the ghost of the Black Dame, who is said to restlessly wander the corridors on moonless nights. Indeed, legend and mystery continue to dominate both this palace and the fortress at Mir. The treasures of the Radzivili family have never been found, although many locations at the two castles have been searched. The dungeons are so large that parts of them are as yet unopened. One of the most intriguing legends is that a cavernous underground passage was constructed between the two, large enough for two coaches to pass side by side. Needless to say, it also has never been found. The beautiful **park and garden** around the palace, which include some delightful ornamental ponds, were not laid out until the late 19th century. The total area is around 100ha, with a number of different styles and appearances to be seen, including a Japanese garden and a Russian wood.

Many of the historic buildings (and most notably the palace) are currently undergoing great works of restoration, although unlike Mir, without the patronage of UNESCO.

Getting there By car, take the same M1 motorway from Minsk towards Brest as if bound for Mir, then take the turn on the P11 road to the south signposted Njasvizh just after the turn for Mir and continue for around 20km. The town is situated on the bus route from Minsk (departing from the central bus station) to Klyetsk, the ride taking around three hours. As with Mir, set aside a full day for Njasvizh.

Where to stay and eat The town has a hotel and a number of restaurants and cafés. Given that independent travel is both time-consuming and complex in rural areas, you will get the best out of a visit by joining an organised excursion from Minsk. You could include a stop here during the course of a day trip to Mir, but that would make for a long day and you would struggle to do justice to either town in the process.

NOVOGRUDOK In the 13th century, Belarus was the nucleus of the great principality of Lithuania and its capital was Novogrudok. The town is dominated by a hill on which the ruins of a 14th-century **castle** stand. At 323m above sea level, the castle hill is one of the highest points in the country and the views over the town and surrounding Nieman River are singularly impressive. At the height of its powers, the town enjoyed extensive trade links with the countries of central Europe, the Baltic, Scandinavia and Byzantium. It also made a huge contribution to the development of the ideas of the Reformation in Belarus. Inevitably, conflict and war gradually weakened its position, so that today, only traces of its former greatness remain. There is little to see of the castle, but the **Farny Transfiguration of the Lord Roman Catholic Church** remains intact at the bottom of the hill. It is a fine example of the 'Sarmat' Baroque style, which is characterised by a fortress-like appearance. The great Belarusian poet Adam Mitskevich was born in Novogrudok and was christened in the church. Other sites within the town relating to the poet include the nearby **Barrow of Immortality**, at the foot of which is a memorial stone, the **sculpture** on the other side of castle hill and the location of the **house** where he was born at number 1, Leninskaya Street, on the original foundations of which now stand a **museum** dedicated to his life and work. In the grounds, certain outbuildings of the original house have been recreated. Elsewhere in the town is another museum devoted to its history and the region. Four other places of worship, two of them Eastern Orthodox, one Roman Catholic and one a mosque are also all worthy of a short visit.

Where to stay and eat The town has three hotels (one of them a health centre) and a number of restaurants, cafés and bars. Situated around 40km northwest of Mir on the P11 road, one way to see it is to pay the town a visit by way of a detour from your excursion to Mir, although as with a trip to Njasvizh, this will make for a long and tiring day. Alternatively, book two separate excursions from Minsk to ensure that you get the chance to enjoy the delights of both at a leisurely pace.

DUDUTKI FOLK MUSEUM (✆ *2 137 25 25 for information;* ⊕ *May–Oct 10.00–20.00 Tue–Sun; admission prices for foreign visitors are US$15 (adults) and US$8 (children), with all other activities extra, including the services of a guide and translator*) Located 35km south of Minsk, near to the village of Dudutki on the banks of the Ptich River, is this former country landowner's estate, where life as it was lived in the 18th and 19th centuries is affectionately recreated. Both an open-air museum (the only one in private hands in the whole country dedicated to traditional crafts and ways of life) and a working farm, there is an original working windmill and other functioning workshops (located in traditional buildings of wood and hay) displaying carpentry, pottery, braiding and other handicrafts, together with a blacksmith, a bakery and a cheese-maker. The craftsmen will be very happy to show off their skills and you will be invited to have a try! Vintage cars are also on display and visitors can take advantage of the *banya* at US$5 per person, as well as taking part in horseriding, sledging and horse-drawn cart rides for around US$15 per hour. There is an outdoor animal enclosure in which wild boar roam (reasonably at leisure) and there is also an ostrich pen, plus runs for standard farm animals such as pigs and goats. For the children, there are horses and rabbits. The atmosphere is extremely relaxed, so you can wander around at will. The riverside paths and farmland tracks make for an inviting backdrop to your lazy meanderings. Then after your exertions, you can visit the excellent **restaurant** (outdoors in good weather) for a splendid meal of locally produced and traditionally cooked fare accompanied (of course) by vodka that is legally distilled on the premises. Bread, cheeses, butter and meat in many forms are all made and reared there. Expect to pay around US$10 per person for your meal. To round off your visit, spend some time in the shop, where you can buy high-quality goods manufactured on the spot at eminently reasonable prices. 'Gypsy performances' and concerts of traditional music are regularly performed, but the best time to visit is during one of the traditional festivals to celebrate, for example, the winter solstice, the arrival of spring, or harvest time, when the whole place is alive with colour and activity. All in all, a visit to this excellent museum is one not to be missed and you could easily spend a whole day here.

To view some excellent photographs and for a background briefing on the history of the site, as well as details of the modern-day activities on offer there, go to www.belarus.net/polyfact before you visit.

Getting there By car, take the P23 road from Minsk, then follow the signs east for 12km. The village is on the bus route from the capital to Ptich, but the nearest stop to the museum is some 2km away. If visiting on a local tour through an agency, most companies allow a half day here, but you will be pushed for time if you want to see and do everything.

ZASLAVL A historic settlement 20km northwest of Minsk, Zaslavl is believed to have been founded in AD985. It was first mentioned in 989 and legend has it that it was the place to which the disgraced Princess Ragneda, the daughter of Polyatsk Prince Ragvolod, was exiled for her attempt upon the life of Kievan Prince Vladimir. Izyaslav, the son of Ragneda and Vladimir left Kiev with his mother for the place that subsequently bore his name. The young prince later received an invitation to come to the throne of the Polyatsk princes, thereby re-establishing its independent dynasty.

Heavily fortified in the 11th century, much of the Zaslavl area has now been designated an area of special archaeological importance. It also boasts the **Reformist Saviour and Transfiguration Church** (built in 1577), where Symon Budny is known to have preached, and the towered **Roman Catholic Church of Mary's Nativity** (built in 1774), a magnificent example of Baroque architecture. Other sights of interest here are the ruins of the castle and its fortifications, the first and the oldest fortification system in Belarus, together with the authentic 19th-century steam mill, the miller's house, an ancient barn, a smithy and a museum of folk art, tapestries and musical instruments.

In 1433, a significant battle took place here between the forces of the mighty and warring neighbours Lithuania and Russia. Each year, historical societies recreate the event in a spectacular festival of great pageantry, including a reconstruction of the siege of the castle. There are concerts of medieval music, interactive sideshows for children and puppet theatre, with shashlik and beer in plentiful supply for the adults.

There is a very informative website (*www.zaslavl.by*). Although it's in Russian only, the photographs are good and the map extremely useful. Half an hour from

Minsk by car or train, probably the best way to see the sights of this town is by means of an organised excursion from Minsk, perhaps in conjunction with a visit to Dudutki. A number of tour operators offer this bespoke package.

RAUBICHY ARTS AND CRAFTS MUSEUM Located 22km from Minsk and less than an hour away by car, this ethnographical museum is situated in the former Krestogorskaya Church. It has numerous displays of folk art from all over the country, including costumes, fabrics, weaving, pottery, carved wood, earthenware and straw goods. Only 10km away is the idyllic **Minsk Lake**, dotted with numerous islets and surrounded by forests of dense pine. Also nearby is the **International Sports Complex**, incorporating ski jumps, shooting grounds, tennis courts, football pitches and an international biathlon course, together with two hotels and a number of eating establishments. Again, organised excursions from Minsk are available.

STROTCHITSY MUSEUM OF EVERYDAY LIFE AND ARCHITECTURE Only half an hour's drive and 12km from the city, this outdoor museum features around 100 buildings from all over the country, including peasant dwellings, taverns, mills, a country school and a church. There are also thousands of exhibits, including kitchenware, tools, earthenware and national costumes.

BELARUSIAN STATE MUSEUM OF FOLK ARCHITECTURE A Skansen-style outdoor museum of century-old buildings from different regions of Belarus, this site is located near to Ozyerto, 15km southwest of the capital and in a very picturesque spot at the confluence of the River Ptich and its tributary the Menka. Many guided tours are available here, together with demonstrations of traditional crafts, including bee-keeping, weaving and linen. Visitors also have the chance to learn about regional folk architecture, as well as myths, legends and fairy tales.

OUT-OF-TOWN MEMORIAL SITES
National Memorial Complex at Khatyn (*Logoysk region, Minsk oblast;* ✆ *745 50 60; 745 57 87 (to arrange guided tours);* e *khatyn@tut.by; www.khatyn.by/en; site* ⊕ *24hrs daily; guided tours and photography exhibition 09.00–17.00 Tue–Sun; admission to the site is free; there is a charge of BYR250 (children and students), BYR1,000 (citizens of Belarus) and BYR2,000 (foreign visitors) for admission to the museum*) If you take only one out-of-town trip while in Minsk, then do try to make it this one. Only 75km from the capital, this memorial complex bears witness to the horrors of Nazi barbarism during the Great Patriotic War. It was constructed on the site of the former village of Khatyn, which was razed to the ground in the spring of 1943 and its inhabitants brutally butchered. At the centre of the complex is a truly astonishing bronze sculpture, the 6m-high *The Unconquered Man*. Before you go, do visit the excellent English-language website (see above) for a full description of the terrible events in 1943 and for further details of the memorial complex that exists today. The tragedy of Khatyn was not just an isolated episode in this tumultuous war, for the experience was replicated many times over on the territory of the Soviet Union. It is said that the inhabitants of 618 Belarusian villages were burned alive during the occupation in SS punishment operations against partisan groups. Of these villages, 185 were never rebuilt and have simply vanished from the face of the earth. Overall, every fourth Belarusian perished during the war: a total of 2.2 million people. This figure included the 380,000 who were deported to Germany as slave labourers, never to return home. A staggering 209 cities and townships and 9,200 villages were destroyed. So catastrophic was the impact on the population that it did not recover to its pre-war total until 1971. Every visitor to Belarus is struck by

Khatyn was once a small but thriving community in a picturesque wooded area, but this hamlet no longer appears on even the most detailed map today, other than as a memorial. The atrocity took place on 22 March 1943, when troops of the occupying German army completely encircled the village. Earlier that day, a skirmish had occurred in the vicinity, when partisans attacked a motor convoy on the highway just 6km away. A German officer was killed in the engagement. Whether or not anyone in the village knew anything about this is a matter of conjecture, but what then happened is beyond understanding even to this day. All of the villagers, young and old, healthy and infirm, women, children and babes in arms were driven from their houses at gunpoint and herded into the barn. No mercy was shown. Among them were Joseph and Anna Baranovsky with their nine children. So too were Alexei and Alexandra Novitsky with their seven children, along with Kazimir and Elena Lotko with their seven children, the youngest of whom was only 12 months old. Vera Yaskevich was also driven into the barn with her seven-week-old son Tolik. Vera's other daughter, little Lena, first tried to hide in the family home, but then she decided to run for the woods. At first she was successful in evading the trailing bullets, but the soldier who ran after her and overtook her showed no mercy, callously gunning her down before the eyes of her helpless and horror-struck father. Among those who found themselves in the wrong place at the wrong time were two people from other villages who by chance were in Khatyn that day.

When everyone was inside the barn, the doors were barred, the roof covered with straw and the building doused in petrol. After setting it alight, soldiers positioned themselves on all sides of the conflagration to machine-gun any of the suffocating people who managed to break out. The village was then looted and the 26 homesteads burned to the ground.

The whole scene is unimaginable. Terror-struck parents hopelessly striving to save their wailing children, throwing them through windows into the murderous gunfire, or else just sheltering them in their arms and with their bodies, helpless and powerless, themselves crying and overcome by panic. People stumbling from the building, their hair and clothes ablaze, straight into a hail of bullets. Choking smoke everywhere, the smell of burning and the deafening screams of despair.

In total, 149 people, including 75 children, were burned alive. The youngest baby was only seven weeks old. Only one of the adults of the village survived; his tale, detailed below,

the large number of war memorials that exist and the extent to which the conflict continues to dominate the national psyche. A visit to Khatyn helps to place all of this into the right context.

So it is to the memory of all of these communities that the vast complex at Khatyn is dedicated. Across a total area of 50ha, the memorial has 26 symbolic chimneys, each with a mournful, tolling bell, to mark the site of each of the 26 houses, the boundaries of which are delineated by low concrete walls with gates, all of them depicted as being open as a metaphor for the hospitality of Belarusian people. Also marked are the sites of the village wells. On the face of each chimney is a plaque bearing the names of each family member who lived there, from aged grandparents to babes only a few weeks old. In itself, this is a truly sombre metaphor, for only the brick chimneys were left standing when the Nazis were burning log houses in Belarusian villages.

As you approach the complex from the car park, the lie of the land slopes gently down to *The Unconquered Man*, who stands facing you. A broad concrete path leads right up to the base of the sculpture, with its centre line planted with flowers. It is only when you visit at flowering time that you appreciate the significance of this, could not be more harrowing. Only three children – Volodya Yaskevich, his sister Sonia and another boy, Sasha Zhelobkovich – had been able to hide from the murderers and would escape death, and by a miracle, two girls from two different families – Maria Fedorovich and Yulia Klimovich – were also spared from death in the barn. Somehow, they managed to escape the fire and crawl to the nearby wood, where they were later found by the inhabitants of the neighbouring village of Khvorosteny, barely alive. But after having survived this horror, the village of Khvorosteny was itself also burned to the ground later in the war. This time, the two girls did not survive. It beggars belief that fate can be so cruel.

Two other children not only escaped from the barn, but also survived the war. They were seven-year-old Viktor Zhelobkovich and 12-year-old Anton Baranovsky. Viktor's mother Anna was holding him firmly by the hand as she staggered through the smoke and flames of the burning barn. Mortally wounded by gunfire, she covered her son's body as she fell. Viktor had been wounded in the arm. He lay on the ground under his mother's corpse until the Nazis finally left the smouldering ruins of the village. Anton Baranovsky was wounded in the leg and also lay still, so as not to be discovered.

As the inhabitants of the neighbouring villages and hamlets slowly picked their way through the ruins, they discovered the two stricken boys, wounded and badly burned. After tending to their wounds, they took them to the orphanage in the small town of Pleshinitsy, where they were raised after the war.

The only adult witness to the massacre at Khatyn was the 56-year-old village blacksmith Joseph Kaminsky. Wounded and severely burned, he did not regain consciousness until late at night, when the fascists were already long gone. As he meticulously searched through the ruins of his village and the bodies that lay there, he came across his injured son amongst the corpses. The poor boy had received bullet wounds to his abdomen and he was severely burned. Joseph tended to his wounds as best he could, but as his father cradled him, he died in his arms.

And so it is that the only human sculpture of the Khatyn memorial complex, *The Unconquered Man* tells the tragic story of Joseph and his son. It is a doleful and harrowing metaphor for the suffering not only of the villagers of Khatyn, but also of all who were bowed under the yoke of oppression and tyranny. When you see this sculpture of bronze for the first time, particularly if you have some prior understanding of what took place here, the power and impact of the image is staggering in its effect.

for the pattern of planting was very deliberately designed to display a long, meandering line of vivid red blooms all the way to the statue: a river of blood.

On your right as you first set foot on this path are two enormous granite plates at an angle. This is the location of the barn in which the villagers were murdered and they represent its collapsed roof. Elsewhere is a mass grave containing the remains of the villagers. There is also a separate cemetery for the other villages that were burned to the ground and are now lost, the symbolic graves bearing an urn containing soil from each one. There is a 'Wall of Grief' to commemorate concentration camp victims, with niches containing memorial plaques detailing the loss of life at each camp. Then set amongst three silver birches symbolising life burns the eternal flame to keep alive the memory of all who lost their lives in the conflict.

In 2004, by decree of the president, further enhancements to the site were undertaken to mark the 60th anniversary of the country's liberation, including the establishment of a small museum and photo-montage to document both the occupation as a whole, this specific atrocity and the history of the memorial complex.

The memory of my first visit here will stay with me for ever. As we walked into the complex on a chilly early spring morning, a rifle shot cracked out in the

Of the five children and one adult who survived the Khatyn massacre, three are still alive.

The village blacksmith Joseph Kaminsky lived for many years in the nearby village of Kozyry after the war. He would often go back to Khatyn and was often to be seen by visitors cutting the grass and tending the site of his former home. He died in 1973 and was buried in Logoysk.

Volodya Yaskevich, who had been born and raised in Khatyn, was subsequently brought up in the orphanage at Pleshinitsy. He studied at vocational school Number 9, before beginning his working life as a turner at the Minsk automobile plant. He served in the Soviet army, before returning to the factory in Minsk in 1952. He then began a new career as a turner and progressed to shop foreman. He retired in 1993 and still lives in the village of Kozyry, the home of Joseph Kaminsky for so long. He has a daughter, a granddaughter, a grandson and a great-grandson.

Sonia Yaskevich was also born in Khatyn and she too lived at the children's home in Pleshinitsy after the atrocity. She studied at vocational school of communication Number 15 in Brest before spending her working life as a typist in a Minsk post office. A pensioner now, she still lives in Minsk. She has two sons and a granddaughter.

Like Volodya and Sonia, Viktor Zhelobkovich was born in Khatyn, then raised in the Pleshinitsy orphanage. After studying at vocational school, he worked as a moulder in a machine tools plant. As with Volodya, he returned there when his army service was over. He then studied at and graduated from university, where he took evening classes specialising in mechanical engineering. He has been working in the design office of a precision engineering company since 1976. He presently lives in Minsk and has a daughter and a granddaughter.

As with the others, Sasha Zhelobkovich was born in Khatyn, then raised at Pleshinitsy. He studied at military school and attended military academy. He served in the armed forces and after retirement, he continued as a reservist lieutenant-colonel. He died in 1994.

After leaving the orphanage, Anton Baranovsky lived in Minsk, but died in tragic circumstances in 1969.

distance. It was probably hunters in the nearby woods. But the effect on us all was both immediate and startling. I have visited a number of times since and I have never failed to be deeply moved. I have taken several Belarusian friends there for their first visit. All were moved to tears. The mournful monotone of the tolling bells in the silence that pervades all around acts as a summons, inviting you to look, learn and never forget.

There are two important contextual points to bear in mind in all of this. First – following the liberation of the Soviet Union, a rampant Red Army took terrible revenge on the civilian population of Germany as the Nazi forces were driven back over the Rhine; then secondly (and with huge irony) – this memorial complex at Khatyn should not be confused with the Katyn Forest memorial, located east of here (and 20km outside Smolyensk in Russia), where in 1943, German forces uncovered the mass graves of more than 22,000 Polish officers and civilians shot by the NKVD on Stalin's orders. Only after the disintegration of the Soviet Union was vicarious responsibility for this atrocity accepted by Russia.

Getting there By car, take the M3 motorway north out of Minsk in the direction of Vitebsk. After 70km, take the right turn signposted Хатынь. The complex is located 5km along that road. There is no reliable access by means of public transport.

'Stalin Line' Historical and Cultural Site As Europe stumbled towards conflict in the 1930s and paranoia gripped the national psyche of countries across the continent, most foreign policies became increasingly obsessed with defence and self-protection. The Soviet Union was no exception. All along the western border of the USSR, from the Baltic to the Black Sea, Stalin ordered a network of defensive military fortifications to be built. In all, 23 fortified zones were built, four of them within the territory of Belarus. At that time, the border was a mere 40km from Minsk. In concept and design, it matched the Maginot line along France's eastern border and it was intended to serve the same purpose.

This network became known as the 'Stalin Line' and on 30 June 2005, a precise reconstruction of a section of the historical layout covering 40ha was ceremonially unveiled in the presence of the president himself, resplendent in full military uniform, near the town of Zaslavl, 35km from the capital. Incorporating authentic equipment from the time (complete with dents from shells and bullet holes), it is an open-air museum of military fortifications, including the defence line itself with trenches, anti-tank obstacles and ditches, anti-personnel obstacles and machine-gun pillboxes Today, visitors can walk around a pillbox and sit in a gun emplacement, stroll along the trench system and clamber over a tank. There is also a museum of military exhibits. Escorted tours are available from guides dressed in uniforms of the day. There are plans to enlarge the facilities available to include a restaurant where you can sample rations as eaten by soldiers of the day, but no work has yet begun on this.

The excellent website (*www.stalin-line.by.com*) is sadly in Russian only, but even without the language, the photographs and maps are extremely interesting.

If you do not have your own car, the complex is best accessed by means of a local excursion from Minsk. The cost per person will be around US$40, with the option of a guide and translator for the group at a cost of US$70. A more costly option (but much better value for money) will be to combine your visit with a trip to the memorial complex at Khatyn (above) and the Mount of Glory (see below) at the same time. Expect to pay around US$100 each for this, with the price of admission to the sites themselves and all extras on top.

'Mount of Glory' To honour the glorious victory of the Red Army over the fascist invaders, this monument atop a manmade hill consisting of scorched earth and soil brought from the nine 'hero cities' of the USSR and battlegrounds of the Great Patriotic War is visible for miles around. Created to mark the 25th anniversary of the liberation of the country from the Nazi occupation, it is located 21km out of the city centre at the side of the main highway to Moscow (where it joins the road to Minsk-2 International Airport). It stands an imposing 70m off the ground at its zenith and is situated in the vicinity of the last battle in the war to take place on Belarusian soil. It consists of four titanium-covered bayonets pointing directly to the sky, representing the four fronts on which divisions of the Red Army, partisans and members of other underground organisations successfully completed the liberation of the country. At the base is a golden circle, upon which images of the faces of soldiers and partisans have been sculpted, along with heroic inscriptions to the glory of the Red Army.

A row of tanks and other assorted military hardware lines the car park at the base of the mound and there is also a café selling the usual refreshments (with an outdoor barbecue area for national holidays and special commemorations). A concrete path winds around the mount to give access on foot to the obelisk itself and the entirety of the memorial stands in 26h of parkland, in which are displayed sculptures of wood depicting folk art.

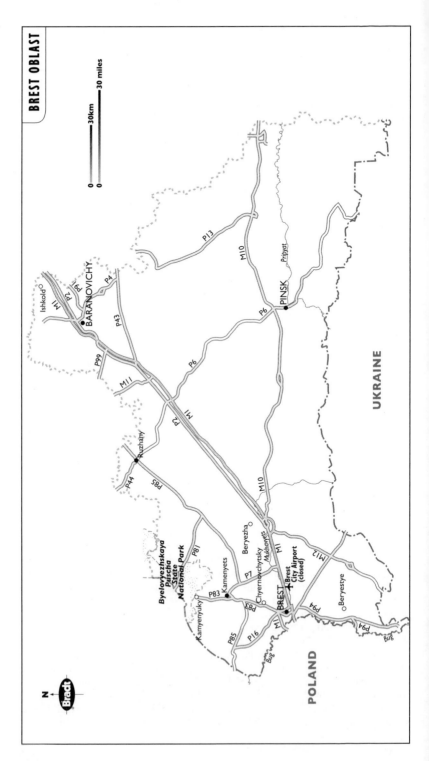

BREST OBLAST

30km
30 miles

Ishkold
BARANOVICHY
P2
P4
P4
P43
P99
M11
M1
P3
Ruzhany
P44
P85
Byelovyezhskaya
Pushcha
State
National Park
P81
Beryezha
Mukhavets
Kamenyets
P7
Chyernovchytsky
Brest
City Airport
(closed)
BREST
Kamyenyuky
P83
P83
P85
P16
M1
M12
Beryestye
Bug
Bug
Bug
POLAND
UKRAINE
P13
M10
Pripyat
PINSK
P6
P6
M10
P94
P94
P83

N

Bradt

4

Brest City and Oblast
Брест

Located in the southwestern corner of Belarus, Brest region has borders with both Poland and Ukraine. The administrative and cultural capital of the *oblast* is the city of Brest itself, which has a population of around 300,000. Only a short distance from the Polish border at the confluence of the Western Bug and Mukhavyets rivers, Brest is closer to Warsaw (200km) than to Minsk (350km). Its geographical position on the main Berlin–Moscow railway line and on the major intercontinental highway from west to east, together with its historical location as the crossing point on which trading routes from all points of the compass converged, has afforded the development over time of a unique environment for different cultures to meet and evolve together. It is very much the case, though, that Western influences predominate here. Brest people, they themselves think, are very outward looking with a greater understanding of life in the West than their more insular compatriots further east. Furthermore, the position of the city, right on the western extremity of first, the Russian Empire, then latterly the Soviet Union, has bestowed upon it enormous strategic importance in times of war and peace. Today, Brest is not only a principal border crossing, but also a bridge: in cultural terms, between eastern and western Europe and politically, between the European Union and the Commonwealth of Independent States. This manifests itself in a number of ways, the quaintest of which is that travellers by train are delayed for several hours here, because of the change in gauge of the track. This means that passengers must watch while their carriage is physically lifted from its Western bogie and placed on another that fits the narrower track in use in the East! All in all, the city very much feels like a major border crossing with a great deal of energetic hustle and bustle, but at the same time, there is a calm and relaxed side that speaks of charm, grace and elegance. In keeping with the city's reputation for energy is a growing culture of sporting activity and fitness. A number of sports complexes have been constructed to international standards and increasing numbers of national and international events are held within the city. I discovered this to my cost on my last visit, which coincided with the opening of the first Eurasian Games, such that there wasn't an available hotel room to be found in the whole of the city.

There are many delightful avenues that are just right for promenading in this splendid city with cosmopolitan restaurants, bars and cafés, where you can stop and watch the world go by. Just watch out for the gargantuan pot-holes in the roads all over the city, even on main streets.

The establishment of the free economic zone over 50 years ago has helped to create an environment in which trade can flourish with confidence. Poland's entry into the European Union in 2004 will also have helped support trade, but the city's greatest claim to fame is its fortress, sited on an island and made legendary by the great heroism and deeds of sacrifice of its defenders during the Great Patriotic War.

Although not on the grand scale of Minsk, there is much to interest the visitor in the architecture of the city. A number of examples of the imposing neo-Classical style so favoured in the last decades of the Russian Empire can be found here (especially in and around the central station square). Not surprisingly, there is also much that is reminiscent of Poland, particularly the Roman Catholic churches, while a number of Orthodox churches are particularly pleasing on the eye. Also worth an hour or two of your time is a slow stroll along the bank of the Mukhavyets River, a pastime much favoured by promenaders of all ages. Just beware of the mosquitoes, so be sure to button up. The river runs east–west and is parallel to Masherova Avenue, half a kilometre to the south of this main thoroughfare. There are pleasant gardens and walkways on the northern bank.

The whole southern part of this region has its own natural and ethno-cultural identity as the Belarussian Polyesye. The main waterway flowing through it from west to east (as far as Chernobyl in Ukraine and beyond) is the Pripyat River and its many tributaries. This is a unique natural environment and 12 reserves and 29 other protected areas have been set up here with the objective of affording it as much protection as possible. Pride of place goes to the world-renowned state national park and biosphere reserve of Byeloyyezhskaya Puscha, a unique medieval woodland area 65km to the north of the city (see page 154).

The territory of Brest *oblast* is rich in culture. There are around 120 historical parks and estates, together with over 2,000 buildings and monuments of historical interest. There is a Byeloyyezhskaya Puscha museum in the village of Kamyenyuky, in the district of Kamenets. It is in that district, standing between the city and the reserve, that one of the most widely recognised national symbols of Belarus is to be found, the Byelaya Vyezha (the White Tower). Amongst the oldest of the sites is the settlement of Beryestye, which has buildings dating from the 11th and 12th centuries, whilst local people are particularly fond of the Roman Catholic church in the original 'Belarussian Gothic' style in the village of Ishkold (Baranovichy district), the Roman Catholic Renaissance church in the village of Chyernovchytsy (Brest district), the Monastery of the Cartesian Order in Beryezha and the church of Saint George in the village of Synkovichy (Lunynyets district). Also of great interest are the part-ruined remains of the 17th–18th-century Sapyegazh Palace in Ruzhany, with its imposing façade of columns and elegant galleries. Finally, the ancient museum town of Pinsk, situated 150km east of Brest, still retains its charm and beauty.

HISTORY

The city of Brest has long been regarded as the traditional Western gate of the country, a city with a glorious and valiant history across the centuries, complemented by a vibrant and hopeful present and future. It was first mentioned in the 'Story of Temporal Years' Chronicle in 1019 as Beryestye, in the context of the struggle for the crown of Kievan Rus between Duke Svyatopolk of Turov and Duke Yaroslav the Wise of Novgorod. A number of theories exist as to the original derivation of its name. Some believe that it comes from one or two Slavic words meaning either 'birch bark' or 'elm', while others are of the opinion that it is Lithuanian in origin, from the word meaning 'ford'. The preponderance of forest and the confluence of two major rivers here mean that either is possible. Brest developed over time as a frontier town and trading centre on the western fringes of Kievan Rus, a wooden castle being built there in the 12th century on the site of the current fortress. The historical chapters of this book repeatedly show how, for many hundreds of years, the territories of Belarus have been the rope in a tug-of-war between powerful and aggressive states on its borders. The strategic location of Brest ensured that it was a regular target for subjugation and it featured heavily in a number of bloody engagements. Early in the 13th century it was part of the Grand Duchy of Lithuania, having formally been a Polish town, before being sacked by the Mongol Horde in 1241. Then in 1390, it became the first city on Belarussian territory to be granted self-determination and government under Magdeburg Law, only a short period after suffering significant structural damage at the hands of the Teutonic Order. .

As its cultural and social influence grew, it became more and more the location for key events. Meetings of certain of the state's most significant *sejms*, or parliamentary bodies with limited powers of local self-determination, were held here; and in 1553, a Calvinist cathedral and printing house were established under Duke Nikolas Radzvili the Black, where in 1558, one of the best known of all Renaissance books was printed, the Brest Bible. In 1569, it became part of the mighty Polish-Lithuanian Commonwealth. In 1596, it hosted the historic council which established the Eastern Catholic (or Uniate) Church to reconcile (or perhaps forge a compromise between) Roman Catholic and Eastern Orthodox believers. Conflict returned in the 17th century, when Brest was first invaded by Russia (in 1654) and then all but destroyed in a series of wars involving Sweden. It was eventually restored to Russian hands in 1795 and renamed Brest-Litovsk on the occasion of the further partition of the Polish-Lithuania Commonwealth. The mighty fortress was constructed between 1836 and 1842, not only as a citadel for the protection of this frontier town, but also as a major component in the defensive structure of the giant Russian Empire. Unfortunately, however, it wasn't enough to protect the city and it fell to the Germans in 1915.

In March 1918, in a ceremony as heavy with symbolism as the fortress itself, Lenin's Bolshevik government concluded the Peace Treaty of Brest-Litovsk with Germany, bringing World War I to an end on the Eastern Front. In this treaty, Lenin ceded vast swathes of territory (Poland, the Baltic lands and much of Belarus and Ukraine), including of course, Brest. This was a master stroke of political compromise and expediency on the part of the newly installed Bolshevik government, which was struggling to impose authority back home. On the face of it, the deal appears to have been a major defeat, but Lenin had little choice: quite simply, the enormous and so-called 'invincible' army of the Russian Empire had collapsed in anarchy and total disorder. In tens of thousands, ordinary soldiers had given up the fight and were trudging home. Mutiny was everywhere. Domestically, all was in chaos and disarray following the Revolution in November 1917. But crucially, the peace bought Lenin enough breathing space to establish and consolidate Bolshevik control over the organs of the state.

The victorious Western powers overturned the German–Russian treaty as part of the settlement that came out of the Versailles Conference in 1919. Under the Treaty of Versailles, the restored but fledgling Polish state took control of Brest that year from the Germans, although during the conflict that ensued between Poland and the Soviet Union, the fate of the city was for it to move from the control of one state to another on a number of occasions. At the conclusion of the war, Brest was under the control of Poland and the 1921 Treaty of Riga formally ratified this position. In essence, for the inhabitants of the city, all of this meant that it was located far within the Polish border from 1921 until the outbreak of World War II.

The fortress suffered very heavy damage during World War I, but it still retained its strategic importance and after the conclusion of the 1921 treaty, it housed a significant Polish military presence. The garrison was pressed into service during the Nazi invasion of Poland in the early days of September 1939, when only four battalions stood shoulder to shoulder to defend the city against the formidable and overwhelming motorised force of the 19th Panzer Corps commanded by highly

4

respected General Heinz Guderian. An intense and bloody battle ensued over four days, before the Poles withdrew. For a while, the focus of attention was diverted from the city, but Brest was annexed by the Soviet Union later that year under the secret (and shameful) Molotov-Ribbentrop Pact. In this unholy alliance of diametrically opposed totalitarian dogmas, the USSR and Nazi Germany callously carved up the sovereign Polish state for themselves, as the democracies of western Europe turned their backs and looked away, in the climate of appeasement that prevailed at the time. But the inhabitants of Brest (and the peoples of the greater Belarussian territories) had no interest in political expediency. In the eyes of many, the single consequence of this act was to bring about the rightful reunification of a single Belarussian nation under the constituency of the Belarussian SSR. Sadly, though, the grim reality was that the Nazis were soon to turn up in force on the western bank of the Bug River, almost at the same time as Soviet forces began to mass on the eastern side.

So it was that the peace was short-lived and the city was first in the line of fire when the Germans attacked the USSR without warning on 22 June 1941 under Operation Barbarossa. The city itself fell within a few hours, but this was the start of the most stirring period of history for the fortress. The unparalleled feats of heroism and courage of its defenders in the weeks that followed have passed into legend. Not without good reason did a grateful nation subsequently bestow the title of 'Hero-fortress' (the city also being granted the status of 'Hero City of the Soviet Union', one of 13 throughout the USSR to be honoured thus). Those soldiers who were first to feel the might and fury of the Nazi war machine somehow held out throughout the summer of 1941 in conditions of intense attrition. Their bravery and self-sacrifice in holding back the invasion for six long weeks (as supplies of food and drinking water dwindled to nothing) gave the rest of the Soviet Union just enough time to gather itself for the withering onslaught that was to follow. To see now the vivid red-brick walls of the fortress, pock-marked and riddled with machine-gun fire, is to gain some understanding of the enormity of the unfolding events that summer. By the time the fortress finally fell, nearly all of the defending troops had been killed. With tragic poignancy and as an enduring mark of their ultimate sacrifice, the last of them had inscribed in large letters on the wall of one of the barracks 'I am dying but not surrendering. Farewell, Motherland!' By this time, the fortress was deep behind enemy lines, almost all of Belarussian territory being by this time under the yoke of Nazi oppression. The years of tyrany that followed were brutal in the extreme. Brest's Jewish population was all but wiped out during the course of 1942, as was the case throughout the whole country, before the Red Army liberated the city in July 1944. The latest chapter in the long history of this cosmopolitan city was begun in February 1945 at the peace conference conducted by the Western powers at Yalta, when it was formally restored to the sovereignty of the Belarussian SSR and the greater Soviet Union. Upon the disintegration of the USSR, Brest became part of the newly created independent nation state of Belarus.

GETTING THERE AND AWAY

The local **airport** is 12km east of the city. Built in the 1970s, it used to operate weekly flights to the capital Minsk and to 15 cities in the old Soviet Union, including Moscow, Kiev and Novgorod. At the time of writing, however, it was closed for commercial flights and there were no apparent plans to reopen it for this purpose. If air travel is your preferred option, then take one of the scheduled routes either to Minsk or Warsaw, then complete your journey by train.

There is easy access from the West and the city finds itself on two major trans-European routes: Brussels to Irkutsk and Vienna to St Petersburg. Furthermore, every single **train** from Berlin to Moscow stops here. Most travellers journey by means of the daily sleeper train that departs from the central railway station in Warsaw for its equivalent in Brest. The journey time is around four hours and the cost of a single ticket is US$15. From Berlin, the sleeper is much more expensive (around US$55). Alternatively, take a train from the Polish border town of Terespol, for the princely sum of € 1. Unfortunately the central railway station in Brest isn't very central and you will need to take a short cab ride into the heart of the city, or hop on any of the buses that pass right in front of the station, a large, neo-Classical building of archetypically pre-Revolutionary grandeur. Built between 1833 and 1866, it is still one of the city's iconic buildings. Indeed, in its heyday, it was one of the most elegant and sumptuous railway stations in the whole of the Russian Empire, before it metamorphosed to bear the mark of classical post-war Stalinist design. It is divided into northern and southern sections, for trains travelling westwards and eastwards respectively. A large and very long station hall divides the two. The usual facilities are on offer, including kiosks for the sale of cigarettes and light refreshments, a luggage store and currency exchange. There is also a restaurant with surprisingly good standards of food and cuisine. All of the facilities are billed as being available 'round the clock', but in reality, it would be unwise to count on this much beyond nine in the evening. Red tape is a painful experience because of the proximity to the national border and every passenger must go through customs and immigration before proceeding onto the platform.

Internally, the rail service to Grodno has been suspended until further notice, but the daily services to Vitsebsk and Gomel are still running. The journey to Minsk on the express from Berlin will take approximately four hours. The electric commuter train is much cheaper (only US$6), but it takes a very tedious seven hours to get there.

Brest is situated on the main transcontinental **coach** route, but although this is a cheap option, the journey times are long and uncomfortable. The bus station is situated in the middle of the city, on Mitskevich Street (✆ *004 for public service information, or 23 81 42 for direct access*). There are daily buses to Grodno within Belarus and to Warsaw and Lvov in Poland. There is also a weekly service to Prague.

And there *should* be easy access by **car** on the main highway that crosses the border here. The Brest crossing is located at the Warsaw Bridge but it is a place of some notoriety, for no other reason than the apparently capricious nature of the guards. Unexpectedly long delays can be experienced, entirely without warning and apparently at the whim of the border guards on duty. Some of the tales told by travellers are approaching legend and waits of up to 12, 24 and even 36 hours have been reported. The average wait appears to be between two and six hours. It is rumoured that the guards are not immune to the odd monetary inducement to hasten the process, but this is singularly not advised. Just sit tight and admire the view; of a line of stationary and immobile vehicles snaking into the distance.

GETTING AROUND

There is no underground system in Brest, but the city centre is compact and most of the sights and facilities are within easy reach of each other. Cabs, buses and trolleybuses are all cheap, efficient, plentiful and easy to use.

Orientation is relatively easy. Apart from the fortress, many of the pre-war buildings are inevitably no longer standing and streets in the city centre were laid

4

out in the trademark chequerboard style so favoured by post-war urban planners. The square in front of the train station is expansive and the large thoroughfare that leads out of it in a straight (southerly) line is Lenin Street, halfway along which can be found Lenin Square, where the old revolutionary continues to stand guard on his plinth, just across the street from the square itself, which is actually in the shape of a crescent. It has been pedestrianised and is attractively laid in bricks of different hues. This is the administrative centre of the city: the House of the Soviet, the offices of the regional and city executive committees and the regional office of the National Bank of the Republic are all to be found here. There is also Saint Christopher's Church. The tourist area of the city, where many of the shops, bars and restaurants are to be found, begins with the pedestrianised end of Pushkinskaya Street, which runs directly opposite Lenin's statue on the other side of the square. Three blocks to the east is Sovyetskaya Street, which is in the heart of the main shopping area. There are also many bars and street cafés here. At the time of writing, Sovyetskaya Street itself was in the course of being developed for pedestrian use only, to match sections of other streets in the area. When the building site has gone, this whole area will be extremely attractive. Already in places, the street scene has been transformed by the addition of attractive lighting, paved areas and furniture. Most sites of interest are located within the compact centre, but the notable exception is the one thing that really is a 'must-see', the hero fortress. It can be found to the southwest of the centre at the bottom of Masherova Avenue, 2km away.

TOURIST INFORMATION

As highlighted previously, it is not always possible to find comprehensive tourist information in Belarus. If there is no information facility in Minsk, then you wouldn't expect to find one in Brest either. How refreshing it is, then, to happen upon a state tourism office inside the Hotel Intourist, at 15 Masherova Avenue (\ 20 05 10; ⊕ 08.00–18.00 Mon–Fri). Turn immediately right as you enter the lobby and take the stairs in the corner to the first floor. What a find it is! The staff are extremely accommodating and only too pleased to help with bookings for guided excursions anywhere in the country. Excellent English is spoken and there is a good stock of tourist literature (in English) on the city and region. English-speaking guides are also on hand to lead any excursions and visits that you might book. Given the paucity of tourist and traveller information anywhere else in the entire country, the value of this facility is impossible to overstate. Any visit to the city really should start here.

A great many national and local tourist agencies have offices in the city (19 at the last count), with new ones appearing all the time. All will be able to book local excursions for you, but not all of them are licensed, so a degree of caution is advisable.

The most well known of these companies, a national agency with a branch office in the city, is **Top-tour** (*120 Kosmonavtov St;* \ *22 02 92/14 13;* e *brest@toptour.by; www.toptour.by*).

Before you leave home, you might find it useful to browse the site www.brest.by. Some pages are in English and the link to information relating to the Byeloyyezhskaya Puscha National Park is especially helpful. Best of all are the pages relating to the heroic fortress siege. Extremely well written, they tell the story in great detail, with some excellent photographs. There is also a large 'photo album' of numerous scenes around the city. Great works of photographic creative art they most certainly are not, but they do give you some idea of what to expect when you arrive.

WHERE TO STAY

Hotel Intourist (122 rooms, 10 suites, 2 apts) 15 Masherova Av; ℡ 162 20 20 83; f 162 22 19 00. Located on the main city thoroughfare leading to the fortress (25 mins' walk from the bus & railway stations), this conveniently located hotel is a prime example of post-war Soviet urban planning. It is a charmless, high-rise concrete monolith, but is nonetheless functional & all basic needs are adequately catered for. There are 62 sgl & 60 twin rooms, plus 10 2-roomed suites & 2 apts. All have the usual facilities. There is a restaurant, 3 bars (one of them 24hr), a banqueting hall, casino, massage room, hairdresser, travel agency, currency exchange & an ATM in the lobby. There is an extra charge for parking nearby in a secure area. All major credit cards are accepted. English is spoken here. *From US$40–60 pp, per night, room & inc buffet b/fast.*

Hotel Belarus (153 rooms, 11 suites) 6 Shevchenko Bd; ℡ 22 16 48; f 22 16 58; e bresttourist@tut.by. Situated in a picturesque location close to the Mukhavyets River (45 mins' walk from the bus & railway stations), this is another functional hotel with the usual facilities & little aesthetic appeal. There is also supervised parking onsite, a shop, travel agency, a dentist (!), a hairdresser, currency-exchange facilities, a massage room, solarium, games room, a conference 'hall' with seating for 18, a restaurant, café & a bar. A casino & bowling alley are located next door. All major credit cards are accepted. *From US$35–45 pp, per night, room & inc buffet b/fast.*

Hotel Vyesta (47 rooms, 12 suites) 16 Krupskaya St; ℡ 23 78 29/71 69; f 23 78 39. Located downtown (10 mins' walk from the bus & railway stations) in a green & peaceful neighbourhood, but guess what? It's another concrete box! Don't let this put you off though, because this place is quite a find & inside, all is rather quaint & cosy. There are 30 sgl & 16 dbl/twin rooms, 1 trpl & 12 suites. Recently refurbished in part, some of the furniture & décor is new, but unexciting. If you can, get one of the older rooms, with wood panelling & 1920s-style décor. Although the unpretentious nature of the hotel lends a certain homely charm, facilities here are somewhat limited; there is a hairdresser, massage room, sauna, 'business centre', café-bar & 1 restaurant. All major credit cards are accepted, but no English is spoken. *Sgl from US$49, dbl from US$76, suite from US$95, rising to US$184, all inc b/fast.*

Hotel Bug (named after the river, one hopes!) 2 Lenin St; ℡ 23 61 70/64 17. Only 3 mins from the railway station on foot, this large & imposing building matches the station itself for grandeur, but inside, it's dark & gloomy, with old-style Soviet service matching the old-style Soviet décor. The restaurant here is unspectacular. *From US$20 pp, per night, room & inc buffet bfast.*

WHERE TO EAT

Brest is a cosmopolitan city with a direct and very large window overlooking the West, so the diversity of food emporia reflects this, although restaurants are not in plentiful supply. Most establishments are of a similar standard in terms of quality and cost, so do experiment. To get the ball rolling, look out for the following:

RESTAURANTS

U Ozero On the shore of the Upper Lake, Brest City Park; ℡ 23 57 63; ⊕ 11.00–01.00. This is a real find & not to be missed. Right by the side of the largest ornamental lake in the city's most beautiful park, this café nestles amongst delightful weeping willows. In the summer, you can sit beneath them, on the terrace, sipping chilled Baltika beer as you watch your shashlik cooking on the BBQ. Traditional Belarussian fare, such as *draniki*, is also available on the menu, along with more substantial main course dishes. *US$10 & upwards.*

Santa Fish Restaurant & Bar 7 Ordzhonikidza St (opposite the central railway station); ℡ 26 36 05; ⊕ 11.00–23.00. Exotic seafood & fish dishes of the highest quality. The prices reflect this. A rarity for this city is that an English translation of the menu is available. Excellent service. *US$30 & upwards for main courses.*

Zio Pepe 4 Shevchenko; ℡ 20 50 53; ⊕ 11.00–04.00. Standard pasta & pizza restaurant, but it's cheap & open all night, largely because it shares the premises with a nightclub & casino. There is also a bar. *Around US$10 for a main course, with drinks extra.*

Restaurant Jules Verne 29 Gogolya St (at the junction with Karl Marksa St); ℡ 23 67 17; ⊕ 12.00–midnight. This is my personal favourite. As you might expect from the name, the décor is pure

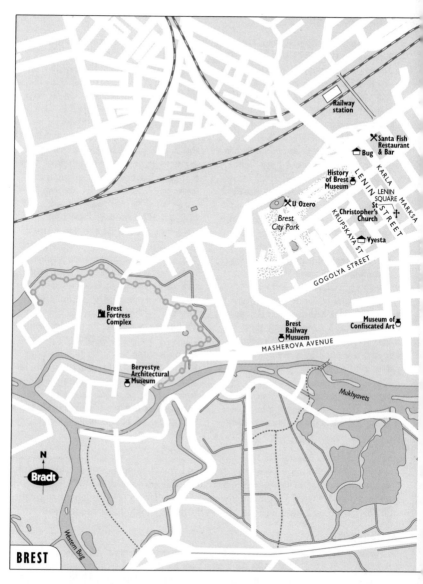

Brest map showing:

- Railway station
- Santa Fish Restaurant & Bar
- Bug
- History of Brest Museum
- U Ozero
- Brest City Park
- LENIN STREET
- KARLA MARKSA
- LENIN SQUARE
- Christopher's Church
- KRUPSKAYA ST
- Vyesta
- GOGOLYA STREET
- Brest Fortress Complex
- Brest Railway Musuem
- Museum of Confiscated Art
- MASHEROVA AVENUE
- Beryestye Architectural Museum
- Mukhyovets
- N
- Bradt
- Western Bug

BREST

Victoriana, with dark wood panelling, mock oil lamps & sepia etchings on the walls. But it's all very tastefully done & the food is excellent. Self-billed as offering 'world cuisine', northern European (particularly German & Scandinavian) & Indian & Thai cuisine are on offer in a comfortable & relaxed setting. We chose

CAFÉS

✗ **Café Magellan** (just before the junction with Komsomolskaya St) ⏰ 10.00–midnight. A personal favourite as a daytime 'shopping' eatery.

Indian & my chicken *massaman* with vegetables & garlic chilli nan was outstanding. The menu is available in English & there is even a special menu for children. Good service & willing staff complement the experience. This place is highly recommended. *Around US$10 for a main course, with drinks extra.*

✗ **Pizzeria** Pushkinskaya St (just beyond junction with Sovyetskaya St). A favourite basement hang-out.
✗ **Zyevs** Next to the Pizzeria. Excellent coffee bar.

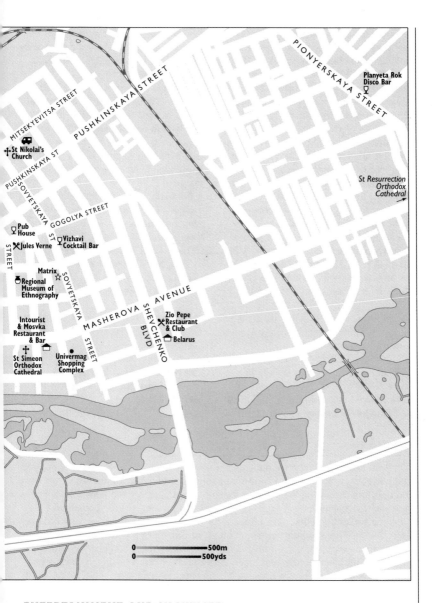

ENTERTAINMENT AND NIGHTLIFE

You would expect to find a wide choice of bars in a city such as this and you won't be disappointed. The following is a reasonable cross-section of what is on offer, but there will be others I haven't yet seen that are equally worthy of mention. If you find any, please write and let me know. All of the bars are open from late morning until 23.00 or midnight, while the clubs do not open until around 20.00, but you can dance the night away until at least 04.00.

♀ **Bar 'Pub House'** Gogolya St; ⏱ 12.00–midnight. Absolutely ideal for a relaxing drink after a

sumptuous meal at the Restaurant Jules Verne opposite (see *Where to Eat* above), this is a cosy, quiet & comfortable bar. Neither busy nor empty on any of my visits, it's a great place to relax & chat.

♀ **Vizhavi Cocktail Bar** 50 Sovyetskaya St; ☎ 23 05 50/14 94; ⏰ 12.00–23.00. Located right in the heart of town, this is a good place to stop off for a drink in the middle of your sightseeing or shopping. Alternatively, come here first to kick-start a night on the tiles.

☆ **Planyeta Rok Disco Bar** 48 Pionyerskaya St; ☎ 46 64 83; ⏰ 12.00–late. As befits the name ('Planet Rock'), this is a loud, brassy venue with thumping music in constant attendance. Relaxing it isn't, but if you're in the mood to burn off some calories on the dance floor with gassy beer for refreshment, this is the place for you. The location, on the northwestern fringe of the city centre, is not ideal.

♀ **Moskva Restaurant & Bar** 17 Masherova Av; ☎ 20 43 23/10 93; ⏰ 12.00–midnight. Right next door to the Hotel Intourist, it looks classy on a cursory glance, but it has always been empty when I've been there. The menu is not unappealing, but it's all just a little tired & sad. Still, if you're staying at the Intourist & not feeling particularly adventurous, it will serve a purpose.

☆ **Club Matrix** 73 Sovyetskaya St; ☎ 23 82 39; ⏰ 20.30–03.30. Standard club facilities that you can find the world over, but this place is actually quite hip & its central location means that it's easy to get there & easy to bale out when you get bored or tired. The name is a bit of a clue & aficionados of the cult movie series won't be disappointed.

☆ **Club Vesuviy** 108 Souvorov St; ☎ 43 03 80; ⏰ 20.00–04.00. Interchangeable with the Matrix in terms of facilities, but it's a very long way southeast of the city centre, in a suburban location.

☆ **Club Zio Pepe** 4 Shevchenko St; ☎ 20 50 52; ⏰ 20.00–04.00. The nightclub & casino arm of the Italian restaurant (see *Where to eat* above) has little to complement your pizza there. Standard club fare.

In addition, the following are all worthy of a visit for the purpose of your own research. All are either centrally located or else on major streets with easy access by public transport:

🖵 **Café Kosmos** 92 Kosmonatov St; ☎ 26 55 15/60 71

♀ **Bar Molodyeny** 6 Komsomolskaya St; ☎ 26 45 31

🖵 **Café Vyesta** 16 Krupskaya St; ☎ 23 78 35/39

♀ **Bar Vizit** 50 Sovyetskaya St; ☎ 23 14 94

♀ **Yubilyeny Restaurant & Bar** 328 Moskovsky St; ☎ 42 37 38/23 48

SHOPPING

Look no further than the central area bounded by Lenin, Gogolya, Kyubisheva and Mitsekyevitsa streets for all of your purchasing requirements. Sovyetskaya Street runs north–south through it. Most of the best of the city's stores and boutiques are here and the convenience of a single, easily navigable location is too good to miss. On Sovyetskaya itself (on the left heading south, just beyond the Church of Saint Nikolai) is a children's store, selling clothes and toys. Elsewhere in this area are many outlets selling fine sweets, presents, souvenirs, fashionable clothes and beauty products. To recharge your batteries, there are many bars and cheap eateries where you can obtain fast but tasty food and refreshments. My personal favourites are the Café Magellan and, in the other direction, the adjacent Pizzeria and Zyevs (see page 144).

I also have it on good authority from my friend Olya that the Univermag shopping complex on Masherova Avenue, 200m east of the Hotel Intourist, is an excellent source of good-value shopping. Clothes, beauty products, traditional souvenirs and other 'present material' are all available here at very competitive prices, she tells me.

OTHER PRACTICALITIES

Currency-exchange bureaux are easy to find in this border town and as it is a free economic zone, foreign currency is in plentiful supply. A useful tip is to have not only Belarussian roubles and US dollars with you, but also small supplies of euros and Polish zloty. After all, Poland is only a very short walk away!

There are also plenty of banks. ATMs are appearing in increasing numbers, but they are not always maintained and stocked, so service can be a little hit-and-miss.

And there is an excellent post office at the top of Pushkinskaya Street (at the Lenin Street end), on the left-hand side as you enter Lenin Square.

Credit cards are not widely in use and may be viewed with suspicion. The concept of travellers' cheques is not understood and they are very difficult to cash. Crisp notes are far and away the best option here.

WHAT TO SEE AND DO

BREST FORTRESS Брестская крепость (*Masherova Av;* \ *20 03 65/00 12;* ⊕ *08.00– midnight Mon–Sun; admission free*) The largest tourist attraction in the city, a visit here is one of the truly 'not to be missed' events during the whole of your stay in Belarus, let alone your limited time in Brest. To do it full justice, you will need to give yourself at least four hours to see everything there is to see. The walk here from the city centre will take around 30 minutes; alternatively, there is an hourly bus service, which stops at points along Masherova Avenue, the main road running straight and true past the Hotel Intourist.

The location was very well chosen by the planners, because the complex holds a strategically important position at the confluence of the Bug and Mukhavyets rivers. It occupies a huge site, its diameter being around 1km, although much of the outer defence line was obliterated in the terrible fighting that took place here in 1941. The stronghold within occupies a small island in the centre of the river, which is connected to the remainder of the structure by three small bridges.

This geographical location was thought to be so important (and the strategic need for the fortress so great), that when it was built in the four-year period from 1838, it was actually necessary to move the whole town, in its entirety, 2km to the east to accommodate the new complex. In fact, the one single piece of architecture from pre-1838 Brest that still exists is situated right in the middle of it. The beautiful **Byzantine Church of Saint Nikolai** (not to be mistaken for its namesake on Sovyetskaya Street) was severely damaged during the 1941 siege and reduced almost to rubble. While the exterior has been mostly renovated, its golden dome being a particularly striking feature, much remains to be done to the interior, although services are regularly held here. For now, the walls are bare brick and plaster (there are neither friezes nor murals), but this throws into even sharper relief the beautiful icons that are mounted in many places. And right in the centre of the church is its most beautiful feature: a huge golden chandelier, delicately suspended from the ceiling almost to head height, adorned with icons and ceremonial *rushniki*. As you pass through the main door, turn immediately right to view the small but informative pictorial display in black and white that reveals the church at various stages of splendour and misery through its cyclical construction and destruction. It is something of an oddity to find such a sanctuary of reverence and piety in this location, when all around tells of conflict and aggression. Devotional objects such as small icons and candles are available for purchase inside in the right-hand corner immediately after you enter.

The fortress had an important defensive role to play in World War I, after which it was used mainly for housing soldiers in the 1920s and 1930s. In 1941, it came to the attention of the world during the first six weeks of Operation Barbarossa, when the Nazis threw everything they could at it to break the resistance of the defending forces. The Germans took the entire town in the first few hours of their attack. Around 90% of the city was destroyed in a furious and relentless barrage of withering artillery fire. The fortress suffered severe damage too, but the two regiments garrisoned inside held out. The Nazis turned the focus of their strategy from attack to attrition and so it was that the siege began. Elsewhere, the German advance eastwards was gathering pace by the day. Six weeks later, they had almost taken Smolyensk, deep into Russian territory, before the resistance of the defenders of the fortress was finally broken. Much of it was in ruins and only a handful of men had survived, but in the context of the wider conflict, an invaluable job had been done. Citizens all over the USSR had been inspired by the daily news bulletins they received from the front line, telling of the heroism of the small band of Soviet troops striving valiantly against their Nazi aggressors. Stalin had been given just enough time to plan his campaign, so that when he issued his rallying call to every citizen of the Union to defend the Motherland to the death, the vast empire at his command swung into action in a patriotic fervour of almost spiritual intensity. Little wonder, then, that the 1939–45 global conflict is still referred to throughout the countries of the former USSR as the Great Patriotic War. At the end of the war, the decision was taken not to rebuild the fortress, but instead to turn it into a huge shrine, a giant monument to commemorate what transpired here. Exactly the same thought process informed the concept and design of the deeply affecting state memorial at Khatyn (see *Chapter 3*, page 131).

Bear all of this in mind as you enter the complex. The approach along Masherova Avenue is long, straight and slightly downhill, with sculptures in the shape and colour of the Soviet flag lining the route, upon each of which is embossed an image of the head and shoulders of one of the defending troops. To the left and adding nothing to the scene is an ugly and incongruous factory with an enormous red and white striped chimney, whilst on the right is the city's railway museum. At the bottom of the avenue is a huge car park for over a thousand vehicles. Last time I was there, it contained six cars. As you begin the long walk towards the fortress, your eye is drawn to the first iconic sight, over 100m in front of you, where an enormous concrete block, grey and sombre, rests on the remains of the outer wall, into which has been cut a gigantic star. This is the entrance. As you walk through, tape recordings are played of stirring soldiers' songs, gunfire, explosions and the radio broadcast that first broke the news of the attack. Coming out of the tunnel and another 150m ahead, the eye is immediately drawn to a massive, glistening bayonet obelisk, 100m high, near to which is an astonishing concrete sculpture (entitled *Courage*), into the top of which has been carved the head of a grim-faced defender. It is almost 34m high and the reverse side has carvings depicting various scenes from the heroic defence. At the foot of the obelisk is the inevitable eternal flame, guarded round the clock by four teenagers from the Corps of Pioneers. In a symbolic gesture of equality, two are male and two are female. The vaguely comical ceremony of the changing of the guard does little to enhance the sobriety of this hallowed place; and if you ever witnessed the same process at Lenin's mausoleum in Moscow during the days of the Soviet Union, you will understand what I mean here. Next to the flame are three rows of symbolic tombstones bearing the names of the fallen heroes.

All of this awaits in the middle distance. For now, take a slow stroll along the paved pathway, past a row of tanks on the left, all the while admiring the beauty and the variety of the trees that line the walkway on the edges of the river beyond on both sides. The willows are particularly beautiful. As you reach the end of the path and enter the circle within, pause for a moment to look around. Immediately to your left is a grim but moving sculpture, starkly entitled *Thirst*. It depicts a soldier, near to exhaustion or even death, lying on his side and half crawling, his right hand holding a machine gun and his left imploringly holding out a helmet for water. Legend has it that this depicts the last soldier left in the garrison when it was finally taken. He (and the handful of his comrades who remained) had gone without food or water for 40 days, so the story goes, and when the Nazis finally broke the resistance of the last survivors, so moved were they by this man's endurance and heroism, that they let him go. This tale may have been embellished in the telling over the years, but like all such stories, much of it is likely to be true.

Behind and all the way around this inner section lies an incomplete circle of two-storey buildings, the former barracks, most of which are still intact. Those to the left house a number of galleries for art and literature (⊕ 10.00–18.00). The work of individual artists and writers is frequently on display here. In front of these bullet-riddled buildings are displays of military equipment. The centre ground is taken by the sculpture *Courage*, with the eternal flame, obelisk and symbolic tombstones. If all of this were not enough to paint a bleak tableau, piped choral music, sombre and doleful, plays at a number of locations. Behind is the Church of Saint Nikolai and to the right, the brick remains of the **White Palace** can be seen, with most of the building's shell intact. Entrance into the shell is forbidden though, presumably for reasons of safety. It was here that Lenin pulled off his masterstroke of political expediency in 1918, when he negotiated the Treaty of Brest-Litovsk with the invading Germans. Further to the right is the **Defence of Brest Fortress Museum** (✆ 20 03 65; ⊕ 09.00–18.00 Tue–Sun; admission *BYR2,500 for locals, BYR4,000 for foreign visitors*), which is well worth a visit. Neatly arranged exhibits tell the story of the construction and history of the fortress, as well as graphically depicting the conditions of the siege. Sadly, explanatory information is provided in Russian only, but non-Russian speakers will still get a good impression of its history.

The White Palace represents one of the entrances to the central stronghold and a small bridge behind it leads to the final small island at the centre. When you get there, it is worth gazing around you; the view of the bullet-riddled red-brick **Kholmsky Gate** is one of the iconic images that you may have seen in books.

You should now take time to retrace your steps back through the entrance, pausing *en route* to look at the many plaques positioned throughout the site, on which a date appears in large letters, followed by a brief description of the key events at each location (sadly in Russian only). And for refreshment and reflection, turn left immediately after you pass the museum and walk down a short but beautiful tree-lined avenue to the Café Citadel (⊕ 10.00–23.00 Mon–Sun). Housed in a series of vault-like rooms in a low, red-brick building; soft drinks, alcoholic beverages and snacks are available cheaply. Expect to find more staff there than customers. Toilets are also available here.

Do remember that the grounds of the complex are open until midnight. A promenade here at dusk is particularly atmospheric.

MUSEUMS

Beryestye Architectural Museum (✆ 20 55 54; ⊕ 09.30–18.00 Tue–Sun; admission *BYR2,100 for foreign visitors*) Situated south across the river from the fortress and with access from inside, this large modern building was constructed around an excavation site. The exhibitions consist of more than 40,000 artefacts in 14 halls from the 11th to the 13th centuries, all relating to the original settlement here 1,000 or so years ago. Most were discovered during excavations during the 1970s. There is also a reconstruction of a Russian town as it stood in the second half of the 13th century. In total, the remains of more than 30 buildings are available for viewing and this museum offers a welcome respite from the sombre experience of cruel and bloody modern warfare that has assaulted you thus far in this place. But do tread carefully around here and do not stray onto any path other than to the museum. After all, you are literally on the border with NATO at this point! Sadly, however, the museum was closed at the time of writing for substantial renovations.

Brest Railway Museum (⊕ *May–Oct 09.00–18.00 Tue–Sun, Nov–Apr 09.00–17.00; admission BYR2,000 for locals, BYR6,000 for foreign visitors*) On the left-hand side of Masherova Avenue as you leave the fortress, 200m beyond the car park, is the open-air railway museum. Opened in 2002, 48 historical steam locomotives from the 1930s and 1940s are on display here, together with a staff carriage dating from 1915. All of them are in full working order. The grounds and exhibits are frequently used for shooting films and as the location for festivals.

History of Brest Museum (*3 Levatyevskaya St;* ↘ *23 17 65;* ⊕ *10.00–16.00 Wed–Sun; admission BYR2,500*) As might be expected, artefacts and exhibits tell the story of the city through the ages. Useful background information for the student of local history. And it's in a pleasant location.

Regional Museum of Ethnography (*60 Karla Marksa St;* ↘ *23 91 16;* ⊕ *10.00–17.00 Tue–Sat; admission BYR2,500*) A branch of the History Museum and located in a historic building (a 19th-century former hotel and theatre), the focus here is more on society and culture. There are extensive collections of artefacts from the region, rare books and archival antiquities.

Museum of Confiscated Art (*39 Lenin St;* ↘ *20 41 95;* ⊕ *10.00–17.00 Tue–Sat; admission BYR3,000*) Known locally as the museum of 'Salvaged Artistic Values', this quirky concept has on display valuable pieces of fine art, including paintings and sculptures, from around the world. The difference is that they were all confiscated by customs officials from would-be art-thieves, at the nearby border! Some really interesting items are shown here.

CHURCHES AND CATHEDRALS

Saint Christopher's Church of Exaltation of the Holy Cross This church was constructed in 1856 from the bricks of Catholic churches and monasteries that previously existed in the old city. Within is the renowned 17th-century icon 'Our Lady of Berestye', richly decorated in gilt and precious stones. Services are held in both Polish and Belarusian. The acoustics of the building are of the very finest quality. This archetypical example of Catholic architecture is located just off Lenin Square, where the man himself remains on duty, ever alert. A nice contrast of ideology.

Saint Nikolai's Church Situated on the northeastern side of Sovyetskaya Street (close to the junction with Mitsekevichskaya Street), this delightful church is one of the most beautiful in the whole of the city. Built between 1904 and 1906 in the pseudo-Russian style to commemorate the end of the Russo–Japanese war, it is a stunning example of Orthodox décor, both outside and in. The deep blue cupolas decorated with gold stars are particularly striking, especially in the sunshine. Closed during the time of the Soviet Union, it was only restored and returned to its parish in the 1990s.

Saint Simeon Orthodox Cathedral This lovely example of 16th-century Orthodox architecture is situated on the south side of Masherova Avenue, right next to the Hotel Intourist and on the way to the fortress; its exterior is lime green in hue. Very lime green indeed. You may be reminded of a highly decorated cake at first glance. Much of the current construction dates from 1865 and this is the only place of worship in the city that has never once closed its doors, whatever the prevailing circumstances outside. Inside and right of centre as you walk in is a tomb that is said to contain some of the earthly remains of the city's Father Superior and martyr

Aphanasyi, who was tortured to death for his Orthodox beliefs in 1648. His statue was erected and sanctified just outside the grounds of the cathedral in 2005.

Saint Resurrection Orthodox Cathedral On the way out of the city in an easterly direction, at the junction of Partizansky Avenue and Moskovskaya Street, stands the imposing Saint Resurrection Orthodox Cathedral. Its silver domes are particularly eye-catching. Built only in 2003, its altar was sanctified by His Holiness Alexei the Second, Patriarch of Moscow and All Russia. Below ground level is a special vault to honour the renowned icon 'Our Lady of Kazan'.

PARKS AND RECREATION

Brest City Park Originally laid out by Russian soldiers who were stationed near here in 1906, the park is only ten minutes' walk from the railway station on the right-hand side of Lenin Avenue. The original area of 4ha has been redesigned and significantly expanded to some 50ha. It reopened to visitors on 1 May 2006 and not unsurprisingly for an ex-Soviet republic, its official title is now 'First of May Culture and Entertainment Park'. It is the largest in the city and a beautiful place to walk and meander, with dozens of species of trees that are not normally to be found in this part of Europe. There are also two delightful ornamental ponds, called the Upper and Lower lakes, which are connected by a canal through which water lazily flows. Newly built bridges of decorative iron span the canal, with another bridge linking the island in the centre of the Upper Lake to the shore. Two fountains complement the overall ambiance. There are also tennis courts and many attractions for children. To complete your self-restoration, visit the lovely café U Ozero ('By the Lake'). When refreshed and relaxed, try your luck in the amusement park, listen to a performance at the open-air concert stage, or perhaps visit the large disco club (or then again, perhaps not!). Many refreshment kiosks are also situated throughout the park.

FESTIVALS If you find yourself in Brest at the end of July, look out for the **city's birthday celebrations**. The official date is the 28th, but festivities take place over a number of days, culminating in the main event on the final Sunday of the month. Activities include parades of revellers in fancy dress, particularly knights, street theatre, concerts and sports events. Visitors come from all over the country to watch and take part, as the whole city swings into party mood in a dazzling display of colour, light and sound.

Then in October, Sovyetskaya Street is the scene for the **Autumn Fair**, a celebration to give thanks for the bounties of the harvest. The thoroughfare overflows with an abundance of natural produce, in a symbolic display of the strength of the relationship between the people and the land.

OUTSIDE BREST

PINSK Pinsk is the ancient capital of Polyesye, with a history enveloped in mysteries and mists. Its appeal and significance over the centuries have been shaped by the geographical location of the town. Formerly surrounded by impassable swampland, it's little wonder that it has always been called, a little disparagingly, 'the land of woods, bogs and fogs'. But its strategic position, traversed by the Pripyat River and at the confluence of the Pinya and Strumen, compensated for this and it quickly gained power and influence as a major stopping-off point along the ancient north–south and east–west trade routes. Nowadays, it is a town with a population of over 128,000 and its significance as a fertile centre of agriculture is assured. There is also a small but specialist industry here manufacturing boats that sail the local rivers.

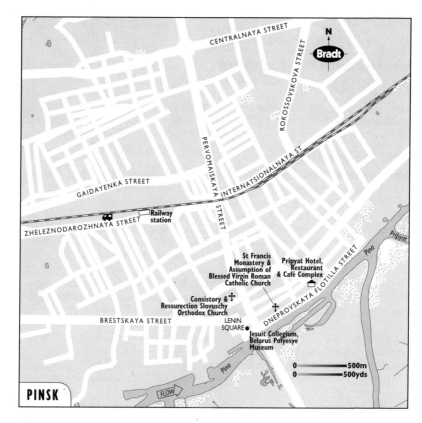

PINSK

History The historical settlement of Pinesk, named after the River Pina that flows through the modern town, was first established over 900 years ago. This makes it one of the oldest Slavic settlements in the country. In strategic terms, it held an uneasy position between the warring principalities of Novogrudok and Halych-Volynya. Although declaredly neutral, its sympathies were with the Novogrudok princes and not surprisingly, it was taken under their patronage in 1320 and subsumed within the Grand Duchy of Lithuania.

In 1569, after the creation of the mighty Polish-Lithuanian Commonwealth, its strategic importance was recognised when it became the administrative centre of the province of Brest. Then in 1581, this status was further enhanced when the town was granted rights of self-determination and government under Magdeburg Law. Its significance and influence continued to grow exponentially. It developed into a large residential settlement, with a wooden castle, 16 churches, monasteries of both Orthodox and Catholic faiths and a synagogue. Indeed and in every respect, it was second only to the Commonwealth's capital Vilno (now Vilnius) in importance and paid the same level of taxes to the Treasury as Polotsk, Grodno and Kiev.

But the period 1640 to 1706 was a time of abject misery for the townspeople. Succeeding invasions and sackings on the part of Cossacks, Poles, Ukrainians and Russians decimated the population, destroyed much of the town's architecture and wiped out the community's infrastructure. Miraculously and in spite of almost relentless conflict, the city not only survived as a settlement, but recovered, as evidenced by the existence of a flourishing print workshop from 1729 to 1744.

From 1793 until 1939, it came under the jurisdiction of first the Russian Empire, then Poland after the Polish–Soviet war and finally the Soviet Union. At the outbreak of World War II, the Jewish community comprised over 90% of the town's total population and during the tyranny of the Nazi occupation from 1941 to 1944, all were interned in concentration camps, most of them never to return. Records are incomplete, but it is believed that as many as 30,000 Pinsk Jews perished during 'the final solution', including 10,000 in just one day. It was liberated by the Red Army and returned to Soviet ownership in 1944, before finally coming under the jurisdiction of the Republic of Belarus in 1991, upon the creation of the new state.

Where to stay and eat There are several hotels and restaurants in town. The largest is the **Pripyat Hotel, Restaurant and Café Complex** (*107 sgl rooms, 103 dbls, 19 trpls & 8 luxury suites; 31 Dnyeprovskaya Flotilla St;* ❘ *35 96 33;* e *pripyat_pinsk@tut.by*). As might be expected, it's a large, multi-storeyed concrete edifice that is archetypically Soviet. Consisting of three separate buildings from two to nine storeys high, it is located on the bank of the River Pina, east of the Saint Francis Monastery. Facilities include a restaurant (⊕ *07.00–01.00 for b/fast, lunch & dinner*), bar, open-air café, disco, ATM, conference and office services. There is also a helpful tourist office, from which excursions and tours can be booked. The railway station is 3.5km away and the bus station 4km. Expect to pay US$25–42 per person per night.

What to see Much the best way to see the sights is on an organised tour from Minsk or Brest with one of the state tourist agencies. Today, the two most interesting visitor attractions can be found on the banks of the Pina River. The first of these is the **Saint Francis Monastery and the Assumption of the Blessed Virgin Roman Catholic Church**, constructed between 1712 and 1730. Founded in 1396, this was one of the oldest religious sites in the Grand Duchy of Lithuania. The original wooden church was looted and burned many times before the Baroque structure of stone that replaced it was completed in 1730. Inside are seven ornate altars, six of wood and one of stucco, together with around 100 sculptures and carvings created by master craftsman Jan Schmitt. There are also several beautiful paintings and frescoes. In the grounds is a belfry constructed in 1817.

On the other side of the road bridge (but on the same bank) is the **Jesuit Collegium**, built between 1635 and 1648. It is an imposing building of three storeys, with features that are both Baroque and Renaissance, walls that are 2m thick and impressive vaulted ceilings. In its day, it was an educational institution for both religious and secular teaching, consisting of classrooms, library, theatre hall, chapel and refectory, all full of sculptures, icons and portraits of its founding fathers. The crypt contains the holy relics of the Jesuit preacher and martyr Andrei Babolya, who was murdered by Cossacks in 1657 and canonised in 1853 by Pope Pius IX. After the abolition of the Jesuit order, the monastery was taken by the Uniates, then became the Epiphany Orthodox Monastery until 1918, when it was handed over to the Roman Catholic faith. The library was emptied of its rich and valuable collections in 1940. They were taken to Leningrad and have never been returned. Today, the building houses the **Belarus Polyesye Museum** (*22 Lenin Sq;* ❘ *35 84 02*).

There is also a more modern structure worthy of a visit at the junction of Gorky and Pervomayskaya streets, north of the river. It is the **Consistory and the Resurrection Slovuschy Orthodox Church**. A wooden church built in 1668 originally stood on this site, before the stone building that replaced it in 1778 was destroyed during the Great Patriotic War. After the war, a cinema was built here,

No piece on Pinsk would be complete without mention of the population and the terrain of the area. Much has been said about the almost mystical relationship between the people of this country and the land, but the unique nature of the 'fogs and bogs' of the Polyesye give an added dimension to this. Many of those living in southeastern Belarus, from Kamenyets in the west to Mozyr in the east, call themselves *Polyeshuky*, so identifying themselves with this area of low marshland along the line of the Pripyat and Bug rivers and their southern tributaries where they live. Those living in Pinsk and its immediate surroundings call themselves *Pinchuki*' and the dialect spoken here differs from Belarussian, Russian and Ukrainian. It borrows words from all three, but also has its own specific words and expressions that can only be found there. The language also has its own distinct accent. In recent times, historians and social commentators have tried to link this ethnographic peculiarity to the name of a Baltic tribe that lived in parts of the Polyesye until the 13th century. This theory to explain the phenomenon is not widely acknowledged, and is far from universally supported. Nevertheless, the originality of the culture of the region is not something that should be overlooked, along with the reality that a significant proportion of the population regard the local dialect as their mother tongue.

but the ground was subsequently reconsecrated and a new church built in 1995. Its black domes are especially striking, particularly under snow.

BYELOVEZHSKAYA PUSCHA STATE NATIONAL PARK AND BIOSPHERE RESERVE

(*Kamenyuky, Kamenyets district, Brest region;* \ *1631 56 122/132; information* \ *1631 56 370/396*) First established as a national park in 1939, it entered the list of UNESCO World Heritage Sites on 14 December 1992, then in 1993 it was granted the status of biosphere reserve, affording unique opportunities for specialist ecological study. There are conference and library facilities here, together with accommodation for up to 100 visiting scientists.

Today, the park is an integral and important feature of around 1,700km² of ancient primeval forest within Belarusian borders, although the woodland stretches across the border into Poland, which jointly administers the park with Belarus. This is all that now remains of a vast canopy that once covered the whole of the huge northern European plain, the former home and playground of Polish princes and Russian tsars. In fact, the last private owners of the forest were the tsars of the Russian Empire, from 1888 to 1917. After the Revolution, it was nationalised and brought under the jurisdiction of the state. Some of the trees here are believed to be over 600 years old. More than 900 plant species have been recorded, including 26 tree and 138 shrub species. Almost two-thirds of them are indigenous to the area.

The forest appeared as the backdrop to news bulletins all around the world on 8 December 1991, when the Byeloyyezhsky agreement, the document that formally dissolved the USSR and established the Commonwealth of Independent States, was signed here by the presidents of Belarus, Ukraine and Russia.

Today, life is much calmer and the reserve is home to around 212 species of bird, including corncrake, eagle owl, white stork and white-tailed eagle, along with 59 species of mammal, including wild boar, wild horses, roaming elk, beaver, lynx, fox, deer, wolf, otter, badger, mink, ermine, marten and perhaps most famously, bison. By 1920, the European bison was almost extinct. Once to be seen roaming the great continental plain in their thousands, only a handful remained. But with careful management and controlled husbandry in the intervening years, numbers have increased to more than 2,500 in eastern Europe. Several hundred are known to inhabit the park.

There is also a zoo within the park and excursions into the depths of the forest are available by horse and cart. The needs of visitors are well catered for with two hotels and a number of restaurants and bars. A relatively recent innovation is the newly established tourist attraction for children of all ages within the forest that enables visitors to call on the 'real' Grandfather Frost (the eastern Slavic equivalent of Santa Claus) in the 'real' fairy-tale palace that he calls home, where he lives with his granddaughter Snyegoruchka, the Snow Maiden. Interestingly, Grandfather Frost is to be found there in full regalia all year round.

The reserve is also home to around 4,000 people, most of whose livelihood is agriculturally based. Sadly, several potential threats to the park exist because of agricultural intensification in the surrounding area and the prevailing economic situation. The greatest hazard is from run-off generated by the 40 tons of pesticide and over 30,000 tons of fertiliser used every year by large state farms on the periphery. Rising inflation, coupled with the lack of investment funding, creates pressures by necessitating industrial intensification. Clearly, there are challenges ahead if this unique environment is to continue to be protected in the future.

Getting there The park is located around 70km north of Brest and 20km from the nearest major town, Kamenyets. Five buses run to Kamenyets from Brest every day, but from there you will still need a cab to get you to the gates of the park; and there is no transport within the park itself, other than that arranged by official tour operators. It is technically possible (just) to drive your own car around, but the state guards this natural treasure very jealously indeed and there are many red-tape hoops to jump through before a permit is granted. Also, this is border country, so security is high. Even the wild animals don't get to cross. It's far better to come here on an organised tour, which is best arranged through the staff at the Hotel Intourist in Brest. If you want to deal with the arrangements before you arrive in Belarus, the national tourist agency Belintourist market a number of very comprehensive tours to this and other sites. Someone else can then take care of the driving and the itinerary; you can just sit back, admire the view and watch the sights.

Facilities on site There are two small hotels within the park dating from the Soviet era (and so just a little tired and shabby), one of them at the Viskuly complex in the village of Kamenyuky, where the park headquarters are also located. Visitor facilities include a number of cafés and restaurants with ethnic-folk floor shows, sauna, swimming pool, basketball and volleyball courts, tennis courts and mini-football pitches. There is also an interesting Museum of Nature in the park, together with enclosures for viewing the wildlife at close quarters. Walking routes and tours on horseback are available, together with specialist photographic safaris and visits to some of the mighty oaks that have been given their own name, such as 'The Emperor of the North' and 'The Tsar Oak'. A number of historical and cultural sites can also be visited, including the former Tyskevich estate, the 'ancient tsar road', the 'ancient man site', old churches and the White Tower (see below).

The town of **Kamenyets** is located on the road from Brest to the national park. Chronicles show that in 1276, Duke Vladimir Vasilkovich despatched his architect to the area to find a suitable location to construct a fortress to defend his lands and to house within its defences a settlement. By 1289, the construction of the **Byelaya Vyezha (White Tower)** was complete. Sitting atop a mound of earth surrounded by a ditch, this cylindrical tower, 30m high and over 13m in diameter, isn't actually white, but despite the inaccurate description, it is a splendid architectural monument in outstanding condition. Originally intended as an enclosed community, it was constructed on the motte and bailey principle, but only the tower is left. You can even still climb to the top, by means either of the internal staircase, or the steps cut inside the walls, which are 2.5m thick. The tower also conceals underground passages leading directly to the nearby river. This is the main landmark of the town. It originally formed a key component of a line of frontier strongholds, but today it is the only one remaining in the country. Others at Brest, Grodno and Novogrudok failed to stand the test of time and fell during wars. On several occasions throughout history, the town of Kamenyets suffered the same fate as other frontier garrisons, of being sacked and destroyed. But the White Tower itself always prevailed and today, it is afforded the full status of a national historic site.

Flax

5

Grodno City and Oblast
Гродно

The region of Grodno is situated in the northwest of Belarus and has borders with both Poland and Lithuania. The administrative and cultural centre of the region is the city of Grodno itself, with a population of 309,000. Situated 278km west of Minsk and just 294km east of Warsaw, it is only 20km from Poland and 40km from Lithuania. Records indicate that the city has been in existence for at least 900 years. Not surprisingly, given its location, it has a significant Polish and Lithuanian heritage. At various times in the past, it has fallen under the control of both.

The greatest wealth of the Grodno region is the leafy groves forming the magnificent tract of natural forestation that occupies more than one-third of its territory to the northeast and southeast of the city, either side of the historic town of Lida. Comprising both coniferous and mixed woodland, it is pleasing to see that pockets of the ancient virgin forests that once covered this whole continent have survived more or less intact here.

From within Belarus, you will approach the city from the south or east. My first visit was when I drove the back roads from Brest in the south, a delightful journey of 150 miles through ancient villages. Given that most of the country is extremely flat, I was surprised to find that 60 miles or so before I reached Grodno, the terrain became much more hilly, with extensive panoramic vistas opening up expectedly. So it is in the city itself.

This is also a land rich in lakes, large and small, but all of them picturesque, with a reputation for clear waters. The renowned Avgustovski canal also runs through the region for around 20km on its meandering way to Poland. Once a year, a festival of culture takes place around the Dombrovka sluice, featuring ethnic craftsmen, folk musicians and performing troupes from Belarus, Poland and Lithuania.

The history of the region, characterised first by conflict and then by the ensuing peaceful co-existence of Baltic and Slavonic peoples, has left its mark on the territory. The original fortress of Grodno, built on the banks of the Nieman River in the 11th century, has now evolved into an elegant, thriving, bustling, energetic and cosmopolitan modern city, where more examples of Classical architecture have been preserved than in any other city of Belarus. Indeed, the national state government has declared the historical centre of Grodno a special architectural zone under the protection and jurisdiction of the state itself. Of the country's six major cities, it is perhaps Grodno that best lends itself to an appreciation of its charms by strolling along its streets, gazing at the richness of the buildings that surround you on every side.

There are also many fine examples of unique architecture in the region, such as unusual military churches. During the 15th and 16th centuries, many of the Eastern Orthodox churches were required to serve the dual purposes of worship and as places of fortified refuge against the attacks of aggressors. Many of those that are still standing look more like towered castles. The best examples of these

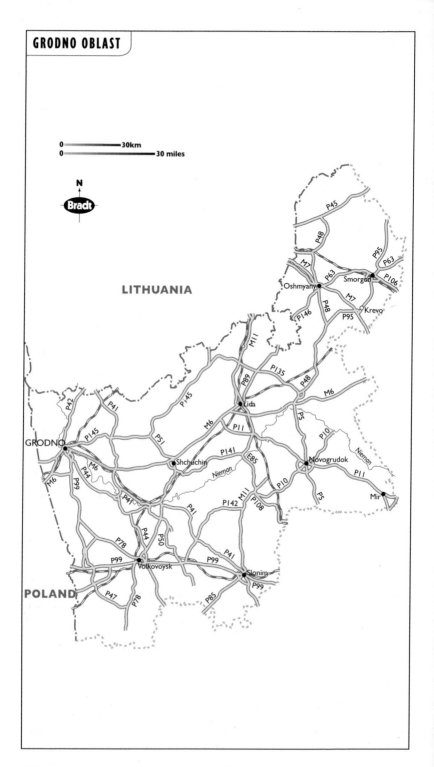

GRODNO OBLAST

fortress-churches can be seen in the districts of Zeiveny (from the late 15th century) and Shchuchin (from the 16th century). In Smorgon, the 16th-century Calvinist cathedral is well worth a visit.

In short, this is a land full of ancient towns and villages that would repay the close attention of admiring visitors many times over. Unfortunately, options for independent travel are extremely limited, so for now, travellers must content themselves with booking onto one of the many organised tours and excursions that are available through the state agencies. It's not as good as independent exploration, but it's certainly the next best thing.

HISTORY

The town of Grodno is believed to have been founded as an important strategic, military and trade centre on the northwestern border of Kievan Rus, although evidence of Palaeolithic settlements dating back over 10,000 years have been discovered in the vicinity of the modern town. Between 1000BC and AD1000, the territory is believed to have been inhabited by confederations of Baltic tribes, but by the middle of the 11th century, the Slavic Krivichi and Dregovichi tribes had begun a policy of expansionist colonisation in the area. It gained its first mention in the Primary Chronicle in 1127 and it is clear that by this time, the geographical location of this Slavic settlement at the crossroads of many trading routes had enabled it to attain the status of capital of an independent principality, possibly as long ago as the 10th century.

Economic and cultural development was swift, such that later in the 12th century, the city had its own architectural school, as evidenced by the splendid **Kolozhskaya Church of Saints Boris and Hleb** (see *What to see and do*, page 166). By 1280, Grodno had been subsumed into the mighty Grand Duchy of Lithuania. Indeed, under the rule of Grand Duke Vitautis, from 1376 to 1392, the town acquired equal status with Vilnius as a second state capital. Conflict with knights of the Teutonic Order lasted into the 15th century and it was from here that Vitautis led the forces of the duchy to victory in the famous battle of Grunwald. Even today, this battle is still regarded as a major feature in the development of modern Belarus. Then in 1496, charter rights of self-determination under Magdeburg Law were granted. The King of Poland and Grand Duke of Lithuania Stephan Batory established his main residence in Grodno during the 16th century for more than ten years. His influence can be widely seen today in much of the city's architecture. From the second half of the 17th century, in the time of the influential Polish-Lithuanian Commonwealth, meetings of *sejms* (a branch of government with delegated powers) were regularly held here, as a result of which the town's influence on regional and national politics grew. The last ever of the Commonwealth's *sejms* took place in 1793, before the final Rzeczpospolitan monarch Stanislas Augustus Poniatowski resigned the crown in 1795, leading to the third partition of Poland. Thereafter, the city passed into Russian hands, in which it served a key municipal function as the seat of a local administration, one of the most advanced in the whole empire. In 1859, the Warsaw to St Petersburg railway was completed through Grodno, which thus became an important junction on the line.

The start of the 20th century saw much revolutionary activity at key locations throughout the empire, most notably the revolution of 1905. At the same time, Belarusian nationalism was developing. Grodno played its part, with the first Belarusian periodicals being printed here.

The city and its environs were once more a war zone during the 1914–18 conflict and German forces were in occupation from 1915. As a consequence of the

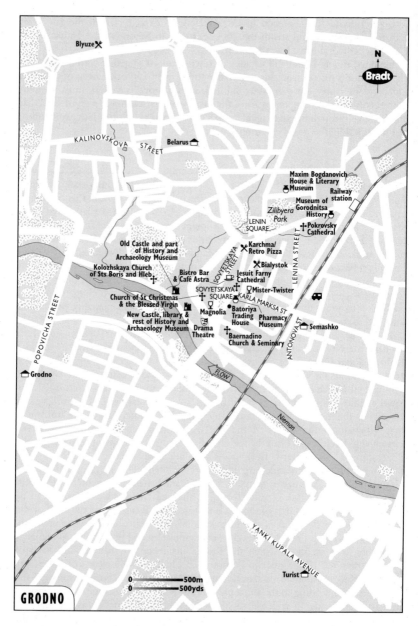

Blyuze

Belarus

KALINOVSKOVA STREET

Maxim Bogdanovich
House & Literary
Museum

Museum of
Gorodnitsa
History

Railway
station

Zilibyera
Park

LENIN
SQUARE

Pokrovsky
Cathedral

Old Castle and part
of History and
Archaeology Museum

Karchma/
Retro Pizza

Kolozhskaya Church
of Sts Boris and Hleb

Bistro Bar
& Café Astra

Bialystok

Jesuit Farny
Cathedral

Church of St Christmas
& the Blessed Virgin

SOVYETSKAYA
SQUARE

Mister-Twister

KARLA MARKSA ST

New Castle, library &
rest of History and
Archaeology Museum

Magnolia

Batoriya
Trading
House

Pharmacy
Museum

Semashko

Drama
Theatre

Baernadino
Church & Seminary

POPOVICHA STREET

Grodno

FLOW

Nieman

YANKI KUPALA AVENUE

Turist

0 ___ 500m
0 ___ 500yds

GRODNO

outrageously callous political expediency practised by Lenin to end Russian involvement in the war, these territories were ceded to Germany by the Bolsheviks under the Treaty of Brest-Litovsk in 1918, following which the first Belarusian nation state was allowed to come into existence.

It did not endure for long. Between 1919 and 1921, the area changed hands many times. Units of the Red Army established Soviet power on two separate occasions, with claims to sovereignty also being made by the newly created Polish state and by Lithuania. Then finally, the Riga Peace Treaty of 1921 incorporated Grodno region into Poland. The city of Bialystok, 100km to the southwest, became the capital of the region and Grodno's economic significance fell into decline, although it had risen again by 1930 with the growth of the Jewish population. Military units stationed here were pressed into action when the Nazis invaded Poland in 1939, then when the country was shamefully carved up by Nazi Germany and the USSR under the terms of the notorious Molotov-Ribbentrop Pact of Non-Aggression, a significant engagement took place in and around the city between the Red Army and Polish troops, as the Russians marched inexorably westwards to establish a buffer to protect the sovereignty of Soviet national borders. Fighting was brutal and bloody. To this very day, each side continues to deny the claims of the other in terms of actual losses, although one fact has now been established without ambiguity. As accepted at long last, thousands of Polish officers who had been taken prisoner were subsequently murdered by the NKVD acting under Stalin's direct orders and buried in mass graves, most notably those discovered in relatively modern times in the forests of Katyn. When Grodno passed into Soviet hands as part of the Belarusian Soviet Socialist Republic, much of the Polish population was dispersed elsewhere within the USSR, before the city once more fell to the Germans in 1941 after the start of Operation Barbarossa. Liberation by the Red Army in July 1944 came too late to save Grodno's Jews, the majority of whom died in Nazi concentration camps. At the end of the war, Soviet sovereignty was restored. This endured until the break-up of the Soviet Union, when Grodno became one of the key cities of the newly established nation state of Belarus.

Today, the grace and charm of the historical centre conceals a competitive commercialism in the wider area. The *oblast* is probably the best developed in the entire country in terms of industrialisation: buses, tractors, combine harvesters, spare parts for cars and agricultural machinery, plastics, fertilisers, manmade fibres and threads, radio and television sets, furniture, textiles, shoes and tobacco goods are all produced here in significant quantity, whilst a favourable climate and fertile soil have helped to promote agriculture as a key component of the local economy.

All in all, this is a very classy city indeed. It's hip and sassy, but at the same time, relaxed and comfortable. Even the high-rise suburbs have a certain elegance. I have stayed in crumbling Soviet-style apartment blocks in four of the six major cities and the urban scene here is by far the most attractive. Certainly, the concrete is still crumbling, but the design and exterior of the blocks is a cut above, with wide swathes of tree-lined parkland in between. I was with my Belarusian travelling companion on her very first visit to Grodno. We've covered much of the country together and she was very impressed indeed. And like everywhere else, impressing the locals is no mean task.

And it is also a truly multi-cultural city. Renowned for its tradition of tolerance and inclusivity, refuge has been given to Tatars, Jews and Prussians (amongst others) in times gone by. Today, communities of over 80 different nationalities exist somewhere in the *oblast*. One-third of the population classes itself as being Polish or of Polish descent, whilst there are also significant Russian, Ukrainian and Lithuanian communities. It's no surprise to find, then, that the city is home to the biannual Festival of National Cultures in June, when the streets become one giant stage for the performing arts. Anyone lucky enough to be in the city when the festival is on has a treat in store. As well as performances, dishes of many national cuisines are in evidence, along with national crafts, dances and music in different languages. There are fireworks and ornamental water displays. The grand finale takes place in the town's central square and continues until dawn. An impressive spectacle indeed.

GETTING THERE AND AWAY

The **train station** (*37 Budenyi St;* ✆ *44 85 56*) is situated 2km northeast of the city centre. Several trains a day arrive from and depart for Minsk, the fastest being service 127, which takes around 5½ hours. The longest, service 615, takes about eight hours. Additionally, there is an overnight sleeper. The service to Brest and Vitebsk is much less frequent. The station is also one of the stops on the main line from Warsaw to St Petersburg. All in all, it is a very busy junction, with some 65 trains arriving and departing each day, from and to destinations such as Moscow, St Petersburg, Minsk, Vilnius, Warsaw and locations further afield. Just bear in mind that even though some services are daily within the country, it is a quirk that there is often one timetable for even days of the month and another for odd days! Remember also that this is almost a border town, so don't be surprised to find arbitrary customs controls and checks in operation.

The **bus station** (*7a Krasnoarmeiskaya St;* ✆ *72 37 24*) is located in the east of the city, due south of the railway station and about half an hour's walk from the centre. Cross over the railway line and head due west along the arrow-straight Karl Marx Street. Today, the cheapest and most convenient way to get around within Belarus is by means of the inter-city bus routes: 60–85 buses leave Grodno every day for destinations in Russia, Ukraine, Lithuania, the Czech Republic, Poland and Latvia, stopping off at the major centres of population within the country *en route*. Buses to Minsk leave every 30–40 minutes and you have two choices: either the 'stopper', which takes 5½ hours, or the express, which makes one comfort stop only in the middle of the journey and takes 3½–4 hours.

The **airport** is situated 18km southeast of the city. It has all of the facilities necessary to operate national and international flights, but there have been no commercial passenger arrivals or departures for some time now, notwithstanding that the airport was regularly in use during the days of the USSR.

GETTING AROUND

Unlike Brest, Grodno's attractions are more widely spread over a larger geographical area, although it is possible to cover a good proportion of the main sites in one walkable sector of the town (see *A walking tour* in the *What to see and do* section, page 169). Unusually for a Belarusian city, the urban scene is particularly hilly, especially in the centre. This gives it an airy, lofty feel, with big skies and surprisingly impressive panoramas when you least expect them, especially from the northern bank of the river. This does mean that walking has its dividends. Furthermore, most of the hotels are away from the city centre, such that access only on foot to see everything will require a substantial investment of time. **Buses** and **trolleybuses** are rather old and generally very full, but they are a great way to see the city and you will feel like a local in the process. A trolleybus ride is one of those experiences that is so totally eastern European, and very evocative. Best of all, they are incredibly cheap: a single ticket anywhere in the city will you set you back no more than BYR220, a handful of pence only. Tickets are available from the driver or at kiosks located at many stops. Just don't forget to punch your ticket when you get on. Checks are frequent from plain-clothes inspectors and fines for violations are rigidly enforced.

Travel by *marshrutka* (scheduled minibus) is also an option. The price is a little higher, but at BYR700, still very cheap. Just expect to be crammed in and not to have the most comfortable of journeys. Either pay the driver when you get in, or else pass your handful of notes over the heads of your fellow passengers if it's really crowded! A tap on the shoulder is most likely to be the next passenger behind you doing the same thing. If you sit on the front seat, you will be expected to act as the conductor! The price is the same for adult and child alike, however long your journey.

As everywhere else, **cabs** are readily available for the more bespoke journeys. Expect to pay around BYR5,000 for a 15-minute ride. Dial 061, 062, 063, 067, 070, 073, 078, 079 or 088 for service.

TOURIST INFORMATION

As with previous chapters, I'd like to begin with the caveat that several details concerning opening hours, telephone numbers and prices for restaurants, bars, clubs, museums (below) proved impossible to establish, despite continued efforts.

That said, much the best web-based visitor resource by far is the excellent www.belarusguide.com/cities/hrodna. Local people have populated its pages with up-to-date information and there are links to other sites of interest. A few hours' worth of research before you go will be useful.

You will be able to buy maps, postcards and some guides (mostly in Russian) from the kiosks present in each hotel, but hours of opening are whimsical and wholly unpredictable.

Locally, dial 001 for tourist and practical information (but in Russian only).

The state tourist agency **Belintourist** has a branch office at 13 Lenin Street (↘ 75 04 01/77 33 99). The helpful staff there will be ready to arrange excursions for you. There are several other agencies, including the national Top-Tour, but not all of the others are licensed, so be careful who you choose before handing over your money.

WHERE TO STAY

Despite its charm and the beauty of the architecture, this is not a great city to find attractive hotels, with the exception of the Semashko. For each of the others that are listed here, décor and facilities are entirely functional and clean, but no more. If you treat your hotel as somewhere to rest your head and not as a place for aesthetic enjoyment, you won't go far wrong. Hotel restaurants and bars are unspectacular and more expensive than those in town, although still ridiculously cheap by Western standards. All in all, look upon your stay as an opportunity to find out what it was once like to travel around the Soviet Union in its heyday. The one exception to this is in respect of the quality of service from staff: most are friendly and accommodating. Officially all major credit cards are accepted, but don't be surprised if you receive a firm shake of the head when you go to check out. It's wise to make sure that you have plenty of cash with you.

🏠 **Hotel Semashko** (23 rooms) 10 Antonova St; ↘ 75 02 99. Located within walking distance of both bus & train stations, this privately owned hotel (the only one in the city) offers an altogether different experience. The décor is fresh & the service slick. Opened only in 2003, there are 13 sgls & 10 dbls, all of which are equipped to Western standards & well appointed. There is also a bridal suite. Facilities include a restaurant, café, open-air terrace bar & 'VIP bar'. Sgl from US$60 per night (inc b/fast), dbl from US$75.

🏠 **Hotel Turist** (158 rooms) 63 Yanki Kupala Av; ↘ 56 65 90; f 26 98 73. Located 3km southeast of the city centre (3km from the railway station & 1.5 from the bus station) in a suburb across the river, this is a 1980s concrete box. A cab ride from the city centre will cost around US$2. There are sgls & dbls, standard & upgraded, plus suites, all of which are adequately appointed. There is a currency-exchange office, travel & excursion bureau, hairdresser, dry cleaner, newspaper kiosk & solarium, along with a restaurant, café, snack bar & disco bars. There are also conference & business facilities. *Sgl from US$38 per night (room only), with the best suites US$118.*

🏨 **Hotel Belarus** (189 rooms) 1 Kalinovskova St; ☏ 44 16 74; ƒ 44 41 45. The city's primary hotel (& another concrete block), the rooms are on 6 floors, ranging from sgls to suites. Quite frankly though, the lobby is awful; it's like the waiting area of a bus station, but with less charm. The higher-specification 'luxury' rooms are well appointed, but

you will pay for the privilege. There is even an apt here. The bus & railway stations are both around 2km away. Facilities include currency exchange, hairdresser, newspaper stand & a watch repairer (!), together with a restaurant, café & snack bar. *Sgl from US$40 per night (room only).*

🏨 **Hotel Grodno** 3–5 Popovicha St; ☏ 22 42 33. Another archetypically Soviet high-rise block of crumbling 1970s concrete. *Sgl from US$40 per night (room only).*

✕ WHERE TO EAT

The city centre is not particularly well served by restaurants. Given that most of the hotels are off-centre too, the logistics of eating out require a little planning in advance. The easy option is to eat at your hotel, but none of the in-house restaurants could be classified as anything out of the ordinary, with the exception of the Semashko, which justifies a visit there just to eat. Those that are listed here can therefore be said to have a certain *je ne sais quoi* which makes the extra effort of getting there worthwhile.

✕ **Restaurant Karchma** 31 Sovyetskaya St; ☏ 72 34 11; ⏱ 11.00–midnight. Hip & crowded, this is a cool place to hang out. The ethnic décor is tasteful & the whole package, from appearance to ambiance, is classy. Belarussian cuisine is served & the standard is good. *Main courses US$15–25, inc drinks.*

✕ **Restaurant Bialystok** 20 Gorodnichaskaya St, just off Lenin Sq; ☏ 44 33 64; ⏱ 12.00–23.00. For the ultimate Soviet-style dining experience, this is simply not to be missed. When you cross the threshold, you will be greeted by a member of staff who will take your coat, show you the toilets & escort you up the stairs (all without a smile) into a cavernous, empty room with a high ceiling & dreary décor. You may very well be the only ones there for the duration of your stay. The staff are bored and discourteous. With some reluctance, one of them will serve you automaton-style. The food is bland & uninteresting (but a lot cheaper than the restaurant in your hotel), & you won't leave feeling like you haven't eaten. *Main courses US$12–25, inc drinks.*

✕ **Café Cronon** 6 Kalyuchinsky St; ☏ 44 12 52; ⏱ 12.00–midnight. This little restaurant-cum-café is unpretentious but cosy. There are only 6 tables, so try to book to avoid being disappointed. The salads are particularly tasty. There is a separate summer house. *Main courses US$10 or less, exc drinks.*

✕ **Mister-Twister Café Bar** 10 Karla Marksa St; ☏ 47 09 89; ⏱ 11.00–midnight. There are 2 rooms for dining here, but it's not as hip & sassy as it thinks it is. The fare is 'American' & acceptable, if unexciting. *Main courses US$15–20, exc drinks.*

✕ **Retro Pizza Restaurant** 31 Sovyetskaya St; ⏱ 11.00–01.00 Mon–Thu, 11.00–02.00 Fri–Sun. Right next door to the Karchma & sharing the same address, the fare is standard pizza-style, but tasty. You can also 'build your own'! I especially rate the 'Mexicana' here. A good range of salads, pasta & meat dishes is also available. The décor is relatively pleasing on the eye, although just a little too orange for my liking. The low ceiling gives it a vault-like appearance, so it can be noisy, but the tables are thoughtfully laid out for privacy & discretion. Service is understated & efficient. *Pizzas US$5–10, sides & drinks extra.*

✕ **Restaurant Blyuze ('Blues')** 1a Vryublevsky St; 33 29 74; ⏱ 12.00–02.00. Situated northwest of the city centre & further out even than the Hotel Belarus (but a very good option if you are staying there), this is a relaxed & hip venue offering good-quality food served with more than a little imagination. *Main courses US$20–30, exc drinks.*

ENTERTAINMENT AND NIGHTLIFE

The main drag on Sovyetskaya Street features a number of bars. None of them stands out from the rest, but all are acceptable places to hang out for a beer or two. For starters, try these:

Bistro Bar 5 Sovyetskaya St; ☏ 72 21 57; ⏱ 10.00–15.30 & 16.00–23.00. Compact, *bijou* & a little frayed around the edges, this tiny bar is one for locals & drinkers.

Café Astra Immediately adjacent to the Bistro Bar on Sovyetskaya St; ⏱ 11.00–02.00. Discreet & infinitely more charming than its neighbour, with a good selection of coffees to go with the usual alcoholic beverages.

Magnolia Bar ⏱ 12.00–02.00. Situated in Sovyetskaya Sq, halfway between Farny Cathedral & Bernadino Church, but on the opposite side of the square. Alcohol, bright lights & dancing. Enough said, but the central location (it couldn't be more central!) makes getting there & back very easy.

And if you have your dancing shoes and fancy a late night:

☆ **Epolyet Night Club** 30 Ozhyeshko St; ☏ 44 83 42. Located at the bottom of Sovyetskaya St (so easy to find), it's brash & noisy, but also a fun night out.

SHOPPING

Confine your shopping expeditions to Sovyetskaya Street (see below) and you won't go far wrong, but if you can't find what you're looking for there, you could try these multi-outlet retailers; just don't expect to find anything else that you didn't find on Sovyetskaya, though.

Batoriya Trading House 10 Stefan Batory St, in Sovyetskaya Sq, 150m down from Farny Cathedral; ☏ 72 39 18; ⏱ 07.00–23.00. The pavement outside is widely used as *the* place to meet friends before a night out, or to just hang around together, especially for young people.

Nemiga Favourite Trading House 44 Leninskovo Komsomolo Bd; ☏ 33 21 00

Central Market 6 Poligrafistov St; ☏ 75 22 34. For the hustle & bustle of market trading Belarussian-style.

Ranitsa Bookstore 33 Mostovaya St; ☏ 72 17 65. It's by far the best book shop in town.

OTHER PRACTICALITIES

There are plenty of banks and currency-exchange bureaux, but only a limited number of ATMs.

The main post office is at 29 Karla Marksa Street (☏ 72 00 60).

Credit and debit cards are not yet widely in use. You might be lucky, but it's better to play safe and take enough cash with you for the duration of your stay.

WHAT TO SEE AND DO

Because the city is located so near to the border with Poland and Lithuania, it has one of the largest concentrations of Roman Catholic worshippers in the whole of Belarus. It is also a centre of Polish culture, with the majority of ethnic Poles in the country residing in the city and its surroundings.

It is hardly surprising, then, that Catholicism dominates much of the architectural heritage. One of the iconic landmarks of the city is the 17th-century Roman Catholic **Jesuit Farny Cathedral** at the top of Sovyetskaya Square. The construction of this fine and imposing example of high Baroque architecture, over 50m in height, was begun in 1678 by Stefan Batory at the same time as he was redesigning the Old Castle 300m or so to the southwest. As if these activities were not enough to keep a man engaged, he was also busy leading the mighty Polish-Lithuanian Commonwealth in a series of continuous and uninterrupted military campaigns at the time. So it was that the cathedral was not actually consecrated until 27 years after work began, in the exalted presence of Peter the Great and Augustus the Strong. Further additions were made in the early part of the 18th century and its late Baroque frescoes and magnificent altars were not finally completed until 1752. In all, there are 14 altars, the main one of which is unique; at 21m high, it was the tallest in all Rzeczpospolita. The interior is simply stunning. Popular belief is that this is the most beautiful Catholic church in all Belarus. To appreciate the grandeur of the exterior, walk across the square in front of the cathedral all the way to the steps of the House of Culture, then look back. The effect is particularly impressive by night.

At the bottom of the square to the left is **Bernadino Church and Seminary**. This 16th-century Roman Catholic complex stands in its own extensive grounds, 200m to the south of the Farny Cathedral, on a hill on Parizhskoi Kamuny Street overlooking the Nieman River. Originally constructed in the style of the Renaissance, it was substantially altered in both 1680 and 1738. It is archetypical of the styles that flourished in the 17th century, from Gothic to Baroque. The interior is considered a masterpiece of so-called Wilno (Vilnius) Baroque. The church suffered some damage during the last war, but renovations were later sympathetically completed. Today, the oil paintings, lavish décor, alabaster statues, religious artefacts and other relics easily match those to be found in Farny, to my mind. The large grounds are host to a number of other monastic buildings, including cloisters, a charming wooden two-storey dormitory, a convent and a Dominican monastery. When you leave by the front door, walk to the end of the garden for an excellent view of the unusual drama theatre directly across the road. If you get the chance, try to do so at sunset. The quality of the light at this time of day is particularly impressive for both back-lighting the theatre and also bathing the front of the church in a rich luminescence, especially when set against a deep blue, cloudless sky.

To the right of the theatre, on the other side of Stefan Batory Street, is the delightful Orthodox **Church of Saint Christmas and the Blessed Virgin**. Constructed between 1721 and 1750, its whitewashed walls beautifully showcase the magnificent domes of matt black adorned with shimmering golden stars. The courtyard is pretty and the interior of the church is well worth a look.

Half a mile beyond the theatre and further beyond the Old and New castles, along the riverbank and on a hillside of its own, at the bottom of neat parkland in a delightful suburb of old wooden houses, stands the oldest remaining building in the city: the **Kolozhskaya Church of Saints Boris and Hleb**. Do try very hard to visit this special place. Three-quarters of the original stone sections remain from the 12th century, the south wall having collapsed in the landslide of 1859. This is hardly surprising. The high hill on which it is precariously perched stands right above the Nieman River. First mentioned in chronicles in 1183, this church is the only surviving example of the ancient style of 'Black Ruthenian' architecture, which can be distinguished from the style employed in the design of other Eastern Orthodox churches by the use of stones of blue, green or red hue, arranged to form crosses and other images on the wall. Inside and outside it is stunningly beautiful. After enjoying the enchanting design of the crosses on the exterior, take a look inside. The original stone walls and pillars are whitewashed and without frieze or other embellishment, but everywhere to be seen, hanging from pillar and wall, or just propped up in alcoves and corners, are countless icons, incense burners and gilt candle holders. I was lucky enough to visit on one of the special holy days of the Orthodox calendar, when a service to commemorate one of the revered saints was in full flow. It was spine-tingling. As the officiating priest recited the holy incantations, a dazzling shaft of sunlight arrowed from the high window, diagonally to the floor at his feet, while incense swirled and danced in the beam. All the time, the choir sang a *cappella* and the parishoners seemed held rapt by the majesty of the occasion, some standing, some kneeling to kiss the floor and all constantly crossing themselves and bowing, time upon time. It was impossible not to be moved. When you have finished exploring within, go back out of the door, turn to the left, walk to the rail at the edge and lean for a while to take in the view. Far to the left is Farny Cathedral and from this perspective, you have a true idea of just how enormous its façade really is. Sweep your gaze westwards (to the right). Next can be seen the old Fire Tower, built in 1912 as a response to the great fires of 1885 that destroyed around 600 houses, half of all the city's buildings. Next can be seen the New and Old castles. You have a good perspective of the hill on which they are built from here. To complete the panoramic tableau, you have a fine view upriver to the forests beyond the city boundary.

The **Eastern Orthodox Pokrovsky Cathedral** should not be missed if you have the opportunity to see it. Away to the northeast of the city on Ozheshka Street and only a few hundred metres before the railway station, this polychrome Russian Revivalist extravaganza dates from 1907. It was built to commemorate the city's army officers who lost their lives in the 1904–05 Russo–Japanese war. The pink-and-white stripes of the façade contrast nicely with the blue-and-gold cupolas, the whole being most pleasing on the eye.

On a hill overlooking the Nieman River from its northern bank stand the **Stari Zamak** and the **Novi Zamak** (Old and New castles). Their lofty perch enables them to dominate the southwestern quadrant of the city and they can be seen for some distance, particularly from south of the river. The Old Castle, which is located on the site of the fortress established by the first Kievan Rus settlers, was originally built of stone in the 14th century under Grand Duke Vytautas. Today, only modest sections of the original wall remain. It was then thoroughly overhauled in the late 17th century in the Renaissance style by the Italian Scotto at the behest of Polish King Stefan Batory, who made the castle his principal residence. He died there seven years later and is interred in Grodno. Several modifications have been made since, but the attractive 17th-century stone arch bridge linking the castle with the city to the east still survives. The main building, which dates from 1678, contains part of the city's **History and Archaeology Museum** (⊕ *10.00–18.00 Tue–Sat (last ticket 17.30); admission BYR2,500*). The collection is extensive and to do it justice, you will need at least two hours here. When you leave, walk down the brick-paved path from the entrance and pause to look over the wall. To the left, you will see cut into the hillside to separate the Old from the New an elegant set of ornate steps going all the way down to the riverside. There are pleasant gardens and walkways to be found here, along with a small cafeteria built in the medieval style, with an attractive outdoor seating area. Along the river to the left lies the bustle of the commercial city and to the right in the distance, extensive forests. In between are attractive old wooden houses set in extensive green parkland on the opposite bank. If you look over to the right of the bridge, you can see the Fire Tower again. Continue now to the end of the paved path and pass through the double wrought-iron gates to find the New Castle, which was built on the other end of the hill as a residential palace for Polish King August III when he'd had enough of the old one. It was completed in 1737. A classic example of Baroque style, the beautiful and sumptuous Rococo interior was completely destroyed when the Red Army expelled the Nazi invaders from the city in 1944. The subsequent programme of rebuilding was much less lavish. In fact, the exterior looks a tad shabby, although inside the works of restoration are most impressive. The lack of attention to detail outside is in strict contrast to the manner of reconstruction elsewhere throughout the western territories of the former

Soviet Union in the post-war period. Today, the section facing the river houses a library, whilst at right angles to it is the remainder of the city's **History and Archaeology Museum** (⏰ *10.00–18.00 Tue–Sat (last ticket 17.00); admission BYR1,600*). As with the Old, the exhibits here are well worth a couple of hours of your time. Returning outside, you will see that the courtyard is neatly laid out and populated with trees of different species.

Standing directly between Bernadino Church and the New Castle is the unusual and slightly unnerving design of the **Drama Theatre** building. Looking like something modelled on the coronet of a Tolkienian king from Middle Earth, it was clearly intended to speak of opulence and wealth, but it doesn't pay to look too closely. The exterior is rather shabby and would benefit from a whole new coat of paint. The intended effect is further prejudiced by the proliferation of empty beer bottles that litter the pavement around the outside. This is disappointing. The design is certainly eye-catching and properly presented, this could be one of the leading images of the city. You might expect it to be illuminated by spotlight at night, but unless a performance there is running its course, it is unlit, dark, gloomy and just a little sad. Someone should have a word with the city's administrators. Happily the image is a little brighter by morning on a sunny day, when the light gives the building a little more sparkle. As with the castles next door, the view across the river from the walkway behind the theatre is magnificent.

It is also worthy of mention at this point that the view from the south bank is equally splendid, although the perspective is reversed of course. As you drive or walk onto the bridge crossing the river, look up to see all of these buildings towering above you.

Sovyetskaya Street is regarded as the main thoroughfare and centre of activity. It's certainly the best place to do your shopping, and it's also a good place to stroll and to people-watch. The city authorities are in the process of pedestrianising this thoroughfare, but at the time of writing, this process is only half finished. This means that the bottom section of the street is one giant building site. There's a relaxed attitude to health and safety in this country, so there are no restrictions on access to the site. Just be careful of the very deep holes in the ground that you could find anywhere in this area, particularly at night. When finished though, it will be delightful. The shopping streets of Minsk are now starting to look like those that we recognise in the West, with vulgar neon and in-your-face advertisements, but elsewhere in Belarus, things remain a little calmer and more understated. In Grodno and particularly on Sovyetskaya Street, small specialist shops, cafés and bars nestle unassumingly behind pastel façades. There are also many Western designer stores, but advertising is almost non-existent. At the top end on the right is one of the city's main department stores Magazin, selling all manner of things on two floors. Some of the items appear to be quite luxurious and will probably be some way beyond the means of the average local resident. You can also buy some reasonable souvenirs here, especially ceramics, textiles and straw-crafted goods. Passing down the street, there is also a cinema, halfway down on the right-hand side. Then a little further down on the left, just after you enter the building site, is the Nieman department store. Relatively new, it is bigger and fresher than Magazin. There is also a delightful street café right outside bearing the same name, selling soft and alcoholic drinks and snacks to customers at tables on the pavement under umbrellas.

MUSEUM OF GORODNITSA HISTORY (*37 Ozhesko St;* ☎ *72 16 69;* ⏰ *10.00–17.00 Tue–Sat; admission BYR3,000*) Devoted to the history of the city, it's a very small museum in a very attractive wooden building just off Lenin Square.

To take in a good selection of the best sights in town, you might like to try this circular walk. If you include shopping time and also stops for refreshments, you could spend a whole day on it. Begin at the Old and New castles, including a walk around the two museums there. Visit the Church of Saint Christmas and head east past the Drama Theatre, before crossing the road to Bernadino Church. When you leave the church, turn right along Mostovaya Street, one of the boundaries of Sovyetskaya Square. Pay a visit to Batoriya Trading House for some souvenirs, before continuing on to Farny Cathedral. Upon leaving there, walk across the square, through the pleasant ornamental gardens and turn right down Sovyetskaya Street to the end, browsing and people-watching as you go. At the bottom, turn and walk back up the other side of the street and through the square, the attractive paved area of which is much favoured by promenaders. And skateboarders. Turn right at the bottom when you reach the Drama Theatre, retracing your steps back to the New Castle. Stroll down to the riverside and rest on a bench in the gardens there. You will have deserved it!

PHARMACY MUSEUM (*4 Sovyetskaya Sq;* ☏ *44 17 09;* ⊕ *10.00–16.00 Tue–Sat; admission BYR2,500*) Situated right next door to Farny Cathedral, the building in which this unusual museum is housed was constructed by Jesuits in 1709, specifically for pharmaceutical research. It served this purpose until 1950, before closing its doors until 1996, when it opened to visitors once more as the country's only charitable museum dedicated to the history of pharmaceutics.

MAXIM BOGDANOVICH HOUSE AND LITERARY MUSEUM (*10 First of May St;* ☏ *72 22 54*). The famous Russian poet lived with his family in this house between 1892 and 1896. It opened its doors as a museum dedicated to the life of the poet in 1982 and exhibits include family photographs, personal belongings and collections of poetry. Some of the rooms recreate the interior of the house as it will have been when the family was in residence.

ZILIBYERA PARK Ten minutes from the Gorodnitsa, back in the direction of the city centre beyond the Pokrovsky Cathedral, is the Zilibyera Park. Once shabby and more than a little seedy, it has received something of a facelift in recent years, so that today it is a place for quiet reflection, gentle promenading and somewhere to sit in an oasis of green to watch the world go by. The walkways are illuminated by night. Further within the confines of the park is an amusement area with rides for children.

OUTSIDE GRODNO

There follows a selection of the picturesque towns and villages that can be found in the greater Grodno region. There are many others, equally as pretty and with similar attractions, that have not even made it into the list. As mentioned in this chapter's introductory remarks, access is going to be a problem, as there is no public transport to speak of that will be easy to use without a good working knowledge of the language. So if you don't have your own transport or a local friend who can drive you, the only option is to book yourself an excursion through one of the tourist agencies in town. You will at least get to see something of the natural beauty and architectural splendour of this lovely region.

Lida is the second-largest town in the *oblast*. Situated 160km due east of Grodno on the A236, it suffered greatly in the chequered history of warfare that dominated the area in the Middle Ages, then again in the Great Patriotic War, when it was extensively damaged. Once upon a time, the mighty structure of the **castle** (*Bd Komsomolskaya;* ✆ *3 22 94/2 13 91;* ⊕ *09.00–18.00 Tue–Sat, 11.00–15.00 Sun; admission BYR1,000, plus another BYR1,000 if you want to take photographs*) must have dominated the town centre, but the structure itself is now dwarfed by a hideous apartment block right next to it. Presently under massive works of renovation and reconstruction, this is one of the biggest castles in the whole country at 80m by 80m. Construction began in the middle of the 14th century. Made of stone and brick, the design and style are very similar to that employed in the building of Mir Castle (see *Chapter 3*, page 125). In the centuries that followed, it was sacked and plundered a number of times. In 1953, it was included in the state's List of Protected Monuments and in 1976, works of restoration began. There is still much to be done. Only the walls and one tower are standing, with a recently added high-level walkway. If travelling by car, park in the large car park at the bottom of the boulevard. The entrance to the castle is 100m up on the right-hand side, through two massive, swinging iron doors. **The Exultation of the Cross Roman Catholic Church** is another of the town's main symbols. Built between 1765 and 1770 in the Baroque style, the interior is exquisite. Also, look out for **Saint Joseph's Catholic Church**. Built between 1797 and 1825 in the Classic style, it was remodelled in 1958 as a sports hall, then as a planetarium, before being converted to a cinema in 1991, then back again to a functioning place of worship in 1995! Other than these sites, the town has little to commend it, being a typically charmless post-war urban planning nightmare. But for a truly authentic Soviet-style experience, leave the castle by the main entrance, cross the boulevard to the hideous apartment block opposite and pay a visit to the canteen to be found on the ground floor (◷ *10.00–17.00 Mon–Sun, then again 20.00–02.00 for dancing, though you will probably want to give this a miss!*)

Oshmyany, a small, 14th-century town that was once a fortress of the Great Dukes of Lithuania, is situated northeast of Lida, just 20km from the border with Lithuania. It boasts the beautiful **Saint Mikhail Archangel Roman Catholic Church**. Originally constructed in the early 15th century, it was rebuilt between 1900 and 1906 in the renowned Vilnius Baroque style. Also here is the brick-built Orthodox Church of the Resurrection. Together, both buildings frame the historical town square. The well-known Belarusian painter Korchevsky (1806–33) was born in the town. He studied in Vilnius and St Petersburg, before leaving the country for Italy in 1829.

Along the M7 road in the direction of Minsk, 30km to the southeast, is **Krevo** which has the limited remains of a 14th-century castle in the style of Lida, Mir and Novogrudok, all of which were part of the same defensive line that was constructed to repel Crusaders.

Some 30km northeast on the P106 road, **Smorgon** is an ancient town standing close to the Viliya River, surrounded by scenic countryside. The powerful Radzvili dynasty that so influenced the historic towns of Mir and Njasvizh had many connections here. Napoleon's long retreat from the gates of Moscow in 1812 passed directly through the town and the emperor himself made a last stop here, before passing over command to Marshal Murat and escaping to Paris with only his personal guard. The 19th-century **Roman Catholic Church of Saint Mikhail** has an extremely unusual structure, comprising an eight-sided base alongside a multi-tiered belfry with a hipped roof and octagonal drum at the apex.

Some 60km due east of Grodno on the road to Lida lies the town of **Shchuchin**, with its rare fortress-church that dates from the 16th century. Near to the town's enormous central square, 100m by 200m, stand the **Roman Catholic Church of Saint Theresa** (built in the Classical style in 1827), the **Orthodox Church of Saint Mikhail the Archangel** (constructed in the second half of the 19th century) and some traders' houses dating from the late 18th to early 19th centuries.

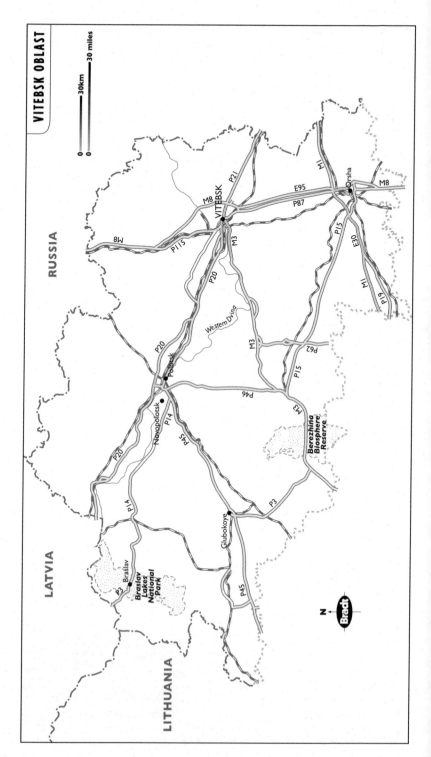

VITEBSK OBLAST

30km
30 miles

6

Vitebsk City and Oblast
Витебск

Bordering Lithuania, Latvia and Russia, the Vitebsk region is situated in the north and northeastern part of the country and occupies almost one-fifth of the country's total territory. The administrative centre of the *oblast* is the charming and elegant city of Vitebsk, with a population of around 367,000.

This whole area is the country's Lakeland, with 11 out of the 19 major lakes of Belarus being found here. It is a region of delightful natural beauty and charm, of deep blue lakes and stunning pine forests, famed way beyond the country's national boundaries. The most precious gem in the entire area is undoubtedly the collection of Braslav lakes, 50 of them in total, covering a surface area of 130km², all incorporated into a national park, with rare species of plant and wildlife preserved in their natural environment.

Situated in the southwest of the region is the stunning Berezhina Biosphere Reserve, over 85% of which is primeval virgin forest.

The concept of sustainable ecotourism is one that the country has been striving to promote, with limited success thus far insofar as visitors from outside its borders are concerned (see *Living the good life*, page 72). Probably more so than in the other *oblasts,* there is real potential for truly developing this concept here, in a manner that complements the natural resources existing in abundance whilst at the same time, securing their protection into the future.

The oldest town in all Belarus, Polotsk, is in the Vitebsk region. Founded in 862, this Slavic settlement is known to have been the centre of Christianity during the time of Rus, the first Russian state.

Vitebsk is widely regarded as being second only to Minsk as the cultural capital of the country and it is the location of the popular 'Slavyansky (Slavic) Bazaar', an international song and culture festival which takes place annually in the open air in late July and early August. Most of the musical programme is devoted to a celebration of ethnic Slavic music. The main participants are artists from Russia, Belarus and Ukraine, but there are also guests from a significant number of other countries, both Slavic and non-Slavic. For one glorious week in high summer, the entire city turns into a gigantic street party. The English-language website www.festival.vitebsk.by/en is a mine of colourful facts and information on the history of the festival and current practical arrangements. As well as the Bazaar, the city also hosts a number of annual festivals celebrating other performing arts, such as modern dance and chamber music. And the original School of Arts founded in 1919 by Marc Chagall continues to thrive. Overall, there is little doubt that the reputation of Vitebsk as an international centre for the promotion of the performing arts and fine art is assured.

HISTORY

It nicely fits the character of the city of Vitebsk (as a place where artistic temperament can flourish) that its foundation is based on the romance of legend.

It is said that whilst travelling through the region in the year 974, Princess Olga of Kiev was so impressed by the beauty of the hill at the junction of the Western Dvina and Vitba rivers marking the site of an old Slavic settlement of the Krivichi tribe, that she ordered a city to be founded in that very spot. At best this tale is apocryphal and at worst a total fiction. But so attractive is it that 974 is the official year of foundation of the city! In reality, it is likely to have first been settled by the Varangians exploring south, during their migration from their Scandinavian homelands in search of trade with Greece.

Whatever the true story, the existence of Vitebsk as a fortified centre of trade and commerce is recorded in chronicles dating from the 11th century. At this time, trade links with the Russian cities Kiev and Novgorod, with Byzantium and western Europe were already in existence along the rivers Dnieper and Dvina. Unfortunately (but not surprisingly), this marked the territory as being prime for invasion and subjugation on the part of warring princes and foreign armies. It became part of the Grand Lithuanian Duchy early in the 14th century and then on 15 July 1410 significant numbers of Vitebsk citizens helped the combined armies of Lithuania, Poland and the Czech Kingdom to defeat the Teutonic Order at the famous battle of Grunwald. In 1597, limited rights of self-determination under Magdeburg Law were granted, only to be taken away when all of the town's Orthodox churches were closed in 1622, following the assassination of Uniate Archbishop Kuntsevich during the course of a riot in the city. Then between 1700 and 1721, Vitebsk suffered considerable damage to both fabric and infrastructure in the Northern Wars that set Sweden against the Russian Empire. The town was almost completely destroyed by fire in 1708 and, over time, trade fell away as the population diminished.

It was annexed by Russia in 1772, leading to limited revival of the city's wealth, but when Emperor Napoleon invaded the country on 24 June 1812, Vitebsk found itself directly in the line of the march to Moscow. Napoleon had bought the loyalty of the noblemen of Vitebsk by promising to restore the right of self-determination that had been the privilege of the city in its time as an administratively autonomous region of the former Polish-Lithuanian Commonwealth. However, the peasants of the region were mobilised en masse by the Russian imperial army; and we all know who won in the end. On 11 July, the Russian army was billeted here on the retreat from Polotsk and then over a three-day period from 13 July, there was very heavy fighting involving tens of thousands of troops on the western fringes of the city. At the conclusion of the engagement, the Russians were forced to retreat eastwards. On 16 July, Napoleon entered Vitebsk. He established his headquarters in the Governor's Palace, high on the bank of the Dvina, but his stay was only a short one. The emperor had more pressing business in Moscow, but as history tells, he didn't quite get there.

In the meantime, incessant war had taken its toll on the city. By 1825, the population was less than 17,000 and it was not until the emancipation of the serfs throughout the Russian Empire in 1861 that its fortunes began to revive, greatly assisted by the construction of two major rail links (Moscow–Riga and St Petersburg–Kiev) which crossed here. The census of 1897 shows that the population was then over 66,000.

In 1892, the famous Russian painter Ilya Repin took up residence in the city. This was the start of its golden age as a spiritual home for notable painters, including Chagall himself, Kazimir Malyevich, Mstislav Daburzhynsky and others. Further, many masters came to teach at Chagall's school. It must have been an exciting time to be around, with the streets being turned into one enormous art studio, where buildings and the sights of the city were brought to life on canvas. Much of the substantial body of work that was created then is still to be found in the city, a rich representation in tableau form of life here early in the 20th century.

Sadly, further deprivation followed in World War I. Vitebsk became a military garrison close to the front line and the population was swelled by a significant refugee contingent. In the climate of unrest and dissatisfaction that prevailed, Bolshevik propaganda was widespread. The town's soviet was established only two days after Lenin took power in the country, but there was more misery in the civil war that ensued. Little by little, things began to improve and the revival continued apace during the intensive industrialisation of the Soviet Union under Stalin, although the population suffered just as much as the rest of the country by reason of the infamous ideological purges of the 1930s.

And this latest phase of industrial prosperity came to an end with the Nazi invasion in 1941. Only days after it began, bloody engagements were taking place in the vicinity of the city. Thanks to heroic rearguard action on the part of the Red Army on the western bank of the Dvina River, a significant proportion of the population and most of the industry of the town was evacuated and moved far to the east. But it was only a matter of time before the town fell. The Germans established a huge garrison and those who remained in and around the city were brutally repressed, not least as punishment and reprisal for the large-scale underground and partisan activity that was established here. The Red Army returned to claim the city once more in June 1944, but only after the fiercest of battles, often involving hand-to-hand fighting in the suburbs. Only 15 of the city's more significant buildings and 186 civilians survived. Nearly a quarter of a million of the region's inhabitants had either been killed in action or murdered in Nazi concentration camps. It was not to be until the end of the 1960s that the city's population reached that of 1939.

Today, the region is home to some of the country's largest industrial and scientific plants, while cultural life and the arts are also flourishing. The great traditions begun by Repin and Chagall continue to be upheld, such that this cosmopolitan city can indeed be said to represent a nexus of the old and the new.

GETTING THERE AND AWAY

Vitebsk is located on a major **railway** route to St Petersburg. The splendid station building is located in a square of pleasant gardens at the western end of Kirov Street, 15 minutes' walk from the town centre. There are also trains south to Kiev in Ukraine and east to Smolensk and Moscow in Russia. There are several 'express' trains a day to Minsk, the journey taking around five hours. Internally within the country, there are also slower and less frequent services to Brest and Grodno. Several trains a day call at Polotsk.

There is a daily **bus** to Minsk which takes around 5½ hours to complete the journey. The bus station is located ten minutes on foot to the northeast of the railway station. Polotsk is two hours away and the service is a regular one. Tallinn in Estonia can also be reached by coach and this is an interesting way to enter the country, if rather long.

GETTING AROUND

The city certainly repays exploration **on foot**, although the relatively modest numbers of sites of interest are spread over a large geographical area. Many of them are located on either bank of the Dvina River, in the vicinity of the Kirov bridge. On a bright and sunny day late in autumn, a stroll along the river here, through the splendid wooded gardens, is a real delight. The other advantage of walking is that it affords an opportunity to enjoy the pre-war architecture at leisure. So, if the weather is fine, don't give yourself too onerous a task by trying to cram in an extra

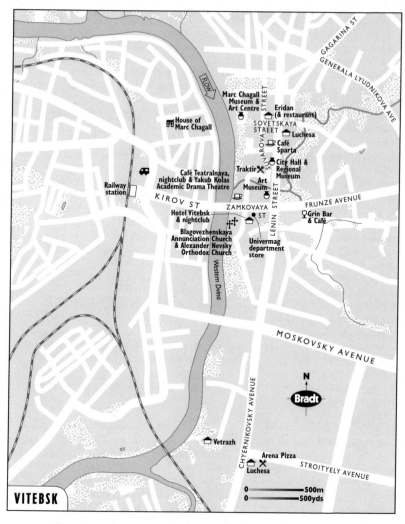

VITEBSK

museum or two; plan to tick less off your list and spend more time ambling. Otherwise, take advantage of the cheap, cheerful and plentiful (but overcrowded) supply of **buses**, **trams** and **trolleybuses**. Most rides, however long, should not cost more than US$0.20. **Private buses** also operate in the city and they won't be as crowded as the public ones, but you will have to pay more. There are plenty of **taxis** and no fare anywhere should be more than US$5. Be sure to agree the price in advance.

TOURIST INFORMATION

As in previous chapters, please allow me again to mention that it has not always been possible to establish comprehensive information on opening times of restaurants, museums, bars and clubs but every effort has been made to do so. A number of tourist agencies can be found in the city, but be sure to check their credentials first. The safest option is to book through the travel and excursion bureau located in **Hotel Vetrazh** (*25/1 Chyernikovsky Av;* ☎ *21 72 04*). For research before you go, visit the excellent English-language website www.vitebsk.by/eng. The information available there, particularly in respect of the history of the city and region, is incredibly detailed.

WHERE TO STAY

⌂ **Hotel Eridan** (25 rooms) 17/21 Sovyetskaya St; ☎ 36 24 56; f 37 44 24. Rated the best hotel in the city, this elegant building dating from 1910 is situated in a charming location in the historical area, just 200m from the Marc Chagall Museum & 2km away from both railway & bus stations. It is an attractive 4-storey building with 9 sgls, 3 dbls & 13 suites (some rooms with balconies). All are comfortable & well appointed. There is also a restaurant, bar, conference hall, sauna, steam bath & fitness centre. The hotel has an enviable reputation for high-quality service, English is spoken here too & there is wheelchair access. All major credit cards are apparently accepted, but do check first. *Sgl from US$56, dbl from US$84, suite from US$112, all inc b/fast.*

⌂ **Hotel Luchesa** (155 rooms) 1 Stroityely Av; ☎ 29 83 47; e reception@luchesa.by; www.luchesa.by. Newly opened in July 2004, this is a concrete monolith in the modern part of town, but it does have the advantage of being at the intersection of major routes, with easy access to the sights by public transport. It is 3.5km to both the railway & the bus station from here. There are 110 sgls, 18 twins & 27 trpls. There is a café serving

Russian & European cuisine, a bar, meeting facilities, a conference hall seating 100, a hairdresser, solarium, a currency exchange & a kiosk selling souvenirs & newspapers. As with the Eridan, check first before relying on being able to check out with your credit card. *Sgl from US$40, dbl from US$65, suite from US$83, all inc b/fast.*

⌂ **Hotel Vetrazh** (147 rooms) 25/1 Chyernikovsky Av; ☎ 21 72 04. Built in 1989 & located not far from the city centre. With rooms on 8 floors, it's pretty standard, Soviet-style stuff, functional, modest, but relatively cheerful. The railway & bus stations are 3.5km away. Services include a currency exchange, laundry, beauty parlour, travel & excursion bureau, restaurant, bar, snack bar & casino. *Sgl from US$25, dbl from US$30, suite from US$69, all inc b/fast..*

⌂ **Hotel Vitebsk** (150 rooms) 5/2a Zamkoyava St; ☎ 37 72 80; f 36 95 36. In the city centre & 1.5km from the railway & bus stations, the hotel is on 12 floors with a range of rooms & suites, a restaurant, bar & nightclub – & lots of concrete. Don't expect too much here, but it will serve a functional purpose at a competitive price. *Sgl from US$28, dbl from US$29, suite from US$79, all inc b/fast.*

WHERE TO EAT

The city's reputation has more to do with culture and the arts than fine dining, but one or two restaurants are worthy of note.

✖ **Restaurant Traktir** 2 Suvarova St; ☎ 37 01 07; ⏲ 12.00–midnight. Widely regarded as the best restaurant in town both for atmosphere & the quality of its menu, this venue is well located, close to the City Hall & in one of the older, more attractive streets in the whole city. Part of the menu is also in English. *Mains from US$8.*

✖ **Café Teatralnaya** 2 Zamkavaya St; ☎ 36 99 66; ⏲ 11.00–17.00 & 18.00–23.00. This is a trendy venue that attracts a large artsy crowd; not surprising, really, as it's located in the vaults below the Yakub Kolas Theatre. The ambiance is excellent &

the food is very good indeed. Traditional Belarusian & European cuisine from a varied & imaginative menu. After the restaurant closes, the venue becomes a nightclub, well into the small hours. *Mains from US$6.*

✖ **Arena Pizza Restaurant** 57/4 Lenin St; ☎ 37 24 63; also at 3/3 Stroityelye Av; ☎ 21 99 49; www.arena-pizza.by; ⏲ 10.00–23.00 daily. A new venture, these two related emporia serve standard pizza fare in a mock Italianate café setting. A delivery service is available until 22.00. *Pizzas from US$2–5; sweets & drinks extra.*

The restaurant at **Hotel Eridan** (see listing above) enjoys a fine reputation for excellent food and service, but it is expensive. There is also said to be a passable

Chinese restaurant located in the vicinity of Restaurant Traktir (the Zolotoye Drakon, the 'Golden Dragon'), where there is an English translation of the menu.

ENTERTAINMENT AND NIGHTLIFE

Vitebsk has a greater than usual number of higher educational establishments for a city of its size and has a substantial student population. Not surprisingly, then, youth culture is reasonably well catered for. This means that you might expect to find a wide choice of bars; and you won't be disappointed. None comes more highly recommended than any other, so this is a good opportunity for you to undertake some exploration of your own. All of the bars are open from late morning until 23.00 or midnight, while those that are also clubs will stay open until well into the small hours for you to dance the night away until at least 04.00. The clubs located at **Café Teatralnaya** and **Hotel Vitebsk** (see listings above) are regarded as being the best places in town for drinking and dancing.

SHOPPING

Vitebsk is famed more for its status as a centre of fine art rather than for the quality of the shopping experience it offers. Chagall-related paraphernalia is omnipresent, but that apart, there is nothing here that you cannot find elsewhere in the country. The **Univermag department store** on Zamkovaya Street has a reasonable array of traditional Belarusian handicrafts on offer (as does the railway station and the open market situated close by). The town's distillery produces some of the highest-quality vodka in the whole country and bottles aimed at the tourist market (in other words, just a little kitsch) are available in shops throughout the city.

OTHER PRACTICALITIES

There are banks and currency exchanges aplenty here, but don't expect to find many ATMs.

WHAT TO SEE AND DO

Of the six major cities in Belarus, Vitebsk has been fortunate to be able to retain a palpable and living sense of history (much more so than any of the other five), notwithstanding the widespread destruction wrought in the Great Patriotic War. To varying degrees, the prevailing influence and atmosphere in those five is certainly the more recent Soviet past, but not so here. Whatever the reason, there is a delicate sense of refinement in this elegant town.

MUSEUMS AND GALLERIES In terms of the arts, it will be no surprise that Marc Chagall's presence dominates the city:

Marc Chagall Museum and Art Centre (2 *Putna St;* ☎ *36 03 87* (*also for booking guided visits*); f *37 27 37;* e *chagall@chagall.belpak.vitebsk.by; www.chagall.vitebsk.by;* ◷ *Apr–Sep 11.00–18.30 Tue–Sun; admission BYR4,300*) Opened in 1992, this fine building is situated in an especially green part of town that is pleasing on the eye, where 300 original works of art consisting of lithographs, xylographs, etchings and aquatints are displayed on two floors. The collection also owns the series of illustrations to Nikolai Gogol's poem *Dead Souls*.

Vitebsk has many sons and daughters of repute whose fame is well known within the country, but perhaps the most internationally renowned of them all is the 'brilliant dreamer', the Surrealist painter Marc Chagall (1887–1985). Born into a family of Hassidic Jews and one of ten children, some of his best works display a charming nostalgia both for his devout upbringing and for the city of his birth. Life was difficult for the family, his father being a menial worker in the local fish factory, although it is clear from the artist's autobiography that his childhood was a happy one, in which he was allowed to endlessly roam the suburbs of the city and the surrounding countryside. But where Chagall was a dreamer, his father most certainly was not. In the absence of support from his parents to pursue his great passion for art, he left the city that he so loved in 1906 to study in St Petersburg. He moved to Paris in 1910 under the patronage of lawyer Max Vinaver. There he was befriended by Robert and Sonia Delauney, in whose circles he found the time, space and inspiration to assimilate and develop Cubist ideas. He returned to Vitebsk prior to the outbreak of war in 1914 and married his fiancée Bella, who was to be a major influence on his later work. After the 1917 Revolution, he was appointed Commissar of Art for Vitebsk, a role that did not come easily to him. He also founded, directed and taught at the School of Arts in the city, but he moved to Moscow in 1920, then back to Paris in 1923. His work was denounced by the Nazis and at the outbreak of war, the family moved to the south of France and then to the USA. When Bella died in 1944, Chagall was overcome with grief at the loss of his muse. He stopped painting for quite some time, although his subsequent relationship with Virginia Haggard (they had a son together) saw a return to his creativity. Returning to France in 1947, he subsequently married Valentine Brodsky (in 1952). In the 1960s, he was commissioned to design stained-glass windows for the Hadassah University Medical Centre in Jerusalem, work that profoundly impacted upon his faith. Further commissions for murals and costume design followed in France and America. He died in 1985. Influenced by Cubism and Surrealism but always an independent artist of unique style, he referred to Vitebsk as 'my second Paris' (although some claim that he actually called Paris his 'second Vitebsk'), and cameo sketches of the city as it was in the early 20th century are reflected in many of the works of this great master. In January 1991, Vitebsk celebrated the first Marc Chagall Festival, then in June 1992 a monument to him was erected on his native Pokrovskaya Street, with a memorial inscription being placed on the wall of his home at the same time. The small wooden house is now open to the public and the city also has a first-class Chagall Museum (see page 178).

House of Marc Chagall (*29 Pokrovskaya St;* \ *36 34 68;* ⊕ *Apr–Sep 11.00–18.30 Tue–Sun; admission BYR2,500*) The artist's father built this house at the end of the 19th century and Chagall spent his formative years here, subsequently recalling his time with great affection in his autobiography. Opened to visitors at the same time as the museum, articles and relics of Jewish family life from the late 19th and 20th centuries have been gathered and stored for display. There are also copies of archive documents and works of art detailing the life of the artist and his family in the city.

And just around the corner is the **monument** to the artist.

Art Museum (*32 Lenin St;* \ *36 22 31;* ⊕ *11.00–18.00 Wed–Sun; admission BYR4,200*) Many of the artists featured here were natives of the region, including Ilya Repin, who is widely regarded as being the founder of the art movement in the city.

6

The Yakub Kolas Academic Drama Theatre *(2 Zamkovaya St;* ↘ *(box office) 36 00 83;* f *36 07 83;* e *theatre@vitebsk.by; www.theatre.vitebsk.by)* Also built in the Classical style and adorned with the same pale orange stucco as the City Hall and Russian Governor's Palace, this theatre is home to a company that enjoys an enviable international reputation. It is only one of two in the whole country (and presumably the world) that presents performances exclusively in the Belarusian language. This should not be seen as a bar for foreign visitors, however, because presentations are usually so vividly striking and avant-garde in nature, that language is only one part of the experience. The theatre's website is a mine of useful information, both on the history of the company and the current repertoire.

CHURCHES Most of the churches in the city (particularly those from the time of the Polish-Lithuanian Commonwealth) have been destroyed, either in warfare or under the communists, but some remain. Others have been rebuilt. Try to see the following during your stay:

The Alexander Nevsky Orthodox Church Situated on Zamkovaya Street, close to the Dvina River, just across the road from the Yakub Kolas Academic Drama Theatre and within the beautiful grounds of the reconstructed Blagovezhenskaya Annunciation Church (described below), this is a tiny but strikingly beautiful reconstruction in wood of the 10th-century church that originally stood on this spot. Regular services are held here, as is daily worship of a less formal nature. The atmosphere is deeply affecting.

Blagovezhenskaya Annunciation Church A church has been standing on this site in Zamkovaya Street since the middle of the 12th century, but the original building, which had been extensively renovated in the 14th and 17th centuries, was reduced to rubble by the communists in 1961. Then in 1992 it was fully restored to its original appearance and magnificence (or at least, to how the architects imagined it to have been). The design technique, limestone blocks separated by two rows of brick, with the exterior being covered with a thin layer of stucco, is classically Byzantine and with the exception of this church, there is evidence of only one other (at Novogrudok) north of the Black Sea. Sadly, the church at Novogrudok was never actually completed and now lies in ruins. Work on both of them was probably undertaken by the same team of Byzantine architects and builders.

The Eastern Orthodox Saint Protection Kazan Cathedral Erected in 1760, the white plaster of the exterior and the matt black of the cupolas splendidly enhance the glittering gold domes and crosses above.

The Roman Catholic Cathedral of Saint Barbara Built between 1884 and 1885, this cathedral was built in the neo-Romanesque style of architecture. It's very red indeed and is perhaps best described as 'gothic' with a capital G.

OTHER BUILDINGS Other historical buildings worthy of your attention include:

The City Hall Located just along Lenin Street from the Art Museum and built in 1775, it has been extensively renovated. The beautifully ornate Baroque clock tower is an especially entrancing feature. Incorporated within is the **Regional Museum** *(36 Lenin St;* ↘ *36 47 12;* ⊕ *11.00–18.00 Wed–Sun; admission BYR3,000).* On display are relics, artefacts and memorabilia detailing the history of the city and region, with a particularly impressive collection devoted to the city's privations during World War II.

The Russian Governor's Palace Built in the early 1770s, this was the location chosen by Napoleon in 1812 to celebrate his 43rd birthday, during the long Russia campaign. A contemporary building of the City Hall, the pale orange stucco and Classical style make both of them pleasing to the eye. In front of the palace is the stone **obelisk** commemorating the centenary of the Russian victory in this campaign.

OUTSIDE VITEBSK

POLOTSK This is the region's second-largest town and one of the most attractive in all Belarus, although it is starting to become swamped by a new and expanding industrial city right next door. Located 105km northeast of Vitebsk along the A215 road, this historic settlement (and one of the oldest cities in the whole of eastern Europe) has a beautiful riverside location on the Dvina, which also flows through Vitebsk. It is often referred to as 'the city of all Belarusian cities' and many people regard it still as the spiritual cradle and first capital.

History The name of the town is derived from the Polota River, which flows into the Dvina. In fact, Polotsk was one of the earliest of the major settlements of the Slavic tribes and is widely regarded as having been the first independent 'Belarusian' state. It was first referred to in the Primary Chronicle of AD862 and it featured significantly in Viking incursions from the north. Norse sagas describe the city as the most heavily fortified in all of Kievan Rus.

Between the 10th and 12th centuries, the greater principality of Polotsk emerged as the dominant centre of influence in all of the lands now recognised as Belarus. It continually asserted its sovereignty over other powerful settlements and administrations of Kievan Rus to become not only a political capital, but also the Episcopal see and the controller of certain subservient western lands occupied by Baltic tribes. In fact, its influence stretched from the shores of the Baltic Sea in the west to the area of Smolensk in the east. Its most powerful ruler was Prince.Vyseslav Bryachislavich. He reigned from 1044 to 1101 and an inscription commissioned by his son Boris in the 12th century can still be seen today on the huge boulder placed near to the Cathedral of Saint Sophia, which was built between 1044 and 1066 as a symbol of the power and independence of the city.

The town became part of the Grand Duchy of Lithuania in 1307. It is believed that its geographical location and the extent of its influence and power made it the most significant trading centre in the whole of the duchy. It was granted self-determination and the right to govern under Magdeburg Law in 1498, but was sacked by Ivan the Terrible in 1563, before being returned to Lithuania in 1578. This signalled the start of a long period of settled affluence and it was granted the status of regional capital in the Polish-Lithuanian Commonwealth until partition in 1772. Cyclical warfare in the region eventually took its toll and the city slipped into a gradual process of steady decline. After partition, it was relegated to the status of a small provincial town of the Russian Empire, then during the invasion of Russia by the French in 1812, two decisive battles were fought here.

Getting there There are several daily **trains** to Polotsk from Vitebsk and it's a two-hour journey. You can also get here direct from Minsk, but the journey is long (up to eight hours). The **bus** station is only 100m from the railway station, with several daily buses running to Vitebsk and Minsk, but to get the best out of a visit here, arrange an excursion from Vitebsk (or even Minsk, which is 250km south on the M3 'motorway').

6

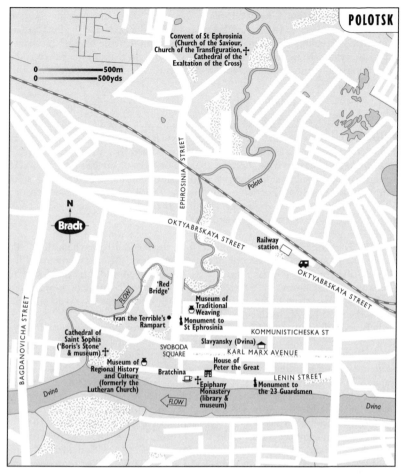

Convent of St Ephrosinia
(Church of the Saviour,
Church of the Transfiguration, ✝
Cathedral of the
Exaltation of the Cross)

0 ━━━━━500m
0 ━━━━━500yds

N

Bradt

EPHROSINIA STREET

Polota

OKTYABRSKAYA STREET

Railway
station

OKTYABRSKAYA STREET

'Red
Bridge'

FLOW

Museum of
Traditional
Weaving

Ivan the Terrible's ●
Rampart

Monument to
St Ephrosinia

KOMMUNISTICHESKA ST

Cathedral of
Saint Sophia
('Boris's Stone' ✝
& museum)

SVOBODA
SQUARE

Slavyansky (Dvina)

KARL MARX AVENUE

BAGDANOVICHA STREET

Museum of ⊙
Regional History
and Culture
(formerly the
Lutheran Church)

Bratchina

House of
Peter the Great

LENIN STREET

Epiphany
Monastery
(library &
museum)

Monument to
the 23 Guardsmen

Dvina

FLOW

Dvina

🏠 **Where to stay and eat** If you have a burning desire to stay over, there are several **hotels**, but most of them are located in the adjoining industrial town of Novopolotsk ('New Polotsk'), which is not particularly pleasant, especially after the delights of Polotsk. The only one in Old Town is the **Slavyansky Hotel Complex** (also referred to as the **Hotel Dvina**) (*13 Karl Marx Av;* ☎ *44 22 35*). Located 1.5km east of Saint Sophia Cathedral, 1km from the railway station and 1.5km from the bus station, there are 48 rooms on two floors, consisting of singles, doubles and suites, starting at US$55 per person per night, breakfast extra. The design of the building is repro-Classical, with a richly ornate and multi-pillared entrance. But inside, it's nothing special, if adequate as a place to rest your head for the night. There is also a **restaurant** (☎ *44 33 93*) of similar standard. Karl Marx Avenue is very much the main drag and other places to eat exist along here. For a snack and a coffee, try the **Bratchina café** (*22 Lenin St;* ☎ *49 07 69*) down towards the river.

What to see The **Cathedral of Saint Sophia** is situated in an elevated position at the end of Lenin Street, from which it dominates the town. When first built, between 1044 and 1066, it was a direct rival of the cathedrals bearing the same name in Novgorod and Kiev. The cathedral bears a striking resemblance to the original Hagia Sophia in Constantinople, a symbol of the authority and prestige enjoyed by the city at the time. A rich library was maintained there which included the Polotsk Chronicle, but everything disappeared without a trace during the 16th century Livon Wars. On the orders of Tsar Peter the Great, it was blown up by retreating Russian forces in 1710, before being rebuilt by the Poles between 1738 and 1750 as a Baroque Roman Catholic Cathedral. Today, only the eastern elevation and some of the basement walls are the originals. Further restored in 1985, it now houses a **museum** (✆ *44 53 40;* ☺ *10.00–16.00 Tue–Sun; admission BYR3,500*) dedicated to its history.

Just outside the rear left-hand corner of the cathedral is the huge boulder of **Boris's Stone**, upon which Vyseslav Bryachislavich's son Boris carved the inscription, 'Dear Lord, please help Boris, your slave' in the 12th century, along with a cross and other Christian symbols. Take the steps down towards the river and you come to Lenin Street. Just along on the left is the **Lutheran church**, a stone and red-brick neo-Gothic building constructed at the beginning of the 20th century at the behest of only 200 Protestants living in the town at the time, whose enterprise and wealth considerably outweighed their modest number. No longer a church, it now houses the **Museum of Regional History and Culture** (✆ *44 27 15*). Further along the street, on the right-hand side and with a lovely river frontage, is the beautiful **Epiphany Monastery**. Founded in 1582, it long served as the primary centre of Orthodox worship and teaching in the town. Now, the building is used as the **Simeon of Polotsk Library and Museum** (✆ *44 57 25*), the only museum devoted solely to book printing in the whole country. If you look along the riverbank from the rear of the museum, you will see the **Monument to the 23 Guardsmen**, erected in 1989 to acknowledge the heroism of soldiers of the First Baltic Front who forced their way across the inner river at this point on 3 July 1944 and who lost their lives holding the position. Across the road from the printing museum is the **House of Peter the Great** (✆ *44 28 55*). Built at the turn of the 18th century with elements of Baroque style, it was the residence of the tsar throughout the summer of 1705, during his time in command of the Russian imperial army during the Norther War that was raging at the time. It now houses a permanent exhibition. Turning away from the river and in towards the town, you soon reach the central **Svoboda Square**. Take the road out of the northwestern corner adjacent to a pretty park, but pause briefly to take a look at the **monument to Saint Ephrosinia** on the right-hand side, the first woman to be canonised by the Orthodox Church and also the country's first saint. Proceed onwards and cross the grimly named **'Red Bridge'** over the Polota River, so called to commemorate the bloody battles that took place near here in October 1812 during the Napoleonic campaign, when around 14,000 people lost their lives.

After 15 minutes or so pleasant strolling, you will reach the entrance to the **Convent of Saint Ephrosinia** (*59 Ephrosyny Poltskoy St;* ✆ *44 56 79;* ☺ *11.00–16.00 Tue–Sat; admission free*) itself. The convent complex contains a number of different buildings of interest to the visitor. After you pass under the belfry, the compact **Church of the Saviour** is directly in front of you. Built in 1161, it is one of the best preserved examples of early church architecture in the whole country. The recently restored frescoes match the beauty of the interior, where St Ephrosinia lies in eternal rest. Each year on her memorial day (5 June), thousands of pilgrims from all over the country come to pay homage to her holy relics and to kiss her sacred cross. Sadly, it's not the original, which disappeared without trace during the Great Patriotic War and doubtless sits in a private collection somewhere. But the replica is still a powerful and mystical symbol of the spirituality of the people of Belarus. To the right is the slightly larger **Church of** the **Transfiguration**. Made of wood, it was built in the 17th century. Left of centre stands the imposing **Cathedral of the Exaltation of the Cross**. Lavishly ornate inside, it houses a large number of holy relics that are widely believed to have mysterious and mystical powers. This is very much a place of living worship.

If you have time as you retrace your steps, there are two other sites of interest along the way. First, pause at **Ivan the Terrible's Rampart** on the right-hand side of the road after you cross the Red Bridge. This 16th-century fortification was constructed on the orders of the notorious tsar after he captured the city in 1562. Then behind the buildings on the other side of the road stands the **Museum of Traditional Weaving** (℩ *44 30 41*). Three halls trace the history of this activity, so critically significant to the culture of the country, in relation to the Vitebsk region. Visitors receive explanations about the holy symbolism of images that feature in designs, along with the ancient myths that are encoded in ostensibly simple patterns.

Nestling in various locations throughout the Vitebsk *oblast* are many **small towns and villages** that are worthy of your time. Sadly, access by public transport is not easy unless you can speak the language and have lots of time to sit on a rattling bus, so unless you have your own transport, best advice is to arrange a tour or excursion through one of the state agencies. Some 50km due west of Vitebsk on the A245 road is the town of **Beshenkovichi**, an administrative centre that was first mentioned in 1460. Located on the Dvina River, noteworthy sites include the 18th-century palace and extensive parkland, together with the beautiful Orthodox Church of Saint Elias, built in 1870. Some 85km southwest of Polatsk on the A235 is the 16th-century town of **Glubokoye**. Numerous buildings in the Baroque style are to be found here, together with the stunning Orthodox Church of the Nativity and the Classical Trinity Roman Catholic Church. Established towards the end of the 11th century and located 70km due south of Vitebsk, at the crossroads of two major inter-continental routes west–east (the M1) and north–south (the M8), the town of **Orsha** is one of the oldest in the country. And as well as being a key port on the Dnieper River, it is also a major junction on the Minsk–Moscow railway line. The station is a glorious building, housing shops and an excellent restaurant. Elsewhere, the beautiful Kuteinsky Monastery was originally home to a renowned 17th-century printing house. And in a stunning riverside location, the beautiful walled Orthodox Church of Saint Illy is a 'must see'.

BRASLAU LAKES NATIONAL PARK The park is situated in the vicinity of Braslau, about 250km north of Minsk and the same distance northwest from Vitebsk, through Polotsk along the A215. Established in 1995 and famed for the unique nature of its aquatic ecosystems, the southern part of the park is mostly lowland marsh and forest, while the central and northern parts consist of beautiful blue lakes interconnected by a labyrinth of hundreds of rivers and streams, set in picturesque rolling hills. No fewer than 189 species of bird live here, including black stork, osprey, tern, bittern and ptarmigan. It is also possible to spot elk, wild boar, roe deer, beaver, fox, raccoon, badger and wolf roaming free in their natural environment, although all are notoriously shy and evasive. There are also complexes consisting of large pens for closer study. Inhabiting the lakes are 28 species of fish, such as eel, whitefish, whitebait, zander, pike, catfish, carp, bream, chub, turbot, tench, perch, gudgeon, loach, ruff and stickleback. The park is rich in flora of more than 800 species. The areas of forestry include birch, black elder and aspen.

Visitors can dip into various organised tours on horseback or by car, as well as on the water or by foot, lasting from one to several days. One of the most delightful trips is by launch across the limpid lakeland waters. In terms of facilities, there is the Slobodka tourist centre, the Drivyaty and Zolovo tourist complexes and a museum, together with a sauna and lodges for hunting and fishing. All tours and excursions can be arranged with the specialist company **Sanatoria & Health Resorts Centre** (✆ *00 90 63/29 22 22;* f *22 62 58*). Alternatively, all of the state tourism companies, such as Belintourist, Vneshintourist, Smoktravel or Top-Tour have a range of tours to suit all tastes.

BERAZHINA BIOSPHERE RESERVE The reserve was opened in January 1925 to preserve and nurture another splendid natural environment, as well as to conserve and protect the valuable wildlife living there, notably beaver. Covering around 85,000ha, this substantial area of wilderness is situated 130km northeast of Minsk and the same distance southwest of Vitebsk. Crossed by the A245 road that connects these cities, it is a land of virginal primeval forests (mostly pine and spruce), marshland (one of the largest in Europe) and lakes, rich in diverse flora and fauna, sitting right in the middle of the watershed of the Baltic and Black seas. The areas of marshland are particularly beautiful. Small wooded islands rise above marsh plains as far as the eye can see. Thousands of years ago, they were proper islands, washed by the waves of the vast glacial lake that is buried now under a thick and impenetrable layer of rich peat. The largest and longest river, the Berazhina, is an integral link in the system that connects the Baltic to the Black Sea. In times gone by, it has been a very important trade route. Today, trade has been replaced by leisure and the river is populated with visitors retracing the routes taken by Vikings and Greeks in history.

Around 52 species of mammal live here, including brown bear, elk, wolf, otter, wild boar, lynx, the once rare (but now flourishing) beaver and the extremely rare European bison, along with 217 species of bird (including the golden eagle and the seldom seen black stork), ten of amphibian, five of reptile and 34 of fish. And mosquitoes. Clouds of them. The vegetation is also richly diverse, with more than 780 herbaceous varieties being found in the reserve, as well as over 200 varieties of moss and lichen.

Facilities for enjoying this special place at leisure are good. Tourists have at their disposal the compact Hotel Plavno, formerly a presidential residence much favoured by Alexander Lukashenko, incorporating a restaurant, billiard room, hall with cosy fireplace and a sauna. If you picture a large wooden ski chalet, with wall-to-wall pine panelling, then you won't be far wrong.

For people who prefer to spend time much closer to nature, there are also a few complexes of small but snug wooden huts that are located in the most picturesque areas of the park.

The state tourist agencies offer various tours, ranging from weekends that include a visit to the nature museum and the open-air pens along prescribed ecological routes, to specialised longer-term environmentalist tours to observe between 120 and 150 species of wild animals in their natural habitat. The emphasis here is on providing enjoyment through education and the raising of awareness of important ecological issues. Visitors have the opportunity to take a close look at local ways of life and traditions, be entertained by ethnic folk troupes, sample local and national cuisine, experience traditional trades, visit sites of important historical and cultural heritage and learn more about the scientific study undertaken here, as well as watching films on an ecological theme, observing nature and taking part in environmental discussions.

To complete your research on this enchanting wilderness before you visit, browse the reserve's useful and informative website (*www.berezinsky.com*).

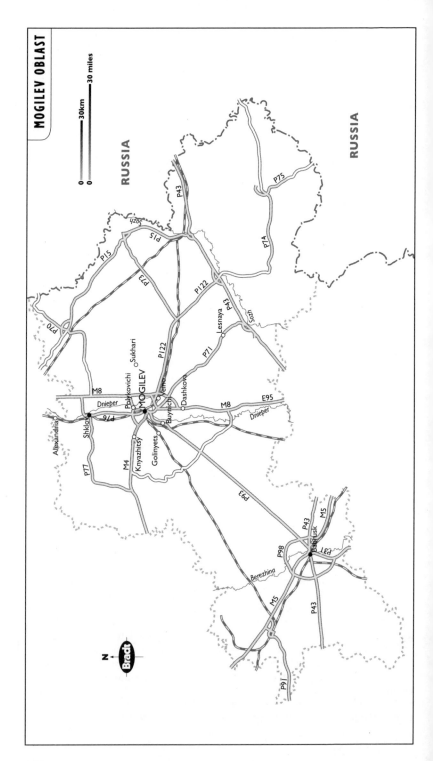

MOGILEV OBLAST

RUSSIA

RUSSIA

P75

P74

P43

Sozh

P15

P15

P73

P122

P70

Lesnaya

P43

Sozh

Sukhari

Polykovichi

P122

P71

P122

MOGILEV

Vieino

M8

Dashkova

Dnieper

Buynich

M8

E95

Dnieper

Shklov

P76

Alexandria

Knyazhitsy

Golinyets

P77

M4

P93

Berezhina

P98

Babrusk

P43

M5

P31

M5

P43

P91

N

Bradt

0 ——— 30km
0 ——— 30 miles

7

Mogilev City and Oblast
Могилёв

Mogilev is a city of 360,000 inhabitants on the hilly western bank of the Dnieper River in eastern Belarus, close to the border with the Russian Federation. It is the capital of a region that has excellent transport links, with main connections to Russia, Ukraine and the Baltic States crossing the territory by road and by rail. Mogilev itself is a major rail junction, and the three large rivers that criss-cross the *oblast*, the Dnieper, the Berezhina and the Sozh, are still used for navigation and transport purposes. In fact, there is a very substantial inland port on the Dnieper. The city itself is one of the main economic and industrial centres of Belarus. At the end of the Great Patriotic War, an enormous metallurgy complex incorporating a number of steel mills was established here as part of Stalin's programme of mass rebuilding and reindustrialisation. There are also many other significant industrial complexes for the manufacture of cranes, tractors and cars, along with a plant for chemical production and many other light industries, particularly those related to tannery. Yet the economy of the region and its social infrastructure has been significantly prejudiced by the consequences of the Chernobyl catastrophe; 35% of the territory was contaminated by radioactive particles in the immediate aftermath of the explosion and there are many areas forming 'hot spots' of radiation that will remain out of bounds for a very long time. No fewer than 13 out of the 21 districts are officially recognised as being in need of specialist measures. Agricultural land makes up over 50% of the territory and between 1986 and 1991, 47,000ha of previously arable but now contaminated lands were taken out of use.

This is all the more tragic because the region is known for its picturesque scenery, with forest covering over 30% of the area. Another 18% is occupied by predominantly low-lying meadows and marshland (not dissimilar to the region of the Polyesye in the south of the country, but less extensive), while the growing of crops (predominantly rye, barley, buckwheat, oats and potatoes) plays a key role in the agricultural sector. Cattle breeding (both for meat and milk production) is also a feature, whilst in a number of districts there are fur, poultry and fish farms. At present, reorganisation of the agricultural sector is under way. Production co-operatives, joint-stock companies and private farms are being established, while for now and for the foreseeable future, collective farms (*kolkhoz*), state farms (*sovkhoz*) and supporting enterprises also continue to operate.

The region has a long and interesting history. These lands have been ravaged many times by fierce battles, with only monuments remaining to tell the tale. For example, near the village of Lesnaya, 55km southeast of Mogilev on the P71 road, stands the memorial complex commemorating the 200th anniversary of the Russian army's victory over the Swedes, consisting of a chapel and a museum dedicated to the history of the region. And the memorial of Buynichskoye Field keeps alive the memory of heroes of the Soviet Union from the Great Patriotic War. Then in the context of contemporary history and current affairs, the village of Alexandria, just to the north of the town of Shklov (35km due north of Mogilev on the P76 road), is famed for being the birthplace of the first (indeed, only) President of Belarus, Alexander Lukashenko. You can visit the local museum in the village school, with its special section devoted to the president, see the location of his family home (2km away) and drink from the spring that can be found nearby at young Alexander's favourite childhood place. The Sports and Tourism Department of the Mogilev Regional Administration is currently marketing this as 'an unusual waterway route for canoe enthusiasts' under the strap line 'Paddle Your Way to President Lukashenko's Home Town'. Yes, really.

Today, the face of the city presents a mixture of the old and new, the traditional and the avant-garde. Nowhere is this better represented than Leninskaya Street. Lovingly renovated and restored, with the enigmatic stargazer street sculpture on display (the one that appears on the cover of this book), it is regarded with much affection by residents and visitors alike. The past and present of the city are also reflected in the displays of the Regional Museum of Local Lore and various museums of fine art.

Each year, Mogilev is home to two very different festivals: Zolotoy Shlyager (the 'Golden Hit Parade', featuring retro-pop) in November and Magutny Bozha ('Almighty God'), dedicated to sacred music, in July and August. There is also an annual film animation festival.

HISTORY

Mogilev can boast many connections with famous visitors who have spent some time here. The people of the city turned out en masse when Russian Tsar Peter the Great arrived by boat on the Dnieper in 1706; Russian Empress Catherine the Great famously met with the Austrian Emperor Joseph II here in May 1780; the great Russian poet Pushkin spent time in the city; from 1915 to 1918, the supreme commander-in-chief of the Russian imperial army was in residence; and in August 1915, the Russian Emperor Nikolai II himself was in town. Indeed, it is widely known that the last tsar paid a significant number of visits to Mogilev.

This and other towns in the area such as Mtislavl and Krichev were founded in the 12th and 13th centuries, although Slavic tribes of the Krivichi and Radimichi had established settlements in the region in the 10th century. The city itself was founded in 1267 by around 200 settlers, although local archaeological excavations have suggested that there were early Iron Age settlements on the site of the current town, specifically where Gorky Park now stands. From the early 14th century, it was a constituent part of the Grand Duchy of Lithuania. After the Union of Lublin and the creation of the Polish-Lithuanian Commonwealth, it was transferred to new royal owners. There followed a period of strong growth in the local economy, due to the advantageous geographical location of the city right at the centre of major trade routes from north to south and from west to east. Crafts such as weaving, metalwork, woodwork, leather processing, gun-making and the art of jewellery manufacture were all developing intensively here. In the 15th century, the city also became a pottery centre. Trading in many different crafts was so significant that it acquired a customs office of its own. Then in 1577, it was invested with new rights of self-government and granted city status by King Stefan Batory under Magdeburg Law. This was a golden age for the city. It was a large river port, more prosperous than Minsk, and many trade ships were to be seen moored there. By the end of the 17th century, there were 15,000 residents of the city living in 3,000 houses. At the same time, Mogilev became a very significant centre for Eastern Orthodoxy, the largest in all Belarus. There were many substantial congregations and a theological seminary was established to protect the faith. Meanwhile, congregation schools promoted the development of education, while printing houses published literature in the Belarusian, Greek and Latin languages. Around this time, Saint Nicholas Orthodox Church, the Epiphany Orthodox Cloister and the Jesuit Roman Catholic Church were built.

During the Northern Wars between 1700 and 1721, the Swedes sacked and destroyed more than half of the city's houses, while Peter the Great himself ordered that it be razed to the ground in 1708. After the First Partition of Poland, it inevitably fell into the hands of imperial Russia, but continued to flourish as the administrative centre of the region. Then during the war against France in 1812, French forces under Marshal Davoilt captured and plundered the city.

When serfdom was abolished in 1861, the social and economic development of Mogilev accelerated exponentially. The city's museum was founded in 1867. July 1883 saw the first issue of the *Mogilev Eparchy News*. In 1885, there were only 124 business enterprises employing 270 workers, but just 15 years later, there were 220 businesses employing 790 workers. The first theatre was built in 1888 and by 1897 the population had swelled to over 43,000, nearly half of whom were literate. In the early part of the 20th century, there were three types of credit institutions, relating to commerce, land and small debtors, together with three printing houses and a number of mechanical workshops.

However, economic crisis and the global depression of the early 20th century widened the gulf between the classes. The year 1901 saw the first significant strike by workers at the dairy plant, followed by workers in the rag trade in 1903. On 1 May from 1901 to 1904, political rallies took place and in late May 1905, there was a strike in the bakery, followed by a walkout of railway workers in December 1905. Demands for improved working conditions continued and in May 1906, hairdressers, shoemakers and tailors downed tools to demand that the working day be reduced to nine hours. At the beginning of World War I, martial law was imposed throughout the region and for the duration of the war, the headquarters of the vast imperial Russian army were located here, with the supreme commander-in-chief in residence. But the political tide was turning and on 22 March 1917, in the aftermath of the February Revolution, the City Deputy-Council of Workers and Soldiers was formed. The power of the collective ensured that in the first half of 1917, Mogilev workers held a number of strikes, seeking various political and economic objectives.

After the ensuing October Revolution, the city remained under anti-Soviet forces for a whole month, until on 18 November 1917, the Deputy-Council of Workers and Soldiers passed a resolution that accepted Soviet rule and took over the administration of Mogilev. There followed the start of a short period of intense instability, when on 18 February 1918 German forces occupied the city, followed by Polish troops on 12 March and then the German army again on 26 May, before it was transferred to the ill-fated and short-lived Belarussian People's Republic. Finally in 1919, it was overrun and captured by Red Army forces, following which it was incorporated into the Belarusian SSR.

It is thought that up to 25,000 people from the *oblast* volunteered for the Red Army in the early days of the Great Patriotic War and from 24 June to 3 July 1941, its western front headquarters were located in the city. By that time, a significant proportion of the major industrial plant and machinery had already been evacuated east. But despite the frenzied construction of two encircling defensive lines in just seven days under the protection of the 172nd division, Mogilev fell to the Nazis on 26 July 1941, after 23 days of intense and savage fighting. A cruelly oppressive regime was immediately put into place by the invaders. Five concentration camps were created in the region and during the period of the war, over 70,000 citizens of the city died and a further 30,000 were taken to Germany as slave labour. Most of

7

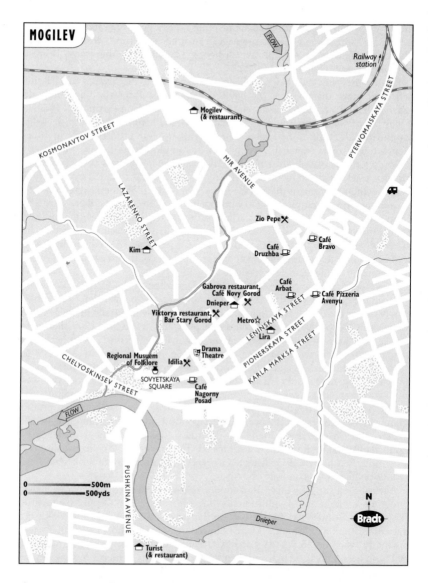

them were Jews. Then on 6 April 1943, the Mogilev partisan army was formed. It very quickly grew to comprise 34,000 active volunteers.

In June 1944, the Red Army launched its Belarusian offensive operation and on the 28th, the city was finally liberated by troops of the 2nd Belarusian Front. On 25 April 1980, Mogilev was awarded the Order of the Great Patriotic War (First Class) for the bravery and resilience displayed by its citizens during the oppression of the war years.

After the war, the city was reconstructed at an astonishing pace and by 1959, the population had spiralled to 122,000 people. New housing estates and 'micro-districts' were springing up all over town and new bridges were built over the Dnieper to cope with the increasing demands on the city's infrastructure. Today, Mogilev's place as a major (and modern) industrial city making a huge contribution to the economy of the country is assured.

GETTING THERE AND AWAY

Mogilev is well appointed in terms of transport links, with major rail and road routes passing through the city. Built in 1902, the railway station is a most attractive building, adorned in pastel stucco. It is located 2km north of the city centre, at the western end of Grishina Street. There are plenty of local trains serving towns in this and adjoining regions. Mogilev is also a stop on several main line routes serving Minsk (several trains a day), Gomel Brest, Grodno and Vitebsk within Belarus and international destinations such as Moscow, St Petersburg, Vilnius and Kiev. There is also a bus station close by, with varied and alternative routes throughout the *oblast*. Several services also arrive and depart from and to Minsk every day. The town is located midway between the cities of Vitebsk and Gomel on one of the country's major routes north–south (the M8). Minsk lies 203km to the west along the M4.

GETTING AROUND

The usual mixture of bus, tram, trolleybus and taxi is on offer, all cheap and all reliable, but you are unlikely to need to go far in this city, as most of the sights are located on the western bank of the river, in a fairly small and compact area around Leninskaya Street. Walking is thus the best option.

Nonetheless, the integrated infrastructure for public transport is particularly impressive in this city. For up-to-the-minute timetables for each (but sadly in Russian only), visit the excellent website maintained by the city's executive committee (*www.city.mogilev.by/rus/articles/transport*). As an aside, this site does have a large number of English pages, providing all sorts of civic, cultural, tourist and administrative information for visitor and resident of the city alike.

TOURIST INFORMATION

Although it contains a considerable number of really interesting architectural features of great appeal to the visitor, Mogilev is not yet geared up for the tourist trade. In this context, it is the least developed of the country's six major cities. Given that it's an industrial centre, most of the focus is on facilities for businessmen. Indeed, sites of interest to the traveller or leisure visitor are not well promoted at all. For example, the city boasts a number of stunning churches, all of which are difficult to find without the benefit of a local guide. There are some tourist agencies in town (including a few located at some of the hotels) offering limited facilities and excursions, but overall, there are very few options. Those agencies that do have offices here are mostly unlicensed, so be very wary of parting with your cash when booking tours from this city. Far and away the best option is to travel here by means of an organised tour arranged before you arrive in the country or from the capital Minsk, with one of the accredited state agencies or international operators (see *Chapter 2, Tour operators*, page 37).

WHERE TO STAY

⌂ **Hotel Kim** (7 rooms) 27 Lazarenko St; ☎ 22 91 11/13; f 22 91 20; e hotel_kim@tut.by; www.mogilevportal.com/res/hotel/kim. Located just off the city centre, this small hotel offers the best value & comfort in town. Only built in 2002 & upgraded in 2005, the specification is of European standard, with all rooms being extremely well appointed. The staff are attentive & keen to please, while the modest size of the establishment gives it a homely & cosy feel. There is a small swimming pool, sauna & café, together with a travel booking service. The railway station is 5km away & the bus station 3km. Highly recommended. *Sgl from US$58, dbl from US$62, suite from US$106, all inc b/fast.*

🏠 **Hotel Lira** (8 rooms) 45 Leninskaya St; ☎ 25 25 43; f 25 29 45. This is another small hotel that comes highly recommended. Only 4 years old & located in the heart of the city, all of the rooms are comfortable & the service is good. There is a small swimming pool, sauna & billiard room, together with a travel booking service. *Sgl from US$57, dbl US$67, suite US$93, all inc b/fast.*

🏠 **Hotel Turist** (153 rooms) 6 Pushkin Av; ☎ 44 56 55/46 75. This is yet another example of the omnipresent concrete monolith so favoured by the Soviet Union in the 1970s & 1980s as the state attempted to expand the tourist trade. The railway & bus stations are 6km & 2km away respectively. Built in 1986 & situated downtown in a park on the banks of the Dnieper, the rooms are on 7

floors, ranging from sgls to suites. All are adequately appointed. Services available include an exchange bureau, travel & excursion office, hairdresser, newspaper kiosk, pharmacy, souvenir shop, restaurant, bar & snack bar. *Sgl from US$40, dbl from US$45, suite from US$115, all inc b/fast.*

🏠 **Hotel Mogilev** (329 rooms) 6 Mir Av; ☎ 26 31 89/46 80 77; f 26 39 41. An even bigger concrete tower block of 13 floors. Located downtown & 3km from the railway station (3.5km from the bus station), the rooms, ranging from sgls to suites, are exactly what you would expect: functional but without charm. It was built in 1972, so the concrete is past its best. Even though it was last refurbished in 1999, it's already looking tired & drab. Services include a casino, restaurant seating 320, bar, swimming pool, beauty parlour, currency-exchange office & shop. *Sgl from US$35, dbl from US$40, suite from US$105, all inc b/fast.*

🏠 **Hotel Dnieper** 29 Pervomayskaya St; ☎ 25 90 41. Functional & adequate, but presently closed for major works of refurbishment.

✖ WHERE TO EAT

✖ **Café Pizzeria Avenyu** 63 Leninskaya St; ⏰ 11.00–23.00 daily. Standard pizza fare. Nothing special, but it's functional & well located. A good choice if you're looking for tactical food between ticking the sights off your list. *From US$4 for a pizza.*

✖ **Gabrovo** 31 Pervomayskaya St; ☎ 22 23 15/76 96/31 15; ⏰ 11.00–midnight daily. Centrally located, this pleasing eatery specialises in Bulgarian cuisine. *Mains from US$6.*

✖ **Idilia** 5/1 Pervomayskaya St; ⏰ 11.00–23.00 daily. A self-service restaurant in a good location. Don't expect haute cuisine, but as with Pizzeria Avenyu, it serves a useful tactical purpose. *Mains from US$4.*

✖ **Mogilev** 6 Mir Av; ☎ 26 39 26; ⏰ 10.00–midnight daily. This is the large restaurant at the even larger hotel of the same name. A very diverse menu, but most of it probably

won't be available. It's all rather average & not cheap into the bargain. *Mains from US$7.*

✖ **Modern** 6 Korolyev St; ⏰ 11.00–23.00 daily. Cosy, with good service. Hot & cold food available. *Mains from US$5.*

✖ **Turist** 6 Pushkin Av; ☎ 44 00 55/21 07; ⏰ 11.00–midnight daily. Also the restaurant in the hotel with the same name. Utterly interchangeable with the Mogilev. *Mains from US$7.*

✖ **Viktorya** 16 Pervomayskaya St; ⏰ 11.00–22.00 daily. Compact & cosy, with a varied & interesting menu of largely European cuisine. *Mains from US$6.*

✖ **Zio Pepe** 35a Mir Av; ☎ 22 37 67; ⏰ 10.00–23.00 Mon–Sat. Cosy interior, good service & fine Italian food, considering it's a national chain restaurant. A solid & perfectly acceptable option. *Mains from US$5.*

ENTERTAINMENT AND NIGHTLIFE

As with the restaurant listings, none of the bars, cafés or clubs has been road tested in this town, although a limited amount of local intelligence has been garnered to assist. The adjective 'cosy' features in just about all of the entries I've seen, but do check this out for yourselves! If you have a desire to strike out into uncharted territory, then perhaps the best option is to reconnoitre along Leninskaya Street, where locals and visitors alike are wont to spend leisure time in surroundings that are known to be safe, pleasing and easy on the eye. It's where you are going to be spending most of your time anyway.

Café **Arbat** 50b Leninskaya St; ⊕ 09.00–15.00 daily. A fast 'mini-café' within the Spartak stadium.

Bar **Beata** 230 Krupskoi St; ⊕ 11.00–midnight daily. Round-the-clock service.

Café **Bravo** 69 Pervomayskaya St; ⊕ 11.00–23.00 daily. Small & cosy.

Café **Druzhba** 32 Pervomayskaya St; ⊕ 11.00–midnight daily. Good food & a large menu.

Bar **Joker** 1 Ostrovskovo St; ⊕ 18.00–05.00 daily. The bar at a nightclub.

☆ **Club Liga** 4 Korolev St; ☎ 23 94 29/91 01; ⊕ 20.00–04.00 daily. Situated to the east of the city centre, there's very little else in the vicinity, but if dancing, lights & loud music are your objective, it's as good as any other venue in the city.

☆ **Club Metro** 36 Leninskaya St; ☎ 25 25 85/87; ⊕ 20.00–04.00 daily. No better or worse than the Liga, but with the advantage of a central location on a very fashionable street.

Café **Nagorny Posad** 13a Leninskaya St; ⊕ 11.00–midnight daily. Centrally located & popular with locals & visitors alike.

Café **Na Slavgorodskom** 3 Dimitrova Av; ☎ 25 44 61; ⊕ 10.00–17.00 daily. In the south of the city & some way from the likely attractions, this is a pleasant venue to while away an hour, but there isn't enough that's different for a special visit.

Café **Novy Gorod** 31a Pervomayskaya St; ⊕ 10.00–15.00 & 16.00–23.00 daily. The location is central & it's a good place to meet & pass the time of day.

Bar **Olimp** 25 Mir Av; ⊕ 08.00–22.00 daily. Slightly to the north of the main central area, this is a venue where the locals go for a beer, but you won't feel unwelcome.

Café **Retro** 16 Lepeschinskova St; ⊕ 10.00–22.00 daily. Cheap, cheerful & fine for a coffee & a short rest.

Bar **Stary Gorod** 16 Pervomayskaya St; ⊕ 19.00–05.00 daily. Delicious food & very good service. Well located for you to be able to do other things, this is a great place to recharge before continuing with your explorations.

SHOPPING

There are no specialist facilities here that cannot be found elsewhere, although the museum shop has some interesting souvenirs to purchase. The best place to browse and to purchase, not surprisingly, is along Leninskaya and other streets in the vicinity. Beware tacky souvenirs, though.

OTHER PRACTICALITIES

There are plenty of banks and currency exchanges in town and even some ATMs.

WHAT TO SEE AND DO

In all probability, your first visit to Mogilev is likely to be on a tour or excursion from Minsk, perhaps with an overnight stay. The area simply is not geared up for independent leisure travel, but the infrastructure for tours via the state agencies is excellent. This will not be to everyone's tastes of course, but until such time as the tourism *industry* develops to match the breadth and quality of the tourism *product* in this country, a guided excursion is going to be the only way for visitors to gain their first sight of the riches on offer in the more remote areas. When you return next time, armed with the knowledge you will have acquired first time around (and preferably, some of the language), it will be a different story. For now, just relax and let someone else do the work while you soak up some local knowledge and climb onto that learning curve.

Here are the best of the sights that you are sure to see:

CASTLE The original castle was built in 1267 when the city itself was established by around 200 settlers. It was then enlarged and considerably modernised between the 16th and 18th centuries. Today very little remains, but it is still possible to appreciate the strategic importance of the location.

KANYESKY PALACE Built between 1762 and 1785, the Kanyesky Palace and its **Memorial Arch** are pleasing on the eye. Georgi Kanyesky was an 18th-century diplomat, writer and philosopher of great reputation.

LENINSKAYA STREET This street is worthy of a few hours' attention. The architecture has been substantially renovated and the thoroughfare pedestrianised, with imaginative street furniture to complement the whole effect. The buildings have attractive pastel-coloured stucco fronts and all is very neat and tidy. But although the restoration work is very professionally done and the intention to re-create Mogilev of old is to be commended, it's all just a little twee. There's even a vague whiff of Disneyland about it all, down to the land train that chugs back and forth along the street, with the few tourists that come here on board. Still, there are some fine pavement cafés and a few shops that are worth a browse. In the central ('star') square, directly outside the Radzima cinema, stands the enigmatic bronze sculpture of a stargazer, pointing to the heavens. It is the work of a modest and unassuming artist, the sculptor Vladimir Zhbanov. A veteran of the Afghan conflict, his work is to be found all over Minsk. His trademark is understatement. All of his creations are aesthetically pleasing, but they do not appear on plinths in the usual places that you might expect sculptures to be displayed. For example, *A Girl from Minsk* stands quietly and without fuss on the pavement of Mikaelovsky Avenue, while elsewhere, a long-legged girl, also of bronze, sits minding her own business on a bench. This is urban art at its best. Do check out the stargazer. This and the rest of Leninskaya Street is the first 'must see' in the city.

DRAMA THEATRE (*7 Pervomaiskaya St;* ↘ *31 00 45; www.mogdt.nm.ru*) Built in May 1888, this charming red-brick building is worth a visit in architectural terms alone. It specialises in contemporary drama, but works of masters such as Gorky, Chekhov and Kupala are also performed here. A night at this theatre was a favourite pastime of the last tsar Nicholas II and his family. Further along the street (*73 Pervomaiskaya;* ↘ *32 66 90*) is the children's **Puppet Theatre**.

THE REGIONAL MUSEUM OF LOCAL LORE (*1 Sovyetskaya Sq;* ↘ *25 10 14/25 14 50/22 01 20;* e *kraimog@mail.ru; www.mogilewmuseum.iatp.by;* ⊕ *1 Oct–30 Apr 10.00–18.00, 1 May–30 Sep 10.30–18.30; closed Mon & Tue; admission BYR4,500*) This place is a real find and a towering monument to the dedication of its founding fathers and those who have kept the aims of the museum alive against all odds. The first history museum was founded in the city in 1867. It survived a number of privations, including revolution and was reincarnated more than once, only for the building to be burned to the ground during the early days of the defence of the city in 1941. The treasures were hidden in a secure facility, but they disappeared during the war and the search for them still goes on. As a result, everything collected in and around the city from 1867 until 1941 was lost. After the war, it took several years for a museum of sorts to be established once more, with a 13-year gap from 1977 while major works of repair were undertaken. Happily the museum is now open for business once more and on display are over 300,000 artefacts, consisting of archaeological finds from the region, coins and treasures, icons and other holy relics, paintings, ethnographic displays, historical documents, war memorabilia and articles of everyday life from the 19th and 20th centuries, all collected since 1944. The reassembled historical collection from 1917 to 1945 is particularly interesting. Located in four halls, great historic events and significant periods of time are covered in considerable detail, including the 1917 Revolution, mass industrialisation, Stalin's purges, the Nazi occupation and subsequent partisan insurrection. Walking excursions of 45 minutes' duration, lectures on the move about history and the environment, can be booked for groups of up to 25 persons, but only in Russian, although with advance notice, an English speaker of sorts might be available. The English-language website is extremely informative. Another 'must see'.

THE ROMAN CATHOLIC CATHEDRAL OF SAINT STANISLAV
Built between 1738 and 1752 in the Baroque style and fronted by four majestic colonnades, it is beautifully decorated with many exquisite murals depicting the entire cycle of the Scriptures. Organ recitals are regularly held here.

THE ORTHODOX CONVENT OF SAINT NIKOLAI
This walled monastic complex has preserved the structure of its magnificent Baroque cathedral, which was constructed in 1668, including the bell tower, walls and gates, together with the original iconostasis and some magnificent frescoes in dazzling colours from the 17th and 18th centuries on the exterior of the elevations.

THE TRINITY CATHEDRAL
Constructed between 1909 and 1911, this is a fine example of retro-Russian design.

THE MEMORIAL COMPLEX AT BUYNICHSKOYE FIELD
Located 5km south of the city centre on the P93 road, just to the west of the small village of Buynichi. It is here that a hugely significant military engagement took place in the early weeks of the Great Patriotic War. For 23 long days and nights, shortly after Operation Barbarossa began, this place was the scene of a heroic defence action on the part of Red Army soldiers of the 388th Infantry Division, who delayed the capture of the city (and thus slowed up the advance on Moscow) long enough for the Soviet Union to gather its strength and resources for the defence of the greater part of the Soviet Union. The heroism displayed by regular Red Army soldiers and partisans here has passed into legend and the Regional Museum of Local Lore in Mogilev has an excellent feature on the engagement. On many days of the year, hero veterans of the Red Army can be seen here, taking part in official ceremonies of remembrance, or else visiting in small numbers to honour the memory of their fallen comrades. It is a sad, solemn, but ultimately uplifting place. After passing through a triple archway of simple but affecting design, the visitor comes to a memorial lake and a chapel of remembrance. There are also displays of tanks and military equipment, together with a memorial stone upon which are inscribed verses of the renowned war correspondent, writer and poet Konstantin Simonov, a veteran of the battle. Upon his death, his ashes were scattered over the field in accordance with his last wishes. There is an excellent English-language website (*www.simonov.co.uk*) devoted to the life and work of this esteemed writer and some research before you visit will help to set the scene for you. Also in the village of Buynichi is an interesting **centre for handicrafts**. There is an amusing play area for children, a reconstructed mill and a number of traditional workshops. And coming soon to Buynichi is a 'new' medieval castle. There is much local interest in historical re-enactments, especially of episodes from the Middle Ages. A number of historical societies exist in the town and when the 'new' castle is built, complete with an inn, hotel and tavern, along with several authentic towers and an encircling wall 7m high, the 1 ha area within will be used for jousting and other knightly activities. It is also planned that the castle towers themselves will contain hotel rooms. Furnished in the, er, medieval style, of course. Watch this space and book early.

Even though the surrounding countryside is attractive, particularly on and around the rivers that cross the region, access by public transport is difficult, for two reasons: first, you're going to need to be able to speak the language and secondly, the infrastructure is not geared up for visitors who want to explore, but for local people who need to get from their homes to work, to market and to school or university. But some of the excursions arranged by the state agencies will include a tour of the rural areas, particularly if you arrange an overnight tour from Minsk. Noteworthy architectural monuments of the district include the 19th-century **Church of the Protection of the Virgin** in the village of Veino, 5km east of Mogilev on the P122 road; the early 20th-century **Assumption Church** in the village of Golinyets, 10km southwest of the city on minor roads; a **farmstead** (from the beginning of the 20th century) in the village of Dashkovka, 15km due south of the city on the E95 road; a **Dominican church** built in 1681 in the village of Knyazhitsy; and the early 20th-century **Assumption Church** in the village of Sukhari, 20km northeast of the city on the P96 road. Finally, there is a small but interesting **military history museum** in the village of Polykovichi, just to the northeast of Mogilev on the P123 road. These are a good reflection of the sites to be seen on an organised tour through the *oblast*, but there are many others further afield that are worthy of your attention. Come back with your own transport and explore one day.

8

Gomel City and Oblast
Гомель

Gomel, also referred to as Homyel or Homel (as a result of some literal and phonetic translations of the name, based on the strong accent that pervades in this part of the country), is the second-largest city of Belarus and the main administrative centre and capital of Gomel *oblast*. With a population of close on half a million people, it is located high above the western bank of the Sozh River, in the southeastern part of the country, 300km from Minsk and close to the borders with Russia and Ukraine. It is also only 120km or so from the now empty Ukrainian city of Pripyat, where the ill-fated nuclear plant at Chernobyl was situated. In the whole of Belarus, this region suffered the worst contamination of all and subsisting levels of radiation are still very high in some areas of its countryside. It will be so for a very long time indeed. There are a number of 'no go' areas in the region to which access is available only by means of official pass. These areas are patrolled by militia. Additionally, strict rules remain in force about the production and distribution of foodstuffs, together with strong government advice about what to eat and drink in terms of natural products. To assist with the mitigation of the consequences of Chernobyl, the Polyessky Radiation and Ecology Reserve was set up in the *oblast* to study the effects of exposure to radioactive material and to undertake some strategic thinking to assist with the development of long-term contingency planning for the affected areas.

The city is a large and significant transport junction at the centre of a rail and road crossroads that connects the rest of the country to the west (and thence to the countries of western Europe beyond), the Baltic States to the north, Russia to the east and Ukraine to the south. There is also an airport (to and from which only a limited number of commercial flights operate) and a river port. Historically, the Sozh was a major trading route. Today, modern Gomel shares with Mogilev the accolade of being one of the largest industrial centres of Belarus. The region's southern position and mild climate also mean that conditions for the development of agriculture are most advantageous.

Away from the city, the countryside is particularly attractive. It is a land of forests and picturesque riverbanks, with low marshland in between. Here is the eastern end of the Polyesye, the unique land of 'fogs and bogs' (see *Chapter 4*, page 154). In the days of the Soviet Union, the fragile balance of nature here was disturbed, as marshes, peat bogs and lakes were artificially dried up with the aim of increasing the proportion of land available for cultivation. Happily, the topography and ecology survived (when the USSR itself did not) and much of the area was preserved in its natural state and condition. Today, the Pripyatsky National Park affords visitors the opportunity to admire this rare environment in circumstances where the ecological balance, the animals that live here and the plants that thrive are nurtured and protected.

In addition to the natural delights to be enjoyed, there are also many manmade creations of great interest. Architectural delights in the region include the Bernadino Roman Catholic Church and Cistercian Monastery in Mozyr, the 18th-century Church and Jesuit College in Kalinkovichy, the 17th–18th-century

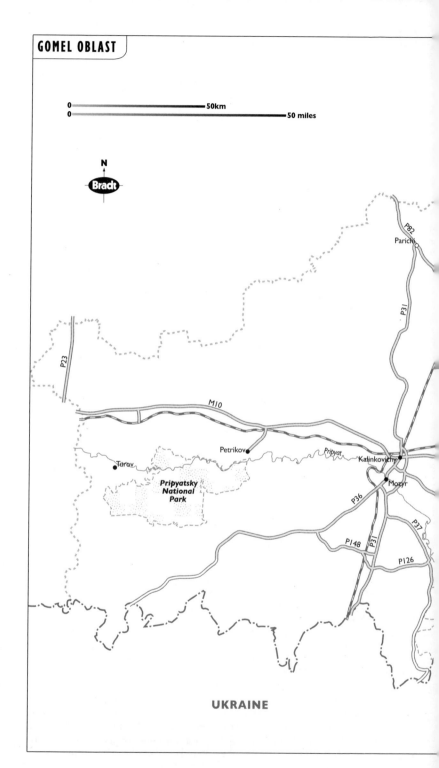

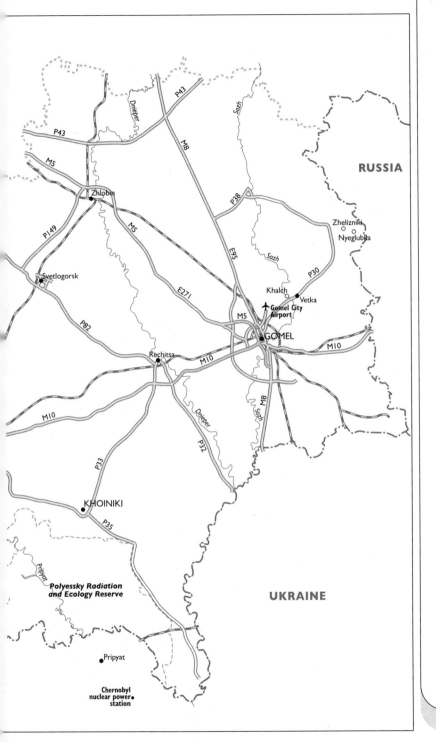

There is little doubt that the tragedy that occurred at the nuclear power plant at Chernobyl has become a defining landmark in the history of this oft-blighted country, dividing it into pre- and post-Chernobyl periods. Nowhere has this been more acutely articulated than in Gomel region.

The damage to the republic as a whole is almost beyond measure. Analysts believe that the cost has totalled in the vicinity of US$235bn; put another way, this equates to 32 annual state budgets of the pre-tragedy period. Practically all spheres of human activity have been affected in the regions, particularly those in the southeast. Farmland and pastures have been excluded from agricultural use, while the use of forest, mineral, organic, fuel and other resources is subject to restrictions. Amongst other losses suffered in the regions are the closure of enterprises and companies, output reduction, significant expenditure for the resettlement of whole communities, the cost of ensuring safe living conditions and social security for residents of the contaminated regions, including their medical care and recuperation. In particular, the cost to the social and community infrastructure is incalculable. And the effect of the 'Chernobyl factor' on the lives of individuals and families continues to manifest itself in all sorts of unexpected ways. The existence of real and readily diagnosable medical problems and conditions is an irrefutable fact, with evidence and data to back up the claims. More difficult to analyse and articulate are the consequences of the despair and lack of hope that follow in the aftermath of such cataclysmic events.

Gomel *oblast* took the biggest hit and bore the brunt of the disaster. In the country as a whole, more than 135,000 people from 470 townships and villages, two-thirds of which were in Gomel *oblast*, had to leave the worst affected territories and resettle to safer regions of the republic. My own adoptive family in Vetka were forced to move many hundreds of miles east into the Urals, almost without notice. It was years before they were permitted to return.

In the years that followed the disaster, the *oblast* developed a system of radiation monitoring and control, as well as a series of protective measures in agro-industrial

Church of Saint Nicholas in Petrikov and the beautifully restored church at Zhelizniki, believed to be the oldest in the entire region (and one of the oldest, if not the oldest, in the country). In the school at Nyeglubka, students are taught the art of weaving on wooden machines constructed exactly as they were many hundreds of years ago, to preserve the old and traditional ways. Many bitter engagements were fought on these territories in the Great Patriotic War; for example at Halch, there was great loss of life as the Red Army strived to cross the Sozh, with Gomel itself almost completely flattened under fierce bombardment. Monuments to heroism and sacrifice are everywhere to be found in this *oblast*.

HISTORY

First mentioned in chronicles in 1142, the original settlement here was established at the place where the Gomeyuk stream flows into the River Sozh. Today, this point is marked by the ornamental swan lake at the bottom of a ravine in the Rumyantsev-Paskevich Park. A number of different Slavic tribes seem to have co-existed peacefully in the area and as with so many other communities in these lands, Gomel's geographic location was extremely favourable when it came to developing trade, because of the river routes connecting northwest and southeast Europe.

Originally included in the estate of Prince Rostislav Mstislavich, it subsequently shared the fate of most Belarusian towns, passing through the hands of one production, which is financed from the state budget. The region is carrying out a set of measures aimed at improving medical services to the victims of the catastrophe. There is also a system of social protection of all categories of the affected population.

Various foreign charitable organisations from Germany, Great Britain, Ireland, Japan, Italy, Austria, Belgium, the USA and other countries render significant support to Gomel in mitigating Chernobyl's consequences. They supply drugs and medical equipment, organise learning and development opportunities for Belarusian doctors in Western clinics and arrange recuperation visits to foreign countries for children from the most contaminated regions. More recently, on the initiative of the United Nations and the World Bank, the *oblast* launched projects aiming to promote the rehabilitation of the contaminated territories, insofar as that can be safely achieved. These projects seek the support of the international community in two ways. First, in securing loans for developing the industrial infrastructure and creating new jobs in the affected regions, thus providing an opportunity for local people to raise their level of social security themselves; and second, in the transference of skills to local people to enable the country itself to rebuild its infrastructure according to its own perception of where the need really lies.

The trouble with radiation pollution is that you can't see it, smell it or taste it. For the most part, everything looks exactly the same. The consequences are there to be seen, in terms of abandoned villages, derelict homesteads and signs by the side of the road displaying the familiar radiation logo barring access down some of the woodland tracks and old roads, but not the radiation itself. It is for this very reason that many people, particularly the elderly, have gradually moved back to their former homes in areas where it is unwise to live, eat the fruits of the forest and drink water from the local streams.

In this region of great natural beauty, radiation is all around: in the water, in the food, in the ground and in the air that people breathe. It is part of the way of life and it won't be going away for a very long time. The challenge is to combat its consequences while making the safest and best use of natural resources, without compromising the health and well-being of all who live here.

conquering warlord after another, from Princes of Kievan Rus to Ivan the Terrible. In 1335, it was ceded to the Grand Duchy of Lithuania and in the 16th century its castle held a strong fortified position high above the River Sozh in major engagements against invading Tatars from the Black Sea. Then in 1670, a significant step in the development of the region came with the grant of rights of self-determination and governance under Magdeburg Law. As in earlier times, tradesmen and merchants were encouraged to return once again as the commercial prosperity of the city and its satellite villages grew. Yet for the next 100 years or so, short periods of economic stability were followed by debilitating conflict as the strength and power of Gomel's warring neighbours waxed and waned.

It passed to Russia after Poland was partitioned in 1772 and then in 1775, Tsarina Catherine the Great gifted the town to one Count Rumyantsev. Brave and a tactically astute militarist, he was not only a hero of the people, but also a personal favourite of the empress herself. His loyalty to her was rewarded with many lavish gifts that included (amongst other things) extravagant jewels, military decorations, ornate silver trinkets and works of art. Emancipation of the serfs was still almost a century away and so the gift of the town also included 5,000 peasants living in the area. Finally (and most significant of all), she gave him 100,000 roubles to build a palace. It took him five years (between 1777 and 1782) to replace the old wooden castle with a magnificent mansion of stone. It was designed by Rastrelli, the architect responsible for the Winter Palace in St Petersburg.

I remember my first visit to the region in 2001 for two particular reasons. First, whilst visiting a large school, I asked the headmaster to explain the purpose of a digital display in the entrance hall, the numbers on the readout constantly changing, apparently in random fashion. He told me that it was a monitor showing the level of radiation pollution in and around the school. Then later that day, I visited a kindergarten. I passed from room to room, smiling fondly at the accoutrements of the toddlers and small children that were all around: toys, books, clothes and in one room, a series of cupboards, the drawers of which were tiny beds for the littlest tots to take an afternoon nap. It made me miss my own children very much indeed. And in this place of youthful innocence and apparent safety and security, my gaze fell on an object resting on the window ledge. When I went over to take a closer look, I saw that it was an old-fashioned Geiger counter.

On a later visit to the *oblast*, I was given the opportunity to spend a day in the restricted zone with two senior local officials, one an elected deputy and the other an ecological expert. On a warm spring day, we took the road from Vetka that leads towards Svetsilovichy and then onwards to the Russian border. It is a long, straight and flat road, with extensive silver birch forests on either side, just beyond the tarmac. Not far out of Vetka is the permanent militia post that is manned 24 hours a day to monitor those who pass through this area. Unsurprisingly, we encountered no difficulty here. Some 5km further on is a road to the left and just before you reach it, you notice the first half-derelict property. As you turn in, there stands the telltale sign warning of dire consequences if you enter, the sinister international radiation logo leaving you in no doubt as to the violation of the natural order that lies beyond. We got out of the car to walk for a while. The sun was shining, birds were singing and everywhere we looked were the signs of new life, of growth and regeneration in the hedgerows and trees. Except that all around us, the insidious, creeping and degenerative radiation permeated the very ground on which we walked. The most obvious sign of incongruity was everywhere to be seen, in the form

Gomel quickly began to take on the architectural characteristics of a major European city. In 1834, Rumyantsev's younger son Sergei sold the palace and grounds to Count Paskevich, who added further features, built the nearby tower and designed the ornamental gardens that are still there today. In 1850, the first telegraphic communication line in all Russia was established between St Petersburg and Simferopol on the Black Sea, passing through Gomel. At the same time, the city found itself on the new highway between St Petersburg and Kiev. Then by 1888, it had become a major rail junction. This was a time of great prosperity, with trade, industry and culture developing rapidly. Another major road route was completed by the construction in 1857 of a bridge erected over the Sozh. By 1913, the town's population had soared to over 104,500 people, including a large and influential Jewish community.

The early part of the 20th century saw much revolutionary activity in Russia and in 1917, the empire fell at last. The first Soviet was established in Gomel in December 1917 and then in April 1919, the administrative area was incorporated into the newly independent but short-lived republic, which then became part of the Soviet Union. By 1926, it had become one of the most significant regions in the Belarusian SSR. Indeed, the 1920s and 1930s saw massive and rapid economic growth in terms of the industrial and infrastructure development of the town. Huge industrial enterprises were established. By 1941, the town was able to boast 264 of them, along with 144,200 inhabitants. Indeed, Gomel ranked third at this time in the whole of the republic in terms of industrial output.

of increasing numbers of buildings that we passed, all with the windows and roofs removed by the authorities to prevent people from living there. The remains of the large village school were particularly poignant. We were assured that it was perfectly safe for us to be here on a short-term basis and indeed, the advice of perceived medical expertise sought prior to the visit confirmed that this was so.

We drove further into the contaminated zone, passing another manned checkpoint as we crossed a small stream. Every time we stopped, I got out of the car to scan our surroundings. The countryside here is stunningly beautiful. Rivers, streams, woodland, marsh and meadow lie between small villages of delightful wooden houses. All empty, or at least, most of them. Very occasionally, we would pass individual dwellings with smoke spiralling from the chimney and a *babooshka* tending the crops in the garden outside. The state turns a blind eye to these people and on the face of it, produce from the land here cannot be sold. Regular checks on the radioactivity of fruit and vegetables are supposed to ensure that this is so. I couldn't help wondering, though.

On another occasion, the extent to which limitations on access into the zone are rigidly enforced was shown to be comprehensive. I was in the second of two cars *en route* back to Vetka from a visit to a farm in Vyeliki Nyemki, a small hamlet north of Svetsilovichy where I and others had been working on sustainable development projects. The state officials accompanying us on the visit were in the first car and I was travelling with colleagues who had never before seen the abandoned village described above. We slowed and turned in, the first car pulling away into the distance. We had only just got out of the car when it returned at high speed, one of the officials leaping out to shepherd us back into our car. I was later told by a colleague who was travelling in the first car that as soon as the officials realised we had turned off, the driver performed a high-speed U-turn to fetch us back. Genuine regulation for all the right reasons, or just bureaucracy? I still can't decide.

By the time of the Nazi invasion in July 1941, the Jewish community had increased to around 50,000, approximately one-third of the city's total population. Some managed to flee in the early days of Operation Barbarossa, but after the city fell on 19 August 1941, those who could or would not leave were confined to conditions of unspeakable barbarity. In the final analysis, over 100,000 people from the *oblast* were to die in five concentration camps and four ghettos, or after having been transported to Germany as slave labour. The city itself was virtually flattened, with 80% of buildings being destroyed. The Nazis stripped the town of all industrial equipment, food reserves and stocks of raw materials for transportation back to Germany.

The region was a major centre for resistance activities of the partisan movement and on 26 November 1943, the town was liberated by forces of the Belarusian Front of the Red Army. In 1946, the process of restoration and reconstruction of Gomel began, based on the preservation of original features in strategic planning terms. By 1959, the population had climbed to 168,000 and in 1962, the first trolleybuses appeared on the streets. Bit by bit in the four decades that followed, Gomel developed once more into a major European city, full of hustle and bustle, as significant new projects were completed, including newly established residential areas and the construction of a pedestrian bridge over the Sozh from the Rumyantsev Park. At the end of the 1990s, the works of construction for the new suburban railway station, another new river crossing and the impressive 'Ice Palace of Sports' (a huge facility for public sports use) were finished, as befitted the country's second city.

The Belarusian state airline Gomelavia is based at **Gomel Airport**. The enterprise was established in 1996 and operates domestic scheduled services and regional charters. Situated 8km from the city (a cab ride from the centre should cost no more than BYR15,000), the airport opened in 1968 and is the second largest in the country. The airline operates scheduled domestic flights to Minsk, Grodno and Mogilev within Belarus and scheduled international flights to Moscow and Kaliningrad in Russia. Its operating partners are Aeroflot and Transaero Airlines. There is one daily flight in each direction between Gomel and Minsk, departing Gomel at 08.30 and returning from Minsk at 20.00. The cost of a return ticket is US$15. The experience is an interesting one. Passengers are ferried across the tarmac to the waiting plane in a 'truck' pulled by a tractor. One of my associates describes how, on his first flight, the twin-engined, propeller-driven aircraft raced down the runway for take-off, only to come to an abrupt halt, before turning around and taking off in the opposite direction! But the flying time is only 45 minutes and this remains by far the quickest means of travel between the country's two largest cities. One further key piece of interesting news is that from 25 March 2007, airBaltic (*www.airbaltic.com*) began operating three flights per week from Riga to Gomel and back. This has begun to transform travel to Belarus. Before, it was only really possible to fly to Minsk from the West, but the country has become more accessible to visitors from western Europe now that this route to the southeast has begun to operate. For the time being, however, it is too early to assess the impact of this new service.

The main **railway station** is located on Privakhsalnaya Square at one end of Lenin Avenue and only 15 minutes' walk from the city centre. It has the facilities that match its role as a major rail terminal. There are frequent trains each day to Minsk (the fastest journey time is just under five hours) and there is also a sleeper service.

The **bus station** is situated just a few hundred metres away. There are several daily services to Minsk (journey time around six hours) and regular routes also operate north and west to the major centres of population within the country and south and east into Russia and Ukraine. Local bus services also depart from here and the coverage is excellent, both in terms of frequency and also the number of destinations served.

Access by **road** is very good too. The M5 motorway heads northwest from here to Minsk and all along the route major works of upgrading are in the course of being implemented. The relatively new ring road around the city of Babrusk (almost halfway between Gomel and Minsk) has made a big difference. Journey times are generally around five hours. Other major roads will take you west via Mozyr to Brest and then into western Europe, north via Mogilev to Vitebsk and then into the Baltic States and finally, east and south into Russia and Ukraine.

GETTING AROUND

The main thoroughfare heading north to south within the city is Sovyetskaya Street. The gradient rises as you head south and at the very top is Lenin Square, where you-know-who still presides over the city from his lofty perch on a granite plinth. Behind is the park where the palace and cathedral are to be found, then beyond and some way below the park is the Sozh River. Lenin Avenue leaves the square from the same side as Sovyetskaya, but in a northwesterly direction and at an angle of around 45°. It's then a straight 15-minute walk to the railway station. To access the bus station, turn left out of the main entrance/exit of the railway station and walk straight ahead for 200m. There are plenty of taxis to be found around here, particularly right outside the main entrance to the railway station.

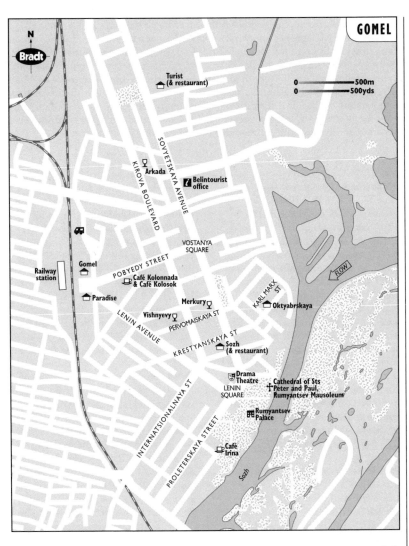

The bus, tram and trolleybus services are plentiful and cheap, if overcrowded. Directly in front of you out of the railway station is Pobyedy Avenue and a straight ten-minute walk along here will bring you back to Sovyetskaya. Turn right to complete the triangle back up to the park. All in all, the centre is compact and everything you will want to see can be easily accessed on foot.

TOURIST INFORMATION

As with previous chapters, please bear in mind that in spite of continued efforts, due to the developing nature of tourism in the country it has not always been possible to ascertain complete information on opening hours, telephone numbers and prices for restaurants, bars, clubs, museums and the like.

The city of Gomel has a number of tourist agencies, most of them on Sovyetskaya. The state agency Belintourist has an office at 61 Sovyetskaya (*56 70 00/72 88/80*

17). Otherwise, the reception desks at the larger hotels will have limited amounts of information. The agency Gomeltourist operates from a base in the Hotel Turist on Sovyetskaya, offering a full range of visitor facilities, including tours around the city and out-of-town excursions. Before you go, take a look at www.gomel.lk.net for some comprehensive history notes and some useful photographs. The *oblast* executive committee's website (*www.gomel-region.by/en*) is packed with information, although primarily aimed at members of the community, but you can pick up some very useful intelligence about facilities and infrastructure. For notes on history and the towns of the area, the best resource is www.goldring.gomel-region.by.

WHERE TO STAY

Hotel Turist (181 rooms) 87 Sovyetskaya St; 56 50 15/57 59 15; f 57 48 77; e gomeltur@mail.gomel.by. Built in 1986 & substantially refurbished in 2004, there's no escaping that this is an archetypical Soviet concrete block, situated 2km from the railway station & 2.5km from the bus station. With rooms spread over 7 floors, you pretty much get what you might expect; drab décor, little warmth in terms of atmosphere, but adequate & functional facilities. There is a currency exchange, Gomeltourist travel & excursion bureau (57 49 49), post office, restaurant spread over a number of rooms (all of which offer live music or evening cabaret), café, bar (24hrs, serving excellent coffee), newspaper stand, jewellery shop, pharmacy, souvenir shop, hairdresser, sauna & massage room. Rooms range from sgls to 3-room suites. All in all, it does the job. Conference attendees & businessmen (national & international) use this hotel, so be wary of the unofficial 'services' that will be on offer, ie: the knock on the door & the late-night phone call after you turn in. *Sgl from US$48, dbl from US$72, suite from US$112, all inc b/fast.*

Hotel Sozh (120 rooms) 16 Krestyanskaya St; 53 81 73/74 81 59; www.hotelsozh.com. Much older than the Turist (& it shows in terms of style rather than disrepair), this classy 4-storey hotel was built in 1960 & refurbished in 2001. Centrally located just off Sovetskaya (close to the southern end) in the heart of the city, there is an excellent restaurant that is highly rated by the locals, 2 24hr bars, currency exchange, beauty parlour & travel bureau. Beware the cheap 3rd-class rooms, though; they really are basic, but excellent value if you just need somewhere to lay your head for the night. This hotel is one of only a handful in the whole country that publicly advertises its different rates, depending on the nationality of the guest: CIS residents pay more than double the rate charged to Belarusian nationals, while foreigners pay almost three times as much. *Sgl from US$28, dbl from US$45, suite from US$60, all inc b/fast.*

Hotel Oktybrskaya (145 rooms) 1 Karl Marx St; 77 68 91; f 77 66 91. Not far from the river, there are sgls, dbls & suites on 6 floors. There are no facilities other than the rooms & b/fast is not available here. It's cheap, but not very cheerful; a last-resort option. *Sgl from US$30, dbl from US$40.*

Hotel Gomel (190 rooms) 1 Privakhsalnaya St; 55 32 45/74 81 59/71 67 25; www.hotelsozh.com. In the same ownership as the Hotel Sozh, but much more downmarket. It's considerably bigger, but it's a sterile, soulless place. There is a restaurant, café & currency exchange. Its big advantage is in terms of location; it's the first high-rise you see on your left as you exit the railway station. *Sgl from US$35, dbl from US$45, suite from US$60, all inc b/fast.*

Hotel Paradise (24 rooms) 1 Privakhsalnaya Sq; 77 69 66/01 49; www.gomelparadise.com. A small hotel, situated on the other side of the station to the Hotel Gomel; turn right out of the main exit. The reception area is wall-to-wall pseudo-marble & it's tacky. There's also a small restaurant here of acceptable standard, serving European, Russian & Belarusian cuisine, plus a laundry, hairdresser & shop. Rooms range from sgls to apts & all are functional, but no more. *Sgl from US$25, dbl from US$35, suite from US$55, apt from US$90, all inc b/fast.*

WHERE TO EAT

Café Irina Lunacharsky Park, off Gagarin St; 70 36 44; 12.00—midnight daily. The dining area inside is small & quite ordinary, but outside is an attractive terraced eating area under cover of a huge awning. There are patio heaters for chilly evenings too. There's also a large BBQ. The cuisine is

Belarusian & European from a varied menu. Service is excellent & the food is of a very high quality. It's my personal favourite in town. *Mains from US$6.*

✘ **Sozh Restaurant** 16 Krestyanskaya St; ☎ 74 81 75/88 02; ⏰ 19.30–01.00 daily. Belarusian & international cuisine of high quality, in an attractive setting & with good service. The best indicator is that it's well regarded & much used by local people. *Mains from US$7.*

✘ **Restaurant Turist** 87 Sovyetskaya St; ☎ 57 59 03; ⏰ 11.00–midnight daily. Situated at the Hotel Turist, there are 3 restaurants in this complex, all serving Belarusian & European cuisine to a high standard, although the service is not the fastest & it's a little frosty too. Live floor shows while you eat will take you back to the days of 1970s-style cabaret. *Mains from US$7.*

ENTERTAINMENT AND NIGHTLIFE

Gomel is home to a larger than average number of excellent universities and higher education facilities, as befits its status as the country's second city. In fact, the State University, with over 10,000 students alone, is actually located on Sovyetskaya Street (*www.gsu.unibel.by/en*). With so many students in residence, the bar and club scene is thriving. And as you might expect, there is a wide choice of establishments. As in the other major cities, the coffee-bar culture that was lost in the West decades ago continues to thrive.

The establishments on Sovyetskaya, the main hub of activity, tend to be lively. The most chic street is Pobyedy, so bars here like to think of themselves as being sophisticated. Three blocks up towards the park from Pobyedy and running parallel to it is Pyervomaiskaya, which is also known for the quality of its bars in terms of atmosphere and facilities.

♀ **Bar Amerikanka** 16 Pyervomaiskaya St; ☎ 78 74 10
♀ **Bar Arkada** 90a Kirov St; ☎ 57 11 91
♀ **Bar Berezhka** 38 Sovyetskaya St; ☎ 77 65 35
☕ **Café Dubravha** 58a Kosmonavtov Av; ☎ 54 06 24
☕ **Café Kolonnada** 16 Pobyedy St; ☎ 77 55 38

☕ **Café Kolosok** 16 Pobyedy St; ☎ 77 47 91
♀ **Bar Merkury** 1 Pyervomaiskaya St; ☎ 53 47 63
☕ **Café Rumyantsyevskoye** 38 Sovyetskaya St; ☎ 77 67 78
♀ **Bar Vishnyevy** 16 Pyervomaiskaya St; ☎ 53 18 15

SHOPPING

A gentle amble up Sovyetskaya Street towards the park will take you past a variety of shops in increasing numbers, including two very good bookshops, one on each side of the road. The classiest shops are to be found in Pobyedy Avenue, off Sovyetskaya Street. An alternative place for purchases is the cathedral, which has two stalls at the rear selling posters, cards, beeswax candles and very cheap artefacts (such as images of icons for your wallet, desk or car) that make excellent souvenirs.

OTHER PRACTICALITIES

As befitting the country's second city, banks and currency exchanges are to be found all over the town centre. ATMs are not commonplace, but they are beginning to appear in increasing numbers.

WHAT TO SEE AND DO

One of my favourite pastimes in the whole of Belarus is to take a stroll along **Sovyetskaya Street**, with its fine 19th- and 20th-century architecture, and into the park. If you begin on the eastern side of the street at **Vostanya Square**, opposite Pobyedy Street, take a look first at the **tank** mounted on a granite plinth on your left. It's a monument to the Red Army heroes who liberated the city in

1943. Head up Sovyetskaya past the circus and in the pretty park that you now reach, close to the pavement, look for the **bust of Andrei Gromyko**. He was the Soviet Union's foreign minister in successive governments for an incredible 28-year period that spanned four decades, notably under Leonid Brezhnev. Gromyko first entered government under Stalin and he was unquestionably one of the giants of Cold War diplomacy. He was born in a small village near here.

Further along, you will pass a series of **murals** depicting key events in the history of the city, beginning with its foundation in 1142. You very soon emerge into **Lenin Square**, a vast area of tarmac with the **drama theatre** to your right and in front of you, the **statue of Lenin**, high on its plinth, gazing magisterially over the entire city. If you enter the **Rumyantsev-Paskevich Park** to the left of the statue, you will find that you are standing directly in front of the early 19th-century **Cathedral of Saints Peter and Paul**. Built to Classicist design, it is an imposing building, but its real delights are to be found inside, for the iconostasis and walls display a wonderful collection of icons. Daily services are held at 08.00 and 17.00 from Monday to Saturday. On Sundays, they take place at 06.30, 09.00 and 17.00.

Turn right out of the cathedral, then right again towards its rear aspect and you find yourself standing in front of an oddity; the pseudo-Classical **Rumyantsev mausoleum**. It's classically Russian and an excellent photo opportunity. Carry on past the mausoleum towards the railings and pause to take in the view over the Sozh. The countryside to the east stretches away in front of you beyond the river. On the far bank are wide groves of trees that come almost to the water's edge, leaving a strip of sandy, light-coloured soil that could almost be a beach. This is exactly the purpose that it serves for local people in the months of summer. Now turn your back on the Sozh, lean on the railings and take in the panoramic view across the park. It was designed at the end of the 18th century by Count Rumyantsev around the **palace** that was built to his orders. Amongst others, the renowned British architect John Clark worked extensively on the project. Here is an exquisite example of classical park design. Covering 25ha high above the Sozh, various species of tree have been deliberately arranged into groups that enhance their features. There is Belarusian maple, ash and chestnut, together with eastern white pine, northern white oak and Manchurian walnut. Standing away to your left, in the middle of the park, beautifully complemented by the woodland all around it, is the palace itself. This isn't the best perspective from which to view its charms; a better one soon awaits you. Head diagonally back towards Lenin Square and make for the ornamental fountain, with benches all around it. Beyond the fountain, along a path, is another seating area. From here, the view of the palace is at its best and by now you will have noticed the light classical music that is constantly relayed over speakers situated all over the park.

This is such a romantic location! I recall walking here one winter's day in watery sunshine, with snow on the ground, wrapped in scarf, gloves, heavy overcoat and hat, listening to the music, watching the sunbeams slanting down through the bare trees and deep in thought. I looked up to see an elderly couple. They were clasped in a tender embrace, dancing to the music, gazing deeply into each other's eyes as they twirled around and around, smiling and laughing gaily.

If you head across the front of the palace and follow the gradient of the path downwards, you find yourself entering a ravine. If you look up to the left, you will see the imposing 39m **tower** added by Count Paskevich after the original palace was constructed, while below you and to your right is an ornamental pond with its resident swans. You have two choices now: you can either climb out of the other side of the ravine and head through the woods until you reach a rickety tower, pay the attendant BYR1,200 and then climb the even more rickety spiral staircase until you emerge on a wobbly platform high above the tree line. The view over the city is simply fantastic, but your perch is a lofty one and it really does wobble quite dramatically. Or, if heights don't suit you, take a turn around the pond and head for the railings by the river, then stroll at your leisure by the side of its fast-flowing waters. At regular points along the riverbank and throughout the park are small café-bars serving soft drinks, alcoholic beverages and light snacks. You can also take a 40 minute cruise along the river from here, with some lovely views across the lower town.

There are several points at which you can turn away from the river and climb back into the park. When you do so, you have two things left to do. First, take a stroll across the high pedestrian bridge to the other side of the river and back, with splendid views on either side; then secondly, visit the palace. Opening hours are rather erratic, but if you strike it lucky it's well worth a visit (*admission for foreign visitors US$5*). The entrance hall in particular is just stunning, and room after room is packed with artefacts and relics from the period.

When you have experienced all there is to see and do in this lovely park, head back down Sovyetskaya, window shopping as you go, to where your voyage of exploration began. Resolve to do it all over again on your next visit, preferably in a different season, when the experience will be very different.

OUTSIDE GOMEL

VETKA This small town, 22km northeast of Gomel and founded in 1685 by 'Old Believers' who had fled from Russia, is my second home and in many ways, my spiritual one. Located on the banks of the Sozh River, it is surrounded by forest and marsh. The name is assumed to have been derived from an island of the same name in the river. It was twice burned to the ground by the tsar's troops, in 1735 and 1764, with its residents being forced to resettle to the outer provinces of eastern Russia. At the time, it was widely known for the unique style of icon painting that was practised here. There was also a specialist school for woodcarving. In 1772, the town was annexed to the Russian Empire and in 1852 it became part of the Gomel administrative region.

In 1880, Vetka is known to have counted around 6,000 inhabitants, 994 wooden and 11 stone buildings, six windmills, a rope factory and a tannery. Anchors were produced at local forges and ships were constructed at the shipyard on the Sozh from 1840. There is still a wharf there today. In the middle of the 19th century, the richest of the town's merchants had their own steamships. During the war years from August 1941 to September 1943, Vetka was under the occupation of the Nazis, who murdered 656 of its residents. Prior to the Chernobyl catastrophe, there were over 40,000 residents, but after a massive resettlement programme to take people away from the areas of radiation pollution, the population had shrunk to only 7,200 by the first anniversary of the disaster. On 1 November 1987, a splendid **folk arts museum** (*13 Red Sq;* ✆ *2 26 70/2 14 49;* ⏱ *10.00–18.00 Tue–Sun; admission BYR5,500; www.vetkamuseum.iatp.by*) was opened here. Its exhibits are of the highest quality and display the unique historical and cultural features of the region. Located in a former merchant's house, its ceremonial entrance doors have beautiful wooden carvings worked by local people. The items on display, including ancient artefacts, icons, manuscripts, traditional costumes and woven *rushniki* (many from the unique weaving school in the nearby village of Nyeglubka) are simply stunning. This is particularly so of the icons. Most of the ones exhibited here were crafted by Old Believers in the 17th century in the style of those on display in Moscow's cathedrals. The founder of the museum was Fyodor Grigorievich Shkliarov, a native of Vetka and a fervent promoter of local

When I first visited Vetka in 2001, the focus for the Orthodox congregation was a small wooden church on one of the roads out of town. It was badly in need of repair. The priest told me that work had started on a new construction in the middle of town, but that the project had come to a halt when the source of funds dried up. Each time that I returned, the half-built shell and surrounding building site felt like a metaphor for all of the infrastructural problems that beset the people of this country. And then, out of the blue, I arrived in town after an absence of 12 months to find the church complete, its golden domes glinting in the sunshine. It was to be consecrated during my visit by the head of the Orthodox Church in Belarus, none other than the Metropolitan Filaret of All Belarus himself, and when I went to see the chief executive of Vetka Executive Committee, Viktor Burakov, to update him on developments with our joint sustainability programmes, I was humbled to receive an invitation to attend.

The day of the ceremony dawned bright, with a cloudless blue sky. We made our way to the church and were greeted by a mass of local people. As we were led through, our eyes fell upon two trails of wild flowers, freshly picked, that lay along the sides of the path from the entrance gates, up the steps and into the church itself, leading all the way to the iconostasis. The riot of colour and the heady aroma presented a glorious living display. Inside, people were crammed shoulder to shoulder and together, we waited over an hour for the Filaret's entourage to arrive. Then, without any warning other than a series of urgent whispers that reached us in a wave from the gates, the invisible choir in the gallery above burst into life with a soaring, a cappella divine liturgy that sent a tingle all the way up my spine and made my heart want to burst with joy.

There was a huge surge as the procession came into view, with priests in ascending order of seniority and bedecked in astonishingly ornate robes to match their status, all of them with huge spade beards, extravagantly swinging incense holders as if their lives depended upon it, responding to the liturgy with chants of their own. Constantly and urgently, people all around me were muttering, bowing their heads, eyes to the ground and crossing themselves incessantly, almost obsessively. It was impossible not to be caught up and swept away by the tide of mysticism and ancient, holy ritual that was washing over us all. Then the Filaret himself appeared, head high, exuding sacred power and influence, his gaze slowly passing over every corner of the congregation. Wherever his gaze rested, if only for an instant, people crossed themselves even more frantically than they had before (if that were possible), while his Holiness periodically responded with the slightest of inclinations of his head.

The entire process of consecration took almost two hours. At one point, the Filaret blessed each of the walls with holy water flung from the bristles of an enormous brush, like something a decorator would use. At least twice, he changed his robes. To do so, he stood in the middle of the congregation, on a slight dais, while junior priests solemnly and reverently removed each layer of robe for him and replaced it with another. Once, he reached inside and produced a magnificent comb with a flourish, before proceeding to preen his flowing beard, deliberately, slowly and with more than a slight air of superiority.

When it was all over, we accompanied him to the local restaurant, where the tables were creaking under the weight of food and vodka. The priests came too. At various points throughout the meal, they broke into spontaneous, soaring a cappella harmonies, delivered ever louder and with more gusto as each empty vodka bottle was replaced by another full one. The celebration lasted long into the afternoon, until the Filaret decided it was time to go. In an instant he was out of his seat and after blessing all those assembled before him, he swept out of the room like a ship in full sail, his entourage trailing behind. An extraordinary day.

culture. He began to assemble artefacts in the 1960s and continued to enlarge his collection into the 1980s. Public interest began to be engaged over the years and these items laid the foundation for the museum. Sadly, Shkliarov died the year after it opened. Today, the museum has a national reputation as an artistic educational centre, where research is undertaken into the study of traditional Belarusian culture. Just across the square from the museum is the **Sozh Restaurant** (⊕ *11.30–23.30, mains from US$5*) serving traditional Belarusian fare. It's a vast, cavernous room that is almost always empty and always cold, but the food is nourishing and good value. On two separate occasions, I have seen it alive with colour and noise. On my first visit, I was honoured to be invited to the wedding of the daughter of a senior local official here. The second time was the lavish lunch given on the occasion of the consecration of the recently completed **church** (see *The metropolitan filaret comes to town* opposite). Located just off the square, it is well worth a visit. Inside, it is bright and airy. Painted on the iconostasis is a fresco depicting the fate of the victims of Chernobyl.

Directly outside is the **memorial stone and church bell** dedicated to the memory of those who died in the immediate aftermath of the Chernobyl explosion, along with the lost villages in the uninhabitable zone whose residents were required to leave their homes for good.

KHALCH This small village in Vetka district, located high on the western bank of the Sozh is notable for its 19th-century **manor house** that is occasionally open to visitors on an ad hoc basis and its small wooden **church**. As you cross the Sozh on the road from Gomel to Vetka and just before you enter the town, look up to your left. The brightly coloured blue church is situated high atop a bluff, looking down over the river towards Vetka. A heroic and bloody engagement took place here in 1943 as the Red Army, supported by groups of partisans, fought to cross the river to liberate Gomel.

There is a regular bus service to Khalch and Vetka from Gomel. If you are driving, the road there runs directly from the bottom end of Sovyetskaya. It's a straight road, heading in a northeasterly direction. Khalch is situated 18km along it, just before you cross the Sozh. Vetka is on the opposite bank.

NYEGLUBKA Located on back roads 45km northeast of Vetka, this is another small village that is pretty but unremarkable, other than in respect of the **village school** there. For it is here that the descendants of traditional weavers are taught the skills and crafts of their forebears on intricate wooden looms crafted in exactly the same way as the originals. The headteacher is pleased to welcome visitors and always eager to showcase the skills of her students. It's difficult to find, but the tourist route devised by the local executive committee includes a visit here and the Belintourist office in Gomel (see *Tourist information*, page 205) will be more than pleased to book you a place on the tour.

Only a few kilometres to the west of here is the tiny hamlet of **Zhelizniki**, where the restoration of one of the oldest Orthodox churches in all Belarus has just been completed. I have visited it several times at various stages of the works and it is a joy to be able to report that all is now complete. A visit here is also included on the locally devised tour.

On the western fringes of the *oblast* is the **Pripyatsky National Park**. Deep within the mystical Polyesye region and covering 82,529ha, it was established in the marshy lowland area between the Pripyat, Stivha and Ubort rivers to protect and preserve the unique ecological systems that are to be found in this area, along with its landscape and biological diversity. The park is of particular interest to ornithologists: around 250 species are registered, including the greater and lesser heron, common crane, eagle owl, serpent eagle and marsh owl. Since 1987, the European bison has been reintroduced here and there are now believed to be 67 individual animals within its boundaries. The park's main town and spiritual heart of the Polyesye is **Turov**, where there is a fine **nature museum** (⊕ *May–Oct 10.00–18.00 Tue–Sun, Nov–Apr 10.00–17.00; admission BYR3,000*) explaining all the visitor needs to know about the history and ecology of the area. Within the park itself are many small communities whose inhabitants continue to practise the traditional crafts and trades developed by their ancestors. There is a **visitor complex** at Lyaskovichy on the banks of the Pripyat River, including a cosy hotel of wood construction where the décor is designed to replicate homes of old. In the depths of the forest is the Hlyupinskaya Buda facility, consisting of three traditionally built cottages with modern conveniences, accommodating up to 20 people. There are even boats that sail up and down the river, which are used as floating hotels. Tours from one to ten days can be arranged through the state tourist agencies.

Appendix 1

LANGUAGE

Russian and **Belarusian** have equal status in Belarus as national languages. Both of them are categorised as eastern Slavonic languages, the wider group of which share so many vocabulary and grammatical similarities that they were originally classified as one: Old Russian. The alphabets are based on the Cyrillic script, from the alphabet of the Old Church Slavonic language, which is still in use in the Orthodox liturgy. Today, the untutored ear and eye would discern very little difference between Belarusian and Russian. Everyone speaks Russian, although Belarusian is becoming more widely used, particularly on public signage. I have replicated the Russian alphabet below in its entirety and added the Belarusian equivalent for the few letters that are written differently. It will be enough for you to be able to recognise these letters to assist with your pronunciation. I have then included some words and phrases in Russian that should help you along the way. Wherever you travel in the world, faltering but earnest attempts at communicating in the language of your hosts are generally well received. This is certainly the case in Belarus. The people here think they are the forgotten country of Europe; and the rest of Europe (and indeed the world) might be on a different planet, given the paucity of interaction between Belarusians and Europeans. So, take a very deep breath and give it a go. You will always be greeted with a smile. Don't forget, though, that English is widely taught in schools and young people especially will be keen to try out their own language skills on you.

Most people are utterly daunted by the Cyrillic alphabet and in a sense, this is perfectly understandable, as you're going back to school to learn how to read all over again. But a little perseverance pays huge dividends. When you master the basics of being able to pronounce a few words, you will be surprised by how much you can begin to understand in a very short time.

If you are embarking on learning the language for the first time, it will probably be overly ambitious to attempt a full language course before you go, or to take grammatical texts and a dictionary with you. But I do strongly recommend that you take a phrasebook. The best two on the market are those published by Lonely Planet and Rough Guides. There is nothing to choose between the two in terms of quality and both balance just the right amount of academic detail with practical expediency. For details of language courses, see pages 62–3.

A1

THE CYRILLIC RUSSIAN ALPHABET

Russian		Phonetic pronunciation
А	а	a, as in *far*
Б	б	b, as in *bill*
В	в	v, as in *violin*
Г	г	g, as in *go*
Д	д	d, as in *do*
Е	е	ye, as in *yellow*
Ё	ё	yo, as in *your*
Ж	ж	zh, as in *pleasure*

З	з		z, as in *zebra*
И	и		ee, as in *eaten*
Й	й		y, as in *coy*
К	к		k, as in *kitchen*
Л	л		l, as in *lantern*
М	м		m, as in *my*
Н	н		n, as in *never*
О	о		o, as in *open*
П	п		p, as in *pillow*
Р	р		r, as in *growl* (but roll your tongue extravagantly!)
С	с		s, as in *suspense*
Т	т		t, as in *tea*
У	у		oo, as in *moose*
Ф	ф		f, as in *face*
Х	х		pronounce *loch* like a Scot!
Ц	ц		ts, as in *fits*
Ч	ч		ch, as in *cello*
Ш	ш		sh, as in *shampoo*
Щ	щ		shsh, as in *fresh shampoo*
Ъ	ъ		hard sign, to keep a consonant hard
Ы	ы		i, as in *mill*
Ь	ь		soft sign, to soften a consonant
Э	э		e, as in *envelop*
Ю	ю		u, as in *usurp*
Я	я		ya, as in *yam*

For the purpose of rudimentary learning to enable you to read signage, all you will need to know is that in the Belarusian language, the letter И и is replaced by I i and that there is an additional letter Ў ў pronounced like a 'w', as in 'how'. And that's all you need to know!

The main problem with English is that the frighteningly large number of rules is only exceeded by an even larger number of exceptions to those rules. This problem doesn't exist with Russian. It's much more phonetic, so when you've cracked the Cyrillic alphabet, the only thing left to worry about is locating which syllable in a word carries the emphasis. In the following pages, underlining shows which syllable to stress. For your first visit, though, none of this should be a problem; if you set your level of expectation appropriately, you won't have too much difficulty in being able to read the odd word, understand a few, have the confidence to utter a word or phrase and have them understood by the recipient. Try these for starters:

FIRST MEETINGS AND NICETIES

Hello (formal)	Здравствуйте	*Zdravstvoitye*
Hi (casual)	Привет	*Preevyet*
Good day	Добрий День	*Dobri Dyehn*
Good morning	Доброе Утро	*Dobroye Ootra*
Good evening	Добрий Вечер	*Dobri Vyeicha*
Yes	Да	*Da*
No	Нет	*Nyet*
Thank you	Спасибо	*Spaseeba*
You're welcome	Пожалуйста	*Pazhalsta*
Please	Пожалуйста	*Pazhalsta*
Excuse me	Извините	*Eezvenitye*
What is your name?	Как вас зовут?	*Kak vas zavoot?*
My name is…	Меня зовут…	*Minya zavoot…*
Pleased to meet you	Очень приятно	*Orchin preeyatna*

How are you?	Как дела?	*Kak dyela?*
Good	Хорошо	*Hurashor*
Excellent!	Отлично!	*Atleechna!*
Bad	Плохо	*Plorkha*
Very	Очень	*Orchin*
Do you speak English?	Вы говорите по-английский?	*Vy guvareetyeh pa angleeski?*
Do you understand?	Понимаете?	*Punimahyetye?*
I don't speak Russian	Я плохо говорю по-русский	*Ya plorkha guvareyoo pa rooski*
I don't understand	Не понимаю	*Knee puneemaiyoo*
Repeat, please	Повторите, пожалуйста	*Puvhtareetye, pazhalsta*
I like…	Мне нрявиться…	*Minye nrahvitsa…*
I don't like…	Мне не нрявиться…	*Minye ni nrahvitsa…*
I love…	Я люблю…	*Ya lyooblyoo*
See you again	До встречи	*Da fstryechi*
Goodbye	До свидания	*Dos sveedanya*
Bye	Пока	*Paka*
Good night	Спокойной Ночи	*Spakoinoi Norchi*
Bon voyage!	Счастливого пути!	*Shistleevava puti!*
All the best!	Всего хорошего!	*Fsevor harrorshiva!*

KEY WORDS

What?	Что?	*Shtor?*
Who?	Кто?	*K-tor?*
Where?	Где?	*Gdyeh?*
How?	Как?	*Kak?*
Why?	Почему?	*Puchyemoo?*
On the left	На лева	*Na lyeva*
On the right	На права	*Na pravha*
Straight ahead	Прямо	*Preeyarma*
Near	Не далеко	*Knee dalyekor*
Far	Далеко	*Dalyekor*

SHOPPING

How much does this cost?	Сколько это стоит?	*Skorlka ehta styeet?*
What is it?	Что это?	*Shtor ehta?*
A lot	Много	*M-norga*
A little	Чутьчуть	*Chootchoot*

FOOD AND DRINK

Bread	Хлеб	*Khlyeb*
Cheese	Сир	*Syrr*
Meat	Мясо	*Myasa*
Fish	Риба	*Reeba*
Fruit	Фрукти	*Frookti*
Vegetables	Овощи	*Orvashee*
Mushrooms	Гриби	*Greebi*
Potatoes	Картошки	*Kartoshki*
Water	Вода	*Vada*
Milk	Молоко	*Malakor*
Juice	Сок	*Sok*
Sugar	Сахар	*Sakhar*

Tea	Чай	*Chai*
Coffee	Кофе	*Korfye*
Beer	Пиво	*Peeva*
Vodka	Водка	*Vordka*
Breakfast	Завтрак	*Zavhtrak*
Lunch	Обед	*Abyed*
Dinner	Ужин	*Oozhen*

ADJECTIVES

Big	Большой	*Balshoi*
Small	Маленкий	*Marlenki*
Hot	Горячий	*Grryachi*
Cold	Холодный	*Khorladni*
New	Новий	*Norvee*
Old	Старий	*Staree*
Beautiful	Красивый	*Krasseevi*
Delicious	Вкусный	*Ffkoosni*

NUMBERS

0	Нуль	*Nool*
1	Один	*Ahdjeen*
2	Два	*Dva*
3	Три	*Tree*
4	Четыре	*Chyetearye*
5	Пять	*Pyats*
6	Шесть	*Shhehst*
7	Семь	*Ssyem*
8	Восемь	*Vorsyem*
9	Девять	*Dyevyats*
10	Десять	*Dyesyats*
20	Двадцать	*Dvahdsahts*
50	Пятьдесят	*Pyatdyesyat*
100	Сто	*Stor*
500	Пятьсот	*Pyatsort*
1,000	Тысяча	*Teesyatchsa*

DAYS, SEASONS AND TIME

Yesterday	Вчера	*Vcherra*
Today	Сегодня	*Sivordnya*
Tomorrow	Завтра	*Zavhtra*
Monday	Понедельник	*Ponyedyelnik*
Tuesday	Вторник	*Vtornik*
Wednesday	Среда	*Ssreda*
Thursday	Четверг	*Chetvyerg*
Friday	Пятница	*Pyatnitsa*
Saturday	Суббота	*Sooborta*
Sunday	Воскресенье	*Voskresyenye*
What time is it?	Который час?	*Katory chass?*
Now	Сейчас	*Saychass*
Hour	Час	*Chass*
Minute	Минута	*Minoota*
Spring	Весна	*Vyesna*
Summer	Лето	*Lyeta*

Autumn	Осень	_Orsyen_
Winter	Зима	_Zeema_
Day	День	_Dyenn_
Morning	Утро	_Ootra_
Afternoon	После обеда	_Porslye abyeda_
Evening	Вечер	_Vyeacha_
Night	Ночь	_Norch_

Wild boar

Appendix 2

Unsurprisingly for a relatively new country that is so little known in the West, very little has been written in English about Belarus. But if you search hard enough, there are some gems to be found. I do urge you to read as widely as you can before you go; any insight that you can gain into the history of this country and its people will only be of benefit to you as you travel around and forge relationships along the way. I have also added reference to a few of the best books on the *Chernobyl* catastrophe; although it occurred outside the national borders of Belarus, no traveller and student of the issues facing Belarusian society today can hope to be prepared for the deeply affecting experiences to be gained from a visit here without at least a rudimentary knowledge of what occurred on that fateful Spring night in 1986.

TRAVELOGUES AND MEMOIRS

The Bronski House by Philip Marsden (HarperPerennial, paperback, ISBN-13 978-0007204526) is a delightful, unusual and intensely moving blend of history, tragedy, romance and travel writing. In the summer of 1992, the author accompanied the exiled poet *Zofia Hinska* back to the Belarusian village of her birth. This was the start of a "rites of passage" journey that was to link the history of this troubled region to a sad family history. It's a very good illustration of the effect of momentous events in shaping the national psyche that endures to this day. Highly recommended.

Among the Russians by the excellent Colin Thubron (Vintage, paperback, ISBN-13 978-0099459293) is a splendid memoir of the extraordinary journey taken by the author across the Soviet Union in the 1980s, when he drove 10,000 miles from the Baltic to the Caucasus and to the Far East of the Soviet Empire in an old Morris Marina. Only the first chapter is about Belarus, his point of entry into the USSR, but the poignant tales that follow about the people he met along the way could easily have been written about Belarusians.

Black Earth City: A Year in the Heart of Russia by Charlotte Hobson (Granta Books, paperback, ISBN-13 978-1862074989) contains only passing references to Minsk, but like Thubron, Hobson has a fine insight into the human condition that at times is reminiscent of *Chekhov*. This moving debut is the story of a year spent in provincial Russia at the time of the break-up of the Soviet Union. And the beautiful cameo illustrations of the warm relationships within the author's circle of friends in Russia might very easily describe those that I have been fortunate to be able to experience over the course of my time in Belarus.

Escape to the Forest by Ruth Yaffe Radin (Harper Collins, paperback, ISBN-13 978-0060285203) is the story of a young Jewish girl living with her family in the town of *Lida* at the start of the Great Patriotic War. Based on a true story (so it's also fiction in part), she describes life under the Nazis, before she fled into the forest to join a band of partisans resisting the occupation and fighting to save Jewish lives.

Burning Lights by Norbert Guterman (introduction), Bella Chagall (author) and Marc Chagall (illustrator) (Random House USA Inc, paperback, ISBN-13 978-0805208634) is an affectionate remembrance of Jewish life in pre-revolutionary *Vitsebsk*. The beautiful drawings are those of the famous Belarusian painter and the text is written by his wife.

POLITICS, HISTORY, ECONOMY AND SOCIETY

The Reconstruction of Nations: Poland, Ukraine, Lithuania, Belarus, 1569–1999 by Timothy Snyder (Yale University Press, paperback, ISBN-13 978-0300105865) is a masterly and scholarly work of analysis into the turbulent history of these Eastern European countries, whose past and present are inextricably interwoven. First published early in 2005, it's right up-to-date.

Revolution from Abroad: The Soviet Conquest of Poland's Western Ukraine and Western Belorussia by Jan T Gross (Princeton University Press, paperback, ISBN-13 978-0691096032) is a compelling tale of life between the two world wars under the oppression of first the Soviet Union and then Germany. It's a very powerful treatise on the totalitarianism of opposing dogma.

Belarus: A Denationalized Nation by David R Marples (Routledge, an imprint of Taylor & Francis Books Ltd, paperback, ISBN-13 978-9057023439) is now a little dated (it was first published in 1998), but as a commentary on the Soviet-style politics that developed in the country throughout the 1990s, it retains its legitimacy.

Belarus (Then and Now) by the Lerner Geography Department (Lerner Publishing Group, paperback, ISBN-13 978-0822528111) is a very brief introduction (at only 64 pages) into the history, geography, economy, politics, ethnography and society of Belarus.

Belarus: At a Crossroads in History by I A Zaprudnik (Westview Press Inc, paperback, ISBN-13 978-0813317946) is also a little dated (it was first published in 1997), but it remains a powerful commentary on the complexities of the country's history and its demographic, social, cultural and political evolution.

CHERNOBYL

Chernobyl Heart by Adi Roche (New Island Books, paperback, ISBN-13 978-1904301981) tells the story of the tireless work undertaken by children's charities to help alleviate the plight of children affected by the radioactive fallout. Adi's selfless commitment is well documented already and the stories recounted here are both tragic and uplifting all at once.

The Chernobyl Disaster (Days That Shook the World) by Paul Dowswell (Hodder Wayland, hardback, ISBN-13 978-0750235617) is a short (64 pages) but very informative, no-nonsense resumé of the 24 hour period in which the explosion occurred. Aimed at the teenage market, it's a brilliant introduction to the key issues. If your time is limited, this is the one to read.

Voices from Chernobyl by *Svetlana Alexyevich* (Dalkey Archive Press, hardback, ISBN-13 978-1564784018) is a collection of intensely moving remembrances from those who lived through the nightmare.

Wormwood Forest: A Natural History of Chernobyl by Mary Mycio (Henry (Joseph) Press, hardback, ISBN-13 978-0309094306) addresses the issues from a different angle; that of the radioactive wildlife sanctuary that appears to have developed in the exclusion zone.

Heavy Water: A Poem for Chernobyl by Mario Petrucci (Enitharmon Press, paperback, ISBN-13 978-1900564342) is based on first hand accounts from people who were there. It's an unusual and extremely dignified piece of work that is also a fitting memorial to the tragedy.

Bradt Travel Guides

www.bradtguides.com

Africa

Africa Overland	£15.99
Algeria	£15.99
Benin	£14.99
Botswana: Okavango, Chobe, Northern Kalahari	£15.99
Burkina Faso	£14.99
Cape Verde Islands	£13.99
Canary Islands	£13.95
Cameroon	£13.95
Congo	£14.99
Eritrea	£15.99
Ethiopia	£15.99
Gabon, São Tomé, Príncipe	£13.95
Gambia, The	£13.99
Ghana	£15.99
Johannesburg	£6.99
Kenya	£14.95
Madagascar	£15.99
Malawi	£13.99
Mali	£13.95
Mauritius, Rodrigues & Réunion	£13.99
Mozambique	£13.99
Namibia	£15.99
Niger	£14.99
Nigeria	£15.99
Rwanda	£14.99
Seychelles	£14.99
Sudan	£13.95
Tanzania, Northern	£13.99
Tanzania	£16.99
Uganda	£15.99
Zambia	£17.99
Zanzibar	£12.99

Britain and Europe

Albania	£13.99
Armenia, Nagorno Karabagh	£14.99
Azores	£12.99
Baltic Capitals: Tallinn, Riga, Vilnius, Kaliningrad	£12.99
Belarus	£14.99
Belgrade	£6.99
Bosnia & Herzegovina	£13.99
Bratislava	£6.99
Budapest	£8.99
Bulgaria	£13.99
Cork	£6.99
Croatia	£13.99
Cyprus see North Cyprus	

Czech Republic	£13.99
Dresden	£7.99
Dubrovnik	£6.99
Estonia	£13.99
Faroe Islands	£13.95
Georgia	£14.99
Helsinki	£7.99
Hungary	£14.99
Iceland	£14.99
Kiev	£7.95
Kosovo	£14.99
Krakow	£7.99
Lapland	£13.99
Latvia	£13.99
Lille	£6.99
Lithuania	£13.99
Ljubljana	£7.99
Macedonia	£14.99
Montenegro	£13.99
North Cyprus	£12.99
Paris, Lille & Brussels	£11.95
Riga	£6.99
River Thames, In the Footsteps of the Famous	£10.95
Serbia	£14.99
Slovakia	£14.99
Slovenia	£12.99
Spitsbergen	£14.99
Switzerland: Rail, Road, Lake	£13.99
Tallinn	£6.99
Ukraine	£14.99
Vilnius	£6.99
Zagreb	£6.99

Middle East, Asia and Australasia

China: Yunnan Province	£13.99
Great Wall of China	£13.99
Iran	£14.99
Iraq	£14.95
Iraq: Then & Now	£15.99
Kyrgyzstan	£15.99
Maldives	£13.99
Mongolia	£14.95
North Korea	£13.95
Oman	£13.99
Sri Lanka	£13.99
Syria	£14.99
Tibet	£13.99
Turkmenistan	£14.99
Yemen	£14.99

The Americas and the Caribbean

Amazon, The	£14.99
Argentina	£15.99
Bolivia	£14.99
Cayman Islands	£14.99
Colombia	£15.99
Costa Rica	£13.99
Chile	£16.95
Dominica	£14.99
Falkland Islands	£13.95
Guyana	£14.99
Panama	£13.95
Peru & Bolivia: Backpacking and Trekking	£12.95
St Helena	£14.99
USA by Rail	£13.99

Wildlife

100 Animals to See Before They Die	£16.99
Antarctica: Guide to the Wildlife	£14.95
Arctic: Guide to the Wildlife	£15.99
Central & Eastern European Wildlife	£15.99
Chinese Wildlife	£16.99
East African Wildlife	£19.99
Galápagos Wildlife	£15.99
Madagascar Wildlife	£15.99
Peruvian Wildlife	£15.99
Southern African Wildlife	£18.95
Sri Lankan Wildlife	£15.99

Eccentric Guides

Eccentric America	£13.95
Eccentric Australia	£12.99
Eccentric Britain	£13.99
Eccentric California	£13.99
Eccentric Cambridge	£6.99
Eccentric Edinburgh	£5.95
Eccentric France	£12.95
Eccentric London	£13.99
Eccentric Oxford	£5.95

Others

Your Child Abroad: A Travel Health Guide	£10.95
Something Different for the Weekend	£12.99

WIN £100 CASH!

READER QUESTIONNAIRE

Send in your completed questionnaire for the chance to win £100 cash in our regular draw

All respondents may order a Bradt guide at half the UK retail price – please complete the order form overleaf.

(Entries may be posted or faxed to us, or scanned and emailed.)

We are interested in getting feedback from our readers to help us plan future Bradt guides. Please answer ALL the questions below and return the form to us in order to qualify for an entry in our regular draw.

Have you used any other Bradt guides? If so, which titles? . . . .
. . . .

What other publishers' travel guides do you use regularly? . . . .
. . . .

Where did you buy this guidebook? . . . .

What was the main purpose of your trip to Belarus (or for what other reason did you read our guide)? eg: holiday/business/charity etc.. . . . .
. . . .

What other destinations would you like to see covered by a Bradt guide? . . . .

Would you like to receive our catalogue/newsletters?

YES / NO (If yes, please complete details on reverse)

If yes – by post or email? . . . .

Age (circle relevant category) 16–25   26–45   46–60   60+

Male/Female (delete as appropriate)

Home country . . . .

Please send us any comments about our guide to Belarus or other Bradt Travel Guides. . . . .
. . . .
. . . .
. . . .

Bradt Travel Guides
23 High Street, Chalfont St Peter, Bucks SL9 9QE, UK
☏ +44 (0)1753 893444 f +44 (0)1753 892333
e info@bradtguides.com
www.bradtguides.com

CLAIM YOUR HALF-PRICE BRADT GUIDE!

Order Form

To order your half-price copy of a Bradt guide, and to enter our prize draw to win £100 (see overleaf), please fill in the order form below, complete the questionnaire overleaf, and send it to Bradt Travel Guides by post, fax or email.

Please send me one copy of the following guide at half the UK retail price

Title	Retail price	Half price
. . .	. . . .	. . . .	. . . .

Please send the following additional guides at full UK retail price

No	Title	Retail price	Total
. . .	. . . .	. . . .	. . . .
. . .	. . . .	. . . .	. . . .
. . .	. . . .	. . . .	. . . .

Sub total . . . .
Post & packing . . . .
(£2 per book UK; £4 per book Europe; £6 per book rest of world)
Total . . . .

Name . . . .

Address . . . .

Tel . . . . Email . . . .

☐ I enclose a cheque for £ . . . . made payable to Bradt Travel Guides Ltd

☐ I would like to pay by credit card. Number: . . . .

Expiry date: . . . / . . . 3-digit security code (on reverse of card) . . . . .

Issue no (debit cards only) . . . . .

☐ Please add my name to your catalogue mailing list.

☐ I would be happy for you to use my name and comments in Bradt marketing material.

Send your order on this form, with the completed questionnaire, to:

Bradt Travel Guides BEL1
23 High Street, Chalfont St Peter, Bucks SL9 9QE
✆ +44 (0)1753 893444 f +44 (0)1753 892333
e info@bradtguides.com www.bradtguides.com

Index

Page numbers in **bold** indicate major entries; those in *italics* indicate maps